D1366782

REGIONS

*The Economics and
Politics of Territory*

REGIONS

The Economics and Politics of Territory

Ann Markusen
Northwestern University

ROWMAN & LITTLEFIELD
PUBLISHERS

For permission to reprint material, we are grateful
to the following institutions:

To the Carnegie Institution of Washington for Figures 4.1 and 4.3,
from Charles Paullin, *Atlas of the Historical Geography
of the United States,* 1932.

To Johns Hopkins University Press for Figure 4.4, from
Robert Fogel, *Railroads and American Economic Growth,* 1964.

To Charles Scribner's Sons for Figures 4.2 and 4.5,
from Kenneth T. Jackson, ed., *Atlas of American History,*
2nd revised edition, 1984.

ROWMAN & LITTLEFIELD

Published in the United States of America in 1987
by Rowman & Littlefield, Publishers
(a division of Littlefield, Adams & Company)
81 Adams Drive, Totowa, New Jersey 07512

Library of Congress Cataloging-in-Publication Data

Markusen, Ann R.
Region building.

Bibliography: p. 267
Includes index.
1. Regional economics.   2. Regionalism—
United States.   3. United States—Politics and
government.   4. United States—Economic conditions.
I. Title.
HT391.3.M37   1987   330.973'0927   87-4359
ISBN 0-8476-7394-4

90 89 88 87
8 7 6 5 4 3 2 1

Printed in the United States of America

For my parents,
Jeanne and David Markusen

Contents

Tables and Figures

Preface and Acknowledgments

This book is about regions and regionalism in the United States. Its central preoccupation is the construction of regions as socioeconomic, often conflictual, collectivities of people, rather than with regions as inert, natural chunks of territory. Regions as units of societal structure are built on concrete economic foundations, with beams roughed up out of political systems, framing set from cultural practices, and finishing overlaid by the ingenuity of their residents. They are bound by the shape of the terrain and the idiosyncrasies of climate. Built to last, they may prove highly resistant to change. Yet the foundations may shift or crack, the beams rot, roofs leak, the siding fall. And concerted human action can raise the roof beams higher, knock out a constraining wall, or add an extension.

In some ways, this book is a companion to my volume *Profit Cycles, Oligopoly, and Regional Development*. Here, I present the political counterpart to the economic analysis laid out in that book, in a less technical, more historical and interdisciplinary manner. Yet its scope goes far beyond the political ramifications of the profit cycle model for regional development. In probing regionalism, it treats received cultures, political institutions, secular economic transformation, and militarism as forces complementary to the dynamics of industrial location.

I began a comprehensive study of the political economy of regionalism in 1978. At the time, I was driven by several concerns. First, I believed that a book of this sort was badly needed because we had no adequate framework for analyzing and interpreting American regionalism. Students trained in the postwar period, as I was, were offered multiple toolkits for dissecting regional phenomena, one in each social science discipline, with little regard for the potential fit among them. And, much like the American resistance to going metric, the separate disciplines found their investments in existing technique so great that despite a resurgent interest in interdisciplinary research, and despite the growth of professions like planning and public policy eager to use its products, they continued to find each other's preoccupations beside the point.

Second, I had spent a number of years, sequentially, in the East, Midwest and Intermountain West. In each location, I found strikingly distinct cultures and political controversies. I became convinced that despite the national consensus forged during the New Deal, and despite the apparent convergence in regional per capita incomes, regions in the United States possess quite distinctive economic structures and developmental dynamics. In the 1970s, these erupted into powerful political antagonisms, along Frostbelt-Sunbelt and East-West lines. I was interested in creating an analytical framework which would be powerful enough to explain the origins, intensity, and outcome of these conflicts. Emerging European theories of regionalism seemed inapt for the United States, chiefly because they were so heavily predicated on a unitary and centralized state and because the spatial patterning of the economies in question was so different from that of the United States.

Third, I found almost all of the existing regional literature remarkably ahistorical, especially in economics and regional science, my fields. It seemed clear that the passions and political effectiveness of regional organizing could be understood only by appreciating the ways in which settlement patterns, livelihoods, social skills, and political institutions had evolved over time. In particular, the North-South conflict of the 1970s seemed incomprehensible without a fairly extensive analysis of these regions' nineteenth-century encounters, which permanently placed their mark on the people, economies, and politics of each.

A final concern was the tendency within the neo-Marxist literature, which I thought to be generally a tremendous improvement on existing scholarship, to belittle the role of human agency and collective action as shapers of regional destiny. The preoccupation with the laws of motion of capital tended to generate the specter of a mechanically relentless capitalism sweeping across regions and altering their fortunes regardless of human response. In my view, capitalism was in turn significantly altered by the resistance of people in places, just as it has been by responses of workers in their workplace. I wanted to demonstrate this empirically.

I also had a strong interest in the normative aspects of regionalism. Involvement in state and local politics led me to believe that nationally oriented political platforms would fail unless they became more sensitive to regional particularities. At the same time, regional movements sometimes become chauvinistic, their constituents succumbing to the view that a problem is the fault of another region, or the federal government, rather than a more complex set of forces. Yet regional movements possessed a great potential which I believed was far too often overlooked or disparaged by both left theorists and those trying to fashion a new progressive alternative.

After the better part of a decade, I still maintain these concerns. Writing this book has not completely resolved the scholastic challenges of regionalism, even in my own mind. That is really a life's project. But I can now offer both scholars and regional protagonists some methods of attack which are interdisciplinary, historically minded, and empirically weighed, and which facilitate an evaluation of the human potential of regionalism.

As with all research efforts, this one has its regrettable omissions, imposed by time constraints. The empirical analysis would have benefited by including Canada, which has a similar political structure and many analogous land-based differentials. Canada, however, has a very different political history and a cross-cutting set of ethnic conflicts not present in the United States.* I chose to leave it for a later, thoroughly comparative treatment, which might include Europe, Australia, and some developing countries.

I also regret not being able to research in greater depth the Populist and New Deal eras as examples of periods when regional antagonisms were overridden by more powerful cross-regional coalitions. Each period would, I think, cast a great deal of useful light on the progressive potential of regionalism and regional alliances in national politics.

My thinking on regionalism, which I still view as a cantankerous topic, has evolved through many years of conversation and correspondence with colleagues and friends. I received a great deal of constructive feedback on several earlier versions of the theoretical work.† This included discussions with members of my Kapitalistate collective and my western urban/regional policy group, particularly Jim O'Connor, Patricia Morgan, Dick Walker, Mike Lugar, Erica Schoenberger, David Wilmoth, Candace Howes, Michael Storper, and Doug Greenberg. Linda Collins helped me with the cultural question.

Over the years, I have enjoyed an intensive debate and extensive correspondence with colleagues from many "regions." In the United States, with Ben Harrison, Ed Soja, Matt Edel, Rick Simon, and Patricia Wilson-Salinas. In Europe, with Doreen Massey, Elizabeth Lebas, Frank Moulaert, Margit Mayer, and Luis Sanz. In Australia, Evan Jones, Frank Stillwell, and John Browett. In Mexico, Jose Luis Medina Aguiar, and in Brazil, my colleagues Roberto Luis and Donald Sawyer at CEDEPLAR. My views also changed under the scrutiny of many of my former students, particularly Marjorie Bennett, Richard Osborne, Jose Curbelo, Sonja Barrios, and Jose Oswaldo Lasmar.

Several people deserve special mention. I would never have pursued the historical material were it not for the outstanding example set by Pierre Vilar in his treatise on Catalonia and his personal encouragement to tackle similar material in the United States. My Berkeley colleagues Mike Teitz and Peter Hall have always been there to muse about things regional and helped set a high intellectual standard. From UCLA, John Friedmann has been this project's single biggest enthusiast, and I doubt I would have finished it without his persistent inquiries. Above all, I owe a great debt to David Plotke, my editor, who raised a number of challenging criticisms about the political analysis and guided me through several rounds of very painful cuts and reorganization.

*For recent analyses of Canadian regionalism, see Schwartz (1974), Stevenson (1979), Knight (1982b), and Matthews (1983).

†Markusen (1979b), Markusen (1980), and Markusen (1983).

A number of people read the earlier versions of the manuscript and offered useful suggestions on content and reorganization, among them John Friedmann, Gordon Clark, Ben Harrison, Niles Hansen, Gill Lim, and John Mollenkopf. My editor at Rowman & Littlefield, Paul Lee, could not have been more charming or patient. Much of the theoretical work was completed in 1980–81, including the Appendix, and does not review the recent outpouring of research, especially in geography and sociology, on "space."

Many people were interviewed concerning or have commented upon the empirical research. On the Native American section, I would like to thank Jack Forbes, Mina Caulfield, Ray Pratt, and Debbie LeVeen. On the South in the contemporary period, and the Southern Growth Policies Board in particular, Bud Weinstein, David Godschalk, Tom Schlesinger, Jesse White, Janet Papke, Bud Skinner, and Sandra Copeland. On the Northeast, my thanks to Ben Harrison and David Merkowitz. On the West, Gail Stoltz, Nancy Owens, Ed Marston, and Margaret MacDonald. My interpretation owes a great deal to conversations with Kit Muller, Ted Nace, and Amy Glasmeier on organizing in the contemporary West.

My thanks to Mel Webber and Margo Gordon, directors, respectively, of the Institute of Urban and Regional Development at the University of California, Berkeley, and the Center for Urban Affairs and Policy Research at Northwestern University, and David Wiley, Dean of Northwestern's School of Education and Social Policy for supporting significant portions of this work. At the Institute, Nene Ojeda and Maureen Jurkowski in particular have helped give the manuscript coherence. Adan Quan, Marge Bennett, Richard Osborne, and Vijaya Nagarajan helped with the laborious bibliographical and empirical work. Ruth Markusen and Janet Soule did a superb job on the index. The Data Center, in Oakland, was a valuable source of supplemental information.

Regions would not have been possible without the sustained support, both intellectual and personal, of Marc Weiss. His relish for and insights into American politics were particularly influential in my thinking. It also would not have been possible without the help and good company of my good neighbors in Cromwell—June, April, Julie, Roger, and Arnold Collman; Siiri and Einar Letty; Betty and Eddie Rostveit; and my cousins Ruth and Martha Markusen. Nor the companionship of my friends Candace Howes, Harriet Cohen, Constance Blake, Louise Dunlap, Amy Glasmeier, Clair Brown, Julie Feldman, and David Taylor. Finally, my thanks to the wonderful childcare centers of California and Chicago—Annie Adams, St. John's, the New School, Dearborn Park Pre-School, Christopher House, and the New City YMCA, for entertaining and challenging David while his mother plunked on the 'writer.

Ann Markusen

REGIONS
The Economics and Politics of Territory

1

Region Building: An Introduction

Struggles over territory have been a dominant form of social upheaval in the world for centuries. Cold war, world wars, wars of independence and national liberation, regional autonomy movements, and urban riots—all appear to refute the Marxist contention that class antagonisms constitute the most fundamental form of social opposition. Unfortunately, we have better developed theories about class conflicts than we do territorial ones. Social science scholars have been remarkably reluctant to tackle the sphere of geopolitics and territoriality. It is one of the projects of this book to contribute some theoretical insights into these confounding phenomena.

In the United States territorial politics have consistently displaced or preempted class politics as a national preoccupation. The Civil War pitted northerner against southerner. Populism attempted to organize southern and western farmers against eastern capital. In the recent postwar period, the Northeast clamored against regional robbery in the guise of job loss, extortionary energy prices, and biased federal aid flows toward the Sunbelt. Indeed, the New Deal period is a singular exception in a long history of powerful interregional antagonisms. Understanding this stubborn phenomenon of American regionalism, which resists reduction to simple class, religious, race, or ethnic differences, is the second project of this book.

Regionalism has been alternatively hallowed and disparaged by scholars with a normative bent. The southern regionalists of the 1930s and some more anarchist-leaning New Left scholars champion regionalism as both a preserver of sound traditional values and a source of great progressive and democratic impetus. Most contemporary Marxists see regionalism as a force impeding the progress of history, as a distraction, or at a minimum, a necessary manifestation of the conflict between the mobility of capital and the immobile nature of reproduction. Demonstrating that regionalism can wear many coats is the third project of this book. Its contribution to history, peace, or prosperity can be evaluated only on a case-by-case basis.

The United States manifests a unique brand of regionalism. As a nation, it lacks some of the pre-capitalist traditions that contribute to regional cleavage in Europe and the Third World—language differences, profound religious disputes, and ethnic groups who are regionally segregated. Thus the United States offers a chance to study regionalism in a more purely capitalist economic setting, with relatively fewer cultural complications. On the other hand, it has a unique political system—federalism—which enhances the possibilities for territoriality in politics.

The richness of the American regional landscape and the eventfulness of the nation's short history have made it impossible to think about doing a full-scale comparison, even with other industrialized nations. The theoretical work is thus tailored for the United States alone, although I believe that it would also fit the Canadian case closely. One of the ideas underlying this research, however, is that the absence of empirically grounded thinking about regionalism is a major contributor to the relative poverty of theory. The particularities of received political and cultural life operate as powerful shapers of territorialism, in ways that may not transcend continental or national boundaries. My hope is that the findings of this volume can be contrasted with those of others working in the European tradition to see where generalities can and cannot be drawn.

I chose to center my research on American regionalism, for several reasons. First, European regionalism is fairly well studied, although I believe that the conclusions I draw from the American case offer insights into that continent's territorial politics as well. The European literature is almost completely devoid of references to American regionalism, and there are no full-scale contemporary treatments of the latter.

Second, the United States is one of the few modern industrialized nations to host a full-scale and heavily regionalized civil war. The conflagration and its aftermath offer an outstanding opportunity to view the formation of regional consciousness. Similarly, the conflict between Native Americans and European colonists, also a violent, territorial encounter, provide another major instance for scholarly perusal. While both these eras have been admirably researched by historians, few inferences have been drawn for regions and regionalism in general.

THE MAKING OF AMERICAN REGIONALISM: TEN THESES

This book advances a set of propositions about American regional politics and their nature, formation, and intensity. Succinctly, they can be stated as follows.

1. *The economic primacy thesis:* Economic antagonisms constitute the principal underlying impulse for regional conflict in the United States.
2. *The cyclical exacerbation thesis:* Regional antipathies wane during

periods of normalcy and wax during periods of accelerated growth or decline, especially if the fruits or burdens fall unevenly across regions.

3. *The federal hothouse thesis:* The strong territorialization of American political power, embodied in the federal Constitution, engenders interregional hostility and channels what elsewhere might be more purely class conflicts into regional ones, as oppositional claims on the central State.
4. *The multiplier thesis:* Even though economic injury may be suffered by a limited group of regional residents, regionwide solidarity will be generated if the livelihoods directly affected constitute an important and irreplaceable portion of the region's economic base.
5. *The cultural leavening thesis:* The successful translation of specific territorial economic complaints into regionalism requires a latent cultural mutuality and the absence of countervailing internal tensions.
6. *The volatility thesis:* Instances of regional sentiment and antagonism are potentially capturable by different coalitions of classes and cultural affinity groups within the region.
7. *The economic capability thesis:* The larger, more unified and robust the region's economy, the more likely that regionalist demands will tend toward separatism or the devolution of State powers, rather than toward the mere redistribution of revenues or program reformulation.
8. *The party politics thesis:* Regions with well-developed, competitive party systems will be less amenable to regionalism than regions with one dominant or several weak political parties.
9. *The mutuality thesis:* When regionalism emerges in one region, it tends to call forth a reactive regionalism, often reluctant and weak, in other regions.
10. *The potentiality thesis:* Regionalism can facilitiate or retard the development of a capitalist economy and/or the transtion toward a socialist alternative.

The first, second, third, and ninth of these propositions deal with the interregional and external face of regionalism—its roots in uneven economic development and nurturance within the American political system. The fourth through eighth theses treat the internal receptivity of regions to the emergence of territorial politics. The final one addresses the normative issue.

Economic Primacy

The United States, with its recent European heritage and Anglo-Saxon hegemony, contains no major cultural cleavages of the linguistic or religious type that compound most instances of European regional strife. It is much clearer, here, that regionalism is a function of economic differentiation. Indeed, regional cultures, such as those evoked by the terms "Yankee," "Texan," "Highlander," and "Dixie," are often of recent vintage, created as unique identities within the last two hundred years.

Three types of economic differentiation, created by the uneven spread of capitalism, have played a role in igniting regionalism in the United States. First, regional struggle may ensue when two contesting modes of production coexist temporally but are differentiated territorially. From the outset, the new American nation became a battleground for this type of struggle between a northern economic system based on free wage labor and a southern economic system based on slave labor. Both regions' elites levied their increasingly incompatible claims on the central State that they had recently collaborated in setting up, driving the southern partner to secession and confederation.

A second type of economic differentiation is the territorial separation of the two dominant spheres of capitalist economic activity—circulation and production. If the bulk of agents of circulation (owners of the means of transportation, financiers, and middlemen in interregional trade) reside in one region, and the bulk of producers (farmers or miners, for instance) in another, then regional conflict may erupt. Economic controversies may encompass freight rates, interest rates, commodity prices, and issues of landownership and foreclosure. Then regional strife of the Populist era, when western and southern farmers found themselves pitted against eastern railroad barons, financial magnates, and grain dealers, provides an extraordinary example of this type of economically founded regionalism.

Third, clashes among participants in territorially differentiated production sectors may also lead to regionalist politics. Sectoral specializations overlay the last two cases of regionalism noted. Southern "King" cotton opposed a northern economy thriving on textile mills, steel, and mixed farming. An eastern manufacturing establishment producing farm implements and consumer goods heightened the conflict between eastern commercial capital and a populist West and South specializing in agricultural commodities. More recently, the energy crisis has produced a new East-West sectoral differentiation which has led to regional quarreling. In all these instances, the commodities produced by one region formed the inputs into commodity production in the other, either as material or capital goods inputs (cotton, plows, fuel) or indirectly as part of the reproduction cost of labor (food, clothing, fuel), creating conflict over the terms of production and exchange in each.

The American regional mosaic lacks two types of economic differentiation that have been important elsewhere: spatial segregation of classes and of landownership. Class structure is not highly regionally differentiated in the United States, although it has been a major source of intraurban conflict. Absentee landownership is relatively unimportant in the United States, at least in the sense that land in any one region is predominantly owned by territorially identified outside interests. The only politically important "outside" landowner has been the federal government, a factor that enhances the role of the State in the formation of American regionalism.

Cyclical Exacerbation

The pace of economic development has a special role to play in engendering regionalism. Slow change, whether it be growth or decline, is more easily accommodated than rapid change. In the former, individuals and institutions have time to find new livelihoods, adapt to dramatic community recomposition, and cope with collective needs. The severe downturns of the nineteenth century helped to ignite regional sentiment, and in the post–World War II period, regionalism resurged once sustained growth ended in 1967. Similarly, rampant growth with its own peculiar brand of unsettling consequences has created regional tensions, as it did on the frontier in the nineteenth century and has again in the late twentieth century in energy and high-tech boom areas.

Cyclical troughs and, to a lesser extent, peaks fail to prompt regionalism only when hardship or benefits are relatively evenly spread. An example is the New Deal period, when overall unemployment levels swamped interregional disparities. The nation had a common cause, captured in Roosevelt's politically astute "One Third of a Nation" phrase.

The Federal Hothouse

The federal structure of the American political system is a factor engendering interregional antagonisms. In the United States, political power is delegated spatially to a degree unusual in advanced capitalist countries (with a few exceptions such as Canada and Australia). Indeed, the initial structuring of the system—particularly the carving out of states in the western portion of the country—was the product of an intense regional conflict between uneasy partners in a national union. In trying to dominate the Congress in the interests of their sectional elites, northern and southern politicians ensured that the distribution of power in that Congress would be highly territorially configured far into the future. As a result, a major task of American political parties has been the transcendence of a narrow regional base, which has often resulted, among other anomalies, in the choice of a presidential candidate from a region where the party in question is relatively weak or weakening. Regional causes have played a major role in the formation of new parties and the demise of older ones.

The Multiplier Effect

Direct economic conflicts between limited sets of regional actors, such as those profiting from the types of differentiated activity mentioned above, easily become regionwide. They may capture the partisanship of the majority of regional residents because of their secondary and tertiary macroeconomic effects. These include the reduced viability of small local firms that supply the sector in decline, the business service sector (banks, advertisers, consultants, insurers), and those segments of the economy that depend upon the existing payroll—retailers, real estate, and the public sector—because their businesses depend upon consumer expenditure.

Critics of regionalism sometimes suggest that working people and other non-elite residents are hoodwinked into regional chauvinism when it is not in their interests. This interpretation is overly facile, because it denies the significance, both economic and physical, of attachment to place. The conditions of reproduction of social life, particularly families, community support systems, public sector facilities like schools, private cultural institutions such as churches—often owned and controlled, at least formally, by working people—are often hard hit when a single sector or ensemble of economic activities endures hard times. The loss of income and jobs, an environmental disruption that negatively affects other sectors, will reverberate through the local economy and touch many lives. With it comes the longer-term fear that the regional economy will not be able to sustain the current community. Outmigration, particularly of younger people, will be forced by the slow evaporation of opportunities to make a living.

Cultural Leavening

However strong the economic peculiarities and hardships of a particular region, they will not necessarily materialize in the form of regional politics. The shape and intensity of regional politics depend heavily upon the existing culture, politics, and economy of the region. Internal unity around regional disruption most often occurs when the local culture is relatively homogenous (or some route around internal differences can be found), can produce indigenous leadership, and possesses a political party structure willing to countenance and embrace the regional cause. Some of the enabling conditions are also economic—class structure, local versus outside ownership, sectoral composition—but others inure in ethnic, religious, and other cultural traits fashioned over the generations.

The Volatility of Regional Coalitions

The dominant members of a regional coalition may change with the evolution of the conflict. At the outset, a regional challenge may be mounted by seriously injured parties without any history of political participation. Their claims will be dramatic and creative, tending toward the radical—farmers in the Populist era are an example. In the effort to gain acceptance and win political battles, the initial leadership may accept or be displaced by more established regional leadership. It is not a foregone conclusion, however, that regional elites will end up controlling a regionalist impulse. In some cases, the control of region politics may pass to a new configuration of interests. The outcome in any individual case depends upon the balance of power between competing interests within the region and on the strategic choices made by the organizers themselves.

Economic Capability

Interregional contests in the United States have consisted for the most part of competing claims levied on the federal government. There are those regional claims which fundamentally challenge the entire edifice of the federal government power and petition for the right to secede or to reorganize the entire representational system. A second type does not challenge the legitimacy of central government but demands that certain of its powers and responsibilities be reallocated among levels within it—that certain categories of public activity, spending, or decision making such as land sales, infrastructure, social services, or civil rights be reshuffled up or down the federal ladder. Finally, there is a third type of claim that accepts the distribution of functions among federal levels but argues for a reallocation of funds among regions or a reformulation of policy to correct regional imbalances.

The type of political claim levied—separatism, federal, functional restructuring or reallocation of federal funds—will depend heavily upon the regional leadership's assessment of its ability to go it alone, its faring under alternative structural arrangements, and its receipts under new federal budgetary practices. These in turn depend upon the growth prospects the region faces and whether its economic trouble derive from a surfeit of older, obsolete sectors, from a disadvantaged position with respect to the terms of international trade, or an adverse distribution of income from outside ownership and control. Regions which are growing at a healthy rate, house their own indigenous finance and industrial capital, and enjoy favorable terms of trade are least apt to register any form of regional complaint and indeed can be expected to be advocates of nationalism. Regions which possess a robust economy but suffer from outside ownership and control and/or adverse terms of trade will be apt to opt for separatism or a decentralization of powers, believing that their economic vigor can carry them alone. Regions which face poor growth prospects will not try to go it alone, but will petition for special treatment. Each of these expected postures depends upon the existing muscle of the region in question vis-à-vis the center of power.

The Role of Party Politics

Since most regionalism does end up in the political realm, at the state if not the national level, the preexisting character of politics within regions plays a powerful role in channeling regional protest and action. Regions with well-entrenched, competitive two-party systems will be less apt to evolve a regionalist politics, since it will be in the interest of at least one party to oppose the program lest it bring too much credit upon the other. An example might be the difficulty in organizing a regional coalition across states when the governors involved hail from opposite parties. Regions with one dominant party will not face this problem. Nor will regions where party structure is weaker and politics is more highly personalized. In the latter, politicians of different stripes will find it less difficult to work together to forge regional unity.

The Mutuality of Regionalism

Regional self-consciousness is a mutually reinforcing process. While regional economic differentiation is linked to larger and perhaps territorially indifferent economic forces, the process of regional identification is quite comparative, even invidious in nature. The self-consciousness of, say, the mid-nineteenth-century South, presupposes another region whose development experience can be compared to its own, against whose progress its own performance can be weighed. That is, to be distinctive is to be different from another region or regions, in this case from both the commercial-industrial North and the diversified agricultural Midwest. One region becomes conscious of its underdevelopment, then, in contrast to another. Often, the region whose economy or elites are on the winning side of this comparison only reluctantly come to see themselves as a distinct region, in response to the vituperative charges of the more troubled region.

The Potential of Regionalism as a Political Force

Regionalism cannot be judged per se as either a reactionary or a progressive force in the evolution of a capitalist economy. Regionalism may galvanize around a program that accelerates a region's integration into the larger capitalist economy or around one which retards it. Major cases of regional self-consciousness and interregional strife may require the mounting of internal cross-class coalitions, but there is no reason to believe that in the absence of such regional social grouping in a cross-regional class conflict would emerge. Indeed, class consciousness may first develop because of regional organizing, and progressive change may evolve within such regional conflicts. Regional conflict is often over legitimate injuries to regional residents, and protest is often a route to a deeper understanding of the operation of the political economy. This tolerant interpretation of regionalism is not inconsistent with a more critical conclusion that most major interregional struggles have ultimately been led by—and profited—a narrow regional elite. By the time the major drama takes place, the positive contribution of regionalism toward progressive change may already have been made. Its advocates may leave the regional coalition to form their own autonomous groups.

THE CASE STUDIES OF REGIONALISM

To substantiate the theses, I chose to research a number of past and contemporary cases of American regionalism. First, I chose to research (through secondary sources) the encounters of Native American groups and European colonists with an eye toward understanding how the regionalization of the continent altered over the sixteenth through eighteenth centuries. Native American "regions," based as they were on a combination of gathering and settled agriculture, were much smaller in size and greater in number prior to the European intrusion. Subsequently, the struggles between the Indians and different groups of colonists yielded dramatically different and regionally diverse land use patterns, boundaries, settlement sizes, and political structures across the North American continent. The contemporary regionalization of the United States bears prominent markings that date from this era and the fact that European settlement took place under siege, yet almost no account of this influence can be found in the regional literature.

It seemed essential to include a study of the origins and politicization of nineteenth-century north-south sectionalism, which culminated in the Civil War.[1] This study, drawn entirely from the extraordinarily rich set of secondary sources produced by American historians, underscores the ways in which the economic issues dividing regions have changed in severity and kind over the past 150 years. It also shows how the federal system of government and the dominance of two-party politics played a major role in precipitating, shaping, and sometimes muting regional impulses. Furthermore, this case study enables me to show how southern regional development and self-consciousness for an entire century to come was strongly colored by the previous north-south discord, creating the material for a renewed anti-Yankee antagonism in the postwar period. The unique structure of the southern economy, its political party system, and much of its contemporary ideology derive from that era. They become strong shapers of the "New South."

For the period following World War II, I have researched the interregional antagonisms that emerged in the 1970s along two axes—first, the popularly termed frostbelt-sunbelt dichotomy, the latter somewhat awkwardly encompassing the Southwest as well as the Old South, and second, a renewed new East-West controversy over energy and resource development. Juxtaposing these recent cases of regionalism with each other and with the nineteenth-century case permits me to illustrate and elaborate upon a number of the theses just presented regarding the types, intensity, coherence, and causes of American regionalism.

I chose not to research the populist conflict as an in-depth case study of regionalism for two reasons. First, its causes and major events are much less well researched and interpreted than are those of the Civil War conflict. A number of provocative studies of the era have been done, but they take quite different positions in evaluating the strength and successes of the populist movement and to an amateur's consternation, do not even agree on which organizations and issues constituted the real core of the movement.[2]

But there is a more important reason for leaving populism out of a study of regionalism and that is that it never became a full-fledged *regional* movement at all. There seem to have been two reasons for this, each operating in a somewhat contradictory fashion. First, the prevailing sectional sentiment and political party concentrations ran along the Mason-Dixon line, still quite warm with the memory of the Civil War. Populist organizers, who sprouted from groups in Texas and the Plains states, tried to create an alliance of western and southern farmers against eastern merchant financiers and railroads, but were thwarted continually by Republicans waving the bloody shirt in the Midwest and upper Plains states and by Democrats invoking the Lost Cause in the Old South. A past regionalism, then, prevented a reconstituted regionalism from arising.

However, it is also true, and quite significant, that the populist movement was much more successfully a class movement than any case of regionalism studied here. The Populists had a specific economic program that they wished to promote for working farmers and free wage labor in all regions. Populism, although it remained highly region-ally concentrated, faced great internal opposition within those regions and consistently claimed to be a class rather than a regional movement. Indeed, it was universally opposed by the pivotal commercial classes in all regions.

Nor did I choose to research the New Deal as an example of an era in which regionalism gave way to strong national unity. In addition to the fact that all regions shared more or less equally in the Great Depression, the success of the New Deal owed much to the ability of Franklin D. Roosevelt to build a unified new Democratic Party out of the more urban and working class northern branch and the heavily agricultural south-ern branch, two groups who had not been on speaking terms for most of a century. New Yorker Roosevelt's success in the South had much to do with personal factors, particularly his strong personal ties, which he deftly parlayed into southern support for his program (Freidel 1965).

The case studies are relatively few in number, although they cover the major instances of American regionalism. They cannot, therefore, be read as definitive proof of the theses presented in the analytical chap-ters. Indeed, to a large extent this regional research effort has been inductive, inferring from the empirical study of regionalism a number of propositions about its causes and shape. The reader should keep in mind that the purpose here is to pioneer a framework for further analyses of regions and regionalism. A comparative study, with regions in other advanced capitalist countries, would provide a further test of the theses formulated here.[3]

A BRIEF NOTE ON METHOD

The analysis laid out in subsequent chapters is not designed to be used as a formal model of regional differentiation and regionalism. It is rather an exposition of the ways in which the method of historical materialism can be applied to these phenomena in the American context. The book argues that this route yields a richer appreciation of regional politics than do other scholarly traditions, including the historians of sectionalism, regional organicism, regional science, and structuralist Marxism. These alternative approaches are reviewed in the Appendix; and while I remain critical, I have incorporated many insights from each where relevant.

The methodology can be succinctly summarized as follows. Marxist political economy, or more precisely, historical materialism, offers the best foundation for an interpretation of regionalism for several reasons. First, it insists on *historical* research—on understanding how the present is shaped by the past and on the great dynamic evolution of social forms. In this it is superior to the rather mechanistic formulations of micro- and macroeconomics, which cannot break out from a framework that sees all change as fluctuation around some essential equilibrium.

Second, the Marxist political economy method begins with a materialistic interpretation of social reality. Of course, standard economics also embraces a form of materialism. But the Marxist formulation is preferable for the task of regional analysis because it emphasizes antagonistic relationships among classes of people and the methodical, wrenching pattern of boom and bust that drives regional prosperity unevenly across regions. Orthodox economics, on the other hand, emphasizes the harmony of interests among classes and permits no analytical room for exploitation.

On the other hand, the use here of the materialist approach should not be interpreted as a claim that economic forces determine all aspects of social life. Indeed, the Marxist approach is far less economistic than orthodox economics. Within the Marxist camp, there exists a great deal of controversy over whether or not economic forces are even primary, whether other aspects of society, such as culture and politics, are to be conceived of as "superstructures" or can be parallel in importance or even dominant at particular moments in history. The strength of Marxism is its intention to capture the whole—to be holistic. Materialism in the broad sense of the term means simply that a good *starting* point for an analysis of social phenomena is the economic relationships among people and the dynamics of the evolving economy in question. This is precisely what the Marxist concept of mode of production does, and as I will show, it is quite helpful for explaining instances of regionalism in earlier periods of U.S. history and the inherited qualities of contemporary regional culture.

Upon this foundation of historical materialism, I have grafted a number of insights and concepts from the behavioral social sciences: economic sectors, political parties, intergovernmental political structure, and sociological and anthropological notions of race, ethnicity, religion, kinship, and gender groupings. The combination permits the foundation of theses outlined above, which are further developed in chapters 2, 3, and 7. The rest of the book consists of empirical applications.

Empirical verification of the strength of the analytical framework is not a straightforward hypothesis-testing endeavor. For one thing, we lack enough instances of regional politics in American history to constitute a reasonably sized sample. For another, we are attempting to draw general conclusions about an historical process of development, rather than specific marginal adjustments to a very specific existing status quo. The institutional framework is thus changing simultaneously with the behavior of participants, preventing the formulation of precise deterministic cause-and-effect models.

The empirical work thus relies upon two types of evidence. First, different instances of American regionalism are compared with each other, both across regions and more cautiously, across time. Thus the proposition that certain political party configurations, for instance, lend themselves to more virulent forms of regionalism than others cannot be rejected if we can say that for all identified cases, regions with those types of party structure did indeed host stronger regional movements.

Second, we can compare the interpretations of other types of analysis with the ones presented here. At times, this must necessarily remain on the level of appealing to the reader that we have told a more plausible story than another tradition does. One way of doing this is to show that empirical evidence cited for an alternative explanation is compatible with the one proposed here, but not vice versa. In many cases, however, alternative scholarly traditions have no well-articulated theory of regional politics, even though they may have much to say about regional differentiation. The present analysis is thus offered as a challenge to those traditions to incorporate regional politics into their bodies of theory.

THE STRUCTURE OF THE BOOK

In chapters 2 and 3, I present an analytical framework for studying regions, since the phenomenon of regionalism rests upon the differentiation of territorial space into distinct units called regions. It is here that the interplay of economic, political, and cultural aspects in the formation of regions and regional consciousness is explored, with an articulation of the specific concepts from the study of each which are useful for analyzing American regionalism. Chapter 2 argues that economic differentiation, of various forms, is a necessary, often motivating force in the formation of regions and regionalism; at the same time seeking to show that economic factors are not sufficient to explain the political outcome. For that, a corresponding analysis of politics and culture must be undertaken. The methodology charted here may be compared to alternative approaches to the study of regions by referring to the Appendix.

Chapter 4 applies this general analysis to two major eras of regional unrest in North America. It first compares regionalization before and after the European arrival, showing how differences in mode of production and political strategy between Native Americans and colonists yielded new patterns of land settlement and political structure. It also contrasts the various encounters between highly differentiated native groups and the Spanish on the West Coast, the French in the Northeast, and the English on the Eastern Seaboard, each with their own quite different designs on Native American land and labor.

Chapter 4 also covers the growing bitterness between North and South that culminated in the Civil War. It lays out the economics of the conflict—the fundamental differences in the mode of production, with strikingly different labor systems, sectoral specializations and mid-century regionwide growth rates—which provoked growing dissension over the proper role of the State. I document how two ruling elites at economic loggerheads translated their political programs into regional claims, attempting to unify all classes internally against an external enemy. The ways in which the political and cultural traits and capabilities of each region mediated these efforts are detailed. The chapter ends with a reflection on the suppression of regionalism in the Populist and New Deal eras.

Chapters 5 and 6 detail the national and international economic context within which postwar regions are differentially nested and privileged. Chapter 5 analyzes the principal features of the new international division of labor and the accompanying spatial restructuring which it has imposed on U.S. regions. In addition, it develops briefly a model of sectoral dynamics which suggests that given capitalist accumulation imperatives, the longer term trajectory of any region, even one enjoying a contemporary boom, is apt to be unstable. Finally, this chapter explores the increasing militarization of the U.S. economy, arguing that its regional effects are highly uneven and that it has created a "defense perimeter."

Chapter 6 illustrates the accelerated economic differentiation of major U.S. regions in the 1970s. Despite an apparent convergence in per capita income, the growth gap among these regions was heightened in the 1970s, recorded in widening differentials in population growth, job creation, outmigration, and unemployment. This cast the various regions in roles quite different from those they had assumed within the national economy. A brief description of the postwar sectoral composition and growth experience of each of the major regions is included in this chapter.

In chapter 7, the translation of economic circumstances into regionalist political expression is modelled for the postwar period. This analysis differs from that developed in chapters 2 and 3 in that the regionalism modelled takes place in a ubiquitously modern, industrialized capitalist economy. Regional cleavage is thus not the product of conflicting modes of production, but of differential sectoral composition and growth rates under capitalism. The model hypothesizes that certain sectoral configurations will tend to produce an internally unified regional politics with a particular set of claims levied on the national government, while other configurations will focus regional energies on internal conflicts. The successful translation of economic pressures into a full-blown regional politics depends upon preexisting conditions within the regions (such as economic and ethnic homogeneity, absence or presence of an ownership class, and political party competition). It will also depend upon interactions among potentially competitive regions. The belligerence of a neighboring or contesting region will tend to heighten internal regional solidarity and consciousness where it was previously slack or moribund.

Chapters 8 and 9 attempt to validate the model by looking at three competing cases of postwar regionalism. Here, the major regionwide political organizations emerging in the 1970s are compared and contrasted. In chapter 8, the new regional consciousness in a decline-preoccupied Northeast-Midwest is explored, particularly in the formation of the Northeast Midwest Congressional Coalition. The same chapter looks at the emergence of an inward-looking, internal growth-preoccupied Southern Growth Policies Board in the early 1970s. An analysis of the ways in which these two regions became combatants in the latter 1970s, and of the legitimacy and resolution of their differences, concludes the chapter.

In chapter 9, the emergence of a new western consciousness and its embodiment in several versions of what ultimately became the Western Governors Policy Office are explored. Western regional policies in this era had both an internal and external face, the former the struggle over the terms of resource development between various groups in the West and the latter a three-way tussle between western residents, an absentee federal government landowner, and outside energy corporations. The growing antagonism between the Northeast-Midwest and the West on energy development issues is also explored.

In the final chapter, a comparative view of these cases, both past and contemporary, is offered. A number of generalizations about the tenor of regionalism under specific circumstances are tentatively drawn. In these final pages, I advance an argument in defense of the progressive possibilities of participation in regionalist politics.

Notes

1. Many writers distinguish between sectionalism and regionalism. One connotation is that sectionalism characterizes larger subnational units than regionalism does. A more important distinction is a normative one made by Odum and Moore (1938), where sectionalism is seen as a nasty, unnecessary set of hostilities while regionalism is the affection held by residents for their interregional unique environmental home and does not dictate any them-us

connotations. Since sectionalism is no longer an oft-used expression, since I am dealing for the most part with large American regions, and since I believe Odum's distinction to be artificial, I will use the term regionalism in this book to encompass both sets of connotations.

2. The best book-length treatment which tries to address these differences in interpretation is Goodwyn (1978).

3. The best intra-European and Canadian comparative work I have seen is Gourevitch (1977). Gourevitch predicts that peripheral nationalisms will be more apt to arise in regions where economic but not political leadership resides; he predicts regionalist sentiment to be low in laggard regions. This does not correspond to the U.S. experience. However, several of Gourevitch's hypotheses are similar to those presented here, especially his notion of "ethnic potential."

2

The Economics of Regions

Because regions are creatures of history, products of contemporary change, and homes to diverse groups, they are multifaceted. In these next two chapters, a working definition of region is proposed and the characteristics of regions are explored using the concepts of mode of production, economy, political structure, and culture. This definition owes much to the vigorous debate among several traditions reviewed in the book's Appendix. The primacy of economic forces is argued in the present chapter but the tempering functions of the state and culture in the translation of economic differentiation into regional conflict is explored at length in chapter 3. At the end of that chapter, we take up the difficult issue of evaluation of regionalism.

REGIONS AND REGIONALISM AS CONCEPTUAL CATEGORIES

Regions interest us because they are the sites of human drama. Regions are distinct from cities and nations as alternative spatial units and are distinct from institutions such as religions, corporations, or political parties. They are social structures that matter in the contemporary world. But do the complex empirical realities we connote when speaking of regions lend themselves to a theoretical conceptualization?

What Is a Region?

A workable definition of "region" must avoid the difficulties that plague much of the dominant regional science literature. It must not insist arbitrarily on the primacy of one or another constituent element. It must be committed to preserving analytically the historical potential of any region as an entity capable of disappearing, of losing significance, or of merging into another spatial form. Furthermore, the conceptualization must capture the tensions between the interior regional dynamic and its exterior environment. Finally, such a definition must acknowledge the relational nature of region, with regard both to other regions and to other spatial entities.

Given these considerations, I propose the following definition. A region is an historically evolved, contiguous territorial society that possesses a physical environment, a socioeconomic, political, and cultural milieu, and a spatial structure distinct from other regions and from the other major territorial units, city and nation. This relational definition delineates regions through both (1) their mutual contrasts and distinctions and (2) their location on the scale of spatial units. The category "region" connotes territorial units with unique physical and cultural traits, whereas the category "city" connotes a special form of human settlement that exhibits regularities of function and spatial structure regardless of location. The category "nation" applies to a special type of region which possesses political sovereignty.[1]

Yet this definition may be too general and fail to compel interest. Instead, one's curiosity is piqued by the *distinctions* promised by the definition—to the breadth and limits of the social content of that category—and by the suggestion of mutual self-definition of regions.

What Is Regionalism?

The conception of regional politics which complements this notion of region is similarly expansive. Regional politics may take two quite distinct forms. First, it may consist of internal struggles around the future evolution of a region. Thus, for example, struggles over plant closings or stripmining become regional conflicts when combattants on either side invoke the specter of a dramatically altered regional economy or environment as a summons to other residents to embrace their cause. Understanding these struggles requires knowing the regional context. Regional identity and consciousness can be engendered (or muted) through these internal events, which evoke (or suppress) an awareness of singularity among residents.[2]

Alternatively, regional politics may take the form of a regionwide movement in opposition to some external entity, be it another region, the larger state or national governments, or an outside economic force.[3] The latter type of regional politics we know as regionalism, a phenomenon similar to but distinct from nationalism, both in setting and in intensity. Regionalism is the rallying around one or more distinguishing characteristics of the region, levied as a territorial claim against one or several mechanisms of the State. Regionalism may be transformed into nationalism, when the demands of a region escalate to the goal of secession and independent statehood, or at least some measure of self-governance.

Regions are products of material forces in history. They bear cultures in which traditional values and meanings, contemporary passions, and future visions are stubbornly arrayed against exterior forces that would erode, undermine, or thwart them. Regions do change as a product of both external and internal initiatives, and their inhabitants engage actively in the process of transformation.[4] The power of this tradition and activism is often overlooked by regional analysts working with structuralist models.[5]

The most compelling questions concern the forces that constitute regional character and motivate regional politics, addressed in what follows. The reader should keep in mind that the analysis is designed for American regionalism, although it applies to some aspects of the European experience which I refer to when appropriate. In keeping with the empirical commitment of the book, I identify throughout the most significant social groups that organize around regional issues and shape the practice of regionalism, a theme I return to in chapter 7.

REGIONS AND MODES OF PRODUCTION

We have defined regions as territorial societies. It is impossible to think of regions as places apart from the peoples who inhabit them. At the same time, the definition encompasses the fact of territoriality and of distinct physical environments. The region, perhaps more than other conceptual spatial units, is the meeting ground of humanity and nature.

Modes of Production Reviewed

The Marxist concept of mode of production is a suitable starting point for comprehending the nature of regions. It offers an analytical framework for examining the interaction between human beings and their natural environment. For analyzing regionalism in the case of the United States, three such modes can be identified: primitive communism (Native Americans), slavery (the South prior to the Civil War), and capitalism (the North, originally, and currently the entire economy). The two cataclysmic territorial wars in the United States were the east-west struggle between mercantile capitalism and Native Americans, and the north-south conflagration between emerging industrial capitalism and slavocracy.

In the Marxist usage, the organization of any human society is fundamentally structured around its mode of production, which governs the *social relations* and *productive forces* sustaining human life. The social relations of a mode include who owns land and other instruments of production (tools, machines, and so on), and who works for whom and under whose control. For instance, under capitalism, workers produce food, clothing, and shelter for the entire population, including capitalists who appropriate the product of labor above what it requires for its reproduction. The ownership of land and particularly the means of production by capitalists allows them to enforce the exploitative relationship; they control the work process and the conditions under which labor can sell its labor power and produce commodities. Slavery as a mode of production operates somewhat differently because slaves as labor power are themselves commodities. A mode's productive forces also encompass the techniques used to produce commodities: for example, machines with mechanical power and automated controls in the contemporary period.

Each mode has a dynamic which results from both conflicts in its social relations and contradictions in the development of its productive forces. Capitalism, for instance, is subject to crises, in part because workers struggle to push wages up and challenge capitalist control of the work process and in part because its internal drive to increase profits through enhanced productivity and exploitation of labor results in periodic overproduction. The dynamics of slavery in the southern United States compelled it to constantly expand extensively in search of exploitable land.

Each mode is characterized by a distributional system which allocates the total output of productive labor among various classes. Under capitalism this is accomplished primarily through wage determination and the process of exchange, although in recent years it is increasingly modified by State intervention for social welfare, regulation of labor-management relations, and attempts to control the aggregate level of economic activity through fiscal policy. The basic features of a mode of production are listed in table 2.1, with examples drawn from the cases of capitalism and slavery as encountered in the nineteenth century and elaborated upon in chapter 4.

Table 2.1　Modes of Production and U.S. Regions, 1830–1860

Mode of production	Capitalism (North)	Slavery (South)
Productive forces		
Productive units	Factories, mills, farms	Plantations
Dominant sectors	Agriculture, textiles, iron, railroads, trade	Cotton (earlier tobacco, rice, indigo)
Techniques	Steam-powered machinery, diversified farming	Hand-cultivated cash cropping
Dynamics	Crisis tendencies, propensity to innovate	Soil exhaustion, tendency to western expansion
Social relations		
Ownership	Capitalists	Slaveholders
Labor power	Wage workers	Slaves
Human settlements	Cities with class and ethnic ghettos, small town and farm communities	Dispersed plantations, small shipping ports
Distribution	Wage income, market exchange	Plantation reproduction of labor power
Political tendencies	Strong central State	Decentralized political power
Ideology	Dynamic, optimistic, expansionist, respect for free labor	Paternalistic, respect for gentility, honor, kinship, hierarchy

Capitalism as a mode of production is more apt to promote regional conflict even though it reduced regional differentiation. Pre-capitalist territorial societies were highly differentiated, due to historical adaptations of human labor and technology to highly varied natural environments. In the process of integrating areas of the globe to a larger world economy, commercial capitalism introduced the diverse regions' technologies (including new food sources, plows, wheels, diseases, and weaponry) to each other with devastating consequences. Furthermore, modern capitalism's continual drive to find new outlets for surplus, cheaper sources of labor and material inputs, and higher productivity through technology systematically intrudes upon the separate regions and confronts each with its neighbors.[6]

Regionalization within Modes

Several features of a given mode of production may be grounds or impetus for conflict with regional manifestations. First of all, the clash of one mode with another, as in the Native American defense against aggressive European colonists, may be grounds for a territorial struggle. Second, the ownership of resources and means of production within a mode may be grounds for regional struggle; an example is the ownership by multinational corporations of resources in many Third World countries, which has provoked wars of liberation. Third, the organization of production itself may be the grounds for struggle, as in some socialist movements and workplace struggles. Fourth, the terms of exchange of labor power (wages), of resources (rent), or of commodities (prices) may be the subject of regional struggle, as in attempts to control export prices, import quantities, exchange rates, and most recently, debt repayment. Finally, the distribution of products via extraordinary means (for example, rationing, charity, welfare, or export-import controls, in capitalist economies) may be the source of regional struggle.

Since it is impossible here to specify theoretically all the different ways in which these features operate in each mode (feudalism, primitive communism, socialism, and so on), the demonstration is left to the following chapter, where an incipient capitalist economy is analyzed in its encounters with Native American and slave modes. In each case, two contesting modes of production were differentially dominant in contiguous regions. Because in each case at least one of the modes was inherently expansionist, territorial wars of aggression and survival erupted, with the dominant political forces of one mode vanquishing the political leadership of the other.

The mode of production model is also a useful starting point for a contemporary analysis of American regionalism. The capitalist mode of production in its current dominant form exhibits the following general characteristics: production of commodities for exchange, production by free wage labor, appropriation of labor's product by capitalist interests controlling the means of production, allocation of labor and means of production toward the end of accumulating more capital, a tendency toward periodic crisis, a methodical tendency toward increasing productivity of labor, a capitalist State which enforces the wage relation and tries to solve the crises and to accommodate new forms of accumulation, urbanization, cultures based on individualism, and so on. But to move from this level of generality toward understanding a given region in any particular period, we must make several additional distinctions.

First, as mentioned above, we can distinguish among stages in capitalist development (such as petty commodity production, mercantilism, and industrial capitalism). Second, we can distinguish structural details in a given time: the specific division of labor in production, the form of capitalist decision making (for example, the small business versus the multinational conglomerate), the degree of competition or cooperation among corporations, the commodity structure which embodies specific gains in productivity, and historic crises in the expansionary process. Third, we must specify the evolving structure of the State and the way it impedes evolution of the capitalist economy and is in turn altered by it.

In the rest of this chapter and the next, I present a framework for looking at the structure and dynamics of a specific mode of production, namely capitalism, as it encounters, employs, and reshapes regions. The exposition places economic determinants of regional distinctiveness and change at the center of the analysis, but contends that political and cultural features are critical for the translation of economic pressures into regional strife and regionalism. The use here of analytical categories such as economic, political, and cultural should not be interpreted as implying that these are independent variables. On the contrary, they are very much interrelated. For instance, the topography of a region constrains the possibilities for spatial settlement patterns, for community cohesiveness, and for economic viability, but the same topography can in turn be reshaped (via highways, soil conservation, earth moving) by economic forces, community traditions, and new forms of settlement. Historically, economic differentiation has been dominant and therefore a good analytical starting point, but the interpretation of any single instance of regionalism requires attention to each category. Yet each category encapsulates a large set of relationships which are differentiable across regions.

REGIONAL ECONOMIES UNDER CAPITALISM

The Marxist literature explains rather well the uneven panoply of regional development as a product of the laws of motion of capital accumulation. While this may serve as a coherent interpretation of the operation of the system as a whole, it is not very useful for understanding the particular qualities and the evolutionary paths of individual regions. Particularly in evaluating the political possibilities of regionalism, we must break down the regional problem further, to get at its constituent elements. We want to know how and to what extent capital-ist-produced uneven development in various regions creates antago-nisms within them, peculiar to their situation, and among them, where the development of one is directly related to the lack of development in another.

Clearly, for the time and place we are considering, the capitalist mode of production ties together a substantial portion of regional economic activity. No region in the United States has constituted an independent economy for at least 150 years. Furthermore, the character or regional economies is constantly changing, with economic crises and hardship taking on different forms in each. The pace of contemporary uneven development has been correctly linked to the accelerated turnover time of capital and the increased freedom of the large multinational corpora-tions, aided by dramatic gains in transportation and communications, to move production across regions, resulting in a constant and rapid reorganization of production spatially.[7]

Corporations, the major institutional actors in this process, exhibit two aspects of the drive toward accumulation. First, they are forced under the competitive conditions of the market (even when oligopolistic) to increase productivity continually. This they do by pursuing both prod-uct innovations and process innovations which will enable them to increase profitability by gaining an edge in the market for short-term superprofits. Second, they pursue enhanced profitability by trying to keep costs as low as possible; that is, by squeezing wage rates, migrating to lower cost labor sites, abandoning physical environments whose resources are exhausted or have become too costly in comparison to new discoveries, shunning jurisdictions where the social wage becomes too expensive, and shifting locations to take advantage of new materials or transportation savings.

Regions, as the economic territories among which corporations move, operate as production ensembles. That is, they are the locus of sets of interrelated economic activities which engage wage labor in the produc-tion of commmodities for exchange. It is the region as production ensemble that is primary in explaining regional differentiation.[8] Similar-ities among regions stem more from the homogenization of social life under capitalism than from any real homogenization of economic activi-ties.

Class Structure, Value Extraction, and Unequal Exchange

A first axis of regional economic differentiation is the tendency for class structure to be unevenly distributed across regions. An example in the United States is the heavy concentration of working-class people in coal-mining areas of Appalachia. In contemporary capitalist countries, exam-ples of pure class structure at this most general level are few, although breakthroughs in communications technologies, where all worldwide operations of a corporation can be controlled from a remote and central location, may increase their incidence in the future. More common is the region whose class structure is distinctive for its mixture of subclasses. Regions with high proportions of small business or individual entrepreneurship in their class structures, such as the American farm belt, have distinctive identities and politics. Or in another variation, some regions have a high proportion of skilled unionized workers, as in the industrial Northeast, or high proportions of low-skilled, nonunionized workers, as in the Southwest.[9]

A second axis has to do with the way surplus is extracted. The underdevelopment of Appalachia has been traced in part to the incomplete subsumption of labor to capitalism in pre-1930s coal mining, where coal companies extracted absolute surplus value from workers rather than raise productivity through mechanization (Simon 1980).[10] Regions dominated by sectors operating in this manner tend to fall behind regions where sectors continually expand by increasing labor productivity. Another variant of surplus extraction occurs when a region's resources can be profitably exploited due to differential natural resource endowments. Regions undergoing an energy boom—the Intermountain West and Alaska in the 1970s, for instance—are highly differentiated economically from industrial regions.

A third source of regional differentiation is the segregation of production from realization activities. In capitalist economies, owners of capital may secure a return in any one of four ways: industrial production, circulation and distribution, finance, and landownership. These avenues correspond roughly to the industrial, mercantile, financial, and real estate sectors in an economy. Any one of these may be regionally skewed in location or operation. Landownership and speculation, for instance, can be controlled by groups outside a given region; a stunning example is the contemporary western Sagebrush rebellion against federal land ownership in the West between the national government, the large energy corporations, and regional land-users like ranchers and environmentalists. This is a battle over land use, land prices, and rents. Mercantile and financial activities have traditionally been skewed toward northeastern cities, serving as a strong regionalizing force during the era of western agrarian populism.

Sectoral Specialization

A fourth feature of contemporary U.S. regional differentiation is the remarkable degree of sectoral specialization among regions.[11] A sector consists of all units (plants, mines, or farms) engaged in producing a similar commodity, whether they are owned by diversified corporations, individual entrepreneurs, or the public.[12] Regional economies are highly structured production complexes centered on individual commodities such as autos, steel, electronics, coal, oil, textiles, and chemicals.

The proposition that sectoral differentiation remains a potent factor in contemporary regionalism requires a rebuttal of the cruder connotations suggested by the term *post industrial society* and its presumed elimination of regional differentials.[13] Advocates of this view argue that (1) service industries account for larger and larger shares of employment; and (2) the composition of regional economies, measured by indicators such as the percentage of manufacturing employment for each, appear to be converging.

But these aggregate figures obscure two tendencies. One, services are highly differentiated internally. Those oriented toward meeting the needs of the working population have been relatively insignificant in growth, except for health services and eating and drinking establishments. Most personal services have actually *declined* in significance. The growth of employment in eating and drinking establishments is a result of the increasing entry of women into the wage labor force, so that labor previously devoted to producing use values in the household, like meals, is now sold to employers while commodity and service purchases are substituted at home for women's direct labor. Thus its extraordinary employment growth in every region is not symptomatic of any underlying shifts. Services to businesses formed the largest-growing segment of services, and these were closely tied to the character of the regional industrial structure. Corporate lawyers were concentrated in New York, Delaware, and Washington, D.C.; geologists in Texas and Colorado; advertising in New York; and media in Los Angeles.

Second, *within* manufacturing, dramatic differences distinguish regional economies, when industries are disaggregated into sectors. The manufacturing base of Santa Clara Valley, California is composed almost entirely of electronics, aerospace, and computer-oriented activities, while that of Detroit is almost completely oriented toward the auto industry. In each case, sectoral complexes have been built around one or several basic commodities, so that even an apparent empirical diversity may be misleading. In Detroit, for instance, the presence of a modest steel industry, and a large machining sector should not be taken as evidence of industrial diversification, since the latter are almost wholly dependent upon the auto industry.

It is not simply the existence of such sectoral differentiation that gives regions their character and shapes their economic life. It is the way in which these sectoral complexes compare to those of other regions and respond to the disruptive events of the world economy as a whole. Individual sectors display differential rates of change in growth of employment and output, depending upon their position in the world market and their profitability at different points in their profit cycle (see chapters 5 and 6 below). These sectoral peculiarities may carry regions with them, so that even in a period of relative prosperity, a particular region suffers dramatically from capital disinvestment.

Sectoral specialization is most apt to produce antagonism when regions occupy sequential positions in the exchange process, especially when market power is uneven. For instance, if one region produces raw materials sold by small firms to another region where purchases are controlled by a few large buyers, then monopoly power on the part of the latter may systematically impoverish the former region by consistent downward pressure on prices. This occurred for fifty years in the Appalachian coal industry, where steel corporations virtually kept the price of coal at the lowest possible level (that is, below that which would have prevailed in a competitive market). In a counterexample, oligopoly in the oil industry in the American West (and subsequently worldwide) has permitted oil companies to extract monopoly profits from oil-consuming regions for many years. (While the western oil consumers were charged similarly, their economic environment was "overdeveloped" by the profit-swollen oil industry, at least to the extent that its accompanying infrastructure and reinvestments were regional.

The State has frequently played a role in such arrangements, which accounts for the frequent targetting of regional protest toward it. Part of the heat generated between the North and the South prior to the Civil War was associated with the question of the tariff. A tariff under conditions of sectoral specialization operates as a license for the extraction of excess profits from one region by agents in the other, depending upon the commodity—in this case cotton or iron—on which it was to be levied. More recently, court suits and congressional battles between the industrial belt and the high plans coal-producing states over a severance tax reflect a similar struggle over exchange rates between producing and consuming regions.

The Relative Maturity of Class Conflict

A fifth source of regional economic differentiation is the historically evolved state of class conflict. In regions which have long been the host of capitalist industrial production, class conflict will have prompted the establishment of unions, collective bargaining, and a local welfare state. At least one political party will champion labor's right to organize strikes, and bargain over issues like job security and work rules.

The United States is singular among advanced capitalist countries in encompassing regions with highly developed institutions of class conflict as well as regions almost wholly without them. This variation is partially rooted in the juxtaposition of two pre–Civil War regional modes of production. The southern slave economy retarded industrialization up to 1860. Afterwards, the conversion of slaves into a semi-free agricultural labor force nurtured the poverty, racism, and violence which was to stunt class conflict in the South for a hundred years.

Slavery and racism are not the only dampers on the historical evolution of class conflict in the United States. In resource-rich regions, union militance has generally been confined to lumber camps and hard rock mines in which it was shortlived, if powerful, due to the impermanence of the resource base. In the interior Northwest and Intermountain West, a sparse population of small farmers and woodsmen are the legacy of these bygone booms.

This uneven development of class conflict in U.S. regions has meant that the more developed regions now confront the outmigration of capital to the lower wage and "better business climates" of the underdeveloped regions. In this situation, regions with differentially developed institutions of class conflict find themselves competing over the *same* sectors—generally those subject to greater competitive pressure to seek out low-cost production sites—such as textiles, shoes, and clothing. Regional struggle may therefore center on the preservation of these institutions in the more developed regions by demanding their imposition on the less-developed area. This case is readily illustrated by the effort of northern unions and the Democratic Party to get rid of so-called right-to-work laws in the southern states.

These types of economic differentiation within capitalist modes of production are listed in table 2.2, which also presents examples of each. The first three—class segregation, differential sources of surplus, and separation of production from realization activity—were more important in the late nineteenth and early twentieth centuries than subsequently. With the increasing penetration of capitalist production and exchange activities into all regions, the latter two—sectoral specialization and differential maturation of class conflict—have become more important in the postwar period. As a result, the substance and form of regional claims which emanate from each type have also tended to change over time.

THE ROOTS OF REGIONAL ECONOMIC SOLIDARITY

The members of a regional society who are directly affected by any one of these economic sources of regional antagonism are generally few. But

Table 2.2 Axes of Regional Economic Differentiation

Source of regional differentiation	Regional examples in the United States
Class segregation	Appalachian coalfields, midwestern farm belt
Differential source of surplus	Appalachian coalfields, Intermountain energy belt
Segregation of production and realization activities	Midwestern and southern farm belt, Great Basin and Plains ranching region
Sectoral specialization	Manufacturing belt, Intermountain energy belt, western defense and high tech region
Maturation of class conflict	Northeast and midwestern organized labor and urban machines; Intermountain and southern weak unions, good business climate

strong forces inherent in the local economy reinforce the importance of their destinies. These forces can be subsumed under the notion of the multiplier effect, or in Marxist terms, the reproductive functions of the local economy. A substantial group of local economic actors derive their income from the provision of the goods and services required by the resident population. Local reproductive sectors found in all but the most sparsely populated contemporary regions include retail groceries and dry goods stores, bottling and baking plants, gas stations and repair services, construction firms, local media, and banking and real estate services. Since the size of the resident population is a function of its ability to "export" commodities to the larger economy, the changing fortunes of this economic, or export, base have dramatic multiplier effects on local reproductive sectors.

Especially vulnerable, and therefore prone to perennial boosterism, are those sectors which in addition to serving the local population possess fixed assets which they cannot mobilize or move to another region. While a small grocer, operating out of a leased space can pack up everything except his steady customers on a truck and follow the general migration west and southward, sizable portions of the real estate, construction, banking, land development, utilities, and communications industries cannot. Nor can the regional media (newspapers and television), state and local governments, and the churches. The management (and sometimes workers) of each of these latter groups would suffer a loss of their wealth, position, or job if the regional economy should decline. Newspapers, for instance, would lose their circulation and simultaneously some of their advertising. Slack in housing demand would push housing prices down, depressing the real estate industry, and producing losses for banks that might have to foreclose. Regionally based politicians would lose their tax base, their constituency, and maybe ultimately their district. These groups, then, to the extent that they cannot convert their spatially fixed assets into money capital (thereby sticking someone else with the devalorization), have a clear material stake in the regional economy and its bolstering.

This segment, which consists of regional capital and is generally prominent in the local chambers of commerce, will not necessarily support workers or small businesses in any particular sector in distress. The ailing sector must be large enough to matter, and its assets must be so specific to that industry that they cannot be easily converted to other uses via the normal operation of the capitalist economy. The single local brewery in numerous medium-sized towns in the United States rarely rallied sufficient local support to survive. If industrial building can be shifted out of production of textiles or furniture into a newer and lighter manufacturing activity, so much the better in the eyes of this segment of the local business community, which is loath to act counter to its ideology of free enterprise. If, on the other hand, a large sector like agriculture, iron mining, or steel is a dominant economic base employer and appears to be in danger of serious disinvestment, the lack of alternative uses for the same resources will tend to drive local chamber of commerce types into a coalition to save the regional economy.

In recent years, regional economies have become even more integrated into the larger world economy than previously, largely because trade and communications improvements have increased imports of manufactured goods into local economies. For this reason, regional economies now have higher trade balances running with the outside world and are even more dependent upon their economic bases than previously. This plus the accelerated rate of world economic integration in the postwar period, with its quickened pace of capital mobility and disinvestment, may have heightened the significance of the multiplier effect. The reemergence of regionalism in the postwar period may have much to do with this larger force and its disruptive consequences on regional economies, a subject we return to in chapter 5.

THE MIX OF ECONOMIC FORCES: AN ILLUSTRATION FROM APPALACHIA

The distinctive economic character of regions resulting from the uneven process of capitalist development is the ensemble of all of these features. It is unlikely that just one such distinction operates in any case of regional disparity. Most regions have at least some form of sectoral specialization, but this may be joined to a distinctive class structure, a unique form of surplus extraction, a segregation of production from realization activities, and a specific level of maturation of class conflict. The blending of these economic attributes tends to produce relatively unique instances of regional expression and coalition. In chapter 3, the major historical cases of U.S. regionalism are examined for their economic underpinnings, and in chapter 7, a further set of hypotheses is proposed for analyzing postwar instances.

A brief look at the Appalachian case will illustrate the potential complexity of this fusion.[14] The most obvious economic force in the history of Appalachia is the coal industry. But the region's underdevelopment had little to do with the simple fact of being dominated by this one sector. First of all, this sector was dominated by small companies in an era when the customers of the industry were largely concentrated in other, adjoining regions. The ability of the latter to keep prices low was a function both of monopolistic power and of the long-run fall in demand for coal, which resulted from the substitution of oil for coal in heating. In turn, the coal companies dealt with the profit squeeze by intensifying the work process, underemploying available labor, and squeezing wages, which they were able to do through their control of the local labor market. This type of absolute surplus value extraction impeded the improvement of mine productivity which might have been secured through mechanization.

This stronghold persisted because of the region's smallholder, subsistence agriculture and the physical remoteness of most Appalachian towns in an era of railroads. The lack of transportation and the ridge-and-valley structure of Appalachian mountains deterred entry by other capitalist employers who might have been attracted to the low-wage pools the coal companies had created. Low wages and unstable work hampered the normal development of local goods and services-producing industries, reinforcing the region's stark dependency on coal. This coal-dominated structure continued to impoverish Appalachia, in contrast to surrounding regions, until the 1930s, when the United Mine Workers successfully organized the coal fields. However, since they were forced to agree to mechanization of the mines, in return for higher wages and job security, the result was a sustained postwar outmigration of mammoth proportions, leaving the region more impoverished than ever.

Thus economic and environmental forces in the Appalachian case consisted of the following: the coal sector's prominence in the regional economy, its extraordinary practice of absolute rather than relative surplus value extraction, the relationship between the sector and its more powerful buyers in other regions, the topography and geology of the region, the maturation of productive forces in the larger economy— especially the coming of oil and the railroads, and the slow development of class conflict. It would be difficult to argue that any one of these constitutes the fundamental or causal attribute, yet all can be reasonably encompassed by beginning with an inquiry into the coal industry.

As in Appalachia, interpreting U.S. regional differentiation in the twentieth century via the study of discrete sectors and their dynamics permits us to identify powerful forces which drive internal regional conflicts, such as the conflict between the principals of an older established sector and a newer incoming one which challenges, economically and politically, the control of the former over the region's productive resources. Similarly, such a method facilitates the analysis of the tendency toward cross-class regional coalitions, between regionally based capital and labor in a single sector, for instance, or between workers, small businesses, and regionally tied capital. Each type of economic differentiation, as we shall see in chapter 7, creates a set of organizational and political possibilities.

Whether these indeed develop into regional struggles, and what intergroup forms and targets they assume, depend upon more than just the economic forces at work. For the Appalachian case, economic analysis alone cannot account for the emerging consciousness of Appalachians in the 1960s, their remarkable militancy in organizing, their commitment to their homes even in periods of intense pressure to migrate to industrial cities, and their resistance to certain aspects of the federal government's Appalachian program of the 1960s and 1970s. To understand these, an amplified framework that includes an appreciation for the cultural and political features of regions is necessary. This is the subject of the next chapter.

ECONOMIC ORIGINS OF REGIONALISM: A SUMMARY

Regionalism has as its precondition the existence of regional differentiation. A primary source of such differentiation is the economic organization of life across regions. Differences in modes of production, if regionally separated, create the possibility for regional consciousness and interregional strife. Similarly, within any one mode, disparities in class structure, trading position, sectoral composition, and class organization can provide the basis for regional antagonism. Linkages within the regional economy may provide cross-class solidarity around a region's programs.

The history of U.S. regionalism, as we will see in chapter 4, has been predominantly based on either wholesale clashes over differing imperatives from contesting modes of production, antagonisms arising from sectoral differentiation, or disparities in the maturation of class conflict. Class segregation, unequal exchange, and differential techniques of labor exploitation have occurred, but mildly, and rarely have formed the basis for a major flare-up of regionalist sentiment. The power of any of these economic forces to ignite regionalism depends crucially on the political and cultural structures of the regions in question, a subject to which we now turn.

Notes

1. Regions generally lie within nations, although it is conceptually possible to treat supranational areas as regions. See the discussion in Knight (1982a, 518–20). Below, I argue that the salience of national political power in fashioning regions discourages this type of region from becoming the subject of regionalist sentiment.
2. Definitions of regionalism are also offered by Matthews (1983, ch. 1); and Knight (1982a, 518). These attempts, as well as my own, grapple with the social and spatial dimensions simultaneously. See Sack (1974, 17), on the complexity of merging spatial dimensions with social content.
3. Sack's work on the knowledge people have of other peoples and places is useful here (1980, 169). Gore (1984) gives the best statement of how all regional policy is explicitly biased against spatially defined groups and implicitly biased in favor of socially defined groups.
4. The mutual interaction between society and place has been a lively topic among geographers and sociologists. Massey (1984) and Cooke (1983) both stress the social construction of space; Massey stresses the "spatial construction of the social" as well (Massey and Allen 1984, 2–6). See also Gregory and Urry (1985, 2–3); and Sayer (1985).
5. For instance, Dulong characterizes the region and regionalism as "an empty

bottle into which the most varied potions can be poured. . . . Precisely because the 'region' has no fixed material referent, it can assume a multitude of meanings . . ." But absence of a single referent does not imply total relativity or malleability. Regions consist of a number of theoretically specifiable fused elements, created and constrained by material reality. A limited range of meanings is a truer statement of political potential than Dulong's "multitude." See the restatement and translation of Dulong in Kesselman (1981, 111). For an alternative and more sophisticated assessment of territory as empty, see Sack (1981, 67).

6. For a provocative statement of this process, see Harvey (1975).
7. See Kay (1975); Holland (1976); Bluestone and Harrison (1980 and 1982); and Frobel et al. (1979).
8. Regions are not the only spatial production ensembles useful for the analysis of capitalist development. Certainly nations constitute production ensembles as well, although they require a different scale of economic analysis from the one offered here to deal with regions.
9. Buck (1979) found for a comparative study of Britain, France, Australia, and West Germany that greater regional disparity in occupational structure within the former two countries seems to be correlated with greater regional antagonism. Efforts to correlate regionalism with class are common in the center-periphery literature; see, for instance, Cuneo (1978). See also the theoretical discussions in Cooke (1983, ch. 9); and Walker (1985). Clark (1984), shows that postwar differentials in U.S. production/nonproduction worker ratios exist and are significantly associated with capital intensification and differential profit rates.
10. See Brenner (1977) for this argument applied to developing countries.
11. Regional science has made significant contributions in this area, particularly in the empirical study of regional-industrial structure and the development of indicators to express it. See Isard (1960) for an encyclopedia of these. Oral tradition credits Wilbur Thompson with the following maxim: "Tell me your industries and I'll tell you your fortunes." The spatial division of labor among regions is a major theme of Massey (1984).
12. A sector in this usage is smaller than an industry, although to relieve monotony I shall use both terms interchangeably. Sectors are *not* synonymous with corporations, but consist only of those decision-making and production units within them that are preoccupied with the commodity in question.
13. See, for instance, Block (1984).
14. This terse history of Appalachia draws on Simon (1980); Rothblatt (1971); Whisnant (1979); and Clavel (1982).

3

The Politics and Cultures of Regions

For the antagonisms embedded in economic disparities to flower into distinctive regional politics, they must take on an organizational form and adopt a political target. In addition, they must be able to mobilize, even create if necessary, an ideology of place. The preexisting structure of the state is fundamental to the success or failure of this translation, as is the inherited culture of the regions themselves. In this chapter, we survey the roles of state and culture in the formation of regional politics. The present discussion operates at a level of generality permitting the analysis of the past two centuries of U.S. regionalism. A more detailed framework, appropriate to the postwar period, can be found in chapter 7.

THE ROLE OF AMERICAN POLITICAL STRUCTURE

Central to a study of this process is the state. Sectoral conflicts at the regional level are fought out within the political forums of the state, for three reasons.[1] First, they often cannot be handled internally, because the complaints are addressed to an external actor, group, or region outside the sphere of influence of the affected group. Second, the state has increasingly come to play a role in the profitability of individual sectors in the economy, at the same time that it arbitrates conflicts between disparate fractions of capital. Initially, federal subsidies took the form of infrastructure provision, land distribution, and land use regulation; but in the recent era they have expanded to include tax incentives, local guarantees, protection from the vicissitudes of internal competition, and procurement policies. Biased distribution of these favors may bring regions into conflict.

Third, as legitimator of capitalist society, the state has increasingly espoused, at least in rhetoric if not in legal principle, the commitment to full employment and community preservation. When sectoral dynamics erode community viability or destroy workers' jobs, groups affected by such conditions increasingly turn to the state for redress.

Yet the prominence of the state as an arena for American regional politics is due to its distinct intergovernmental form in the United States. It is accessible and in more than one form. The spatially decentralized structure of the U.S. state is unusual among developed countries.[2] It lends regionalism and regional struggles a quite different character from European cases. It is helpful, therefore, to review briefly the evolution of the state in the United States and to offer an interpretation of the remarkable territorialization of its structure. Why did the United States, a country organized late in the evolution of mercantile capitalist development, evolve and maintain such a strongly decentralized political structure at the same time that nationalism and centralized States were arising in Europe?

The Evolution of the Territorialized State

The answer lies in the initial territorial texture of the potential members of the American nation-state.[3] These dictated a sharing of power between state and national levels of government relatively unique among industrial nations (and similar to Canada and Australia). Subsequent regional antagonisms and adroit use of entrenched democratic rights at the state and local levels preserved the joint power between federal and state governments. To begin with, the thirteen colonies united in 1776 were composed of disparate societies whose livelihoods and cultures were highly differentiated versions of European society. Economic specializations were often determined by the mercantilist charters of the companies that started each colony; they recruited labor suitable to the area's prospects, from a robust fur, timber, and wheat trade in the North to a lucrative trade in slaves, indigo, cotton, and rice in the southernmost colonies. Yet their respective elites transcended intercolonial antagonisms and united against their common enemies, also territorially based: the Native Americans, whose resistance initially brought the colonies together, and the mother country, England, which as a State protected its mercantilist monopolies by suppressing colonial development and taxing the colonists to do so.

In fashioning the new nation, each participating colony desired to protect its own economic, religious, and political identity and interests, demanding shared powers between federal and state levels.[4] The subsequent aggression against Native Americans and the growing cleavage between North and South over slavery, and then between East and West over agrarian demands, continually strengthened the federal structure by proliferating colony-sized states carved from conquered Native American lands and by permitting experimentation at the state level. Distinct pasts thus produced a government structure that permits regionalism its voice today.

Political organization, as a result, revolved around territorial units, with the result that national parties have never been very strong. Nor have class-based parties flourished. Representation in the national legislature is based on territorial jurisdictions, and the presidency must be won by accumulating state electors. This explains the modesty of formal regional policy in the United States. Since regional politics operated at both the state and congressional levels, via territorial representation, mechanisms for regional policy are already built into the political system. One can argue, for instance, that the domination of the congressional committee system by southern Democratic congressmen for decades produced a deliberate policy to stimulate southern development by the disproportionate location of military bases there. Or, that the committees dealing with the interior were dominated by representatives from western states who made sure that national policy toward infrastructure (dams, water policy) and land disposal were favorable to the business interests of those regions. The threads of this interpretation are explored more thoroughly in the chapters which follow, particularly those on the North-South struggle and the final two chapters on contemporary regionalism.

The Contemporary Role of Federal Structure

The regional complexion of the United States state, then, is both a consequence and a cause of regional differentiation. A great deal has been written on the growing domination of the national government in the United States. While this fact is central to understanding international politics and certain aspects of domestic life, I do wish to stress the importance of the intergovernmental structure of the state for illuminating regional politics. As sectors have been argued to be the key analytical entry point for studying the contemporary economy of a region and its economically based politics, so the federal structure of the state in the United States is the key institutional entry point for studying the politics of regions.[5]

To begin with, the current boundaries of political jurisdictions, the intergovernmental distribution of state powers and responsibilities, and existing party politics form the arena of possibilities for regional contestants.[6] Whether or not a particular group with a territorial base can succeed in pursuing its ends, economic or otherwise, at a particular level of the state depends upon its size and potency. For instance, the auto industry, including both the corporations and the United Auto Workers, have been able to wrest concessions from Michigan's state government in a way that they have been unable to in other states where they form a smaller portion of the economy. Yet Michigan has not been able to cope with the latest crisis in the auto industry, which has forced the corporations to turn to both local government (Detroit's $50 million General Motors tax abatement and land giveaway) and the national government (the Chrysler loan guarantee) for help. In another example, farmers are much stronger in North Dakota (where they won a State Bank during the height of agrarian radicalism) than they are in more industrial states like Ohio. Native Americans are, by design, marginalized in the states in which their reservations lie.

Second, even when regional concerns erupt in new spatial configurations, pressures for territorial organization at scales other than local, state, and federal are shaped around the existing political apparatus. Thus, for instance, the Appalachian Regional Commission and new regional lobbies like the Western Governor's Policy Office are constructed with states as the building blocks. Metropolitan governments, in places like Minneapolis, St. Paul, and San Francisco, are composed of local city governments, while the regional commissions of the 1970s, like the Great Lakes and Old West, were constructed upon county units. In each case, regional problems and consciousness arose around largely sectorally based similarities and interests, but were forced into the framework of the existing political apparatus. The effectiveness of the Appalachian Regional Commission was diluted by its extremely broad coverage, a function of the need to win sufficient support in Congress. The program ultimately covered portions of thirteen states, only three or four of which account for the region's underdevelopment.

Most contemporary regional politics are sectorally based or at least sectorally related. Both intraregional and interregional struggles often take the form of claims by contending groups or coalitions on the state. The level of the state at which they are first levied will be that level most closely corresponding to the territorial extent of the conflict. Depending upon the ability of a protagonist group to link up with related groups in other regions, and upon the powers of the particular level of the state in question, the conflict may escalate to a higher level of the state. For instance, in the Youngstown case mentioned in chapter 7, the worker-community coalition for taking over the closed steel plants required large investment funds, available only at the national level. But the lack of national labor leadership commitment to plant closing issues and the absence of similar concerns in other regions enabled the steel industry to pressure the Carter administration into refusing the requested aid.

THE INTENSITY OF REGIONAL POLITICAL CLAIMS

Regional claims on the state take one of three forms representing successive degrees of intensity: demands for changes in policy, demands for redistribution of state power (usually through decentralization or devolution), and demands for independence and sovereignty. These variants and examples of them are listed in table 3.1

Three Levels of Regional Challenge

First, and most common, regional coalitions can contest issues of policy, where they protest the actions of the State that are perceived to propagate regional bias. In the United States, such issues have long been present at the national level, and frequently divide state legislatures as well. The tariff question, the infrastructure question (where will canals, railroads, highways, and pipelines go and how will they be paid for?), the

Table 3.1 A Typology of Regional Political Claims

Intensity	Substance	Examples
Policy shift claims	Tariffs, infrastructure, public lands, fiscal and monetary policy, urban and regional policy, revenue sharing	Midwestern and southern Populists (Free Silver); Northeast, postwar period (urban policy)
Power shift claims	Devolution, autonomy, nationalization or denationalization of responsibilities or resources	South in pre-Civil War era (states' rights); Intermountain West in postwar Period (Sagebrush Rebellion); Northeast in 1980s (nationalization of welfare and labor regulation)
Separatist demands	Secession, nationalism	South in Civil War era, Native American movements

issue of the disposal and management of public lands, and monetary issues (the National Bank and the soft currency questions) have all surfaced at moments as significant interregional struggles. That they may simultaneously be the subjects of intraregional struggles is also true, and will be quite apparent in the discussion of the North-South conflict in the nineteenth century. Nevertheless, dominant regional coalitions have come to face each other in mutual antagonism over such questions.

If unity within a region is strong enough, and the nature of differences between regions severe enough, political struggle may escalate to a demand for a shifting of power and resources either up or down the federal structure—for devolution or for strengthened centralism. Autonomy, for instance, is the demand of the Catalonian nationalists, whose well-developed economy (and distinct language and culture) has been the target of persistent discrimination by the central government since the Republican loss in the Spanish civil war. Alternatively, a region that might hope to dominate a strengthened national government, and thereby exploit a regional partner, may work for a reallocation of power and resources to the center of a federal system. This was the position of the northeastern-dominated Federalist party in the early American period, and of the unionist north in the Civil War epoch. Changes of this nature generally require an organization on the scale of political parties, such as the Republican party during the pre-Civil War era, or the contemporary Welsh and Scottish Nationalist parties in Britain, and the independent Catalonian Communist and Nationalist parties in Spain. The emergence of such an autonomy movement generally goes hand in hand with the construction of an ideology that celebrates the distinctive character of the region in a manner designed to extend its political base internally.

Finally, a regional conflict may become so severe that one region demands that the entire apparatus of the State be dismantled to create two separate nation-states, each with sovereignty. This occurred when the South seceded in 1860 and when Native Americans struggled to found their own nations, and it periodically threatens to occur in some European regions.[7] A region-become-nation must not only have at least one political party that expresses its cohesiveness, but it must also be in the process of constructing a competing nation-state, as the South did in its confederacy. The new structure of such a State often seeks to rectify the claims that the region previously levied against its former parent. In some cases, these principles are very difficult or costly to implement. Thus when the South made states' rights a founding principle of the Confederacy, it immediately found itself engaged in a military struggle, the prosecution of which was hamstrung precisely by this commitment to a decentralized political structure. Furthermore, the cohesion that underlay the South's solidarity began to fall apart as class differences within the region came to the fore, particularly over issues of who would fight in and feed the southern army.

The Shaping of Regional Claims

The level at which regional demands are pitched is a function not only of the grievousness of the claimed injury, but also of the region's size and internal economic, political and cultural viability. A small or economically weak region does not usually demand devolution of powers or separation, but is more apt to prefer changes in regional policy and resource distribution. A large, diversified but economically troubled region is likely to pursue a similar course. A medium-sized or large region with a rosy economic future but complaints of bias in taxation, policy, or exploitation by institutions in other regions will be more likely to pursue devolution, autonomy, or separatism. Such a region may not be highly diversified economically, as the cases of the pre-Civil War South and the postwar Intermountain West demonstrate. In the former, all parties believed that the mid-century cotton boom would ensure a lasting prosperity for a southern nation, while the Intermountain West, the most vociferously anti-big government region in the contemporary United States, is betting on its agricultural, tourist, and energy futures.

Regionalism may alternatively be explained as the lack of congruence between political and economic power among regions within a nation. Gourevitch (1977) argues that most cases of European regionalism are attributable to the initiative or regions whose economic prospects are superior to those of the nation as a whole, often because the latter has been thrust into a period of prolonged recession and painful restructuring, but whose political weakness vis-à-vis the nation permits the siphoning off of profits or maintenance of oppressive policies, as viewed from the plaintive region. Gourevitch cites as evidence Scotland, Catalonia and the Basque provinces, Flanders, Croatia, and Quebec—all regions with either traditionally or recently strong economies.

The lack of congruence principle operates as a dependable signal for identifying potential cases of regional revolt, but Gourevitch's cases all involve the shift of economic power away from a core where political power resides. A modification of the model must be made in countries like the United States where political power is much more highly regionalized, with a fluctuating center of gravity. Accession to or erosion of political power can thus also provide the impetus for a region to mobilize. For instance, the South, which was politically dominant in the Congress and presidency until shortly before the Civil War, seceded in order to avoid the incipient rule of northern industrialists whose economic policies were sure to be prejudicial to the southern cotton economy. With the postwar energy boom in the West, demographic shifts have enhanced the presence of these states' interests in Congress in ways which have emboldened their economic claims.

In the American case, the lack of congruence is thus not generally caused by economic development outpacing political restructuring. In most eras, political power has been more decentralized than economic power. Indeed, in the United States, regionalized political power has often led to the decentralization of economic development through the agency of federally funded infrastructure (railroads, highways, dams, public lands, flood control, waterways, and electrification) and military spending (bases, shipyards, arsenals, ammunition plants, aerospace facilities, and high-tech enclaves). This history of interaction between economic and political power dispersion—from the Northeast toward the South and West—complicates the analysis of regionalism and underscores the necessity of including the states as a major force in its evolution.

Successful regional mobilization also requires permissive regional political infrastructures. At least one political party within the region must be convertible into a vehicle for regionalist demands. In the mid-nineteenth-century South, the hegemonic Democratic party became such an instrument for the creation of the Confederacy, while in the North, the Whig party failed to take up that region's cause because it was so fiercely committed to a nationalist program. Regions either with one dominant political party that is not also hegemonic nationally or with several relatively weak parties are more apt to nurture regionalist movements than are regions possessing strong but evenly balanced parties with well-developed national ties. As a result, the South and Intermountain West have been historically friendlier to regionalist movements than the Northeast, the South and the Pacific region.

These political configurations—the structure of the federal state and regional variations in political parties—should not be viewed as completely exogenous forces in American history. The origins of each can be traced to past events in the political economy of American spatial development. But they become features of the political landscape in ways that are not consonant with and certainly not simply products of the ongoing evolution of the capitalist economy. For this reason, they deserve a theoretical status of their own in the analysis of regionalism.

THE CULTURES OF REGIONS

The analytical approach discussed so far is designed specifically for interpreting regionalism in the United States. The primacy of certain constructs—particularly sectoral differentiation and federal political structure—may not hold for other cases, particularly countries where capitalism developed out of a feudal mode of production. The secondary status of culture as a regionalizing force may reflect the relative homogenization of culture in the United States compared to other nations. Language, for instance, which played a central role in turn-of-the-century socialist international debate on nations, is only a factor in the United States for the most oppressed and/or recently arrived minorities—Puerto Ricans, Latinos, Native Americans, and Asians. The political demands of these groups, with the exception of the Navajo Nation, have not taken a territorial form but have been expressed as demands for bilingual education, affirmative action, neighborhood policies in cities, and reservation policy. Generally, cultural groups that play a major role in local level politics, from the neighborhood to the city level, are either not strongly concentrated regionally or, in places where they are, have not been able to capture the regional stage. American exceptions include the Mormons in Utah, the Latinos in some areas of the Southwest, and the Navajo Nation.

Cultural attributes are often strong ingredients in the buildup of regional consciousness. Yet they do not lend themselves to an easy scheme of classification. For this reason, many Marxist theoretical treatments of regions omit the cultural dimension. The underplayed significance of culture in Marxism generally has been articulately confronted by Marxists like Hall (1981), Laclau (1979), Williams (1973), and Hirst (1979), who challenge the base/superstructure dichotomy in Marxism and argue that not all struggles can be reduced to their economic base. Reviving Gramsci's work on ideology as a distinct force in history, they argue that a sufficient Marxism must shun a tendency to overtheorize and must focus instead on the roots of consciousness and intentionality, on the ways in which people construct their own reality.[8] Laclau, for example, argues that people's actions do not reflect their class position automatically, but are developed by means of specific struggles in specific periods. The attention to empirical detail suggested by this literature is reflected in the following discussion, which is more a list of cultural factors operating on regionalism than a cohesive model of cultural determination.

American Cultural Variants

Significant cultural distinctions do characterize U.S. regions today.[9] Regional accents, for instance, remain prominent despite nationalization of culture on television and in the movies. Regional traditions are kept alive in folklore and in commercialized place names and products— Lumberjack Mall, for instance, is the name of a new shopping center on the outskirts of Cloquet, Minnesota—a wood and pulp factory town where wage workers' ancestors once felled trees in the nearby woods. Regional lifestyles are celebrated in festivals and art forms—the clam-bake, the hayride, the square dance, the blues. Some regional cultural traits are direct descendants of immigrant cultures, as for instance the radicalism of Finns in the upper Great Lakes and the Mexican architecture and food of the Southwest.

Religion is sometimes highly differentiated across regions, as the concentration of fundamentalist religions in the South and Southwest illustrates. Perhaps the most striking contemporary case in the United States is the predominance of the Mormon religion in the Great Basin, where it is tightly interwoven with regional capitalist interests. Yet the Mormon church was a scale-tipping force in the recent successful coalition to keep the MX missile out of the region. In earlier periods religious missions were often an outpost of cultural imperialism, as in the Christianizing of Native Americans and slaves, and in the taming of Appalachian mountaineers.[10]

Regional cultures also differ in the presence of subsistence production, the extent of kinship ties, the household structure, and particularly the role of women in each of these. Women still garden, raise animals, sew clothing, and collect wild foods in some regions, while in others they are more apt to be working for wages. Men and women both may haul wood for heating, construct their own housing, and fix their own machinery. Regional struggle may include defense of the conditions under which such subsistence is produced. Alternatively, subsistence options may also hamper the effort to organize around job-threatening sectoral changes.

Preservation of patriarchal institutions or efforts to destroy them frequently plays a role in regional struggles. The "home" in the wide-spread sentiment "fighting for God, home, and country" refers euphe-mistically to the patriarchal household. The currently dominant faction in the nationalist struggle in Iran defends a severe patriarchy as one primary aim of the struggle against imperialism. On the other hand, liberation forces, as in many of the socialist revolutions, are often committed to the abolition of the worst forms of patriarchal oppression as a concession to women active in the struggle. In other cases, regional struggles have evoked a consciousness of the issue of women's oppression as a counterpart to that of other groups (for example, the link between abolition and women's rights in the Civil War era).

Not least, a difference in what we might call political culture exists across regions. Political cultures consist foremost of electoral and other organized political groups, but include popular traditions of participation, activism, civic-mindedness, and political awareness. The propensity of any group to engage in combat on any particular issue depends greatly on its past experience with politics, even if around a completely different cause. For example, the formation of a permanent regionwide tax-base sharing arrangement in Minneapolis-St. Paul can be traced to the area's Scandinavian heritage, upper-Midwest populism, and the success of the Democratic Farmer-Labor Party. No other metropolitan area has been able to fashion as farreaching a proposal with such grace.

Protected by the federal system from nationalizing influences which have weakened regionalism elsewhere, political cultures in the United States have remained quite distinctive and durable over the decades. Northern and northwestern states tend toward a heavily moralistic politics (cooperative, with strong populist, grassroots, and localistic strains), midwestern state politics are more thoroughly individualistic (competitive and highly participatory), and southern states' politics more traditional (paternalistic, with relatively low levels of political participation). Empirical evidence suggests that these three broad types have persisted since the mid-nineteenth century (Elazar 1966; and Paddison 1983, 110–12).[11] Glenn and Simmons (1967) found that regional opinion became even more polarized in the postwar period, despite the advances of mass media.

Few of the sociological studies pursuing cultural categories have been applied to regional character in the United States. An exception is Collins' study of "Okies"—poor whites, some with mixed Native American blood, from Oklahoma. She argues that family and kinship structure was extremely important in the Okies' ability to withstand dustbowl conditions, proletarianization, and migration to California during the 1930s; these same ties enabled them to cope with subsequent changes in California agriculture and gave the Central Valley part of its distinctive culture (Collins 1978). Another example is Jorgenson's study on Native Americans, showing how collective attitudes toward land and its use (not exploitation) resulted in a continued regional clash between two entirely different cultures (Jorgenson 1978). Yet another is Simon's study of regional revolt in Appalachia in the late 1970s, which demonstrates the crucial role of what he calls "the development faith" in stopping a coal strike short of broader demands for restructuring the economy (Simon 1979). Cultural traits and experience go far toward explaining the degree of cohesion among people in a region, their organizational proclivities, and the tenor of their regional outlook. This will be demonstrated for the cases studied in latter chapters.

Culture and the Reproduction of Daily Life

There is another sense in which the cultural category is essential for understanding regional politics. This has to do not with differences among regions, but with the widely observed tendency of people to cleave to their own place, to identify with and defend their region. This may be as true of newcomers to a region as it is of older residents. It is suggested that there is an entire sphere of human practice, organized outside of the workplace, which has strong territorial aspects to it. For comparability, we may call this the sphere of reproduction, as opposed to that of production. Of course the reproduction of human society is fashioned by institutions and cultures that reach far beyond regional boundaries. But many of the institutions and activities involved in reproduction—such as households, kinship, schools, churches, community centers, fairs, dances, clubs, friendships, and sports—are strongly regionally identified.

Much of people's knowledge of the world, their common sense, their passions, and their collective practices are anchored in this regional setting. In a world increasingly controlled by national superpowers and living under the threat of nuclear annihilation, the defense of place, of home—rightly or wrongly—is associated with the guarantee of conditions of safety, comfort, neighborliness, and security. People may feel more powerful, more connected with events in their region than they do with similar ones on a larger scale. Cultural practices and traditions, therefore, provide a language for the legitimization of political changes, as a means of defending or developing a way of life. In turn they may fundamentally alter the course of a regional conflict and even alter the working boundaries of a region.[12]

The proximity and concreteness of the region suggest a tractability, a chance to shape the environment, that is not there for most people on a larger scale. People know firsthand the local power structure, and they see daily the changes wrought in their milieu.[13] Not all groups, of course, express this affinity with the region in which they live. Many are forced by economic circumstances to stay in a place where they feel insecure and powerless. Others may feel more grounded in a remote cabin, a neighborhood, or a cosmopolitan circuit (Webber's community without propinquity [1972]). Yet people's regional pride and affinity are based not only on a region's distinctiveness but also on the simple fact of familiarity with it in contrast to the strangeness of other places.

Each of these types of cultural content in regionalism may be undermined or deformed by other pressures, just as they may throw a wrench in the otherwise machinelike operation of the economy. A distinctiveness that was cultivated during periods of isolation, such as occurred in Appalachia or in Native American populations, can quickly be eroded by cultural imperialism. Consider the Christianizing of African slaves and Native Americans alike. More indirectly, the commodification of culture can wrest control of it from the people whose heritage it is and make of it something entirely different, as blue grass music, for instance, has become on national television.

Complicating the struggle for cultural survival is the role of cultural institutions in the region—such as schools, churches, newspapers, radio, television, and professional sports. While each has a clear stake in preserving some indigenous loyalty and identification, it also conveys the larger national culture into the region. When writers like Dulong (1978) worry about the susceptibility of regional populations to a chauvinism instrumental to capitalist ends, they are focusing in particular on the second form of cultural behavior reviewed above and the plasticity of its content. Defenders of regionalism per se, on the other hand, are struck by the resiliency of regional traditions and regional culture and see in regionalism a means of harnessing the love of home to the preservation of a priceless heritage.

The acknowledgment of these cultural components complicates the analysis of regionalism immensely. If they cannot be associated one-to-one with the economic conditions surveyed above—and they cannot—then they represent a cross-cutting set of relationships which must themselves be investigated. Cultural differentiation may prove the basis for, or at least an exacerbating factor in, the antagonism between regions, particularly if one culture has a record of oppression of the other historically. The cultural feeling of southernness bred by the Civil War and its aftermath engendered an antagonism toward "Yankees" that has lasted to this day. While southerners feel an identity with being southern, northerners possess less a sense of community with their fellow frostbelters than a victor's contempt for the losers, a view of southern culture as backward, poor, prone to viciousness, and slightly immoral.

Cultural differences also help explain the diverse responses of particular regions or subregions to similar circumstances. Cultural differences can be expected to correlate along class lines in some regions, and to cross-cut them in others, with profound effects upon the structure of regional conflicts and coalitions. The demonstration of the powerful and elastic role of culture must be left, at this point, to the empirical chapters.

EVALUATING REGIONALISM

Many politically minded readers may be more interested in the political facets of regionalism than in its causes. Is regionalism a conservative or progressive force in national political life? Does it deliver on the issues it fastens upon? These questions require a shift to a normative level of discussion.

A normative evaluation of regionalism is complicated by the fact that judgment depends upon the judge's vision of good performance. Socialists may tend to measure regionalism's value by its ability to advance the transition from capitalism to socialism. Populists and civil libertarians may evaluate it by its success in persevering in or furthering democratization. Single issue-oriented groups may gauge it narrowly on its ability to guarantee environmental production, women's rights, and so on. In what follows, contentions among various progressive groups are reviewed as demonstrative of the normative possibilities.

The Debate Among Scholars

As with nationalism, substantial debate surrounds the merits of regionalism and regional politics, especially among socialists. On the side disparaging territorial struggles, both national and regional, are those who follow Marx's basic line of reasoning, hammered into an article of faith by Luxembourg. Marx believed that the working classes inevitably lost out in nationalist clashes, since these were dominated by the protagonist bourgeoisie. In defense of internationalism, he argued that "the workers have no Fatherland" (cited in Bloom 1941, 24–25). Marx believed fully in agitating for working-class ends within ongoing national struggles, but argued that nationalism subordinated working-class issues and weakened international solidarity among workers.

Contemporary Marxist scholars such as Hobsbawm have carried forward this view. Hobsbawm (1977) argues that nonclass antagonisms, like racism, sexism, and cultural chauvinism, can be handled amicably in the transition to a new socialist society, whereas they are unlikely to be eliminated without that transformation. Hobsbawm cites an impressive number of cases in which nationalism undercut working-class struggles, and he contests Nairn's (1977) suggestion that an independent Wales or Scotland would be more progressive. Both Hesseltine (1944) in the United States and Dulong (1978) in France have roundly condemned regionalism, arguing that it deflects attention and energy from the larger project of reshaping capitalism. Both believe that since any regional coalition necessarily involves members of the petty bourgeoisie or regional capital, such coalitions only coopt working-class movements and put off the reckoning with the real culprit—capitalism—which operates on a worldwide basis. Stillwell (1979) has expressed doubt about the historic role of regional struggles, as I have (1976, 1983) in previous papers. Marris (1976), who affirms the legitimacy of an attachment to place, argues that "Participation in spatial form divides people against each other, confusing the campaign of each interest for recognition of its claim on society at large." A similar concern has been aired in the longstanding debate on black separatism in the United States.

The other side, however, has its partisans as well. Both Debray (1977) and Williams (1981) have written almost mystically about the need for radicals to embrace regionalism. Debray argues forcefully that the various Communist Internationals, which were supposed to be spreading and supporting proletarian internationalism, were in no case directly responsible for organizing any of the most significant socialist revolts in history—the Paris Commune, the Russian revolution, or the Chinese revolution. On the contrary, he argues, socialist regimes were more apt to evolve out of strident nationalist movements, building upon national or regional traditions, as in Cuba. Friedmann and Weaver (1979) advocate regionalism, basing their argument on the sense of place and accessibility to power referred to in the discussion on culture above. In a paper unusual for a regional scientist, Hansen (1978) makes an argument moderately indulgent of regional separatism along lines of a Tiebout-type vote-with-your-feet political competition model. Both Nairn (1975a) and Carney (1980), in the Marxist tradition, are cautiously optimistic about the new regional separatist movements developing in Europe. As I argue in chapters 9 and 10, the new regionalism in the United States gives one less to be sanguine about, and yet it cannot be dismissed altogether. Its various manifestations display degrees of elasticity that might follow alternative courses in the future.

The Complexity of the Issue

As the conceptual richness of the topic affirms, abstract normative judgments on the nature of regionalism cannot be made, for four reasons. First, any regional coalition is bound to include members of more than one class and to exclude at least some residents of a region. It is apt to have complicated interrelationships with other groups in other regions. It is apt to contain more than one claim or issue, so that elements of differing moral quality are fused within a regional ideology. Finally, the targets of such a movement are somewhat variable, depending upon its internal politics, its ideology, and its disaffection with existing channels. Each of these features is worth exploring briefly, using European examples to illustrate the complexity of political issues. We shall see below, in chapter 4, the extent to which these features hold for the major instances of American regional conflict, and in chapters 8 and 9, their facets in the contemporary American case.

The social group whose circumstances and claims give the region its character will not be the entire population of that region. Frequently a regional struggle is led by a group who will gain most from a particular political victory, because new politics or decentralized control of the state apparatus will permit them to pursue their class, gender, cultural, or other political ends with greater success. Other members of that territorial unit may favor the existing political arrangement, fearing that they will be worse off under the domination of the group leading the regional revolt. Yet others may participate in the regional struggle, hoping to bend it to their ends in accompanying and successive internal struggle.

Second, the precise regional lines drawn around parties to a regional struggle will depend on alliances that the initial group can form with other groups with whom they might have a common cause or whose position is ambiguous but winnable. Because of this, the boundary of a region may be set by the particular nature of the struggle. In some cases, boundaries become an object of the struggle, as when the antagonists wish to define the region differently in order to enhance their political or military power. For instance, in the mid-1970s the Spanish central government attempted to define the Basque region as one containing seven provinces, while the Basque separatist and nationalist movements accept only three, sometimes four; the centrists hoped to blunt the power of the separatist movements and sway autonomy elections in their favor by imposing this definition.

The multiple roots of regional struggles result in a complex pattern of social relations that can be expressed in regionalism. When sectoral, class, cultural, and political claims all manifest themselves in a regional struggle, the chances are that no simple characterization of the social relations involved can be constructed. In these cases, multiple and competing claims over the goals of regionalism, and perhaps multiple definitions of the region, may be put forward. In Catalonia, for instance, both class and cultural identities operate in the autonomy movements. But since some members of the Catalonian working class are Andalusian (20 percent) and thus do not speak Catalan, which is one of the political demands of the movement, they oppose it as members of a different culture even though Catalonian autonomy might further the goals of the working class in Catalonia as a whole. Mastery of this complexity of the social relations of regionalism requires concrete historical analyses of each case.

Emergent regional strategy will depend upon which classes, sectors, parties, and cultural groups are represented in a particular regional movement, and which among them control the existing and neighboring state apparatuses. The regional bourgeoisie in Scotland, Nairn (1977) argues, has supported a narrowly cultural and nostalgically militaristic Scots nationalism without real ambitions to independence from England; it has profited from riding along on the coattails of British imperialism, Scots soldiers doing much of the fighting. On the other hand, the Catalonian bourgeoisie has favored strong autonomy for its region for forty years because the central regime denied national political power and economic privilege to the Republican-supporting Catalonians.

Working-class groups, too, may opt for different strategies at the regional level. Lovering (1978) argues that Welsh workers would be better off eschewing the Welsh nationalist movement (which he characterizes as petit-bourgeois-based) and staying with the Britain-wide labor movement. Nairn argues on the contrary that Welsh workers are attracted to Welsh nationalism because they are fed up with the Labour party, in which they have persistently formed a left-of-center caucus. In Catalonia and Andalusia, the left-wing, working-class-based parties support demands for regional autonomy because they believe that regional control of culture, social spending, and economic regulation is the only route toward working-class political power in Spain as a whole.

Internal disunity within a regional movement, especially a cross-class movement, will frequently be expressed in disagreement over political targets. Each class fraction will perceive that one type of political claim will best serve its ends. A Catalonian bourgeoisie will favor cultural autonomy and freedom from economic discrimination by the central State, but oppose any greater independence or any real devolution of economic power onto a regional government that might be left-dominated.

For all of these reasons, evaluating any regional movement requires a thorough analysis of its composition, its target, its forms of political expression, and its possibilities. Undoubtedly, some regional movements are purely system-reinforcing (and there are those who would welcome this outcome). An organization of working-class people and regional capitalist interests around northeastern sectoral decline, for instance, which pushes only for more federal aid, for national government absorption of the social wage, and for massive subsidies to private capital may simply shore up capitalism. Alternatively, a regional working-class and small-business-based movement that proposes dramatic industrial restructuring under new forms of state and community/worker control might thoroughly destabilize and/or begin to supplant capitalist forms.

In either case, it is worth asking about what would happen to the same organizing energies if devoted to other ends. If some national project presents itself as an alternative—a labor party, for instance, with a program of economic restructuring, drastic controls on plant closings, and a plan for transition to socialism—then regional organizing might better be joined to such an effort. On the other hand, regional organizing may be the best alternative, even within a system whose infirmities are national if not international in scope, in the absence of accessible channels for political energies at these larger scales. Regional organizing and coalitions can serve as training grounds and experimental laboratories in politics and strategy.

A more fundamental normative quandary concerns the validity of territorial experience of groups more specific than class—be they sectoral, gender-related, ethnic, cultural, or otherwise. Since regional struggles contain elements of all of these, they must be judged on the moral content of each aspect as well. A working-class, place-based struggle can be racist and sexist. An ethnic struggle may be pro-capitalist. As Hall, Laclau, and others have argued, most left movements must battle on a terrain that is complicated by people's "non-class-belongingness," by their common sense and moral practices, and by their limited range of experience. Aspects of people's morality—love of home, for instance—can be appealed to by both right-wing and left-wing coalitions.

In summary, regional movements present a potential forum for struggling over unique regional conditions, largely but not fully traceable to capitalist evolution and uneven development, and for moving toward a broader national and international transformation of society. At the same time, they may channel consciousness and energies into a territorial them/us conflict, paralyzing efforts to solve the broader, systemic problems associated with modern capitalism and nationalism. One of the tasks of this book is to examine the conditions under which the meaning of regionalism is more or less positive, from a progressive point of view.

Notes

1. I will not attempt here to review the complicated debates over the theory of the state. I accept the view that the state is a semiautonomous agent in capitalist society, responsive both to the imperatives of capitalist accumulation and to the struggles between classes and among fractions of classes over state policy. See Saunders (1979), O'Connor (1979) and Fainstein and Fainstein (1985) for interpretations of the state in this vein. See also the analysis in Cooke (1983, ch. 8).
2. Paddison (1983, 123) argues that regional economic conflicts tend to be especially acute in federal countries compared with those in unitary states.
3. Sack (1980, 178) argues the generic case that whatever else a state may do, it is territorial. But few nation States are as internally and formally territorialized as the United States.
4. Of course, various Machiavellian (in the honorable Gramscian sense) politicians such as Madison saw this separation of powers as strictly instrumental to securing the needs of mercantilist capital in the national sense. See the debate in the *Federalist Papers*, discussed at greater length in chapter 4.
5. Others have argued for the importance of state structure and politics in analyzing regional development. See for instance Duchacek (1970); Walker (1980); Beer (1973); and Sack (1981). Taylor (1982) distinguishes between politics and the state as objects of study.
6. The point was made well by Jensen (1951), who argued that as culture was becoming universalized, and the role of government increased, political areas—states and provinces as well as nations—increasingly tend to be the forms into which regional identities are cast.
7. See Nairn (1977), for instance on Britain; or Mandel (1963) and Carney (1980) on Belgium.
8. I am indebted to Howes (1979) for an overview of this debate.
9. The best full-length treatment is Gastil (1975). For an extended discussion of regional variations in religion in the United States, see Gastil (1975, 47–54).
10. Whisnant (1981) offers a compelling account of how the missionary mentality has oppressed Appalachian people since the turn of the century.
11. See the discussions of formation of regional political cultures in House (1983, 50–55); Gastil (1975, 55–70); Sharkansky (1970); and Patterson (1966). Of course, political cultures can be altered in the regionalist anvil as well. See the discussions in Wattenberg and Miller (1981, 346–57); and Tabb (1982, 138–40).
12. See Cooke (1985) for a contrasting analysis of working-class practices as a force in shaping Welsh nationalism in a similar coal economy.
13. See Marris (1976) and Friedmann (1981) for examinations of this phenomenon, which Friedmann calls the "life space" as opposed to "economic space."

4

Regionalism in American History

Contemporary American regionalism possesses a sturdy geneology. The United States as a nation was highly regionally differentiated from its birth. Irreconcilable antagonisms rooted in different modes of production bred territorial conflict between Native Americans and European newcomers, and between an industrial capitalist North and a slave economy South. The resulting internal wars along east-west and north-south axes bequeathed to future generations a uniquely marked landscape, strongly etched regional cultures and a set of resilient political institutions. Yet regionalism did not dominate national politics in every era. Late nineteenth-century populism retained its essential class character, rather than forging a regional common front between Plains, Midwest, and South against the East. Regionalism was at its least powerful as a divisive political factor during the New Deal and World War II.

In this chapter, the forces behind regional differentiation over the past several centuries of American history are surveyed. The translation of regional differences into interregional conflict is analyzed in the two most prominent instances of conflict. Each case is investigated as a function of the economic, political, and cultural conditions in each region, and tentative conclusions are drawn about several of the general hypotheses regarding regionalism. Each instance also produces institutions and practices which become the legacy of the next era of incipient regional conflict.

NATIVE AMERICAN REGIONS AND EUROPEAN ENCOUNTERS

Over the course of the seventeenth, eighteenth, and nineteenth centuries, the indigenous peoples of the North American continent experienced successive incursions into their territory by several sets of Europeans and Americans. Highly disparate modes of production characterized the two cultures thus brought into contact. Among Native Americans, each region had its distinctive economic system. The colonialists who encountered each of these subcultures had their own specific colonial goals and found different ways to exploit and interact with Native groups. As a result, outcomes were quite regionally distinct.[1]

The Native American Mode of Production: Primitive Communism

The dominant form of productive system in seventeenth-century North America was communal hunting, fishing, and gathering, and in some regions, settled agriculture.[2] Productive units consisted of kinship groups of various sizes, using tools and implements of wood, stone, bone, primitive metals, clay, animal hides, and reeds to harvest food, clothing, and shelter from the land. Their technologies included highly developed knowledge of these materials, of the attributes of hundreds of plants, and of the behavior of animals of all forms. Some six hundred distinct Native American tribes inhabited the present United States (fig. 4.1) (Driver 1969; Kroeber 1963; Swanton 1952).

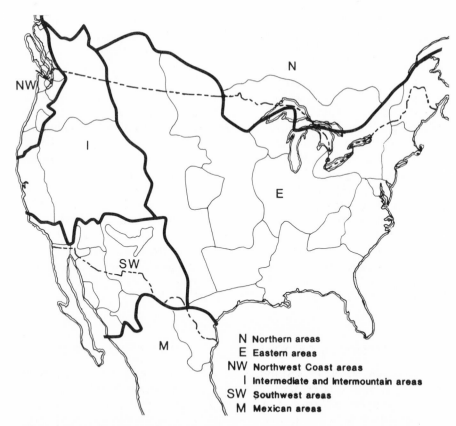

N Northern areas
E Eastern areas
NW Northwest Coast areas
I Intermediate and Intermountain areas
SW Southwest areas
M Mexican areas

Figure 4.1   Native American Regions on the Eve of the Colonial Era. From Dixon Ryan Fox, *Harper's Atlas of American History* (New York: Harpers, 1920, p. 6; Charles Paullin, *Atlas of the Historical Geography of the United States* (Washington: The Carnegie Institute, 1923), Plate 33.

Native American productive forces were periodically improved upon and altered, although not at the pace inherent in the supplanting capitalist accumulation process. The most important changes over the preceding centuries had been the migration northward of mesoamerican techniques of corn, bean, and squash cultivation, which by the time of Columbus had reached along the Gulf and Atlantic coastal plains as far as present day New England (Driver 1969, 66; McNickle 1971).

Social relations within the Native American mode of production consisted of communal or kin ownership of tools and shelter. There was no concept of land ownership as we know it under capitalism, but rather a notion of the rights of use and stewardship. Work was highly differentiated by age and gender, but all members worked so that there was no class system based on the exploitation of labor. The fruits of labor were generally shared around to all members of the tribe or kinship group. The size of the distributional unit often varied according to the particular crop or food involved; for instance, Great Basin Indians would gather in large groups for the fall fishing season but disband into smaller groups for gathering nuts and plant foods (Herndon 1967, 290–92; Trigger 1969, 52–56; Smaby 1975).

Political decisions within tribes were structured along patriarchal and kinship lines. Leaders made decisions, but adult members of the tribe were frequently consulted. Religions and rituals were highly variegated, but always encompassed a strong respect for the earth and sky, expressed as a naturalistic spiritualism. Native American regions were necessarily highly differentiated because the climate, soils, forestation, and wildlife differed so dramatically across the continent.

As a result, each group had its distinctive language, economic practices, and culture. Trade among regions was well-developed in most parts of the continent by the time of European arrival. Occasionally, famine and other migratory pressures would precipitate territorial conflict among Native American groups, engendering precolonial enmities. But for the most part, the Europeans found quite regionally distinct cultures with few formal political or economic links among them.

Four Variations in Colonial–Native American Encounters

Because of this regional differentiation, and because the intruding European cultures brought their own distinct national cultures and economic projects, the course of territorial conflict ran quite differently in different portions of the continent. Cases can be compared: the trading relationship developed between the northeastern Indians and the French and English; the slave labor relationship imposed on Californian Indians by the Spanish; the competition for land which developed first on the east coast and then toward the interior between Native Americans and the English; and the later competition for land and mineral resources between American frontiersmen and Plains and mountain Indians. The reader should keep in mind that there were many variations on these patterns in neighboring areas of the continent.

By the sixteenth and seventeenth centuries, the commercial capitalist nations, especially Portugal, Spain, England, France, and the Netherlands, were engaged in an intense struggle to discover, claim, plunder, and colonialize the other continents of the globe. The precise aim of each nation with respect to a particular piece of territory depended upon its strategy and practices in this intercolonialist rivalry. For instance, the Spanish and Portuguese colonialists, sponsored by the State, were more interested in finding slaves, gold, and silver and in establishing garrisons to lay claim to vast territories than were the French and English, whose trading companies sought raw materials and commodities like timber, furs, and fish to import back home.

The Northeastern Tribes and the Fur Traders

In the northeastern forest region, first French and later English fur traders established contact with Native American tribes for purely commercial purposes. The fur trade yielded immense profits for the trading companies, since they could exchange relatively cheap items like cloth, beads, knives, pots, guns, and liquor in return for the highly valued fur. This trading relationship was in many ways more benign than other European-Native American encounters. Since the native Americans produced the hides, their knowledge of the north woods access routes and habits of fur-bearing mammals was invaluable to the Europeans, and required that they be treated with a modicum of friendliness and respect. For this reason, French racism against Native Americans was much less virulent than the version of English colonialists to the south; French traders intermarried with Indians and sometimes joined their tribes.[3]

Yet in the longer run, the arrival of the European fur traders undermined the Native American economic base and culture in the northeast as irrevocably as did genocide in other parts of the continent. European diseases slaughtered huge proportions of Native Americans, who had not evolved immunities (McNeill 1976, 70–71, 177–78). Tribal division of labor and settlement patterns were restructured by the intercontinental fur trade. Men would leave for prolonged periods in the summer months. Small forest settlements gave way to larger riverside encampments completely dependent on the fur trade. As nearby forests were depopulated of furbearing mammals, the traders moved farther and farther inland, creating intense intertribal rivalries for territory and trade networks. In these latter conflicts, the various tribes would often team up with one or the other imperial power—England or France—and with their nearer neighbors against weaker groups. Such was the nature of the Iroquois confederation of five Indian nations and the origins of the French and Indian War.[4] By the end of the eighteenth century, Indian cultures were almost completely decimated in the northeast and control of the territory had passed into colonial hands.

The California Indians and the Spanish

Compared to the northeastern Indians, who were rather sparsely settled in a climatically demanding region, the California Indians enjoyed a mild climate, a bountiful terrain of fruit and nut trees, and ample fish and gaming grounds. California supported a higher density of precolonial peoples than any other North American region, and fewer tools and techniques were required to reap the fruits of the land (Jones 1971, 89–90; Driver 1969; Bean 1973, 6). The Spaniards who arrived in the eighteenth century found an amiable, gentle people whom they initially rather easily enslaved. These incarcerated Indians performed the labor for the gardens and cattle-raising on military compounds designed to stake the Spanish claim to California soil. The accompanying missions attempted to inculcate the Indians with Catholicism, which served as an ideology in support of this rather miserable life (Cook 1971; Forbes 1970, 29–31; Heizer and Almquist 1971).

The Spaniards' system, a variant on the encomienda system they implanted so successfully in other part of the new world, was unique among North American colonial encounters for its successful employment of Indian labor. This labor permitted a large-scale form of agricultural distribution that was untenable elsewhere on the continent—huge tracts of land were deeded to white Spanish or Mexican settlers to be worked as ranches with Indian labor. However, California Indians resisted so tenaciously, both through self-destructive methods like abortion and suicide, and through escape and retribution, the latter aided by acquisition of the horse, that the Spanish were never able to move much beyond their coastal California outposts (Forbes 1970, 34–36; Cook 1971). The prolonged conflict was nevertheless fatal to the native population. By the nineteenth century many tribes had disappeared altogether.

The Eastern Agricultural Indians and the English

On the east coast of the future United States, from Plymouth to Virginia, the earliest English colonialists found settled agricultural tribes. Initial accounts reported a quite sophisticated knowledge of agriculture, a varied and rich diet, and a high level of skilled crafts, all of which the Indians were willing to share with the strange white people. Indeed, in some early instances, the settlers learned from and coexisted peacefully with native peoples, especially in those colonies of persecuted peoples fleeing from European intolerance.[5] But the majority of early colonists were supported by trading companies who had invested in their settlements as ventures to find tradable commodities—agricultural products such as tobacco and forest products such as wood and fur from Indian lands.

Almost immediately, a conflict developed over land ownership and occupation, initiating approximately 250 years of east-west warfare between land-hungry white settlers (and their commercial backers) and a retreating Native American culture.[6] This encounter was more violent than in the north and west and engendered severe forms of racism against Native Americans, captured by phrases such as "bloody savages."

The prolonged battle was costly to human lives on both sides, and was won ultimately by the white settlers because they possessed deadlier technology—a by-product of emerging industrial capitalism—and more highly elaborated military organization. Against these, a highly decentralized, language-divided and sometimes internally warring Native American political network did not prevail (Driver 1969). The greed for land was so pervasive that lands were pilfered even when Indians had peacefully assimilated Christianity and capitalist farming. This was most dramatically evident in the forced migration of the southern Cherokees to Oklahoma, the disastrous "Trail of Tears" (Van Every 1966; NcNickle 1962).

The Western Indians and the Americans

By the mid-nineteenth-century era of the famous Indian-fighting so celebrated in American folklore, Native American cultures had been radically altered by their encounters with European capitalist cultures. The Plains Indians, for instance, who had previously been nomadic hunters and gatherers on the fringes of the inhospitable high plains, penetrated deep into that region on Spanish-introduced horses, becoming completely dependent upon the buffalo for food, clothing, shelter, and trade commodities (Spicer 1969, 82–83; Brown 1971, 259; Debo 1970, 15). Tribal cultures changed as well, becoming more hierarchical and patriarchal with the evolution of the trade in buffalo hides.[7]

As the plains and intermountain interior lands became attractive to white, eastern Americans for their precious metals and cattle-raising opportunities, conflicts began to build between these last Native American holdouts and the frontiersmen, the latter accompanied by their surveyors, soldiers, homesteading families, and missionaries.[8] Through the course of the nineteenth century, Indians were dispossessed of their rights to own or use almost all of the western lands, except those most undesirable and unproductive at the time. These latter became reservations onto which Native Americans successively defeated in military actions were driven and where the way of life and livelihoods were irrevocably altered and impoverished (fig. 4.2)[9]

The Regional Legacies of Native American Resistance

Few treatments of American regionalism or indeed, American politics in general have accorded the struggle with Native Americans its power in shaping aspects of the American physical and political environment. While not all the imprints can be catalogued here, several deserve mention.

First of all, Native American nationalism is still a powerful force in

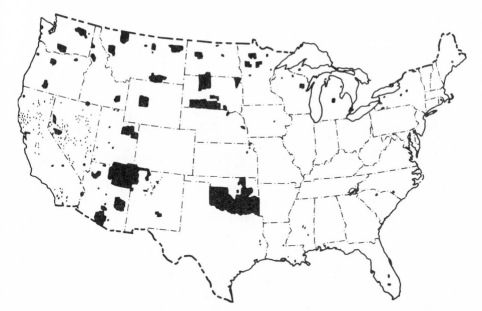

Figure 4.2 Native American Reservations Today. From Kenneth T. Jackson, ed., *Atlas of American History,* 2nd rev. ed. (New York: Charles Scribner's Sons, 1984), pp. 200–201.

some parts of this country. The cultures of Native American groups have remained strong, despite, or perhaps because of, their economic immiseration. In the Intermountain and Plains West, regions where people's grandparents were often homesteaders and Indian fighters, racism against Native Americans remains a strong and divisive force, especially with the postwar renewal of a Native American movement that has vociferously questioned the disposal of its land and the contemporary allocation of resources like water and mineral rights.[10]

Despite geological intelligence at the time of reservation designation, these territorial units of often vast size have recently been discovered to be the sites of valuable mineral deposits. As we shall see in the chapter on the postwar Intermountain West, Native Americans have been able to build strong intertribal alliances and at times, coalitions with other western interests, to create new forms of regionalism.

Second, much of the political geography of the United States can be explained by the progress of the clash between modes of production. The border between Canada and the United States follows the territorial division between groups of colonially allied fur-trading Indians at the moment of the War of Independence. The borders of many states, and the territories out of which they were carved, were established as frontiers between white and Indian territories. An outstanding example is the Proclamation Line of 1767 by which the British designated everything west of the Appalachian crest as Indian territory to appease their Indian allies (McNickle 1962; Horsman 1967). Furthermore, most state borders in the old Northwest Territory follow topographical features which can be defended in warfare and easily policed in peacetime—riverbeds, lakefronts, and mountain crests. The result is an American landscape in which natural ecological units, like river basins, are unnaturally severed by these political boundaries, a situation that has hampered environmentally-oriented planning of all sorts during successive decades.

Third, land ownership and settlement patterns were profoundly shaped by the Indian wars. On the one hand, early settlements in all regions had an important defensive function, which often dictated their placement and size; many important interior towns had their origins as Indian-fighting forts. But perhaps more important, the unique pattern of land distribution in the American interior had much to do with the necessity to compensate a large militia for its service in ridding the territory of Indians. Small homesteads became both a reward for service and a cause for further westward movement against the resisting tribes. Large landownership of the type prevailing in Europe and introduced on the west coast by the Spanish was not possible in an era of fierce resistance to expropriation and enslavement by the native population. This difference between landholding patterns in California and the rest of the country persists today in the highly differentiated structure of agriculture—immense corporate farms in the former and smaller, family owned and managed farms in the ranging and agricultural interior.

The political structure of the new American nation has been suggested by some to owe a debt to Native American political forms. Ben Franklin is said to have been impressed with the federal structure of the Iroquois tribes, whom he visited on a "peace-making" expedition. Clearly, the disparate origins of the colonies who banded together to secure their independence from Britain also figures in this political formation. But the continued threat of Native American resistance was a strong force in prompting the original thirteen colonies to maintain their unity as a nation, preventing their fragmentation into smaller national units as occurred in other parts of the colonial world.

Finally, a powerful lasting imprint of the struggle between Native American cultures and "white" newcomers is the ideology captured in the "Western," that moving picture portrayal of American culture which, while it permeates the entire society (as vividly demonstrated in the Viet Nam episode), is most virulent in the contemporary West. There, newcomer exploitation of the land is legitimized as worthy adventure against a hostile environment and celebrated as a triumph of man over nature. It is not a simple task to harness this strain of western ideology to the preservationist goals of a more recent regional population, opposing new rounds of exploitation like mining and missile installation. We shall return to this theme in the chapter on the contemporary West.

THE CIVIL WAR BETWEEN THE NORTH AND SOUTH

Towards the end of two centuries of east-west Indian wars, the young American nation found itself riven in two along a north-south axis in the bloody conflict known as the Civil War. In this, the initiative belonged to the South. Of all U.S. regions, the South has been and remains the most distinctive. A southern regional culture was rooted in an evolving mode of production, slavery, which compared poorly to its northern neighbors' capitalist economy, and which nurtured an ideology of paternalism and gentility fundamentally at odds with the liberalism and entrepreneurial spirit of the North. Its persistence after the failure of secession was a function of both the enormous bloodshed of the war and the incomplete conversion of southern agriculture to a capitalist mode.

The intense regionalism of the Civil War era was a product of three features of the mid-nineteenth-century American political economy. First, the American colonies adopted strikingly different economic systems—cash-crop agriculture in the South and international commerce buttressed by small-scale farming, artisanry, and nascent industrial capitalism in the North. Each economy employed a different dominant form of labor—slaves in the South, proprietors and wage workers in the North. Social life was built upon these distinct labor systems, generating profoundly different outlooks and problems, arrayed on a territorial basis.

Second, by mid-century, their economies were propelled by spectacular booms and structural changes that placed them on a collision course. An insatiable world demand for cotton, associated with the textile revolution, created pressure on southern land and labor, exacerbated by the curtailment of the slave trade and by soil erosion. In the North, the agricultural subjugation of the Midwest and the advent of manufacturing created a symbiotic boom which placed even greater demands on northern land and labor. As a result, each regional economy generated contradictory demands for resources on the national government, especially over the rules governing westward expansion.

Third, the existing political structure of the young nation facilitated regionalism, especially in the territorially constituted Congress and the electoral competition for control of the presidency. Common enemies (Native Americans and the British) had driven thirteen disparate colonies together into one nation-state. But as the next century wore on, this uncomfortable union increasingly proved dysfunctional for the elites in each region, destroying national political parties and motivating the beleaguered southern leadership to seek national sovereignty in a separate confederacy.

Regional Differentials in Mode of Production

Although commercial capitalism stretched across the globe by the eighteenth century, creating the context for European colonialism, quite disparate forms of production took root in the various regions prior to the advent of industrial capitalism. From the North American colonies, transoceanic commerce was fed by Native American hunting activities, subsistence farmers' and fishermen's sales of surplus fish, grain, and timber, and slave and indentured servant production of tobacco, rice, indigo, and cotton.

The Southern Slave Economy

The American South proved an attractive region for specialization in cash crops because of its climate, its cheap, productive lands easily wrested from native Americans, and its ready access through many tidal rivers. But the slave labor mode of production of the southern colonies was not a self-contained economic system; it was embedded in a larger world capitalist economy.

The profitability of the southern plantation was dependent upon a world market for its produce, on the one hand, and an external supply of labor, on the other.[11] In the eighteenth century, the flourishing slave trade satisfied the latter need.[12] By the early nineteenth century, a vigorous demand for cotton from the newly industrialized European textile mills provided the stimulus to the wholesale conversion of southern agriculture to cotton production. The location of the plantation slave production system within this larger world economy is illustrated in table 4.1, which shows its dependence upon exchange relationships on both sides of its market.[13]

The structure of the slave economy. Yet despite its insertion in the larger capitalist economy, southern slavery was a dominant and distinct mode of production, especially after 1792.[14] As a labor system, it differed fundamentally from feudalism, subsistence farming, or capitalist wage labor. Slaves were a commodity, a form of labor power owned directly by planters who controlled the disposal of their agricultural product. As lifetime and fungible property of their owners, slaves could be employed in ways not available to capitalists who hired free wage labor, with profound consequences for the evolution of the southern economy.[15]

First of all, the southern plantation system extracted absolute rather than relative surplus from its slaves. Slaves were driven harder, worked longer hours at a faster pace, than did agricultural wage workers in the North.[16] The result was a retardation in agricultural productivity which would have come had the planters chosen the diversified farming route of northern farmers, who adopted labor-saving techniques. Yet the system was lucrative. Profit rates on the order of 10 to 15 percent a year were recorded (Conrad and Meyer 1958), and the high price paid for slaves testified to the massive creation of surplus.

Second, the availability of slave labor twenty-four hours a day meant that much of the capital stock and equipment could be built on plantations rather than purchased from craftsmen or manufacturers. Since a trained slave was the property of his or her master, the investment (in

Table 4.1 Sequence and Location of Cotton and Textile Production and Trade, 1790–1820

Commodity capital sequence[a]	S	x	M	x	S'...C	x	M'	x	C'...T	x	M"	x	T'
Activity	Enslaving		Exchange		Production (cotton)		Exchange		Production (textiles)		Exchange		Consumption
Producer					Slave labor				Wage Worker				
Appropriator	Enslaver		Slaver, trader		Planter		Cotton merchant		Capitalist		Textile merchant		
Region	Africa		New England (English, Dutch)		Southern U.S.		New England (English)		England, New England		English		World-wide (U.S., India, Argentina, etc.)

[a]Capital letters represent prices, not values, of commodity and money capital.
Connectors: x represents an exchange transaction; "..." the transformation of labor power into commodities.
S, S': Slaves; M, M', M": Money Capital; C, C': Cotton; T, T': Textiles. Primes indicate that a commodity is augmented in value from its previous form.

the sense of labor foregone in the fields) in skills needed for blacksmith-ing, construction, and repair work could be recouped by the planter far into the future, unlike that advanced for the training of a wage worker, who was free to leave. Slaves also produced many of the domestic goods and services for their masters, as well as reproducing their own labor power through gardening, cooking, and garment-making. All of these supplemental activities meant that the demand for capital and consumer goods which would normally have emanated from an economy specializ-ing in cash crops was severely truncated.

Third, and central to the unity of the South in the prewar period, the slave labor force reproduced itself intergenerationally. In the words of a southerner of the time, "Slaves . . . are not wasted by use, and if they are, that waste is supplied by their issue.[17] The value of slave children as future workers and potential commodities encouraged an ideology of paternalism on the part of slaveholders, who as a class protected their slaves from a too-killing pace of work. (American slaves were the *only* slaves among all the colonial empires successfully to reproduce them-selves in bondage.) After the transoceanic slave trade was closed down in 1808[18] and as soils were exhausted in the upper South, planters there profitted from the sale of slaves toward the south and west, which tied them economically to the slavery system even when they no longer relied upon slaves directly as agricultural laborers.

Finally, the business ethic of slaveholders differed dramatically from that of their northern counterparts. The drive to accumulate capital under slavery was weaker than under industrial capitalism. Planters might choose to amass capital in the form of land and slaves, but few owned manufacturing assets in the prewar period. The predominant type of expansion was a continual push westward to find new, produc-tive soils, but this was a form of replacement activity, rather than real growth in the cotton economy. As a system, the tendency was to squander profits on elegant consumption practices—travel, a townhouse in a coastal city, balls, and fancy imported clothing, furniture, and foodstuffs. In general, southern plantation ideology disdained the ac-quisitiveness celebrated by northern advocates of free labor and capital-ist entrepreneurship. Thus quantitative additions to the stock of produc-tive factors (arable land, labor, physical plant) compared poorly with those amassed within the capitalist dynamism of the North.

The performance of southern slavery. In comparison with the North, the southern economy grew slowly in the period from 1790 to 1860. It was less productive, less innovative, and more environmentally destructive. Relatively low levels of mechanization resulted from the practice of intense exploitation of slave labor and the weaker accumulative drive of the system. Low productivity was also a product of slave resistance—sabotage, mistreatment of machinery and animals, and deliberate slow-ness. Gains were retarded, too, by the system of labor discipline; it was easier to oversee a gang of undifferentiated field workers than to encourage specialized agricultural skills.[18] Cotton grown in this fashion consumed relatively greater amounts of land and labor, and less of capital and technology, than it would have under a wage labor system. A by-product was the extraordinary soil exhaustion rates which propelled the center of gravity of the system westward (Genovese 1967, 43–69).[20]

Nor could diversified farming by non-slave-owning southerners flourish in this environment. Small farmers were squeezed onto less fertile upland soils, where they grew cotton, tobacco, wheat, and corn for market. But demand was weak in a largely self-sufficient plantation economy with few urban dwellers and the slave labor force producing its own food, except for limited amounts of corn and pork. Midwestern and coastal markets were difficult to reach, because the planters had provided themselves with a transportation system (canals and railroads) designed to link their plantations with ports rather than unify the interior (Sydnor 1948, 18; Fishlow 1965, 9). Lack of an indigenous capital market separate from the plantation system curtailed credit to smallholders. As a result of these supply and demand inadequacies, small farmers in the South remained largely marginal and subsistence producers up through the Civil War period (Gray 1933, 477; North 1961, 130).

The structure of southern agriculture had a dilatory effect upon southern manufacturing. Because of its cotton, the South should have been a major textile producer by mid-century; instead, its share of national textile output declined from 33 percent in 1815 to 25 percent in 1860. Supply side forces were largely responsible for this. Not only were capital and entrepreneurship for industrial enterprise scarce, but labor was also hard to find. European immigrants, who swelled the ranks of the northern labor force, were discouraged from settling in the South because of low wages and planter suspicions of radicalism. Planters were opposed to free blacks working for wages and were ambivalent about poor whites doing so, fearing the growth of a free wage labor challenge to slavery. Planters did rent out slaves to work in tobacco and cotton mills, but only when demand from cotton production was sluggish.[21]

Capital goods sectors—metal machinery, railroads, and construction—were similarly depressed by these supply factors. In addition, these sectors lacked demand that would have emanated from a dynamic, diversified agricultural sector. The dispersed pattern of southern agriculture, with its relatively small coastal entrepots, failed to produce the urban agglomeration economies which were so important in the growth of northern industrial cities (North 1961, 126).[22]

The Industrializing Capitalism of the North

In contrast, the North had followed a very different economic path. Not blessed with land easily convertible into cash crops like cotton, its early growth was based on vigorous commercial activity in collecting, stocking, marketing, and shipping the specialized products of the far-flung colonial regions. Commercial profits feeding the growth of its port cities included lucrative returns from the slave, rum, and cotton trades, as well as from carrying North American dried fish, grains, dairy and wood products, and animals to West Indies planters, and returning with their slave-produced sugar. Busy centers of shipbuilding, banking, merchanting, and insurance, like New York, Boston, Philadelphia, and Newport, in turn consumed large quantities of agricultural produce from their hinterlands. By the beginning of the nineteenth century, this internal orientation began to take precedence over the transoceanic trade, and state and territorial assemblies pushed vigorously for turnpikes and canals to penetrate the interior (Greene 1942, 316; Williams 1961, 108–9; North 1961, 49–51).[23]

During the next half century, the North evolved subregions of growing specialization in agriculture and cities in manufacturing, each stimulating innovation and expansion in the other. In an era of relative labor scarcity, demand for the products of mixed farming—wheat, oats, barley, corn, milk, butter, cheese, and meat for a growing city population, and horses and oxen for transportation and horsepower—led to dramatic agricultural innovations in reaping, harvesting, and mowing machinery, whose adoption was facilitated by the entrepreneurial form of family farming and the relatively high quality of agricultural labor (Hobsbawm 1975, 180; Main 1970, 115–17).[24]

Farm commercialization in turn created a vigorous demand for capital goods (plows, reapers, wagons, and scythes) and consumer goods (pots and pans, textiles, and furniture), which engendered an enlarged artisanry as well as the nascent iron and machinery sectors. The coming of the railroad reinforced east-west ties between farmers and industrial cities, opening up new lands and creating quantitative leaps in demand for iron and machinery.

Since slavery crowded out the development of a free wage labor mode of production in the South, it is worth addressing briefly the reasons why slavery did not take root in the North. Slaves were imported into the northern colonies; in 1750 slaves could be found in almost every occupation. Yet they never accounted for more than 5 percent of the population in any one colony, and had peaked in numbers by 1765. Unlike southern cash cropping, northern diversified farmers in small family units found slaves less profitable than hired hands; grain-dairy-meat farming had less need for a year-round workforce.[25]

Furthermore, in both agricultural and artisan sectors, a repugnance for slavery along the lines of the evolving individualist and libertarian European philosophies was beginning to take hold in the North, abetted by a growing free labor ideology. Many slaves were simply freed by their owners. In addition, slaves were expensive after the close of the slave trade, and their relatively lower marginal productivity in northern shops and farms encouraged their sale to southern cotton planters.[26]

Mid-Century Divergence in Growth Rates

The southern economy was distinctive only in comparison with an implicit standard of northern normalcy and was underdeveloped only by contrast to the benchmark of northern performance. That the two economies were starkly differentiated by their respective modes of production can be demonstrated forcefully by looking at regional slave population shares in 1860 (fig. 4.3). By that year, the southern planter class controlled $4 billion worth of slaves and real estate, which was worked by more than two million slaves, while northern entrepreneurs possessed almost $2 billion worth of manufacturing plant in which one million men, women, and children labored for wages (Phillips 1918, 373; Hesseltine and Smiley 1960, 189).

The secular progress of the two economies was such that the southern economy was slipping behind. It was more highly specialized, its industrialization was faltering, and it remained oriented toward an external market rather than forging a unified internal economy with its own self-

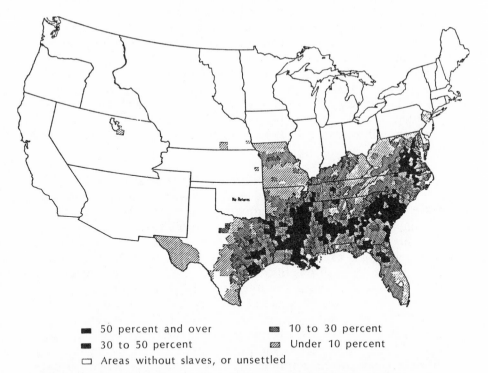

■ 50 percent and over	▨ 10 to 30 percent
■ 30 to 50 percent	▨ Under 10 percent
☐ Areas without slaves, or unsettled	

Figure 4.3 Regional Incidence of Slavery, 1860 (percent of slaves in total population). From Charles Paullin, *Atlas of the Historical Geography of the United States* (Westport, Conn.: Greenwood Press, 1932, 1975).

generated growth. It was increasingly unable to compete with the North in attracting immigrants and supporting population growth, evident in the North's superior pace in settling western lands. Had extraordinary mid-century booms not occurred in both North and South, slavery might have given way less violently to capitalist agriculture in the South.

The peculiar dynamics of the southern economy in the decade before 1860 explains the optimism with which the southern planter class sought sovereignty. A spectacular boom in the cotton market created a hefty derived demand for both slaves and land, causing the cotton economy to appear deceptively strong. At the aggregate level, the rate of southern productivity gains from 1840 to 1860 matched those registered in the North in the latter decade. Even manufacturing output per capita grew faster than in the rest of the nation, although this was a function both of a smaller base and the Panic of 1857 in the North.[27] Speculatively inflated slave and land prices in the 1850s reinforced planters' views of the viability of their economy and tied planters in the older and upper South regions to those in the Deep South.

But high levels of short-term profitability and inflation in asset prices obscured the slave economy's vulnerabilities. For one, the cotton boom was a relatively short-lived phenomenon, the product of rapid substitution of manufactured textiles for homespun and woven products. After the war, it was many years before cotton demand again reached prewar levels, partly because European factories had found other sources in the interim. For another, the option of expanding westward was just about exhausted; cotton could not be grown in the arid and colder regions to the north and west of east Texas (Phillips 1936, 373–75, 392; Wright 1978).

These constraints were not faced by the North, which was preoccupied with the restructuring introduced by the railroads and the settlement of western lands. By the 1850s, northern promoters had built 10,000 miles of railroads, integrating new farm areas with older manufacturing centers. In the ensuing decade, farmers totally rerouted flour shipments from the Mississippi River Basin to the east-west railroads, switching the bulk of livestock and animal shipments to this axis as well. As a result, western shipments to the South declined absolutely and by 1860 total west-south trade amounted to only one third of that between the West and the Northeast (Fishlow 1965, 8, 263–65, 279–83; Fogel 1964, 277). These rail links, which demonstrated clearly the regional differences in spatial and trade orientation, are shown in figure 4.4. The North during that decade was rapidly expanding iron capital and consumer goods production in its growing cities, building new towns at relatively high densities on the agricultural frontier and laying rail at unprecedented rates. These activities led to new sets of northern claims levied on the federal government, often at loggerheads with those of the South and slavery.

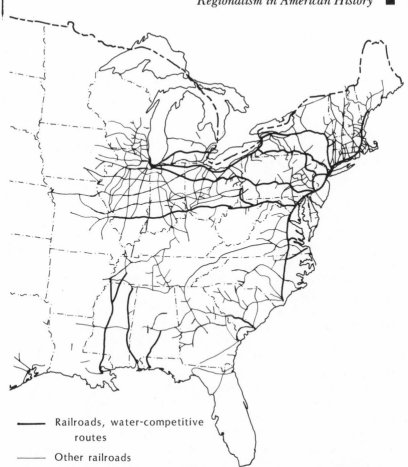

Figure 4.4   North-South Transportation Infrastructure, 1850s. From Robert
Fogel, *Railroads and Economic Growth* (Baltimore: Johns Hopkins, 1964).

Regional Coalitions and Party Formation

The translation of this growing economic cleavage into bloodshed was
facilitated by the peculiarities of federal political structure, by the
irreconcilable nature of claims on the State emanating from each mode,
and by creative leadership by regional elites in fostering internal solidarity. During the decade preceding 1860, national political parties failed in
their attempt to maintain cross-regional political bases and were either
extinguished or replaced by new purely regional party formations. In
each region, a powerful ideology emerged which expressed, sometimes
in ambiguous terms, the values and aims of the hegemonic coalition.

The Political Setting

Regional elites in the two economically antagonistic regions found
themselves battling over a fragile and only recently constructed nation-

state. Indeed, it was remarkable that they should have elected to join together since issues like the slavery trade, slavery in the territories, slave enumeration for voting and tax purposes, and the enlisting of blacks as soldiers had divided northern capitalists and southern slaveholders from the outset. In 1793, James Madison had observed

> The greater danger to our general government is the great southern and northern interests of the continent, being opposed to each other. Look to the votes of Congress, and most of them stand divided by the geography of the country, divided into different interests not by their size, but by other circumstances; the most material of which resulted partly from climate but principally from the effect of their having or not having slaves. [Lynd 1967, 161–62]

But the common desire of mercantilist colonies to throw off the English yoke and protect frontier settlements from Native Americans overcame these early signs of incompatibility. The issues dividing a slave from a free wage-labor economy were resolved with gerryrigged and eventually unworkable compromises.[28]

By the 1830s skirmishes in the national Congress over land, improvements, territorial expansion and national economic institutions began to escalate into a struggle over political structure, captured in the increasing southern demand for "states' rights," and finally into the movement for secession. The political structure of the young nation played a major role in this deepening of animosity. Already, a two-party system had evolved, with a commercial, largely northern elite advocating strong centralized national economic power (in banking and monetary matters, trade regulation, and so on) against an agrarian coalition favoring decentralized state rule. The innovation of the American presidency, with its highly visible direct election and considerable powers independent of the Congress, tended to destabilize party politics and heighten awareness of regionalism.[29]

Squabbling was furthered by the original agreement to carve new states out of the western acquisitions with instant political parity and by the Constitutional provision which permitted southern planters to dominate the presidency, Congress, and especially the Senate, far beyond their numbers, because each slave "earned" three-fifths of a vote for his owner. Meanwhile, a more representative House, which controlled appropriations, began to step out of southern control as early as 1840. These initially manageable conflicts ballooned into a struggle over which regional elite would control the central machinery of the State, partly because that machinery was so awkwardly composed.

The Issues and Their Regional Advocates

Histories of the Civil War recount the hostilities between the contestants "North" and "South" as conglomerate actors.[30] Yet each side consisted of fragile political coalitions among particular economic and social groups, led by a capitalist entrepreneurial class in the North and by the planter class in the South. The dominant coalitions were far from representative of the unanimous will of all regional residents; the dominant mode of production in each region supported a class structure with its own internal antagonisms, and these in turn were overlaid with significant racial, ethnic, and spatial subdivisions. The issues which dominated the interregional arena evoked affinities of differing strength from these various groupings within each region. In the highly summarized and simplified characterization which follows, I have relegated many of these exceptions and complications to footnotes.

By the 1850s, internal improvements were a seasoned controversy. In the North most classes favored nationally underwritten internal improvements—merchants whose trade would thereby mushroom, western farmers eager to reach expanded northeastern markets, and northeastern manufacturers eying amplified internal markets.[31] Southern planters favored internal improvements until, after 1831, these increasingly took the form of northeastern-midwestern rail and canal links. Hoping to finance a southern transcontinental railroad rather than contribute to the impending northern link, planters argued that states should be the major actor in internal improvement schemes.

A second demand, free disposal of federally owned western land, was espoused most adamantly by white western farmers, farmers-to-be, and their artisan-professional-shopkeeper complement. Congress had been auctioning off large portions of its territorial holdings to finance the public debt and internal improvements. Speculators had grabbed up the bulk of this land, selling it to small farmers at much inflated prices. In response, farmers demanded the right of preemption—the protection of frontier squatters from usurpation. Preemption matured into demands for a homestead law which would grant public acreage free to farmers who cleared new farm land and made it productive.

This issue pitted small farmers in both regions against their respective ruling elites. Free land was opposed by planters, whose comparative edge in agriculture and whose national political power would be diluted by rapid small farm expansion in the Midwest; those with expansionary ambitions favored competitive sale of southwestern public lands. Northeastern capitalists feared the depletion of their pool of wage labor, while merchant and banking capitalists preferred schemes that were capturable for more speculative purposes. A few visionary industrialists and merchants saw the expansionary potential in the western market that would result from a more generous land policy: a greater demand for manufactured goods and cheaper food to keep wage costs down. If immigration could solve the labor supply problem, they could support free land (Stephenson 1967; Sydnor 1948, 149, 154).[32]

A third controversy revolved around the protection of young industrial sectors. The tariff issue was the darling of a group of Middle Atlantic industrial capitalists and had formed a central plank in the

American System, the Federalist program for an industrial America, in the early decades of the century. Long subject to trade restrictions favoring British manufacturers in overseas markets, the newly independent American manufacturers sought similar aid by requiring Americans to buy domestically. Southern planters were the strongest opponents of the tariff, which would raise prices of imported goods but would not apply to cash crop markets, particularly cotton, which they dominated. Until the war, they received backing from northeastern commercial and banking interests, and from farmers and urban workers who would face higher prices for clothing, tools, and other manufactured goods (Hesseltine and Smiley 1960, 326; Foner 1970a, 177).[33]

A fourth issue concerned monetary policy. The establishment of a national bank which would control the creation of money and place the young United States on a sound international credit basis was a major demand of the merchant-banker Federalists and their successors through the first half of the nineteenth century. The bank, which would pursue a tight-money policy, thus favoring creditors, was opposed adamantly by debt-laden western farmers. The bank was also opposed by southern planters who, for the most part, profited from relatively cheap money.[34]

These economic controversies were accompanied by two complementary legal issues of tremendous import to the regions: free soil and abolition. "Free Soil" referred to the status of slavery in the territories, especially those petitioning for entry into the Union as states (see fig. 4.5). The extension of slavery was most vigorously opposed by the midwestern farmer and independent artisan classes, whose antipathy was founded on fear of competition from slave labor, fear of competition for land from southern planter capital, and racism. Free Soil was the counterpart of the broader principle of Free Labor, referring to the workers' rights to mobility, to a wage, and to an opportunity to become small-scale independent farmers, artisans, and entrepreneurs (Berwanger 1967; Foner 1970a, 12–17). Free Soil was also backed by northeastern industrial and merchant classes who saw clearly that the entry of new states on a slavery-free basis would clinch their control of a Congress and presidency stubbornly in the hands of the "Slave Power."

Abolition was a final issue, one that was to become central to the struggle. American sentiment against slavery was nurtured by an international climate in which the fact of human bondage clashed with emerging European notions of individual liberty and free labor, in turn a function of industrialization amid a labor surplus released from capitalist agriculture. In the North, small abolition societies of militant activists—some black, some white, and a few with interracial membership—agitated for abolition, first by northern states, and then in the territories and in the South. The black groups, such as those joining in the Negro Convention movement in the 1830s, advocated slave rebellion and led the operation of the Underground Railway.[35]

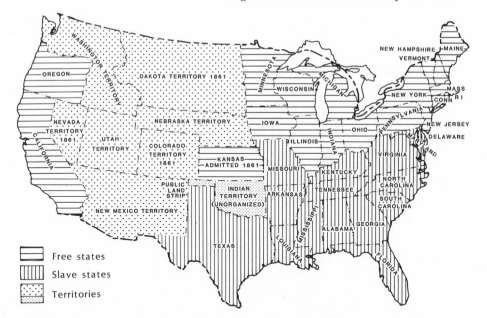

Free states
Slave states
Territories

Figure 4.5   Slave States, Free States, and Territories, 1861. From K. T. Jackson, ed., *Atlas of American History* (New York: Scribner's 1978).

White abolitionist societies arose with the new cultural currents of evangelical religions and romanticism. While not ever numerous and with many internal battles, the abolitionists with their propaganda and militance did much to raise northern and midwestern consciousness about the exploitative conditions under slavery in the South and the incompatibility of slave labor with a free society. Finding a constituency among the independent farmers, small businessmen, shopkeepers, and professionals (lawyers and preachers) of the small town and rural areas of the North, and among the white middle classes in cities, they enriched the sound of "free soil, free labor" with a moral tone that heightened the intensity of regional feeling.[36] However, most northerners did not actively favor abolition. At least three-quarters of the northern population were still neutral on slavery in 1859 (Nevins 1950).[37]

Of all the "northern" issues, abolition was the most threatening to the southern planters because it proposed eliminating billions of dollars of southern wealth and an entire labor system which generated substantial profits and permitted a gracious southern planter class lifestyle. Many small white southern farmers joined the planter class in their opposition, particularly if they owned a slave or believed that such ownership was possible. Many, too, were related to the planter class by blood and identified with their rights to ownership in their land and slaves (Stampp 1974, 63–65; Foner 1970a, 156).

Across this set of issues, certain classes and regional groupings had greater potential unity than others. First, groups such as the southern white farmers, the northern artisan-professionals, and merchants in all regions had potentially divided stakes on more than one issue. They were thus not as cohesive as classes and were vulnerable to divide-and-conquer tactics or cooption by other more powerful class and regional groups. Second, the slave and working classes were relatively unorganized or nonpoliticized on a large number of issues regardless of region, even though their potential strength was enormous, and their conduct during the war played a strong role in its outcome. Third, the issues with the greatest potential to unify the North and the Midwest were internal improvements and opposition to slavery in the territories.

Cross-sectional to Intraregional Parties

In the thirty years before 1860, the issues of free land, free soil, free labor, protected industry, internal improvements, nonextension of slavery, and abolition fueled a dramatic national politics marked by inept and unrepresentative presidents, bitterly fought congressional and court cases, and the ascendancy of purely regionally based parties of national coalition. Figure 4.6 shows the major politically active class constituencies of each region and the issues potentially binding them to the neighboring regions. Each major contending party chose carefully among these issues; their cross-regional strategies are represented by the hemispheres encompassing specific classes in neighboring regions. The issues closest to the center were those which posed the greatest difficulties for each party's effort to bridge the regions.

The Democrats, or "Democracy" as the party was then known, dominated national politics from 1828 to the 1850s. It built its strength on agrarian classes, particularly in the South and West, and on urban workers, especially the Irish. Democracy promulgated an egalitarian ideology of the common man against the plutocracy of the eastern capitalists; its hero was Andrew Jackson. The party championed westward expansion, including vigorous Indian fighting and preemption, and opposed the tariff and eastern-biased improvements schemes. Democracy foundered on the issue of slavery, especially its extension into the territories. In the end, it could not hold together the western farmers and the southern planter class, and in the 1850s became an almost purely southern party.

The Whigs, the major political opposition throughout the period, appealed to large and small businessmen in all regions and espoused a program of economic nationalism—a national banking system, centrally subsidized internal improvements, and opposition to free land. Strongest in the Northeast, it successfully recruited planters, especially from the upper South, who had ventured into manufacturing and finance or found the egalitarian philosophy of the Democrats repugnant. Henry Clay is an outstanding example. The Whigs often chose presidential candidates from that region to "elevate to the Presidency southerners

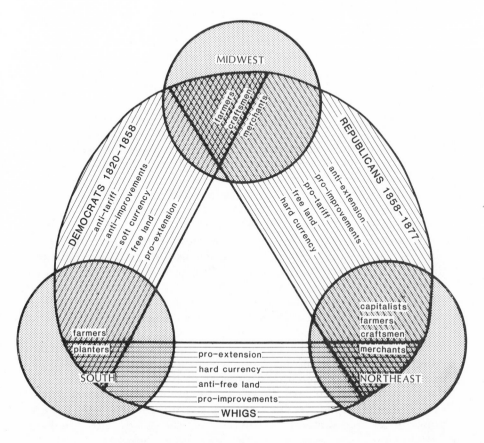

Figure 4.6   Civil War Regions: Classes, Parties, Issues

who were westerners in the public eye or northern with southern principles."[38] But the Whigs were unable to surmount the fundamental contradiction between slavery and capitalism as systems of labor. They also split along regional lines on issues of extension and national enforcement of the right to slave ownership, southern planters drifting back into the Democratic fold in the 1850s.

As the national Democratic and Whig parties disintegrated, there ensued numerous attempts to form a new coalition that could gain control of the presidency and Congress.[39] Success fell to the Republicans, who in 1856 forged an alliance among merchant-professional classes, western farmers, eastern manufacturers, abolitionists, and some working-class whites. They overcame northeastern capital's opposition to free land by arguing that western settlement would generate a strong demand for manufactures, provide a cheap source of food for urban workers, and require further transportation infrastructure.[40] Farmers, alienated from the Democratic party by its hedging on the free soil issue, joined the Republican party with assurances that a good homestead act would be a primary commitment of the party, and that a tariff would stimulate American industry, thereby boosting the urban demand for agricultural produce. The Republican slogan became "Vote yourself a farm, vote yourself a tariff." In four short years, this new coalition, purely regional in nature, won the presidency.[41]

This swift rise of the Republican party revealed the intractability of old cross-regional coalitions. Nationally the most pressing and contentious claims on the state had assumed a predominantly regional, rather than class or cultural, form, a derivative of strict territorial differentiation in modes of production. All substantial efforts at cross-regional coalitions failed to bridge the enmity between southern planters and northern industrialists, commercial interests, and farmers.

Regional enmity flowed not only from the social relations of each mode, but also from the growth of their respective productive forces. The pace of economic growth in the previous forty years strengthened the ties between the Northeast and Midwest and permitted them to outdistance the profitable but monocultural cotton economy of the South. The relative disadvantage of the South in converting economic power performance into political power was manifest in its failure to propagate slavery in the territories and its relatively low population growth rate, both of which eroded the southern vote. Cities like Baltimore and Louisville moved away from the southern fold as their manufacturing and commercial activities molded them increasingly in the image of northern cities. By the 1850s, it had become patently clear that if southern planters had not enjoyed disproportionate political power due to the three-fifths provision for each of their four million slaves, planter class national political power would have been broken.

Intraregional Cohesion

Each regionally dominant party—the Democrats in the South, the Republicans in the North—faced the formidable internal challenge of successfully creating a regional platform and ideology that would unite disparate groups behind them, especially as the thunderclouds of war loomed. In the South, the Democrats faced opposition from upper South planters, from commercial classes, and from planter-led small farmers. The former were won over by the lucrative nature of the decade's intraregional slave trade. Entrepreneurs, merchants, and traders were wooed by the prospect of repudiation of $3 million in debts owed to northerners. Small farmers, who formed the ranks of the Confederate army, were recruited through appeals to racial superiority and economic opportunity.

Buttressing the direct appeal to these groups' economic interests was an ideology which celebrated slavery as a benign labor system[42] compared to the brutality and anomie of capitalist "wage slavery" and branded the North as imperialistic. Southern leadership accused northern capital of creaming off southerners' hard-earned profits and depicted the federal government as its handmaiden, permitting monopolization of the coastal trade and undertaking only those southern improvements, such as harbor lights and seamen's facilities, which would benefit northern merchants.[43] Southern self-defense and states' rights were stressed against northern aggression, which included abolitionist demands for immediate emancipation, the refusal of northerners to cooperate with the nation's fugitive slave provisions, and their collaboration with the Underground Railway.[44] Southern ideology played up family ties between small farmers and planters, warning that interclass mobility would be threatened by the demise of slavery. Racism was invoked by raising the specter of competition from free black labor and indiscriminate violence which rebelling black slaves might inflict on whites regardless of class (Wright 1978, 34; Benson 1972, 316–18; Hesseltine and Smiley 1960, 195).[45]

Despite all this, southern internal unity was incomplete.[46] The Confederacy did not claim to represent the South's four million black slaves. Southern white farmers, especially those in areas of western North Carolina, eastern Tennessee, and northern Alabama, with no cotton and few slaves, resisted the secession of their states, set up guerrilla warfare bases, and sheltered fleeing slaves and dissidents. West Virginia seceded from Virginia in 1860 as an overwhelming number of its mountain subsistence farmers refused to follow Tidewater leadership into the confederacy (Degler 1974).[47]

In the North, Republicans faced organizational complexities as well. From 1789 on, notes Kenneth Stampp (1974, 2) the North never lacked a party or at least an organized faction committed to a legislative program that suited its economic needs. But the Federalists and Whigs had been continually thwarted by their identification as the party of big business and wealth, especially as the Democrats successfully extended the votes to white working men and farmers. The Republicans needed to overcome this class-biased image to succeed as the party of a united North. Three internal axes of conflict confronted them. The first, and most successfully resolved, was the class antagonism between western farmers and eastern capitalists. The Republicans convincingly argued that macroeconomic benefits would reverberate back to the farmer for accepting the tariff and to the eastern capitalist for accepting free land, overriding short-term economic losses.

A second problem was the affinity of many northern workers, especially the Irish, for the Democratic party, which had given them the vote and was the basis for newly powerful urban machines. While independent craftsworkers were easily won to the party of free labor, and groups like the ironworkers, especially after the Panic of 1857, were won to the party of the tariff, other workingmen's groups remained hostile, especially toward the wartime draft and repression of unions. A third internal conflict, between manufacturers who demanded a tariff and a radical anti-Slave Power stand and commercial capitalists who preferred free trade and a conciliatory stance towards the South, was resolved temporarily by stressing to the latter the preservation of the Union and a strong national economic program as central Republican concerns (Foner 1970a, 170, and 1970b, 204–5; Holt 1973).[48]

Accompanying this diversified platform with something for everyone, the Republican party coined the ambiguous slogans "Freedom" and "Antislavery." "Freedom" referred variously to free soil (nonextension of slavery, but suggested free homesteads as well), free labor (mobility), and free man (antipathy to bondage). The antislavery plank was equally ambiguous; slavery could be interpreted as a system, an expansionist program, a political coalition, a chattel labor force, or a moral outrage. For capitalists, antislavery expressed their desire to unseat the Slave Power, which had consistently thwarted their economic development plans in the Congress and presidency. To midwestern farmers, antislavery referred to their hatred of the Slave Power's expansionary designs for western lands like Kansas. To abolitionists, antislavery was a call for the elimination of a morally repugnant form of servitude. To workers, antislavery was a commitment to ending an unfair system of labor (Berwanger 1967, 1, 121; Foner 1970b, 18–19, 32, 209; Montgomery 1967).

By sticking to these catch-all phrases, the Republicans were able to champion modernization, independent entrepreneurship, and the dignity of labor simultaneously. They adroitly emphasized different planks and different connotations to appropriate audiences (Foner 1970a, 193, and 1970b, 209; Van Duesen 1965, 12–13).[49] Theirs was a positive program of economic growth and development, contrasted to the lack of economic enterprise and self-discipline of the southern system, which they heavily criticized. While their programs, particularly the war, never received full support among urban workers and formerly conservative Whig merchants and financiers (Sharkey 1959, 175–83; Cole 1934, 277–82; Green 1965), the Republican North was less hampered by lack of internal unity than was its southern opponent.

The War and Its Aftermath

When states' rights was clearly no longer a winning regional strategy and with the victory of the Republicans in electing Lincoln, the South chose to secede and form its own state, the Confederacy. The Republican leadership chose to deny their right to do so, and war followed quickly. The North was able to prevail over the South in four short years because of the developmental superiority of its economy, reflecting the emergent superiority of capitalist versus slave modes of production. The distinctive productive forces and social relations of each strengthened or sapped its war effort respectively.

First of all, the North's diversified economy served it well. Its dynamism over the previous thirty years had swollen its population base and labor force so that by 1860 it accounted for two thirds of the nation's population and 80 percent of men of military age. It could furnish more soldiers as a result. The North boasted 110,000 manufacturing plants with 1.3 million workers to the South's 18,000 with 110,000 workers (Frederickson 1975, 58; Hobsbawm 1975, 143). The North possessed 70 percent of all existing rail, and unlike the southern network, these lines tightly integrated agricultural with urban industrial regions.[50] Northern diversified farms easily fed Union troops, while vittles for the southern army were scarce (Frederickson 1975, 58; Hobsbawm 1975, 143).

But just as importantly, the social relations of each region's system contributed to the lopsided outcome. Whereas workers and farmers could be drafted in the North, planters dared not permit their primary labor force, slaves, to fight, for it would be too dangerous to arm them. When harnessed as food producers and industrial workers, slaves resisted and fled on the order of a general strike. Even worse, some 500,000 fought in the northern army and acted as laborers, servants, spies, and camp helpers. Nor were southern white farmers universally willing to bear arms for the Confederacy. Some 300,000 southern whites fought for the Union side; over the course of the war, 200,000 deserted the Confederate army. While graft, corruption, and desertion also plagued the northern army, it was less encumbered because it had a larger pool of labor upon which to draw (Cole 1934, 293, 314–18, 336; DuBois 1935, 63, 80; Degler 1974, 174).

The political and cultural features of each region's mode of production were also critical to its ability to prosecute the war. Northern entrepreneurship led to striking innovations in military tactics, in agriculture and in mass-produced war supplies—ready-to-wear shoes and men's clothing, meat-packing, and the reaper were all credited to this period.[51] The predilection for a strong central State meant that few balked at the extraordinary wartime powers assumed by Lincoln or at sweeping changes like the Emancipation Proclamation.

In the South, the decentralized, anarchic slavocracy wasted precious time squabbling internally over tactics. Some states refused to cooperate with the Confederacy, withholding men, money, and munitions from their armories; and others refused to support a southern draft. With the ideological commitment to states' rights strong, no centralized administration that might effectively wage war was constructed. No taxes on land or slaves were levied, so that the war was financed through huge inflationary loans. Even southern military strategy was affected by political ideology. Contending only that they were *defending* the right to secede, and were thus not warring with the North, they refused to advance into northern territory, leaving themselves vulnerable along a lengthy porous border from the Appalachians to the Mississippi (Frederickson 1975, 69–71).

The costs of the war fell heaviest on the South, since most of the fighting took place on southern ground. Tremendous damage was wreaked on southern infrastructure—railroads, warehouses, mills, gins, depots, and government buildings; much livestock and farm equipment had been destroyed or plundered. Southern assets, worth $4.3 billion in 1860, were valued at $1.6 billion at the war's end. Much of this, however, represented the disappearance of property in slaves and the accompanying deflation in land values. In reality, the major productive assets of the southern economy remained in place—land and a huge black agricultural labor force.[52]

The underdevelopment of the southern economy, which was the most profound product of the war era, was less a function of the war itself than of the extraordinary compromise over restructuring the southern economy.[53] The Radical Republicans tried to redistribute political power in the South to a coalition of blacks and progressive whites. But since they could not, being heavily based on industrial capitalist support in the North, redistribute nonhuman property, specifically land, they paved the way for a system of sharecropping in which black former slaves, refusing to become wage workers but not given land to farm independently, became only a semi-free labor force, with devastating consequences for the southern economy.[54]

The sharecropping system, like its antecedent, resulted in low levels of productivity, primarily because of black withdrawal of labor, but also because conservation, maintenance, innovation, and investment were relatively discouraged compared to northern agriculture. Furthermore, the emergent power of the merchant-creditor led to excessive acreage in cotton (surplus appropriation could occur only if farmers raised a commodity which had to pass through their credit-marketing system), and too little devoted to food production for domestic consumption. Despite challenging problems in cotton cultivation (the variability of soil types, the uneven ripening patterns of bolls, genetic possibilities, and variations in cultivation patterns), no entrepreneurial class had the resources to pursue innovative solutions. Southern agriculture changed little during the subsequent decades. In 1910, the standard plantation still had ten tenant farms, with thirty-eight acres each (Mandle 1978, 60–67, 41).

Just as it had in the prewar era, the dominance of cotton and the income distribution structure within it retarded industrialization regionwide. The South's share of manufacturing establishments *fell* from 17.2 percent in 1860 to 15.3 percent in 1904, while its share of the nation's capital assets fell as well (Wiener 1978, 185; Rabinowitz 1977, 109; Woodward 1951, 1904). Cotton cultivation, even with the railroad, fostered the growth of rural cotton centers and small interior cities. There credit and marketing functions took place, and news of prices and sales could be handled by telegraph. The lack of a growing middle class of industrial labor force and the impoverishment of the vast majority of the agricultural population resulted in the continued absence of a stimulus to manufacturing for the regional market. Cities remained administrative centers, preoccupied with keeping blacks unskilled and segregated. Reconstruction, plus the railroads, brought a few new cities, like Atlanta and Dallas, to prominence. But for the most part, the South remained underindustrialized and underurbanized (Rabinowitz 1977, 97–99; Smith 1954, 28–33; Ransom and Sutch 1977, 116–17).

Equally formidable as future determinants of regionalism were the political and cultural legacies of the war epoch. The Democratic party became so entrenched in the South, and the Republican party so hated, that it stifled the expression of internal dissent and over time won the southern states greater congressional power under the seniority system. Within the South, Democratic party conventions continued to allocate votes on the basis of population rather than voters, so that black belt landlords from counties with lots of disenfranchised black sharecroppers dominated state level politics (Hicks 1931, 21–22, 36–39).

White supremacy became a dominant cultural theme. It was enforced through a regime of terror and violence, initially aimed in preserving the black rural labor force. At the same time, the infamy of defeat made itself felt in a culture of conservative Christianity stressing personal salvation. This cult of the "lost cause" engendered an enduring sense of distinctiveness, of being southern, which never elicited a counterpart in the North.

It is impossible to interpret contemporary regional antagonisms without taking into account these products of the Civil War era. We return to this north-south axis of conflict in chapter 8. The underdevelopment of southern agriculture and industry, the one-party political system, the South's unique version of racism, and the culture of defeatism are powerful forces distinguishing the South from the rest of the country and prompting regionalism well into the second half of the twentieth century.[56]

REGIONALISM DURING THE POPULIST AND NEW DEAL ERAS

During two periods of economic upheaval in the United States, regional settlement was subsumed, either through displacement or by incorporation, by the emergence of a new hegemonic national coalition. In the first case, the populist challenge, an incipient east-west antagonism was quashed through the joint agency of a cross-regional alliance of the commercial classes and the invoking of Civil War era sectionalist sentiments running along north-south lines. The result was a profoundly conservative and pro-business victory. In the second, the New Deal, a carefully crafted cross-regional alliance of those worst hit by the depression ushered in an era of diminished regionalism and relatively progressive, albeit capitalism-preserving, reforms. Each era is surveyed briefly here, probing the role and vigor of regionalism in each.

The Populist Challenge

The populist movement surged around thoroughly economic issues. In the 1870s and 1880s, dramatic changes had taken place in both the South and the West. In the South, the prewar planter class had been permitted to maintain political power and ownership of land, while northern financial, commercial, and industrial interests remade the South as a thoroughly capitalist economy, at least outside agriculture. With its physical devastation and its routing of slavery, the war returned the South to the frontier stage of development, quite similar to the West. The small farmer, often debt-ridden and renting or sharecropping the land, became the predominant type of agricultural producer in the South. In the West, expansive settlement patterns had created a large class of small farmers whose livelihoods depended, if less on landlordism, then equally on the banks, railroads, and grain merchants (Hicks 1931, 21–22, 36–39).

Especially at its outset, the populist movement was particularly regionalist in rhetoric and reality. Almost all of its support came from an arc running through the plains states to Georgia and South Carolina; it was particularly strong in Texas, Kansas, and some of the black belt states. Complaints about freight rates, lending practices, and elevator policies bound farmers from the two regions, South and West, together.

> The aggrieved easterner at least suffered from the persecutions of other easterners, whereas the southerner or the westerner was convinced that he suffered from a grievance caused by outsiders. In both sections, the description of railway oppression was incomplete without a vivid characterization of the wicked eastern capitalist who cared nothing for the region through which he ran his roads and whose chief aim was plunder. This deep-seated antagonism for a common absentee enemy was a matter of the utmost importance when the time came for bringing on joint political action by West and South. [Hicks 1931, 74]

The cleavage ran along sectoral lines, with the commercial and financial control based in the East, and the agricultural producers predominantly in the West and South. Analytically, this constitutes a case of spatial separation between circulation and production in agriculture, the latter being the most important economic activity of that era in terms of livelihoods.

This economically induced conflict was exacerbated by the economic cycles of the late nineteenth century. In the 1870s and 1880s, an expansive monetary policy and unusually heavy rainfalls in the West generated an accelerated supply and demand for mortgage money for farms, culminating in tremendous land speculation and overvalued land prices by 1887. In that year, the rains stopped abruptly and land prices plummeted, creating widespread hardship and outmigration from the middle and western portions of Kansas, Nebraska, and parts of Texas (Hicks 1931, 19–27).

The political demands stemming from the Populist movement centered around the dual issues of who, the banks or the government, had the right to issue money and how much of it should be in circulation at any one time. These became the "soft money" and "free silver" claims carried to Congress and into elections by southern and western farm groups.

"We feel that through the operation of a shrinking volume of money, which has been caused by Eastern votes and influences for purely selfish purposes, the East has placed its hands on the throat of the West and refused to afford us that measure of justice which we, as citizens of a common country, are entitled to receive." [Senator Allen of Nebraska, quoted in Hicks 1931, 90]

However, populist economic demands were increasingly cast as class issues, rather than regional ones. In a nation of farmers, workers, and commercial classes, with the important cross-cutting qualifier of race, the organizers of the rural populist movement chose strategically to throw in their lot with that of urban workers. They built on the image of the "producing classes," arrayed against the moneyed elites. By the 1890s, the movement had transformed itself from the Farmers' Alliance to the National Farmers' Alliance and Industrial Union to the People's Party. Indeed, this was the correct analysis of the situation, although kit turned out to be a losing strategy. For in each region, the political machinery was controlled by commercial groups whose wealth and income were tied to the eastern financial establishment. Populism became, then, a powerful challenge to the business classes of all regions in the early 1890s, rather than a regionalist revolt (Parsons 1973; Goodwyn 1978, 113–14).

Ironically, it was regionalism, or "sectionalism" as it was then known, which proved one of the greatest stumbling blocks to the populist effort to organize across regions. In the post-Reconstruction period, both major parties became narrower business-dominated machines, each based in its section. In the North, the Republican party reneged on its abolitionist commitments and sold out its free soiler constituency by taxing it heavily for infrastructure and forcing it to sell in unprotected markets while it bought in protected ones. In the South, the Democratic party represented large planters and entrepreneurs, setting up the machinery which institutionalized the system of debt peonage for small farmers (Hicks 1931, 81–86; Goodwyn 1978, 280–81).

Yet each party was consistently able to appeal, within its region, to the common experience of the Civil War. Well into the 1890s, all occupational segments "voted as they shot" in the Civil War, with the exception of some urban working-class northerners. In the South, "the Lost

Cause" was tirelessly evoked, while in the North, "waving the bloody flag" became a shortcut to closing ranks behind the Republican party. Indeed, populism floundered, according to one of its scholars, in the intensely nonideological climate created by sectional politics, where war-related emotions, not political ideas, dominated. Populism was not lucky, either, in that it proved much harder to educate and rally people around complicated issues like the fiat currency, with "Dixie" and the "Battle Hymn of the Republic" ringing in people's ears (Goodwyn 1978, 4–9).

The wrench thrown by this inherited political and ideological apparatus was further twisted in the South by the culture of racism. The southern Democratic leadership consistently used racism to destroy the credibility of a third party effort. As one prominent southern Populist, Tom Watson, put it, "The argument against the independent political movement in the South may be boiled down into one word—*nigger*."[57] The Democracy was ceaselessly championed as the white man's party. In Georgia, whites were exhorted to stay with the old party to avoid "negro domination," and in Louisiana, the populist platform was disparagingly called the "Populist-negro social equality ticket" (Goodwyn 1978, 189, 195). And indeed, populist elements did organize black and white together. They fought the efforts of rich black-belt planters to restrict suffrage. The elite's desperate appeal to racism, massive vote fraud, and violence all indicate just how powerful a threat the Populists had become.

In the West, Populists confronted charges that they were working for a Democratic front group, since the Alliance was based in the South. Western Populists had to grapple with racist innuendos as well and seem to have done so fairly successfully (Kousser 1974). But in the end, the north-south sectionalism so opportunistically employed by the business elites (and newspapers) in each region, provided an insurmountable obstacle, chiefly by sabotaging the formal organizational efforts of the movement. In the West, the Republican party was so clearly pro-Big Business that it was easy for populist leaders to argue for and form a third party. But in the South, the populist strategy was to reform the Democratic party, a relatively successful course and one made necessary by the racist slurs on a third party. The westerners could not switch to the Democrats, nor were they able to convince the South to take the third party route (Nugent 1963; Hackney 1969, 324–26; Goodwyn 1978, 139).

The populist movement was as successful as it was because of the strategies it chose. These included the cross-regional organizing effort and the worker-farmer coalition they built. But it also owed much to the central and successful role of the farmers' coops that it promulgated as immediate relief from the excesses of capital and a route to mutual self-sufficiency. In addition, the Populists were successful in evolving a strikingly democratic organization, "constructing a mass schoolroom of ideology and a mass culture of self-respect" (Goodwyn 1978, 336).[58]

Ironically, this class-based movement's greatest product was the defensive consolidation of their class opponents, whose common stake in suppressing the revolt helped them to overcome sectional differences and establish firm cross-regional business control over the federal government.

In summary, then, populism was a case where a potential regional coalition, economically motivated and quickened by the business cycle, was blocked by the political and cultural apparatus of the respective regions, masterfully deployed by regional elites whose economic interests were heavily tied to those of national capital, based in the Northeast. Regionalism played a negative role in this case, but then, it was not primarily a region-building era. The regionalism involved was an older holdover, once economically based but now embedded in political party structure, cultural practices, and ideology. Yet a progressive regionalism would not have been possible, precisely because the populist initiative came from the less powerful groups in all regions and was so thoroughly radical in its challenge of capital.

New Deal Nationalism

With the New Deal, born during the worst of capitalist crises to hit the U.S. economy, regionalism was suppressed. A new national coalition, revolving around the Democratic party, spanned several classes and many diverse places, and it was to last well into the late 1970s as a predominant political force. A major reason for the shrinking importance of regionalism during this period was the compelling reality of the depression, equally severe across all regions. Indeed, if anything, the depression overrode existing wide regional differentials in per capita income and poverty with a common concern—the "one third of a nation" unemployed and impoverished. Urban-rural differences figured more prominently than regionalized ones, but even here, farm and factory alike were thrown into a precarious condition if not bankruptcy and closure.

Some signs of regionalism remained, especially during the early 1930s. In particular, southern regionalists wrote in defense of the traditions and agrarian nature of the South, arguing for a mutually respectful regionalism that would preserve and build upon the peculiarities of each region. Twelve Vanderbilt University academics defended the Jeffersonian ideal of small, subsistence farming in a famous statement, *I'll Take My Stand*, an emotional celebration of the Old South (religious, ritualistic, localized, formal, refined, and relaxed) contrasted to the pace, gross materialism, and vulgar capitalistic thinking of modern life (Odum 1935 and 1936; Conkin 1959, 25–26).[59]

Few clear-cut regional differences in support for the New Deal were evident in voting patterns. Roosevelt had overwhelming support from 1932 onward, although its spatial complexion did change modestly over time. In 1932, Roosevelt's victory was more a southern and western phenomenon; his support in eastern cities was less wholehearted. By the mid 1930s, his massive urban-oriented programs had increased his support among urbanites, while the mixed results from his agricultural programs had weakened rural and small town support, especially that from the traditionally Republican Midwest.[60]

Roosevelt's political strategy was forthrightly "something for everyone." Urban parks for the cities, scenic parks for the countryside, dams for the arid west, flood control for the South, trees for deforested regions; and rights for workers, aid for farmers, food and housing for the indigent. Not only that, but most of his programs served more than one constituency. "Multiple purpose" was the hallmark of New Deal policies. Take the Tennessee Valley Authority, for example. It provided fertilizer, rural electrification, flood control, recreational lakes, agricultural extension services, and even bookmobiles for residents of the region. Yet despite its pluralism, the New Deal in reputation and reality came increasingly to represent the gains of the big cities (Dorsett 1977; Allswang 1978, 86).

Thus Roosevelt had to work particularly hard to extend his coalition and maintain it among the more rural interests in the South and West. Roosevelt personally believed that the Democrats would remain a minority party as long as it allowed itself to be divided by urban-rural and regional splits. In 1925 he said, "This talk of combination between South and East or between South and West is wicked as well as destructive in the long run" (cited in Freidel 1965, 19–20). His political advisors sought alliances with groups that were not traditionally Democratic, such as the Non-Partisan League and the Progressives in the upper Midwest; they were successful in bringing states like Wisconsin and Minnesota into the Democratic fold. But Roosevelt's greatest challenge was the South, where conservative Democrats opposed the very essence of his programs.

Roosevelt's success in the South through the late 1930s must be credited to the staunch party loyalties of southern Democrats and to his extraordinary personal charm and savvy in handling southern dissent. At the outset, southern leaders were ecstatic about the displacement of the hated Republicans from the White House, and this party affinity carried them along for several years. On the other hand, Roosevelt's view that poverty was the South's greatest problem clashed with their view that maintaining white supremacy should be the party's number one goal. While the South appreciated the aid, especially the higher agricultural prices set by administration programs, they abhorred many of the New Deal innovations, particularly minimum wages, limits on working hours, the elimination of child labor, and the implicit threat to institutionalized racism present in its economic programs (Freidel 1965, 36; Allswang 1978, 120).

Roosevelt's hold on the South was aided immeasurably by personal ties. Beginning in 1924, Roosevelt sojourned annually in Warm Springs,

Georgia, where he went for relief of his polio. He became fond of his neighbors, well versed in their cultural proclivities, and personally interested in the South's problems. According to at least two scholars, Roosevelt was admired by southerners for his strenuous efforts to walk again, for his willingness to laugh at their jokes, and his easy adoption of their oratorical style (Freidel 1965, 18–20). Roosevelt noted the fondness of southerners for pomp and built southern patronage and honors into his New Deal.

But Roosevelt also made political compromises, some not particularly admirable. He backed off from some of the stronger proposals for tenants' rights and relief. In rhetoric, he supported states' rights, although with the exception of his support for local options in repealing prohibition, his record was highly centralist. Most significantly, he refused to support anti-lynching legislation before Congress, fearing that it would be the last straw breaking the back of tenuous southern support for the New Deal (Freidel 1965, 30, 86).

But these regional tensions are minor themes in the history of New Deal coalition building. The major theme is its extraordinarily class-based composition. The New Deal drew its strength from the poorer, less well-educated, more foreign, more urban and working-class segments of the American populace. Despite the fact that it was very pro-business, and arguably redeemed American capitalism, it was almost universally hated by the upper classes and business spokesmen (Allswang 1978, 44–46, 58–61).

In summary, then, the New Deal succeeded in creating a class-based coalition which, if less radical in not challenging basic capitalist institutions, did overcome the sectionalism which had previously prevented the populist revolt from achieving national power. It could do so because of the universality of the depression, diminishing perceived regional differences. It benefitted, too, from regional party configurations, which automatically guaranteed southern support despite the extraordinary modernism of the program. But it also owed much to the personality and choices of Roosevelt, who managed to hold on to the southern wing of the Democratic party through means that would probably not have been available to any other northeastern politician.

SUMMARY AND REFLECTIONS

Thus two powerful regionalized conflicts—between Native Americans and European colonizers, and between the North and the South in the Civil War—arose fundamentally from divergent modes of production. In each case, the productive relations and dynamics of the modes led to explosive situations which became increasingly difficult to resolve.

Of the two eras, the second produced full-blown regionalism, while the first was merely regionalized. It seems awkward to call the Native American-European conflicts instances of either "nationalism" or "regionalism," since both terms assume a geopolitical structure and outlook that were quite foreign to Native American society.[61] Yet it is clear that Native American production technologies and the developmental dynamic of their economies brought them into irreconcilable conflict with an expansionary European society whose productivity, imperialism, and methods of destruction were much further advanced. The ensuing conflict became profoundly territorialized: Native American confederacies were forged to defend the interior while colonists, traders, and other scouts of European economies were marshalled into a mercantilist vanguard.

Several reflections on the emerging South as an instance of regional formation are in order. First, the existence of a southern region presupposed another region whose development evolved in distinction to its own, and against whose progress the qualities of its differentiation were etched and weighed. That is, to be distinctive is to be different *from* another region or regions, in this case from both the commercial-industrial North and the agricultural Midwest. One region becomes *under*developed, then, in contrast to another, as the disparate economies of each show relatively superior and inferior growth performances.

Second, the ways in which contesting modes of production shaped political conflict lay not only in the sectoral specialization and class structure of each region, but in the forces and timing of change within each which created immediate issues around which political consciousness formed. If any of several elements had been missing—the end of the transoceanic slave trade, the introduction of the cotton gin, the mid-century cotton boom—the course of the conflict might have been entirely different.

Third, the roots of north-south regional differentiation were fundamentally economic, based on two divergent labor systems which created incompatible demands on the State. But cultural qualities and political institutions strongly shaped regional development and political prospects in each region. In particular, southern planter paternalistic attitudes toward their slaves and contempt for acquisitiveness played a central role in the growing antagonism, as did incompatible juridical systems of labor control.

The evolving antagonisms between regional ruling elites were registered as a set of dissonant political claims on the State. At first substantive policy issues (the tariff, land sales, and slavery in the territories), these escalated into demands for institutional restructuring of the political apparatus, especially in the States Rights Doctrine. Ultimately, they burst still further into a nationalist struggle over reconstruction of the nation, the South challenging the Union by asserting its right to secede. In order effectively to operate on each level of this competition, contending regional political coalitions had to quell internal dissent and present a unified regional face to the other. The effort to do so created persistent regional ideologies—Yankee and Dixie.

Finally, economic and cultural endowments profoundly affected the ability of each coalition to prosecute the war. Dynamism in manufacturing and commercial farming meant that northern troops were better armed, clothed, fed, and transported. Black workers, both freemen and runaways, helped supply and eventually fought in the northern army, while in the South, they were not trusted to bear arms. Northern entrepreneurship and acceptance of strong centralized leadership contributed to successful war planning, while southern commitment to states' rights and a purely defensive posture hamstrung the Confederacy's strategy.

The singular role of leadership and ideology in the making of the Civil War underscores the significance of human agency and political strategy in shaping regional conflict. In this sense, the Civil War was not "inevitable," but a collective human artifact. The pressures bred by the confrontation of two very different productive systems could have been handled in other ways, as they were in almost all of the other slave-holding colonies in the new world. The same can be said of Native American encounters with colonial forces. The Populist and New Deal eras demonstrate how heavily regionalized economic strife can be transformed into powerful national political coalitions. These great American historical dramas demonstrate the variability and challenge of regionalism.

Notes

1. This section is a truncated version of the analysis found in my paper, "Native American Origins of American Regional Structure," Working Paper, Institute of Urban and Regional Development, University of California, Berkeley, 1983.
2. This discussion follows the general framework for using the notion of mode of production laid out in chapter 2. For examples of the model applied to other pre-capitalist cultures, see Alavi (1975), Banaji (1972), and Kelly (1979).
3. See Innes (1970, 10–18); Nash (1974, 99–108); McNickle (1962, 20); Martin (1974, 24); and Pope (1966, 53). It is also significant that the French were Catholic, as opposed to Protestant; historians have noted that throughout the Western Hemisphere, the Catholic colonial powers were more prone to treat indigenous peoples as humans and thus as potential converts to Catholicism than were Protestant colonialists.
4. Trigger (1969, 17, 23–25); McNickle (1979); Innes (1970, 20–21); and Otterbein (1964, 59–60).
5. Van Every (1966, 5); Horowitz (1978, 18–23); Thomas (1976, 14); and Herndon (1967, 283–93).
6. Horowitz (1978, 27, 32–36); Thomas (1975, 12); Nash (1974, 47); Thomas (1976); Horowitz (1978, 159). There is evidence that mercantile interests engendered small mountain settlements both as a lucrative market for speculatively held land and as a buffer zone to protect seaboard cities and plantations from Indian attack.

7. See Pope (1966, 55–57) for an excellent discussion of the transformation.
8. Gates (1979), Miner and Unrau (1978), and Gilman (1970) all treat the frontier settlement process.
9. See Horsman (1967), Prucha (1962 and 1976), and Jorgenson (1978) for a survey of Indian policy. For a Marxist interpretation, see Pratt (1978).
10. See, for example, Weltfish (1971), and Forbes (1970).
11. Native Americans resisted enslavement, and although indentured servants had cultivated tobacco, in the Tidewater region, after 1750, slaves proved more profitable. The reasons for the superiority of slave labor are explained in Mintz (1969, 29), Stampp (1956, 16), Gray (1933, 364, 370, 474, 479–80), and Handlin and Handlin (1950, 211).
12. The introduction of slave labor into the American South in the seventeenth century presupposed the availability of slaves. See Genovese (1967, 76) and Davis (1969, 617) on the early roots of the slave trade. Over three centuries of mercantilist capitalism, Davis estimates that ten to fifteen million slaves were brought to the cash-cropping regions of the Western Hemisphere by slave traders of six major European nations.
13. The interoceanic links among markets, agents, and regions are shown in table 4.1. The dots represent a production process, where labor power is spent in producing a commodity which is subsequently exchanged. The process begins with the "production" of slave labor power (S) by either African or American slaves (more accurately, reproduction, as analyzed in the following section). Slaves are sold (exchanges are represented as x) to transoceanic or intra-Southern slave traders (generally, the former up to 1808 and the latter after that date), who for a higher price (S') sell them to cotton planters. Slaves produce cotton (C) sold to cotton merchants, who resell it at premium price (C') to capitalist manufacturers. The latter, using wage labor in factory production, sell the resulting textiles (T) to textile merchants, who resell it for a yet higher price (T'). The transformation of slave labor into cotton (S' . . . C) and cotton into textiles (C' . . . T) by wage workers encompass the only two points in the process where enhanced use and exchange values are produced. But planters, merchants, and industrial capitalists will not advance money capital to purchase slave labor, wage labor, and materials (cotton) unless they reap a profit on the amount advanced. Thus *prices,* as opposed to values, increase with every exchange in the sequence; this enhancement, which includes a transfer of appropriated surplus value from one sector to another, is mirrored in the price captured by merchants, which is augmented at each step (M, M', M").
14. At the time of the revolution, many believed that slavery was an anachronism and would soon fade away. The invention of the cotton gin in 1792, an event not unrelated to the generous subsidies which southern state legislatures lavished on efforts to make the upland-grown short staple cotton profitable, together with the boom in cotton demand associated with the industrial revolution in England, reversed the declining prospects of slavery in the South (Wright 1978, 13–14; Sydnor 1948, 13). The slave population in the colonies, which had been only 150,000 in 1763 and 700,000 in 1790, rose steeply with the new cotton economy to two million in 1820 and four million in 1860 (Nash 1970, 4; Franklin 1967, 186).
15. Alternatively, slavery has been characterized as either feudal of capitalist. The capitalist case is made by Wallerstein (1976, 1211–13), who argues that masters pay a form of "wage" in kind and that slaves are "proletarians." This characterization has been criticized as confusing a system of production with one of exchange (Genovese 1967, 19; Brenner 1977; Kelly 1979). Genovese

argues that by the nineteenth century, southern slavery had matured into a separate mode of production in conflict with capitalism which he labels a "pre-capitalist" system (1967, 23). Gray (1933) and Benson (1972), writing in the non-Marxist tradition, argue for a concept of "the plantation" economy, both pre- and post-Civil War, in which capital is advanced and planters act as profit-maximizing businessmen.

16. This ability to extract excess surplus labor is comparable to but not, strictly speaking, equivalent to the Marxist notion of absolute surplus value in capitalist production, where employers force workers to work longer hours, or at a faster pace, in order to increase output per worker per wage cost. A considerable body of work exists on the impact of slavery upon slaves. A relatively sanguine view of slavery, first formulated by Phillips (1918), has been advanced by some cliometricians, especially Fogel and Engerman's pathbreaking treatment (1974). The work of Stampp (1956) is perhaps the best known of the opposite school. Criticism of the Fogel and Engerman interpretation can be found in David, Gutman, Sutch, Temin, and Wright (1976); Gutman (1975) and Stampp (1980, ch. 3).

17. On the reproduction of slaves as assets, see Genovese (1971, 98), Gray (1933, 658–63), Stampp (1956, ch. 6), Franklin (1967, 178), Sutch (1975, 185–93).

18. A compromise had been struck during the Constitution-making period whereby southern and northern antagonists agreed on 1808 as the year in which the external slave trade would cease. While some surreptitious importing continued, the slave trade became largely internal after that date. (Phillips 1936, 131–49; Franklin 1967, 152; Du Bois 1970, 70).

19. See Bateman, Foust, and Weiss (1974, 297), Genovese (1967, 17, 26; and 1974).

20. Various authors have cogently criticized Genovese's preoccupation with land exhaustion under slavery, arguing that capitalist production may be easily as rapacious and that the coincidence of expansion of cotton production westward with declines in coastal production confuses tobacco and cotton cropping and ignores the fact that the Louisiana Purchase and frontier settlers' clearing activities independently brought marginally more attractive land into production. (Wright 1978; Benson 1972; Gray 1933).

21. Starobin (1969); Mitchell (1968, 23); Genovese (1967, 224–33); Wade (1964); Goldfield (1977, 66); and Goldin (1975).

22. See Earle and Hoffman (1977, 27–51), for a detailed account of the causes of this dispersed pattern.

23. See the debate over whether farming on the frontier constituted a distinct mode of production in O'Connor (1975), Sherry (1976), O'Connor (1976), Kelly (1979), and Post (1982).

24. While outpost settlements were frequently self-sufficient (Main 1970), the frontier moved rapidly and conversion to commercial farming followed quickly. Bruchey (1965) shows that few farms did not produce some commodities for sale and all aspired to increase such sales. Commercial activities included land speculation; see Hacker (1940), Decker (1969), Sweirenga (1968), Gates (1942), and Danhof (1969).

25. On the failure of slavery in the North, see Franklin (1967, 89), Greene (1942, 321), Sutherland (1936, 47, 48), Phillips (1918, 105), Zilversmit (1967, 4), and McManus (1973, 40–41).

26. Franklin (1967, 94, 103–6); McManus (1973, 27, 52–53); Moore (1971, 27); and Zilversmit (1967, 45).

27. Easterlin (1975, 95, 99); Easterlin (1961); Bateman, Foust, and Weiss (1974,

278); Hesseltine and Smiley (1960, 254–55); Engerman (1967); Conrad and Meyer (1958); and Stampp (1956, 388).

28. Analyses of the compromise over slavery in the Constitutional period can be found in Freehling (1972), DuBois (1970), Lynd (1967), and Davis (1975). Interpretations stressing the mercantilist nature of the revolution and class antagonisms within the process of nation building can be found in Harper (1942), Hacker (1935), Mayer and Fay (1977), Lockridge (1973), Greene (1973), Beard (1913), and Main (1961).

29. See Benson (1972) for an interpretation of this presidential role.

30. See Benson's (1972) criticism of the body of Civil War history for this usage. On the other hand, class analyses (Hesseltine and Smiley 1960; Hacker 1940; Moore 1966; Beard and Beard 1927) have also been criticized (Green 1972). See Sharkey's (1959) study showing that northern merchants/bankers and industrial capitalists had directly opposing interests on both the currency and tariff issues.

31. Commercial and banking capitalists in New York and New England opposed western improvements in the 1820s because they feared the loss of commercial leadership to their counterparts in New Jersey, Pennsylvania, Delaware, and Maryland. While most classes favored improvements, they battled among themselves on the means of financing them. Northeastern merchant-banker interests argued that funding should come from the sale of federal lands. Manufacturers espoused financing them from the protective tariff. The westerners favored redistribution of western public land sale moneys to build improvements themselves, while southerners increasingly opposed any additional tariff or redistribution on the grounds that either would strengthen their competitor regions. See Stephenson (1967, 28–87), Dowd (1977, 155), Hesseltine and Smiley (1960, 121–23), Sydnor (1948, 138–39).

32. An excellent source on the western land issue, though analyzed in terms of political parties, not classes, is Stephenson (1967). See also Danhof (1969, 103–4).

33. Not all manufacturers supported a tariff. Those relying on cheap imported materials (e.g., cotton and pig iron) and those distantly located from the midwestern resources market (e.g., New England ironmakers) opposed it. Pennsylvania was the major state providing pro-tariff leadership. The tariff was also supported by midwestern and Vermont wool growers (Hofstadter 1938, 50–55). Exceptions, too, occurred among the ranks of southern planters; hemp growers, wool producers, and sugar planters supported the tariff. Descriptions of intraregional and intrasectoral conflicts on the tariff issue are presented in Coben (1959, 125–32), Sydnor (1948, 326), Foner (1970a, 177).

34. Sharkey's masterful study of currency views by class from the Civil War period on demonstrates that class posture toward monetary policy was quite sensitive to cyclical changes in the economy. He argues that farmers were relatively indifferent during the prosperous '60s, and that manufacturers, particularly in iron and steel, became opponents of postwar contraction because greenbacks had stoked their profits in the war era.

35. Racism within white abolitionist groups made black activists suspicious of white reformers, and for a brief time they experimented with an independent black political party. At the same time, black abolitionists tended to espouse free labor ideology and to view capitalist social relations relatively benignly, although they urged economic cooperation along racial lines and considered colonization schemes, both within and without the United States,

as more feasible routes to economic independence (Meier and Rudwick 1966, 109–12, 124–31; Dillon 1969; Duberman 1965).

36. Symptomatic of the difficulties that abolitionist groups had in forging unity was the 1840s split between the Garrison and Weld-Tappan factions. They differed adamantly in their views of slavery as a moral versus political issue and on their willingness to engage in coalition politics. See Meier and Rudwick (1966, 112–24), Benson (1972, 278), Dillon (1969).

37. Benson (1972, 246) argues that less than 5 percent were in favor of abolition in 1860. The banker and merchant classes were not keen on interfering with a southern labor force that indirectly produced profits for them, through trade activities and purchases of cheap cotton. Fearing black competition for jobs and expressing societywide racist sentiments, the northern urban working classes engendered some pockets of strong anti-abolitionist sentiment, resulting in occasional riots where white workingmen (mostly laborers) attacked both black and white marchers. The use of blacks as strikebreakers and the antipathy of organized labor to any impending civil strife that would damage national union solidarity and work place gains fed this antagonism. (Sharkey 1959, 176–78; Moore 1966, 134.)

38. Brown's (1966, 59) description. See also Degler (1974, 93).

39. Increasing politic instability led as early as the 1840s to splinter group formations and new political parties representing narrow sectional class programs or new cross-sectional coalitions. In 1840 a new explicitly abolitionist party was formed in Albany, the Liberty party. Its candidate, who downplayed the tariff and bank issues, scored Whig candidate Clay for pandering to southern slavery and drew from the Whigs sufficient northern votes to ensure the Democratic candidate, Polk, the election. In subsequent years, Free Soil, Know Nothing, Independent, and People's parties formed in and across various sections, mostly originating in the Northeast and upper Midwest.

40. Chief among these capitalists was Thaddeus Stevens, an iron and steel manufacturer, who was to become a national leader of the Republicans for the next two decades. Shortreed (1959).

41. The Republicans would not have won, however, had not the older party representing the alliance of southern and western agricultural interests finally begun to fall apart. In 1860, the Democrats failed to nominate a candidate satisfactory to both sections. Douglas rallied those northern farmers and eastern working men who remained loyal to the Democratic party to force a minority platform at the convention which would not explicitly obligate congressional protection of slavery in the territories but which would leave the question to popular sovereignty. The southerners withdrew en masse from the convention and eventually nominated their own candidate, Kentuckian Breckinridge, who was solidly pro-planter. What remained of the old southern Whig element, mainly southern manufacturers and merchants and some seaboard planters, formed the Constitutional Unionist party and nominated Tennessean John Bell. Abraham Lincoln was able to win the presidency only because three other contending candidates competed for the vote of the Democratic coalition, which continued to dominate the Congress and the Supreme Court.

42. See Genovese (1971) for a vivid and detailed account of the origins of the Positive Good argument.

43. This argument was made most forcefully in 1860 by Thomas Kettell in his book *Southern Wealth, Northern Profits*, where he purportedly documents the annual northern extraction of $231 million in profits from southern com-

merce. Kettell was a northerner who argued the northern merchants' view that the North had a stake in southern slavery (Green 1965). See also Hesseltine and Smiley (1960, 203), Stampp (1974, 63–64).

44. The tendency to translate regional demands from purely policy aims into a states' rights stand had existed from the early days of the American nation. Any time a particular region found itself in the minority, with regional goals subordinated to national ones, it tended to emphasize the states' rights aspect of the national Constitution, which reserved to the states all activities not explicitly allocated to the national government. From 1820 to 1840 alone, southern states lost three seats in Congress while the rest of the country gained twenty-two; strict construction amounted to the best protection for slavery (Sydnor 1948, 331; Brown 1966, 58).

45. Nonslaveowning whites have been the least well-studied of antebellum southerners (Foner 1970b, 210). The most extensive study is Owsley (1949), a romantic, Turnerian view of southern white farmers.

46. The working out of the southern strategy and plans for secession took place at the Commercial Convention of the 1850s (Takaki 1971, 150; Bernstein 1966, 24; Cole 1934, 71). Johnson (1977) argues that the desire to establish planter hegemony *within* the South was as important a motive for secession as the threat from without.

47. Degler documents that southern antislavery sentiment was almost entirely confined to the upper states of Kentucky, Tennessee, Virginia, and North Carolina. These states generated a Constitutional Party in 1860 that was pro-union but silent on the issue of slavery.

48. Those merchants who profited directly from circulation activities involving southern or southbound commodities (cotton, tobacco, and imports) were particularly sympathetic to the South. See Green (1965).

49. For instance, racism was emphasized in the West. Illinois Senator Lyman Trumbull, a close friend of Lincoln, stated in a Chicago speech in 1858: "We, the Republican party, are the white man's party. We are for free white men, and for making white labor respectable and honorable, which it can never be when Negro slave labor is brought into competition with it." Litwack 1961, 269–71.

50. Fogel (1964, 227) believes that without the railroads, the northern generals would have lost the war and a southern-western alliance might have held.

51. DuBois (1935, 84) argues that the Proclamation was necessary to recruit black soldiers (up to 1863 blacks were almost entirely excluded from the northern army) and to gain support both internally and from Europe. Agricultural progress is documented in Fredrickson (1975, 66–68). Gates (1965) shows that even though one-third of all northern agricultural labor joined the wartime army, agricultural output increased.

52. Sellers (1962, 81, 86); Coulter (1974, 3); Engerman (1971, 373); Ransom and Sutch (1975, 13, and 1977, 41).

53. The cliometric literature tries to discriminate for the south between the economic costs of war itself versus the causal effects of its consequences (e.g., the restructuring of southern labor discussed below, and the exogenous events in the world market for cotton). See Engerman (1971), Goldin and Lewis (1975), and Temin (1976).

54. Ransom and Sutch (1977) provide the best detailed account of this restructuring. Mandle (1978), Wiener (1978), and Rabinowitz (1977) offer rich interpretations of subsequent land ownership, economic performance, and urban structure of the southern economy.

55. The South did not regain its antebellum per capita share of national income until 1950 (Fogel and Engerman 1971).
56. See Billings and Blee (1986), for a forceful statement on the need for historicity in interpreting contemporary southern social relations.
57. People's Party Paper, 1892, quoted in Hicks (1931, 238–39). See also Woodward (1938).
58. Goodwyn argues that the Populist effort demonstrates that coherent reform politics are not simply prompted by economic hardship, but are the product of insurgent cultures, in this case, the Alliance Cooperative Movement (1978, 61).
59. Other scholars developed a critique of regionalism in the same era, espousing nationalism in its place. See the discussion in the Appendix under the regional organicists.
60. Of course, Roosevelt was nominated in the first place because he was relatively acceptable to all regions and his election was primarily a profound rejection of Hoover's policies and arrogance (Allswang 1978, 9, 13, 62, 103; Freidel 1965, 30).
61. Sack (1980, 170–77) provides an analysis of primitive cultures in which people and place are conceptually fused, and the separation required to imagine alternative spatial configurations is absent.

5

The Economics of
Postwar Regional Disparity

In the postwar period, American regions have again been host to major political disagreement. These antagonisms have arisen from unique sectoral specializations within the capitalist economy, from disparate pressures exerted on regional economies in the process of international integration, and from dramatically skewed military spending patterns. This chapter is the first of two which explore conceptually and empirically regional economic and demographic alterations since World War II in the United States. Chapter 5 reviews the major contemporary forces operating on regional economies, while chapter 6 presents evidence on the magnitude and timing of the resulting developmental differentials. Both chapters set the stage for the theoretical analysis of political tendencies in chapter 7. Taken together, the three chapters argue that postwar cyclical and sectoral dynamics produced disparate regional economic traumas, which in turn prompted regionalist antagonism and incompatible demands on the national government.

In this chapter, three forces shaping contemporary regional economic differentiation and change are charted: (1) the growing specializations of individual regions in the new international division of labor, (2) the profit cycle behavior of individual sectors, and (3) the growing militarization of production in the United States. Each has contributed to the unique set of issues and adjustments confronted by north versus south, east versus west, and interior versus perimeter. The final section treats the interactions among all three. The net result has been the growing disparity in north-south growth rates, an exacerbation of east-west sectoral distinctiveness, and a growing cleavage between coastal regions and the interior in both rate and composition of economic development. These set the stage for renewed regional hostilities in the 1970s and 1980s.

THE NEW INTERNATIONAL DIVISION OF LABOR

The growing integration of the international economy has dramatically affected existing domestic economies.[1] Restless geographical expansion has been a hallmark of capitalist development for the past century and a half. However, the pace of change does seem to have accelerated, creating adjustment problems on a massive scale. In addition, irreversible institutional alterations are channeling economic energies in novel directions. The underlying dynamic is the incessant search on the part of owners and managers of capital to find new markets, cheaper labor and raw materials, and more congenial public sector attitudes. Business strategies may concentrate on reshaping an existing built environment or labor force, as for instance downtown urban renewal has in the postwar period. Or, more significant for regionalism, they may take on an explicitly spatial dimension, where production activities are shifted from one region to another to secure higher levels of profitability and to discipline labor and political coalitions in the regions of origin.[2]

Several features of evolving capitalist economic structure are particularly central to an interpretation of regional politics in the postwar period: accelerated market penetration, the transformation of labor market characteristics, the rise of international oligopolistic firms with spatially segregated functions, and the state as a major planner and distributor. Together these forces have undermined the status of the United States as the preeminent industrial economy. Internally they have left their mark most dramatically in growing sectoral differentiation and in severe north-south and coastal-interior growth differentials.

Accelerated International Market Penetration

First, there has been a qualitative leap in the degree of market interpenetration in the postwar period. Aggressive international marketing was first pursued by corporations from advanced capitalist countries—Coca Cola is perhaps the best known example—and was a complement to the search for raw materials (furs, precious metals, and agricultural produce). By the postwar period, more than two centuries of imperialism had irreversibly destroyed the older forms of subsistence economy prevailing in most Third World countries and had imposed upon them a wage labor, commodity exchange economy. Textiles, shoes, toys, and apparel began to be produced in these countries and imported into industrialized countries.

By the mid-1960s, consumer goods imports were joined by durables like autos and producer goods like steel. Heightened competition also came about through expanded trade and new investments by leading multinationals in each other's territory. By the mid-1970s, the growing competitiveness of both these types of imports resulted in an acceleration in their successful penetration of new markets. Steel imports into the United States, for instance, rose from about 5 percent of the domestic tonnage consumption in 1960 to about 22 percent by 1980 and 26 percent by 1985. Overall, by early 1986, manufactured imports had reached 21 percent of the domestic market.

This massive interpenetration of national economies owes much to improved techniques of communication and transportation. The net effect of telecommunications innovations and of new commodity-moving machines such as the super-tanker and the cargo airplane has been to lower the cost of negotiating exchanges across space. Where transport costs were once prohibitive, the Japanese can now import coal from the American west and iron ore from Australia, make steel in Japan, and reship it back to the West Coast of the United States, where it has so successfully undersold its domestic competitors that virtually all integrated steel capacity is in danger of final shutdown. Furthermore, rapid and cheap communications technology permits very rapid servicing of these American markets by plants in Japan without large inventories.

The 1970s acceleration of market interpenetration is also a product of the extraordinary destruction and subsequent wholesale rebuilding of industrial capacity in the losing nations after the war. Investment is always a relatively lumpy process, where new rounds of construction of the most modern plants put a newcomer country or region at the lead of an industry for a decade or more. The full impact of the extraordinary reinvestment in Japan and Germany following the war tended to bunch up in the late 1960s and 1970s, when their relatively new and "best practice" plants (in steel, chemicals, autos, and consumer electronics) far outdistanced the serviceable but outdated American capacity, which dates back as far as the early decades of the century (in the case of steel) or to the interwar period (autos).

In response to heightened competition, corporate leaders in most industrialized countries have found a means of overcoming their domestic cost disadvantages by directly locating plants in newly industrializing nations or by selling them the technology they need to build their own. The largest, most modern steel mill in the world is currently under construction in South Korea; the Japanese steel corporations have been willing advisors and suppliers of the technology. Increasingly, U.S. corporations are producing major components for their domestically assembled autos overseas—particularly high-value-to-bulk items such as engines and transmissions. Where corporations in advanced capitalist countries once maintained their competitiveness by constantly harnessing the most superior technologies, enabling them to pay workers relatively higher wages because productivity was so much higher, this route is no longer a viable one. Technologies themselves have become commodities and are now available in very short order to any would-be producer in any global location. In addition, institutional changes in the nature of corporations and financial institutions (addressed below) have made money capital much easier to shift around spatially.

The major spatial consequences of this market interpenetration are (1) the dramatic sectoral recomposition of the U.S. economy and (2) growing regional disparities in growth rates. Manufacturing sectors which had been major exporters as well as domestic suppliers shrank under the inundation of imports, first in consumer goods and more recently in capital goods. Business, finance, and transportation services, on the other hand, boomed. Spatially, this dramatic new specialization in the U.S. trade role meant the displacement of large segments of manufacturing in the Northeast, and later, Midwest, while the new world cities of New York, Los Angeles, Miami, and Chicago (international agricultural trade) transformed their central city economies. Meanwhile import pressure accelerated internal migration of capital from the older, unionized manufacturing centers, including parts of California as well as the "rust belt," to the underdeveloped, nonunionized south.[3]

Qualitative Changes in the International Labor Force

Increasingly, then, the high level of market interpenetration, with its consequences in the diminished ability of any one nation to police its own economy, is a product of the elimination of barriers to commodity, capital, and technology movements across national boundaries. These changes have taken place without a concomitant removal of barriers to labor movement across the same boundaries. As a consequence, the differential development of the labor force among nations becomes the major distinguishing characteristic of the new international division of labor. The nature of the labor force—its skills, its culture, its degree of internal homogeneity, its own class institutions—in any one country is of course a product of a long period of cultural evolution. In the twentieth century, the nature of the labor force in both industrialized and Third World countries has changed dramatically both as a result of the maturation of class conflict between capital and labor, and as a product of the role which the state has taken on in arbitrating this conflict and in paving the way for capital internationally.

While capital and corporations have become increasingly international, even to the point of losing their national identities, the labor force in most nations remain highly local in character. At best, in advanced capitalist countries, it may have a national organizational and political presence. But to date, it has no international unity or presence to speak of. Two parallel transformations have occurred over the course of the last century in the industrialized and Third World countries of the capitalist sphere and each is central to the character of contemporary regional labor differentiation.

In the industrialized countries with capitalist modes of production, important segments of the working class have managed to surmount ethnic differences, corporate and state violence (Carnegie's Pinkertons or the state militia, for instance), intraclass distinctions (such as occupational differences), cultural proscriptions (religious virtues such as meekness), and prior threats of corporate mobility to build strong working-class economic and political institutions. In Europe, these not only encompass workplace organizations which are joined into national industrial unions (although with competing political ties) but include national political parties which are significant contenders for State power. In the United States, where this latter phenomenon of a national labor party is absent, trade unions have a major role within many basic industries and do form a respectable caucus within the Democratic party. In many industrial regions within these countries, the role of unions in social life and community politics is even stronger.

As a result of continual struggle over the past century or more for gains both in and out of the workplace, these working-class organizations have achieved substantial gains. Among them we might list the forty-hour work week, a living wage, child labor laws, the legal right to organize, time-and-a-half for overtime, seniority rights, pensions, unemployment compensation, the right to bargain, the right to strike, social welfare programs, social security, a national commitment to full employment, occupational health and safety, automatic cost-of-living adjustments, and a clean and safe environment. Each of these represents a fetter of some sort on the organization of production and thus an additional charge on the cost of doing business, which cuts into corporate profitability.

It is logical that capitalists and their organizations, both corporate and political, would choose to oppose these innovations and that they would seek to avoid them in whatever manner possible. As long as barriers to international trade and production kept individual economies isolated, labor was relatively "scarce" and capital had few alternatives. Indeed, as Hobsbawm has argued, the relative scarcity of labor explains much of the inducement to substitute highly productive machinery for men in nineteenth-century American agriculture. It also kept wages relatively high for a large portion of skilled laborers, resulting in a tremendously strong internal market for manufactured commodities that helped propel U.S. industrial development. Yet once new reservoirs of cheaper labor opened up, and despite the extraordinary depressive effects on the home economy, corporations have been eager to escape a well-developed set of working class institutions for more acquiescent sites elsewhere.

The creation of these new sources of labor through the transformation of work and subsistence in Third World countries is the accompanying process which permits successful relocation of production abroad. The traditional rural subsistence economies of many Third World countries have been irrevocably altered by the introduction of capitalist agriculture. Tremendous consolidation of landholdings and dispossession of native groups has often accompanied this centuries-long pattern of supplanting cultivation for use with cash crop exports. In addition, large productivity increases in some forms of agriculture make small-scale commercial agriculture unviable, so that even in cases where an indigenous population maintains ownership of the land, modest levels of trade that provide a little cash income dry up. Both land ownership patterns and productivity changes have converted a large portion of rural subsistence farmers into wage laborers in agriculture. Since the structure of the agricultural sector does not absorb enough of the displaced subsistence workers, many become members of a migratory wage labor force drawn to cities where job possibilities exist in industry and the informal economy.

This newly formed labor pool is not attractive to industrial employers, however, unless it lacks the organizational strength, wages demands, working conditions, and social services that prevail in advanced capitalist countries. In developing countries, the more youthful labor force is relatively less skilled and acculturated to capitalist workplace behavior. While there are instances of labor organizing in Third World countries, in most cases the absence of a long-term stable urban community, the repressive attitudes of government, and the wariness of multinational corporations about any effort to assert working-class rights all contribute to a pacific labor front. As a result, wages are in some cases one-tenth of what they are in industrialized countries, and there are few work stoppages, few demands for a safe and healthful working environment, and no well-developed employer-supported unemployment compensation systems. It seems probable that workers' rights to organize and to a decent wage will indeed be pressed in the future in these countries. But for the present, great discrepancies between the cultures and standards of living of workers in the two spheres are major inducements to relocate production abroad.

Ironically, and despite the formidable border barriers erected by industrialized countries, this same discrepancy serves as a tremendous incentive to Third World workers to migrate to the United States.[4] Particularly in regions like the Southwest and Florida, they have been relatively successful in avoiding immigration restrictions, often with the collaboration of agribusinesses who are eager to use them in seasonal, low-paid field work. In these states, they increasingly form a low-skilled labor pool, which in turn has lured apparel producers and other light assembly operations to these regions. Due to fear of deportation, these workers are often difficult to organize and do not demand the same rights as resident workers. And so, to a certain extent, the international division of labor seeps home, even without the legitimacy and resources available to the movers of capital. In sum, then the quantitative expansion of the international labor force available to capitalist firms and its qualitative tranformation toward a more highly skilled but less organizationally developed pool quickened the international migration of capital toward southern locations. This shift was complemented by the considerable immigration of workers from poorer nations into southern and coastal regions, where they broadened the labor pool and involuntarily constituted a damper on wage rates and unionization efforts.

Qualitative Changes in Corporate Form and Behavior

Several evolving features of twentieth-century business structure have important implications for regional differentiation and change. These are: (1) the dominance of oligopolies in major commodity lines since the turn of the century; (2) the increasing tendency within the corporation to institutionally separate its planning, management, and production activities; (3) the emergence of the conglomerate as the major new form of corporate structure; and (4) the increasingly multinational nature of operations. In some cases these have merely accelerated existing tendencies toward spatial decentralization. In other cases they have had distinct retarding or reorienting effects. Each deserves separate consideration.

The arrival, beginning in the late nineteenth century, of the oligopoly as a common form of producer collusion to control the market ushered in quite distinctive forms of corporate behavior. Oligopolies, such as U.S. Steel and its few sizeable competitors, the Duke Tobacco Trust, or the pure monopoly Aluminum Company of America (ALCOA), could engineer the stabilization of price levels which had previously formed the major element in market competition. Their attention could then be turned to managing the market through market research, sales efforts, product rather than price competition (as in the frequent style changes in consumer commodities), the exercise of political power, and efforts to discipline workers internally.

The invidious competition among the few giants in many of these industries and their mutual need for mutual monitoring of each other's actions resulted in a tendency for these firms to overcentralize production in the locations where the oligopoly was first formed (Pittsburgh in steel, Detroit in autos, Milwaukee in brewing, and Akron in rubber). Concomitantly, newly developing areas which might otherwise have sprouted their own indigenous firms were retarded in their receipt of new capacity, often (as was the case with west coast steel) through direct buy-outs of local firms by the dominant corporations and their decisions continually to expand capacity in the core regions. In some cases, including steel and autos, this spatial imbalance was reinforced by the popularity of the "basing point" system for colluding on prices—an automatic price leadership system where all steelmakers would quote the "Pittsburgh Plus" price of delivered steel regardless of their own location or cost of production.[5]

At the same time, the prominence of a particular oligopoly within a region, while providing more direct jobs locally than would a competitive structure, will tend to squeeze out entrepreneurs in unrelated sectors whose entry might have helped to diversify the region. The dominant sectors—again, steel and autos are an outstanding example—have first pick of the labor force, create the regional social structure for white collar employees, control internally a large portion of regional capital, and have extraordinary sway with local politicians. All of these features make the particular regional economy quite vulnerable to a downturn or the permanent demise of the oligopolistic sector around which their economies have been structured.

The increasing size and concentration of corporate operations has also produced a qualitative change in the nature of production activities at any one site. It used to be that the corporate headquarters, research and development labs, planning and sales divisions, division management, and actual production all were sited on the same large lot. As multidivisional corporations emerged, these began to be located in separate buildings although often within the same urban area. But beginning in the interwar period and accelerating since World War II, these various functions, each of which has quite different land, labor, and transportation requirements, have increasingly been spatially segregated.[6] Nowadays, a headquarters may be located in New York (where it may have moved from more provincial origins), its R and D labs may be in Chapel Hill, North Carolina; its divisional management in regional centers like Des Moines, Iowa and Denver, Colorado; and its actual production facilities in small towns like Cloquet, Minnesota and Cedar City, Utah.

As a result, the labor force across these locations is becoming increasingly segregated. There are significant differences in the composition of streams of labor migration from and toward each type of city (professional and technical workers to Silicon Valley and Boston, for example, and lower-skilled production workers to the outskirts of Phoenix). In addition, most sites now have spatial competitors rendering them much more vulnerable to punitive closings actions by the absentee management. Headquarters cities like New York, San Francisco, Los Angeles, and a few others may be exceptions, but in a similar manner, they may now be forced to compete with each other to fill newly built downtown office space with trade and management-related business services.

The evolution of the conglomerate as the dominant form of large corporation has also contributed to an acceleration in the patterns of regional differentiation and change. The conglomerate, which combines disparate types of commodity production under one organizational roof, permits a super layer of management to treat each of its product lines as an element in a larger "portfolio." Acting as its own internal banker, broker, and capital market, it can shift profits from one operation to another or decide to close lower-return operations in order to diversify into yet other lines, often by merger rather than in-house expansion. Bluestone and Harrison (1982) offer convincing evidence that the conglomerate form hastens the dispersal of production activities to lower-cost sites and tends to encourage the "milking" of relatively efficient but older plants to provide short-run returns without reinvesting in plant, equipment, and maintenance.

In addition to diversifying across sectors, the major corporations are also increasingly operating across national boundaries. This gives them greater flexibility in trading off among differently composed ensembles of productive environments. Multinational capabilities are embodied in nonproduction headquarters personnel whose job it is to research the international production and market possibilities, make connections with foreign suppliers, brokers, and governments, and plan global output and exchange. The transnational character of leading corporations leads to an exacerbation in the segregation of management, control, and production functions discussed above and accelerates the rate at which capital can be redeployed across national boundaries. In some cases, through joint ventures, the national character of corporations is itself disappearing, with dramatic implications for the role of national governments.

All three of the forces analyzed so far—international integration, labor force transformations, and alterations in corporate structure, have contributed to internal realignments in U.S. economic structure. The resulting regional differentials are paradoxical, for it would seem that each force ought to contribute to increasing homogenization across territory. Yet the opposite is occurring—the net result has been greater spatial separation of production versus circulation functions, heightened sectoral differentiation, and increasingly divergent growth trajectories. Capital's ability to take advantage of land-based and labor-based differentials leads to greater growth disparities in eras of rapid territorial expansion.

Changes in the Role of the State

It is often alleged that national governments are more involved in the economy today than they have been in the past. This growing role is perhaps overstated—consider the role of nation-states in the mercantilist eighteenth-century and the American land disposal and infrastructure programs (especially railroads) in the nineteenth century. However, the nature of central government intervention has indeed changed over time and certain of its present features are important, though often unintended, contributors to regional change.[7]

Domestically, the federal government has been a major contributor to regional differentiation through the enormous defense budget. This phenomenon is explored at greater length in the next section. The interstate freeway system, initiated in 1956 and still under construction, has been a second major contributor to regional differentiation. Its network of highways has dramatically shifted low-cost locations from central city to suburban areas and from the manufacturing belt to outlying areas. The energy programs of the federal government in the 1970s, which rapidly stepped up the pace of exploration, construction and production from Alaska through the Black Mesa in Arizona, is a third major contributor.

Federal government actions with less explicitly regional orientations have also contributed to the changing economic structures of regions. The national tax code, for instance, particularly the nature of the investment tax credit and the allowances for accelerated depreciation, have consistently favored new plants over older ones, and new investment over maintenance as a survival strategy.[8] Similarly, housing policies granting tax breaks for new construction have played a similar role. On another front, the failure of the federal government to assume responsibility for uniform welfare standards across the country and for the guarantee of worker's rights to organize in all states have both exacerbated the interstate movement of jobs and capital.

A final and perhaps unintended federal government factor in internal spatial restructuring has been the increased mobility permitted students and retired people from the federal education and social security programs. When students and older people were largely supported by their families, their residence was much more closely tied to the latter's. A significant portion of the internal migration of recent years, both interregional and from urban to more rural areas within regions, has consisted of people in these life stages.

Not only has the role of the State contributed to a growing internal division of work and residence and to diverging rates of regional growth (reviewed in the following chapter), but it has been a major player in the international sphere, helping to create the extraordinarily favorable conditions for the international migration of capital. Aggressive marketing (often tied to aid) of U.S. commodities like agricultural surpluses, with their depressing effects on Third World countries' abilities to develop their own agricultural sectors, led to the latter's efforts to build "import-substituting" sectors and later, manufacturing export sectors, to help adverse balance of payments from debt, agriculture, and capital imports. International agencies like the World Bank, largely under the control of the U.S. government, were central in selecting the countries and sectors to be favored with large loans for industrialization. Support for repressive regimes has helped to create the docile and disenfranchised labor pools that multinational corporations find so attractive in the contemporary period. Thus, State posture has augmented the uneven regional development created by private sector internationalization.

PROFIT CYCLES AND SECTORAL DIFFERENTIATION

The new international division of labor has indeed placed generic stresses on regions with differential degrees of capitalistic maturation. However, differences in contemporary regional experience cannot be laid solely to these economy-wide phenomena. Cities like Detroit, Pittsburgh, Cleveland, Chicago, and St. Louis have had highly varied fortunes recently despite their common membership in a larger manufacturing belt with well-developed working-class organizations and a local state commitment to a decent social wage. What distinguishes them from each other are the relatively unique sectoral configurations of their local economies. Regions and cities manifesting strong regional consciousness or severe planning problems often owe their politics and predicament to one or more sectors which dominate the local economy.

It can be argued that individual sectors (aluminum, autos, brewing, chemicals, and so on) display quite distinct forms of competition and corporate strategy at any given time.[9] Most sectors do appear to pass through a life cycle across which the conditions governing profitability are quite different in sequential periods. Production and marketing decisions, including where to locate plants and jobs, vary in a relatively predictable manner as the source of profit changes. In a formulation I call the profit cycle, four stages can be identified: an innovative stage of superprofits, a competitive stage of "normal" profits, an oligopolistic stage of monopolistic profits, and an obsolescence stage of profit squeeze.

1. Innovation, Superprofits, and Agglomeration

When a new industry is "born," as for instance the steel industry in the 1870s or the electronics industry in the 1960s, it generally enjoys an initial era of extraordinary growth and high returns.[10] These superprofits, defined as the difference of revenues over cost per unit, arise from the special use value that the new commodity has in contrast to existing methods or products.[11] In the short run, potential competitors will have a difficult time entering the new market, for lack of expertise, delays in organizational formation, and the discouraging presence of patents. Superprofits will not necessarily make original entrepreneurs rich, since they will immediately be plowed back into new capital expenditures and experimentation to expand the business and to maintain market leadership.

In an innovative era, the firms forming a new sector will tend to cluster around one or a few nodes. These sites may be close to existing pools of professional-technical labor and corporate headquarters, or they may be in quite accidental locations (an inventor's or founder's residence).[12] Wherever this initial site, the rapid growth of the industry in its youth will tend to reinforce the importance of these sites as agglomerative centers.[13] New firms are frequently formed from employees' spinning off older firms. Competitive efforts will focus on product design, on prototype construction and testing, and on organization building, all activities which rely heavily upon a skilled labor pool, skewed toward the professional-technical categories. The young firms will tend to recruit labor from outside the region and to attract subcontracting firms and suppliers around them. Any inclination to disperse production to cheaper peripheral sites will be tempered by the need to be near the center of ongoing innovative activity and to have ready access to new information about the evolving market. Shoemaking in the Boston area is an early example of this type of innovative agglomeration; autos in Detroit, rubber in Akron, steel in Pittsburgh, farm machinery in Chicago, brewing in Milwaukee, flour milling in Minneapolis, oil in Houston, cereals in Battle Creek, and electronics in Santa Clara Valley are others.

2. Standardization, Normal Profits, and Dispersion

As firms successfully perfect the product and set in place a standard process for large-scale production, much of the strategic need to be near the centers of origin disappears. Organizational attention turns toward market penetration and away from the innovative process itself. The superprofits of the previous period disappear under heightened competition from new entrants, increasing the volume of sales to capture economies of scale and spread organizational overhead thus becomes the major source of expanded profits.[14] At the same time, firms in this stage require fewer experimental and innovative personnel and have less interest in remaining close to competitors.

In this stage, corporations will find it more attractive to migrate to or site new plants at least-cost locations and near developing markets. Textile plants have migrated to the American South and offshore in the past fifty years because labor costs at these sites are so much lower; Coca-Cola bottling plants have been located in every major metropolitan area. In some cases, higher costs at the initial location—because of labor organizations and pressures on locally scarce resources like land and air quality—will help push production out. In general, then, industries in this stage will tend to disperse from original sites under the discipline of normal competition.[15]

3. Market Power, Monopoly Profits, and Uneven Development

Yet a third era characterizes those industries that develop a substantial degree of concentration of market power in the hands of a few firms. The spatial tendencies associated with such power depend upon whether or not oligopoly appears early in a sector's life cycle or later, once standardization has taken place. In the former case, the emergence of market power will tend to retard decentralization and reinforce initial agglomerative tendencies. However, unlike the product-testing and market-exploration activities that hold innovative industries to their youthful centers, it is the market-policing activities of oligopolies, discussed in the previous section, that encourage their continued commitment to centralized operations. Thus while agglomeration can be viewed as economically rational in innovative sectors, in mature but monopolistic sectors it is an aberration from the interregional patterns of production which would otherwise develop in the absence of market power.

On the other hand, if oligopolistic power emerges late in a sector's development, as appears to be the case in brewing, for instance, after it has become relatively dispersed, then it may have the effect of accelerating a spatial reordering which will selectively close some regional plants while consolidating and enlarging the position of others. Those plants closed will be the older, higher-cost plants, often where labor is unionized, while the new clusters of ultra-modern plants will tend to be arrayed on the outskirts of major metropolitan areas drawn by both markets and a relatively unorganized labor force. This tendency may also occur in industries with a long history of oligopoly where profit margins are being eroded by substitutes from other sectors or heightened competition from new levels of import penetration.[16] In this case, the adverse consequences for original centers will be severe because, having been overbuilt and underdiversified as discussed above, they will be particularly vulnerable to shutdowns. Oligopolies will have the size and resources to clear out very rapidly, as the steel industry has done in Pittsburgh, Youngstown, and Buffalo.

4. Market Decline, Profit Squeeze, and Plant Closings

A final era is characterized by shrinkage of output and the decline of profit rates to a less-than-average level. Most commodities in capitalist society face ultimate extinction as substitutes emerge to replace them—a function of the relentless search for new profit arenas that is endemic to capitalist systems. Take for example copper. Most major U.S. mines have shut down in recent years, in part due to depletion and import penetration, but in large part due to the substitution of fiber optics in communications uses, of polyvinylchloride in sewer and water pipes, and aluminum in radiators. If such substitutes are not pioneered internally, the industry producing the older commodity will find its market demand dropping and its profit rate falling. It will respond by trying to rationalize—closing down older capacity, and if entrepreneurial, modernizing existing operations and diversifying into new product lines.

Generally, the net effect of this behavior is the systematic elimination of capacity in the older regions, with maintenance or at least fewer closings in regions of more recent entry. As a result, the industry will appear to be shifting spatially, even reconcentrating its capacity at the more youthful sites. Take the textile and shoe industries, for example. Once almost entirely a New England phenomenon, newer plants were dispersed to lower cost locations in the southeastern Piedmont and the Kentucky-Tennessee interior throughout the first half of the twentieth century. Once heightened competition from imports pressed domestic producers, the older New England plants were eliminated so that both of these sectors now seem to have reconcentrated in a small number of southeastern states.[17]

These four types of profitability experience, generally found sequentially,[18] and their behavioral counterparts are quite helpful for distinguishing among regional growth dilemmas at any one point in time. It helps explain why, even in an era of rapid market interpenetration and huge wage gaps across countries, some regions of the United States are still hosting job growth. Indeed, this profit cycle model enables us to distinguish between two very different forms of regional growth. A large increase in employment registered in a region may mean either the birth of a new sector or the dispersion or relocation of a more established sector from some other region.

The local consequences of these two types of sectoral growth are dramatically different. In the former, we might expect the generation of a highly skilled labor force and associated agglomerative activity, which can set off a major long growth spurt.[19] In the latter case, long-term growth prospects may be an illusion, as the relocation is due solely to the response of corporations to the relative underdevelopment of the regional economy.[20] As this new presence helps create a local labor market, pushes up wages, and encourages unionization, these very benefits may choke off any further growth. The same cost-cutting insistence that encouraged the original relocation may lead to a further round of relocations to offshore sites, rendering the promise of sustained regional development even more ephemeral.

These distinctions between stage status of incoming sectors have dramatic consequences for development potential. If the new activities are in the superprofit stage, they introduce the inmigration of technical and professional labor, dramatic expansion in local business services, pressures on housing, transportation infrastructure, and air quality—in other words they bring robust job growth rates with disruptive land use and public sector consequences. If the incoming sector is a mature, profit-squeezed activity fleeing high tax and wage levels and lured by financial and other incentives, it will bring to its new host problems similar to those of the region it left—heightened capital-labor conflict and the threat of closure or overseas relocation—as well as pressures on local carrying capacity. Thus, the Deep South's efforts to attract post-normal-profit stage corporations will result in a very different developmental path for the region than will the Southwest's defense and the electronics-induced growth.

In addition to aggregate employment levels, the spatial behavior of sectors at different points of the product cycle affects both the occupational composition and structures of the business community within regions. Firms in the initial, superprofit stage will tend to have relatively high proportions of professional-technical workers. As the productions workforce grows subsequently, a dual workforce emerges in the region.[21] Corporations in the last two stages will tend also to have a bifurcated class structure—managerial and production—but it is more likely to be spatially segregated inter- or intraregionally. The growth of employment, therefore, will result in very different occupational structures locally depending on which stage of the profit cycle—agglomeration or relocation—is involved. Class conflicts on the regional level will be a direct function of class structure and sectoral dynamics, as we will see in chapter 7.

Entrepreneurial and unionization structures at the local or regional level will also be affected by sectoral type and dynamic. Regions with dominant sectors in the early stages of development will tend to have a large and robust entrepreneurial class composed of managers and proprietors of small firms. An example is the nineteenth-century agricultural Midwest, the basis, as we saw in chapter 4, of the birth of Republicanism. Regions of origin with dominant sectors in the oligopolistic normal-profit-plus stage will produce a resident regional capitalist class that has a discouraging effect on other entrepreneurial aspirants. Unionization will be advanced in these regions, with patent consequences for regional politics. Regions hosting new dispersals or relocations from existing corporations in other regions will experience an absentee capitalist class, quite distinct from local small business persons in the tertiary sector. Unionization will not typically be extensive in these locations, although efforts to organize workers will sooner or later develop.

In summary, then, the determinants of profitability for sectors at different developmental stages will create differential locational impulses. Superprofit sectors will agglomerate, creating pressures for new infrastructure and amenities required for their professional stratum employees. Profit-squeezed sectors will disperse in search of lower production costs and more efficient market penetration. Oligopolistic market structures will retard dispersion, if they appear early in the profit cycle, but are capable of accelerating it in periods of retrenchment. Three distinct regional experiences and linked to the profit cycle's rhythm: regions losing profit-squeezed sectors, regions gaining the same, and regions hosting youthful, superprofitable sectors. Each, I argue in chapter 7, is associated with specific political tendencies.

THE MILITARIZATION OF THE ECONOMY

A major difference in postwar urbanization patterns between the United States and its European industrialized partners is the degree to which population has migrated internally and shaken up the hierarchy of major cities and regions. A major cause of this remarkable recomposition is the growing role that the military plays as a consumer of manufacturing output. As weaponry has changed over the past two centuries from manual and mechanical to electronic, the location of arms production and deployment has also changed. In the postwar era, for strategic, bureaucratic, and cultural reasons, the industries serving the U.S. Department of Defense have located at suburban sites in the nation's "defense perimeter." Here, they have created relatively homogeneous, politically conservative, suburban communities favoring white male professional and technical workers. They have pointedly shunned the industrial heartland.

Military-led Innovation

World War II was won with American technology. During the war, the U.S. government began shifting massive resources into many technological areas which paid off militarily—proximity fuses, penicillin, nuclear weaponry, autopilots, crypt-analytical machinery, and advances in radar. By the war's end, warfare had emerged into the electronics era. Subsequently, the goal of strategic defense became the creation of ships and planes that would move faster, maneuver better, and be undetectable and deadly. Indeed, this is the basis of the postwar high-tech revolution, a notion that has had its military connection obscured.

These preoccupations led to increasingly greater government domination of the inventive and innovative process in the United States. Up to World War II, the federal government accounted for only about 15 percent of research and development funding. By the 1960s, this share, the bulk of it in military matters, had increased to above 60 percent and has not declined since (Markusen 1986d).[22] Unlike the lumpy process of private sector innovation, which tends to be cosmetic in boom times and more revolutionary in troughs, military-led innovation has been more or less continual. It is a natural counterpart of the cold war, the goal being continually to render obsolete the opposition's weaponry.

These innovations have had spin-offs which have dramatically affected nonmilitary sectors, particularly by automating production. The commercial counterpart of "removing the soldier from the hazards of duty" has been the removal of workers from the process of production. By constantly revolutionizing the means of production, this military-initiated stream of innovations has mitigated the tendency towards overproduction. Yet it has created new contradictions. One is the accelerated displacement of workers in traditional manufacturing. Another is the enlarged burden on the State sector, manifest in huge budget deficits that represent the cost of this role of increasing militarization.

This militarization of innovation has produced a new trend in the location of military-related hardware production. Increasingly, the bulk of the expenditure goes towards electronic and related devices, new synthetic materials, and sophisticated and custom-made communications systems designed for aircraft or submarines. The type of labor required is largely professional and technical, heavily skewed toward the engineering occupations. Generally speaking, this stratum of the workforce prefers to live in relatively urbanized settings with a high level of amenities. The salaries that contractors are willing to pay under cost-plus arrangements permit the realization of these goals. Both the corporation and their employees find sites close to good research universities and/or government labs and testing facilities an added attraction. As a result, the major portion of defense-related production has taken place in suburban areas attached to preexisting standard metropolitan statistical areas (SMSAs) or medium-sized towns. Indeed, military-related communities appear to have pioneered much of the suburban "California lifestyle" so widely imitated throughout the country.

The Defense Perimeter versus the Industrial Heartland

The preference for major research presence and nice living quarters for their professional-technical workforce does not satisfactorily explain why military-related production has shifted so decisively away from the industrial heartland. That the shift has occurred is fairly well established empirically. Prime contracts, which in 1951 were skewed toward the northeastern and north central states, had shifted by 1976 toward the southern and western states, by both aggregate and per capita measures. This bias continued into the 1980s. If subcontracting patterns are added in, the picture does not change much. Input-output studies in the 1960s and 1970s showed that nondefense priorities would have shifted economic activity back toward the manufacturing belt, at the expense of California and Texas in particular.[23]

In the 1980s, the shift has accelerated with the Reagan military build-up. Hardware purchases by the Department of Defense (DOD) are now so high-tech–intensive that the demand for the Midwest's industrial output, even the capital goods so concentrated in that region, is minimal. The Department of Defense alone accounts for a large share of output in the high-tech sectors of radio and TV communications equipment (63 percent), aircraft (46 percent), missiles (80 percent), engineering instruments (34 percent) and electronic components (20 percent). Computers and related electronics sectors are the largest gainers under the Reagan build-up. Department of Defense–originated demand for computers is estimated to increase 141 percent from 1982 to 1987.[24]

In contrast, the sectors in which the industrial belt specializes—steel (79 percent), fabricated metals (79 percent), machine tools (79 percent) and metal stampings (9 percent)—sell very small shares of their output to DOD-related contractors. Even with a large increase under the Reagan build-up, none will sell as much as 10 percent to the military sector by 1987. Meanwhile military priorities are cutting deeply into orders that might otherwise come from nondefense priorities—social spending, infrastructure improvement, industrial rehabilitation. Nor is there research money available for badly needed innovation in industries like steel.

The new high-tech industries that dominate the current defense hardware budget have by and large not grown in the industrial belt, stretching from New York through Detroit, Milwaukee, St. Louis, and Baltimore. The newer sunbelt SMSAs garnered the greatest shares of high-tech job growth in the 1970s. While Chicago was the nation's number 2 high-tech center in 1977, principally because of its prominence in the machine tools industry, it fell far below a number of newer SMSAs in absolute job gains. Indeed, half of the top ten in 1977 failed to rank in the top ten in terms of absolute job growth, not to mention percentage growth rates. All but one of these were in the industrial belt (Chicago, Detroit, Philadelphia, and Newark).[25]

The major defense-related high-tech job growth since the early 1970s has taken place on the "defense perimeter," an area stretching from the Boston area south through Connecticut, Long Island to Newport News, Huntsville (Alabama) and Melbourne (Florida) across the gulf states to

Dallas and Houston, and encompassing much of the Intermountain West as well as the Pacific Coast. Metropolitan areas like Anaheim (next to Los Angeles), Worcester (next to Boston), Dallas, Houston, and Lakeland (Florida) were among the top ten job gainers.

Regionally, the Pacific region tops the list for military expenditures per capita (table 5.1). The only other regions which show a greater than national average share are the mountain states, New England, and the South Atlantic region, in that order. Among the beneficiaries of military outlays, New England and the Pacific states rank extraordinarily high in procurement outlays, while the Mountain and South Atlantic states receive a disproportionate share in the form of military base personnel and pay. However, the South Atlantic region is the single largest recipient, share-wise, of research and development expenditures. Remarkably, none of the four interior regions, the "centrals," came within 90 percent of the national average of military receipts (Stein 1985).

When measured a different way, by shares of manufacturing shipments directed toward the military, the same ranking occur. Certain states within the regions account for the bulk of military shipments, even when normalized for different size production complexes. In the West, California, Arizona, and Utah all rank within the top five defense shipment location quotients, meaning that their manufacturing sectors are heavily dependent upon the military (table 5.2). Oregon and Idaho, on the other hand, have almost no military-related manufacturing. Similarly, the South Atlantic, Florida, Maryland, and Virginia are the big winners, while the Carolinas and West Virginia rank near the bottom.

Table 5.1 Relative Regional Per Capita Military Receipts, 1983

Region	Total Receipts ($ bills)	Procurement ratio[a]	Personnel ratio[a]	Research ratio[a]	Total ratio
New England	18.21	2.06	0.74	1.57	1.44
Mid-Atlantic	24.18	0.83	0.44	0.61	0.64
East North Central	18.02	0.45	0.44	0.14	0.43
West North Central	15.03	1.07	0.60	0.91	0.85
South Atlantic	53.38	0.97	1.67	2.27	1.35
East South Central	10.05	0.53	0.84	0.41	0.66
West South Central	23.39	0.81	1.08	0.21	0.89
Mountain	18.40	0.96	2.08	1.14	1.47
Pacific	56.69	1.85	1.44	1.75	1.66

[a]The ratios represent the regions' per capita receipts divided by the national per capital expenditure for 1983.
Source: Jay Stein, "U.S. Defense Spending: Implications for Economic Development Planning," Working Paper, Georgia Institute of Technology, City Planning Program, 1985, table 3.

Table 5.2 Highest and Lowest Ranking States in Military Shipments, 1983

Rank	Top states	Military shipments location quotient	Rank	Bottom states	Military shipments location quotient
1	California	2.62	50	Arkansas	0.001
2	Connecticut	2.49	49	West Virginia	0.02
3	Missouri	2.49	48	Idaho	0.06
4	Arizona	2.30	47	North Carolina	0.07
5	Utah	2.10	46	South Carolina	0.08
6	Maryland	1.97	45	Kentucky	0.10
7	New Hampshire	1.88	44	Nebraska	0.12
8	Kansas	1.85	43	Alabama	0.26
9	Massachusetts	1.71	42	Montana	0.27
10	Vermont	1.66	41	Wisconsin	0.28
11	Virginia	1.55	40	Tennessee	0.30
12	Rhode Island	1.35	39	Oregon	0.33
13	Florida	1.25	38	Iowa	0.33
14	Colorado	1.23	37	Delaware	0.43
15	Texas	1.17	36	Michigan	0.45

Source: Breandan O hUallachain, "Some Implications of Recent Growth in the American Military-Industrial Complex," Working Paper, Northwestern University, Department of Geography, 1986, table 1, p. 4. Data are from the Department of Commerce's *Current Industry Reports* and were weighted by 1982 employment levels to reflect the lag between production and final delivery.

The state figures for manufacturing shipments bear out the defense perimeter argument. With the exception of Missouri and Kansas, no other noncoastal state between the Appalachians and the Rockies ranks in the top fifteen. Symmetrically, the bottom fifteen states are predominantly interior states, and include some of the more significant manufacturers like Wisconsin and Michigan. The magnitudes of the differences are quite striking. While California ships out military material at a rate in excess of 150 percent of the national average, for manufacturing, states like West Virginia and Arkansas are more than 90 percent below that average. This disparity has intensified under the Reagan build-up. From 1977 to 1983, the states of Massachusetts, Texas, and California, all large to begin with, increased their shares of defense purchases at the expense of most other states (O hUallachain 1986).

Why Defense-Related Manufacturing Is Where It Is

In the literature on high-tech location, a skilled labor force and amenities are often cited as the dominant locational factors (Rees and Stafford 1983; Joint Economic Committee 1982). However, it is apparent that skilled labor is highly mobile, especially in these industries. The Department of Defense permits its contractors to earn a profit on the cost of relocating engineers. Many first-rate engineering schools exist in the Midwest, and anecdotal evidence suggests that currently as many as half of California's new hires come from these midwestern universities. In a large-scale regression analysis of all 277 U.S. metropolitan areas, we found that research and development funds at area universities were *not* an important influence on high-tech growth.[26] This must be because many industrial belt states have superior engineering schools yet are not gaining the high-tech spinoffs.

Furthermore, amenities variables were only modestly important in explaining high-tech location in the 1970s. More consistently important were per capita defense expenditures and percent black (negatively related). While climate was significant in the model, there are stunning anomalies here—both Minneapolis and Boston are lodged in the frost-belt. These findings suggest that factors other than skilled labor, engineering schools, and amenities are driving the distribution of defense dollars, which was not highly correlated with any of the other twelve characteristics.

Why defense-related manufacturing has located far from the preexisting industrial centers of the country is a complicated matter. The present pattern is the product of five decades of location decisions, and the dominant locational factors do change over time. Three factors that loom larger than labor and amenities are strategic choices by the military itself, the geopolitics of congressional operation and Pentagon constituency-building, and the cultural proclivities of military-related managers in a liberal democratic society.

Clearly, strategic decisions made by the military have shaped the longer-term spatial patterning of high-tech and defense spending. Among these are sitings of military bases, many made before the era in question. Base locations were often the determining element in early aircraft assembly relocation, since military airfields and pilots would provide accessible (and often free) testing facilities to manufacturers. Some of the relocation to the Sunbelt, especially of aircraft assembly during the 1930s, can be explained by this proximity.

But even more significant was the opening up of the Pacific Front in World War II. During the brief war years, a tremendous number of civilian and military personnel were transferred to the West Coast, and an industrial complex that included shipyards, steel mills, machining factories, and electronics was underwritten by the federal government. This immense wartime physical plant persisted after the war and drew around it a new and distinctive aerospace and communications complex.

In contrast, the postwar industrialists of the manufacturing belt, whose factories had also been converted to wartime production, dismantled their operations and reconverted them into consumer and capital goods production, to feed the immense pent-up wartime demand. Only those areas of the country without a diversified industrial base became permanent military-industrial complexes. The outstanding examples are Los Angeles, where 44 percent of all employment in the Los Angeles-Long Beach area was derived from defense and space activity, and New England, whose older textile and shoemaking activities were destroyed during the 1950s (Harrison 1984).

Geopolitical power is also an important determinant. During much of the postwar period, presidents hailed from the defense perimeter. Johnson, in particular, is often cited as a major political force behind the space program's location in and around the Gulf states. During the postwar era, military appropriations committees were dominated by southern conservative Democratic leadership, with the result that military bases and contracts often were skewed toward their districts. While prime contracts in recent years have been too concentrated to correlate with congressional status, some evidence remains that informal relationships between the Pentagon, its contractors, and politicians reinforce the Sunbelt-oriented pattern (Rundquist 1983; Adams 1981). More recently, political scrutiny appears to have encouraged the Pentagon to engage in geographical constituency building, in which it carefully scrutinizes the regional distribution of contracts and lobbies congresspersons for support in return.

A third factor, and one that appears to be growing in importance, is the apparent repugnance of both the Pentagon and military contractors for the cosmopolitan, liberal democratic culture that characterizes the older manufacturing belt. The institutionalization of capital-labor conflict in the collective bargaining process, the commitment on the part of state and local governments to high levels of social spending, and the political machines that dominate most cities embody cultural traits antithetical to the military model of labor and command. Military contractors are frequently vehement opponents of organized labor, even those whose unions date from World War II, when they were largely imposed by the government in return for industrial peace.

The Pentagon has gone out of its way to aid and encourage contractors to move away from unions, to engage in union busting, and to automate their production processes to rid themselves of blue collar labor (Markusen 1985c). They fear organized labor not because of wage issues but because of the threat of work stoppages, a severe problem for performance-oriented contractors. Former military officers now turned corporate managers may prefer the military model of loyalty, hierarchy, lack of employee mobility, and absence of adversarial relationships in the newly constructed defense communities.

In summary, then, defense expenditures and even more powerfully, defense-led innovation have fueled the shift of capital goods production toward the defense perimeter and away from the industrial heartland. They have had a major role in determining the siting of new, superprofit sectors like electronics, when they agglomerate around these initial regions. The sheer size of these government-engendered sectors and the unique geopolitical and strategic forces which shaped their regional distribution explain in large part why the United States has had such massive postwar internal redistribution of productive capacity, unlike any other major industrialized nation.

INTERRELATIONSHIPS AMONG SECTORAL DYNAMICS, INSTITUTIONAL CHANGE, AND MILITARY-LED INNOVATION

It is useful to illustrate the interconnections between the forces just surveyed using two instances—others will arise in the case studies which complete this volume. First of all, a strong relationship appears to exist between innovation in individual sectors, the periodicty of long waves, and increasingly, military-led technological change. Several scholars have observed that the initiation of new sectors and the demise of older ones seem to bunch up in the troughs of long waves.[27] During times of prosperity corporations are preoccupied with retaining market share, with product differentiation, with streamlining production processes, and pseudo-innovation. Only during times of economywide stagnation are corporate resources directed toward basic innovation. This suggests that ensembles of new sectors may emerge in tandem, not continuously over time, and that whole new eras may be characterized by a set of such fundamental innovations. The regional implication is that during the trough of a long wave, as many believe we are currently experiencing, differences in the age and type of sector may be much more significant in explaining the divergence in regional economic fortunes than would be the case in more stable periods. If the state, via the military budget, is playing an increasingly powerful role in this process, then its locational preferences will exacerbate uneven regional outcomes.

A second example is the interaction between the existence of market power in a sector and the changing role of the state. Hypothetically, any large industry with relatively few corporate competitors will have greater clout in political arenas, although this of course is mediated by such factors as the degree of regional spread, which suggests the number of congressional votes that can be easily influenced. Small-scale competitive industries, such as agriculture, can substitute trade association strength for lack of existing organizational leadership, although this example is perhaps an exception.

An outstanding illustration of the way in which an oligopolistic industry has been able to bend government policy to its ends is the energy industry, dominated by large oil and electric corporations. Although the federal government initiated a huge program to make the United States energy self-sufficient, it shunned small-scale, decentralized, renewable energy resources like solar power for expensive corporate owned, built, and operated programs such as nuclear energy and synthetic fuels, preserving throughout the dominance of the energy corporations and their monopolistic profit margins. Similarly, the Pentagon appears to support a structure of several large firms in each of its major weapons markets to the detriment of smaller would-be competitors.

Many more instances could be cited of how the profit cycle behavior of individual sectors is tempered by epochal changes in the structure of the international economy and the growing role of the military. In the chapter which immediately follows, the growing economic rifts among major American regions in the 1970s and 1980s are explored and linked to the sectoral composition of each, to the maturity of such sectors, to the region's position vis-à-vis the military industrial complex, and differential pressures induced by major upheavals in the international economy. Following that, in chapter 7, hypotheses are drawn from the profit cycle model to analyze the specific political pressures mounting within disparate regions and the resulting cleavage among regions.

Notes

1. This discussion draws upon Frobel et al. (1980), Sassen-Koob (1982), Noyelle (1983), Hansen (1979), Bluestone and Harrison (1982), Friedmann (1986), and Friedmann and Wolfe (1982).
2. Both Harvey (1982) and Bluestone and Harrison (1982) suggest that capital is increasingly employing this "spatial" strategy as a part of its new attack on labor gains in the postwar period in advanced industrial countries.
3. Evidence on the magnitude of north-south investment differentials is contained in Browne (1980).
4. A substantial portion of this immigrant workforce has been aggressively recruited, both historically and currently. See Piore (1979) for an account of this strategy.
5. This argument and that of the next few paragraphs are developed at much greater length in my companion volume, *Profit Cycles, Oligopoly and Regional Development* (1985c). A similar argument can be found in Chinitz (1960) and for steel in Stocking (1954).
6. First hypothesized by Hymer (1972), this analysis has been expanded upon by Cohen (1977) and Noyelle (1983). Noyelle and Stanback (1983) have tried to allocate metropolitan areas into categories based upon which type of corporate activity is most prevalent in each.
7. Wolfe (1977) has constructed a typology of changes in forms of state promotion of private capital. O'Connor (1973) offers the best Marxist-based conceptual approach to evaluating budgetary components of the federal governments. Castells (1980) and Mollenkopf (1981) both analyze changing public sector impacts on growth of cities.
8. See Luger's (1981) documentation of this bias. A general overview of the distributional pattern of federal aid and outlays can be found in Markusen, Saxenian, and Weiss (1981b).
9. The following material is a brief summary of my argument in a companion volume, *Profit Cycles, Oligopoly and Regional Development*, chs. 3–6. The debt to both Marxist and Schumpeterian traditions should be clear and is discussed at length in Markusen 1986b.
10. A new industry or sector (to avoid tedium I use these terms interchangeably) can be distinguished from new products or processes in existing industries by the tendency for wholly new firms to be formed around the new innovation.

11. The phrase "superprofits" was coined by Mandel (1975).
12. Taylor (1975) argues that most firms originate in the founder's home town, although Feller (1974) argues that there is no necessary relationship between inventive activity and subsequent location.
13. On the relationships between innovation and agglomeration, see Thompson (1965), Pred (1976), and Friedmann (1973).
14. Similar observations are made in the product cycle literature, originating with Kuznets (1930) and Burns (1934) and reviewed by Vernon (1966) and Hirsch (1967).
15. The normalcy of agglomeration followed by dispersion was first hypothesized by Hoover (1948). See Persky (1978) and Hansen (1980) for a debate over the extent to which postwar north-south differentials can be attributed to product life cycle-spatial filtering processes. Bergman and Goldstein (1983) show that noncyclical structural change has been a prominent feature in U.S. metropolitan shifts in the 1970s.
16. Postwar additions of new auto assembly plants and breweries have both followed the Hotelling-type pattern of clustering around new regional nodes. Hotelling (1929) hypothesized that industries with a strong market orientation and limited numbers of competitors would tend to cluster around a central place whereas unlimited numbers of competitors would disperse throughout the market area. See my studies of autos and brewing in the companion volume, and of steel in Markusen 1986e.
17. See the separate accounts of the textile and shoe industries in chapters 9 and 10 of Markusen (1985c). See also Harrison (1982).
18. Some sectors may skip the competitive era altogether and this may be increasingly common. Some may become oligopolistic even after profit squeeze has set in. In a study of fifteen 4-digit manufacturing sectors, I found only one—wineries—that did not pass through clear sequential stages and that case was unique because of Prohibition.
19. The interrelationship of high-tech sectors and a professional-technical labor force is acknowledged in the literature, but no consensus exists as to whether or not one follows the other spatially. See Oakey, Thwaites, and Nash (1980), and Ewers and Wettman (1980).
20. Several researchers have documented that branch plants, particularly in maturer sectors, are less apt to spawn other new businesses and more apt to close down than nonbranch plants. See Thompson (1969), Thwaites (1978), Johnson and Cathcart (1979), Erickson and Leinbach (1979), Hansen (1979), and Erickson (1980). Bluestone and Harrison (1980) reported that textile plants were closing in the South at a faster rate than in the North, although their entry into the former region is more recent.
21. See Saxenian (1980) for empirical documentation of this phenomenon in Silicon Valley.
22. The material in this section is treated at much greater length in Markusen (1985a, 1985b, 1986a, and 1986c).
23. McBreen (1977), Mazza and Wilkinsons (1980), Anderson (1983), Karaska (1967), Rees (1982), Malecki (1984), Leontieff et al. (1965), Bezdek (1975).
24. Figures are from Henry (1983). They do not include the defense portions of NASA, Department of Energy and other non-Pentagon military programs.
25. See Markusen, Hall, and Glasmeier (1986); Glasmeier (1986).
26. See Markusen, Hall, and Glasmeier (1986).
27. See in particular, Mensch (1979); Abernathy (1978); Hall (1981); Freeman, Clark, and Soete (1982); and Rostow (1977).

6

The Regional Development Consequences

Regional development and change in the postwar era are the product of three sets of forces—one encompassing the international economy, one characterizing individual sectors, and one reflecting the growing militarization of the economy. Together they operate on historically evolved economic and cultural identities. In this chapter, the combined results of the new international division of labor, changes in the unique sectoral configurations of regional economies and the growing role of military production are investigated from the perspective of three major U.S. regions: the Northeast-Midwest manufacturing belt, the Old South transformed into the New South, and the Intermountain West.

These three regions were chosen because their recently renewed self-consciousness forms the basis of the chapters on politics which follow. Each has had distinct pressures operating on its economy. The territorial coverage of each is mapped out in figure 6.1, which shows the state by state membership in the major new regional organizations as of 1980. The reader should note that this grouping does not encompass the entire country. Some portions of the Pacific Coast, Appalachia, and the Great Plains region are not included. These states had such diverse local economies and historically divided loyalties that no clear regional affiliation emerged. It is remarkable that neither California nor Texas joined any of the new regional groupings. Both were large enough to be significant actors in the national struggle for resources without joining up with smaller neighbors. In addition, both are microcosms of the national economy—each contains subregions dominated by superprofit or military-oriented growth sectors, others by resource-based activities (oil and agriculture), and still others by profit-squeezed heavy industry (steel, autos, and machinery). Interregional struggles tended to be mirrored in these two states by substate conflicts of a similar nature.

In this chapter, I give a brief descriptive overview of each major region in the postwar period. Each is shown to be characterized by a unique, historically evolved set of sectors. In the 1970s, the decade of greatest regional antagonism in the period, these sectoral ensembles exhibited growing divergence in profit cycle status—the Northeast with

116

Figure 6.1 State Membership in the New Regional Organizations, 1980.

a preponderance of profit-squeezed industries, the Old South on the receiving end of the same sectors, and the West booming with resource-based, and to a lesser extent military-led, growth. The second portion of the chapter reviews the aggregate evidence on jobs, joblessness, migration, and population growth differentials in the postwar period.

THE MAJOR REGIONS OF THE 1970S

The Northeast-Midwest

This region consists of the older, industrial areas of the Great Lakes, New England, Middle Atlantic, Ohio River, and upper Mississippi. It stretches from cities like Duluth south to St. Louis, east to Baltimore, north to Boston. In economic structure it is very similar to the Canadian Great Lakes regions of Ontario and Quebec, which face it on the other side of the border. It resembles, too, some of the older industrial regions in Britain and France, which are also suffering relatively high degrees of economic dislocation. It hosts many of the great cities of the industrial era—New York, Boston, Philadelphia, Pittsburgh, Cleveland, Detroit, and Chicago—whose origins date back to the mercantilist era preceding the era of manufacturing.

In the postwar era of accelerating integration of the world economy, this region has found itself increasingly unable to maintain its industrial base. Lower transoceanic transportation costs and rapid but low-wage westernization in Third World countries entice profit-seeking corporations to set up plants abroad for the production of basic consumer goods. The new conglomerate form of the corporation and the increasing internationalization of the capital market permit both capital and goods greater ease in traversing national boundaries by lowering transaction costs and decreasing risk. The Northeast, with its sophisticated, unionized, and often militant workforce, is at a great disadvantage in this more integrated world economy. The expanded role of the state, especially at the local and state government levels, has led to higher social wages in this region, including public sector wage and social welfare programs, with concomitantly unattractive tax burdens for businesses.

In tandem with these general forces, a significant number of sectors in which this region had specialized for a century reached profit squeeze and abandonment stages of their profit cycles in the postwar period. Especially in New England, the decline of sectors such as textiles, shoes, and fishing, reaching back to earlier decades, had not been matched by compensating growth of innovative manufacturing sectors. One recent study found that real earnings in several prominent New England sectors had peaked in the mid- to late 1960s: textiles and primary metals in 1966, transportation equipment in 1967, apparel in 1968, and food products in 1970. In the Mideast (approximately the middle Atlantic states), the peak years were 1967 for transportation equipment; 1968 for apparel; 1969 for lumber, furniture, fabricated metals, ordinance, non-electrical machinery, and electrical equipment; and 1970 for food products. From 1969 to 1976 alone, New England lost 10 percent of all jobs in women's apparel, 4 percent in metalworking machinery, 18 percent in shoemaking, and 3 percent in aircraft engines. The worst throes of restructuring seem to have moved from New England in the early 1970s to the Middle Atlantic states in the mid-1970s and finally to the Midwest in the last years of the decade. As the data below confirm, the northeastern quadrant of the country had been suffering comparatively low rates of growth in employment and even greater lags in population expansion in the entire postwar period. Plant closings were the primary cause of declining job growth rates.[1]

The adjustment problems posed by the decline of these mature industrial sectors were magnified in selected regional subeconomies by the presence of a dominant oligopoly. The vulnerability of a Pittsburgh, an Akron, or a Detroit became apparent as the pressures of heightened competition from imports and from substitutes mounted. The major auto, rubber, and steel corporations hastened to diversify into entirely different product lines and to disperse production to lowest cost, often international, locations, leapfrogging potential sites in other regions in the process. With expansions in auto, steel, and rubber operations no longer providing the growth stimulus, the lack of diversity in these local economies left them with relatively few alternative sectors upon which to pin their hopes for economic regeneration.

In the 1970s, this growing disparity between the Northeast and the rest of the country was exacerbated by two recessions in five years and by the very uneven regional consequences of the energy crisis. Following the first recession, from 1970 through 1972, northeastern commentators began to note with alarm that the region was not recovering as fast as others, a break from the historical past for this region, whose manufacturing employment might be more cyclically sensitive but had always rebounded before. A second recession in 1974 deepened the crisis. Furthermore, the rapidly escalating price of fuel following the 1973 oil embargo hastened the outmigration of capital and people from the region. Production cost differentials between mild sunbelt climates with cheap natural gas and cold energy-poor northeastern sites induced corporations to accelerate the dispersal of industry in cost-sensitive sectors. Working-class people—professionals and blue collar alike, especially those who had retired—stepped up their migration rates in response to climatically harsh conditions, the high cost of living, and electricity prices which in New York exceeded those in Houston by 170 percent.

But not all the functions associated with industrial production emigrated at the same pace. Those that centered on the management, planning, marketing, and research activities of major, increasingly multinational, corporations tended to remain in the downtowns of the largest metropolitan areas, especially New York but to some extent Boston, Pittsburgh, and Chicago, and for reasons quite political, Washington, D.C. Thus within sectors, the more significant, centralized, and "modern" functions become spatially segregated from the more standardized activities of production, sales, and service. This phenomenon intensified the pressure on land and labor markets (especially for professional-technical, management, clerical, and some types of service workers) in these circumscribed city centers, creating minibooms of intense building activity for primarily highrise office uses. The office boom, grafted onto widespread industrial decline, dramatically altered the occupational structure of the labor force and the spatial configuration of cities, but was not sufficient to reverse the lower growth rates of the region as a whole.

The longer-term secular trend toward lower growth rates in the Northeast had not gone entirely unnoticed, despite the general nationwide prosperity of the era. In the early 1950s, and again in the latter half of the 1960s, academics and government agencies alike brooded over the regional problems of New England, which they variously ascribed to the paucity of the region's raw materials, its trade disadvantages, its high cost of labor, or its specialization in "mature" sectors. One analyst traced a tradition of pessimism regarding the region's future back as far as 1836 (Harris 1952, 55),[2] a date which corresponds closely to the opening up of the Erie canal and the emergence of the partnership of midwestern agriculture and Middle Atlantic-based industry, which was to supplant New England's commerce as the dominant developmental force in the young nation's economy. Two massive studies analyzed the development problems of the New York and Pittsburgh metropolitan regions.[3]

Developmentally, these patterns had severe consequences. First, the labor force became increasingly bifurcated into professional-managerial workers on one end and low-paid, service sector or clerical personnel on the other, as the old "middle" of relatively well-paid blue-collar assembly and craftsworker jobs shrank in both relative and absolute numbers. Second, the region's old spatial integration around metropolitan cities began to come apart. Central business districts became increasingly segregated from and inaccessible to the largely minority residents immediately surrounding them. In some cases, like Detroit's Renaissance Center, whole new office complexes at new sites displaced the functions of the older downtown. Massive rapid transit systems conveyed suburban white-collar commuters into the central city at considerable expense, while some office functions began to suburbanize to take advantage of housewives' search for part-time work. Meanwhile, new manufacturing plants were either decentralized to the region's periphery (clothing to Maine, for instance) or concentrated in industrial parks where pools of high-tech workers could be harnessed to innovation in sectors like electronics and pharmaceuticals (Route 128 in Boston, for example). But even the ability of this region to keep its newer high-tech sectors has been placed in doubt.[4]

In the 1980s, a rift in the Northeast's common identity began to develop, parallel to the regeneration of New England, the partial recovery of the Middle Atlantic states, and the worsening of the restructuring in the Midwest. Both extraordinarily high levels of defense spending and a growing role as the entrepot of international trade and finance reversed the postwar decline of the more northerly seaboard states. Although their growth rates remained below those of the nation, they posted low rates of unemployment by the mid-1980s.

In the industrial heartland, in contrast, total employment remained below what it had been in the late 1970s and unemployment mounted. Hard hit by a deteriorating trade balance in both agriculture and capital goods, these states (Ohio, Michigan, Indiana, Illinois, and Wisconsin) received few compensations in the form of military spending. This parting of the economic ways between New England, New York, and the Midwest diluted the will to work together, as we shall see below.

The Old South Turned New South

Southern development problems in the postwar period have been a product of rapid rates of industrialization and immigration and of the particular sectors which compose that growth. On the one hand, southern economic development proceeded quite rapidly throughout the 1970s, as population, employment, and per capita income rose at rates quite substantially above national norms (see next section). On the other hand, much of this growth was composed of older manufacturing sectors shifting away from locations in other regions. In a world of increasingly competitive Third World economies, where the South is so to speak "flanked" by even lower-cost regions, the development promise of these new industries is ambiguous.

The rapid industrial growth of the South was in large part a "catching up" of this region to the rest of the country, as the economic legacies of cash crop slavery, discussed in chapter 4 above, finally began to lose their grip on southern institutions and labor markets. For one thing, the mechanization of cotton picking following World War II eliminated much of the demand for black agricultural labor which had kept southern elites committed to a system of discrimination against blacks in industrial employment. For another, the civil rights movement successfully challenged the restrictions on blacks' access to jobs and education that had previously retarded the development of a southern labor force. The ranks of a growing wage-labor force were also swollen by both white and black outmigration from Appalachia, where coal mining jobs disappeared precipitously from the depression onward.

Yet the persistence of racism and its past role in discouraging unionism kept wages relatively low. Employers in search of a cheap but moderately skilled labor force increasingly found the South an amenable location for relocated plants or for expansion. The fact that the indigenous political system also favored business development, made unionization difficult, and kept tax rates low by maintaining a very low level of social wage also contributed to the region's pull. The southern boom was also aided by two aspects of the new federal government role as a major economic agent. First, its TVA project, begun in the 1930s, improved both commercial agriculture and provided vast new accretions of cheap electric power for the Tennessee Valley, engendering new manufacturing growth. Second, large shares of the federal military expenditures on military bases and personnel went to southern jurisdictions, in part because of the power and longevity of southern congressmen, in turn a feature of the one-party system dating from the Civil War.

The development consequences were several. Average per capita income grew significantly. Several southern cities, perhaps best exemplified by Atlanta, boomed under the stimuli of industrial growth, and its accompanying regional finance and transportation functions. A large proportion of new employment, however, was not located in these centers but at rural and small town sites throughout the South, to be closer to a surplus rural labor force. Considerable increases in jobs in both urban and rural locations drew out new entrants to the labor force, not only rural residents, but many blacks who had migrated to northern cities during earlier industrial booms and, increasingly, many Latinos who migrated via southern Florida. Such rapid growth brought conflicts over land use and resources, as urban sprawl and central city decline, water shortages, and environmental degradation began to surface as serious problems.

But at the same time, these growth dilemmas were unlike those experienced in Silicon Valley or the Houston area, because they accompanied the entry and growth of sectors for the most part in the latter stages of their profit cycles, rather than new, superprofit innovating sectors. The South was increasing its share throughout the postwar period in sectors such as textiles, shoes, autos, fish processing, lumber, soybeans, and apparel. But even as its share increased, it experienced absolute employment losses in some of these, such as canned fish and shoes.[5] Thus overlaid on the region's growth-minded concern was a somewhat contradictory worry over conserving the favorable cost conditions to which business in these profit-squeezed sectors had been attracted in the first place. This was exacerbated by the distinct possibility that industries such as textiles, apparel, shoes, and even chemicals and aluminum would find overseas locations more attractive, a possibility registered in the not infrequent plant closings in southern locations. The rate at which large manufacturing facilities closed in the South from 1969 to 1976 exceeded that in any other part of the country (Harrison and Bluestone 1981, 13–14).

This threat of truncated southern industrialization has resulted in pressure to keep labor costs and public sector tax rates low. Thus, in terms of human development, many southern workers are members of the "working poor," in that their wages and work opportunities are not sufficient to keep them above the poverty line. Poverty rates remain high in the South. In addition, some of the worst industrial diseases have been detected in the South, specifically black lung disease and brown lung, associated respectively with coal mining and textile mills. The desire to keep labor costs down, and the weakness of unions, have made progress in recognition, treatment, and prevention of these conditions difficult.

At the same time, a new type of industrialization is rising up around military and space facilities in places like Melbourne, Florida and Huntsville, Alabama. Associate high-tech growth has directly engendered tremendous growth in pockets such as these. It brings with it pressures to modernize—to create the amenities and lifestyles favored by the engineers and technicians who are recruited to these locations. Together with other elements of the "New South," they have imported ideas like growth controls, environmental protection, planned urban expansion, and better education, all of which threaten to erase the business climate differentials between this region and the rest of the country. These internal conflicts have come to play a major role in contemporary southern politics, as we shall see below.

The Intermountain West

The American West has played the role of the frontier in American history, a rebellious and challenging role in the drama of regional formation. It is still a frontier of sorts, especially in the sense that its prosperity rests upon the geological materials underneath its surface. Large corporations and independent prospectors with only a jeep are still exploring the recesses and depths of the Rocky Mountains and its basins for wealth that can be excavated at a profit. The land-based activities of agriculture, mining, and tourism continue to form the heart of the region's economic base. In 1970, for instance, the three energy-rich counties of northwestern Colorado had 14 percent of their work force in agriculture and another 9 percent in mining compared to 4 and 1 percent respectively nationwide; these same counties had only 3 percent of their workforce in manufacturing, compared to 27 percent across the country.[6]

This nonrenewable resource-based economy had been relatively stagnant regionwide for several decades prior to the 1970s. In certain areas, like northwestern Colorado, sectors like agriculture lost between one third and one half of all jobs in the postwar era, resulting in serious rates of depopulation. Routt County, for instance, lost 34 percent of its population in the decade of the 1950s. A dramatic turnaround was induced in this sectorally declining region by the energy crisis of the 1970s and the nationalist Project Independence, which boosted prices for energy commodities tremendously. For the first time in almost a century, high plains coal in Montana, Wyoming, and North Dakota could be profitably mined. Extensive oil drilling, the "high-tech" mining of oil shale, and production of synthetic fuels like gasified coal became feasible corporate ventures. The western states were slated, under the project and the neighboring Southwest Energy Complex and North Central Power Complex, to host 250 major new coal mines, 150 new coal-fired power plants, and twenty major new synthetic fuels plants, plus pipelines, transmission lines, railroad spurs, and new roads to transport the energy product. Into the rural areas of the region, then, these energy sectors produced huge discontinuities in settlement patterns, both in population magnitudes and composition, and new conflicts among competitors for nonrenewable resources (Hayes 1980, 88; Baldwin 1973).[7]

While the ideology of the West stresses independence as the touchstone of its frontier culture, the region is in fact heavily tied into the international economy. This has been true since its nineteenth-century settlement by whites, many of whom came to mine ore or run cattle under the auspices of eastern and even British and French capital. In the most recent period, the dramatic boom in energy sectors is a consequence of international oil politics, including the decades long strategy of American multinational oil corporations. Responding to a substantial realignment of international prices in energy commodities, the national government pursued an explicit policy of subsidies and incentives for new levels of resource exploitation in this region, including an array of policies directed towards the leasing and use of its extensive land holdings. And, as we shall see in chapter 10, the energy revival of the 1970s had by 1980 become linked to an export policy concerning both Alaskan oil and western coal.

The western economy can be distinguished from that of the rest of the country by a number of distinct features: poor internal linkages, severe intersectoral competition for scarce natural resources, substantial outsider ownership of land and establishments, and an extraordinary level of federal government land and facility management. Unlike the manufacturing belt in the Northeast, western subsectors have very few interlinkages as suppliers-clients. Instead they are most often found competing over resource inputs while selling to client sectors outside the region.

In addition, many of the subsectors occupying the regions' economy are solidly based on nonrenewable resources of relatively high value. Extraordinary profits may draw and support hundreds of claimstakers and other hopefuls. Yet once the strike proves false or the well runs dry, fortune seekers and their support systems move on to new areas. High-value, nonrenewable sectors in communities with no other economic base sectors create booms and busts of tremendous magnitude in subregional economies.

In addition to the absence of the intersectoral industrial ties found in the Northeast, industrial ownership and management predominantly reside and operate from outside of the western region. Traditionally, the economic bases of mining communities like Lead, South Dakota and the Trinidad-Pueblo area in Colorado were controlled by the Hearsts and the Rockefellers, respectively. Late nineteenth-century ranches and railroads were financed by British as well as eastern capital. Postwar oil booms in Wyoming, urban renewal in Denver, and ski resorts in Steamboat Springs, Colorado have been financed and managed by Texan entrepreneurs.[8] The coal revival has been almost totally the province of the largest national coal companies such as Peabody, Continental, and Westmoreland. The fact that the economy is so dependent upon land-based productive factors, which are commodified via the land market and the rent relationship, introduces an additional set of conflicts between landowners and producers over the division of returns to production and the laws governing land use and transfer.[9]

A distinguishing feature of western economies is that individual producers and corporations alike frequently operate on federally owned land. In the late 1970s, 93 percent of all federally owned or controlled land was located in twelve western states, where it constituted 30 percent or more of each state's land bases. Intermountain WESTPO states host federal land ownership as follows:

Montana	30%	Wyoming	48%
New Mexico	34%	Idaho	64%
Colorado	36%	Utah	66%
Arizona	43%	Nevada	87%
California	45%	Alaska	96%

This profile contrasts strikingly with eastern and southern patterns of tenure where no single state has more than 9 percent of its land area in federal ownership, and states like Texas (2 percent), New York (1 percent), and Maine (0 percent) have essentially no dealings with federal land-managing agencies (Leroy and Eiguren 1980; Blakemore and Erickson 1981). Grazing rights, leasing provisions and other use issues have long strained relationships between the federal government and the region. The cold war military build-up also increased the federal government's role in the Mountain States. Deployment and testing sites for fighter planes, missiles, and nuclear explosives brought limited economic activity to some states. They also created tensions between residents and their government. But even more important was the impetus to defense-oriented manufacturing in places like central Utah and Colorado Springs. Boosted more recently by the Reagan build-up, these areas are among the fastest growing in the nation, though they remain highly specialized military-space complexes.

Under renewed resource development activity in the 1970s, western cities burgeoned. Because of the depopulation of rural areas, and the land-extensiveness of western agriculture, the population of the West is paradoxically more urbanized than in the rest of the country. In the 1960s, front range cities and suburbs had grown in population by 38 percent while the western slopes had increased only 9 percent. As the energy boom commenced, large cities like Denver and medium-sized towns like Billings became centers for professional and service activities related to peripheral energy development. Denver in the 1970s hosted twenty-seven major new office buildings, housing an estimated 2,000 energy-related companies. The service sector had a distinct character in such cities—Denver had as many as 4,000 geologists selling their services to energy corporations (McDonell 1979, 5; Ingram, Lancey, and McCain 1980, 106). These fast-growing urban areas produced their own resource-based demands and contributed to the intersectoral conflict for resources.

However, by the early 1980s, the energy boom had become a bust. The growth dynamic in these states shifted away from the resource poles and toward military facilities. Denver's boom subsided as Colorado Springs' boom accelerated. States like Montana and Idaho, which had relied heavily upon resources like copper, coal, and timber, but have very little military-oriented manufacturing, posted growth rates in the 1980s far below those of their neighbors to the south. These growing disparities undermined the earlier unity the mountain states had demonstrated in addressing the energy era.

THE ECONOMICS AND DEMOGRAPHICS OF
POSTWAR U.S. REGIONS

I have argued that the new international division of labor, unique sectoral dynamics, and skewed patterns of military spending are the major postwar factors shaping regional politics, at least through the 1970s. It would be a formidable task to construct and test a model that would allocate regional growth differentials to each of the three. However, the magnitude of their joint impacts can be inferred from two sources: (1) the regional literature at large, and (2) empirical data on variables influenced by sectoral dynamics: population change, employment change, sectoral composition, migration, and unemployment. They document a strong divergence in growth experience by region, particularly in the 1970s.

Sectoral Growth Patterns

First of all, it bears noting that sectoral differences in the spatial pattern of economic activity have not always manifested themselves at the macro-regional level. In the mid-century period, that is to say from 1929 to about 1960, sectoral change did not occur primarily at the interregional scale. On the contrary, the dominant feature of uneven development in that era was the systematic decline of later-stage inner-city sectors, and their dispersal to suburbs and surrounding states, resulting in an emergent city versus suburban politics which peaked in the early 1970s. Before that, the dominant spatial tension was between rural and urban areas, as declining (at least in terms of employment) sectors in agriculture, fishing, lumbering, and mining, and consequent migration from rural to urban areas, produced a country-city politics. Nevertheless, the historic role of uneven sectoral growth rates in determining interregional differences for more than a century has been confirmed by most students of U.S. regional inequality (Williamson 1980, 55). And by the 1970s this interregional divergence had once again, as it had in the late eighteenth century and the middle of the nineteenth century, taken precedence as the major national spatial antagonism.

Empirical proof that profit cycle-related sectoral features, coincident across significant numbers of sectors, underlie regional political impulses would require demonstration that (1) sectors are highly differentiated across regions, (2) concentrations of sectors in later stages and earlier stages are systematically found in different regions, and (3) across regions, actors associated with sectors in superprofit versus profit-squeezed stages exhibit similar political demands. With regard to the first, regional research for much of the postwar period has been preoccupied with the very palpably uneven distribution of sectors spatially. Indeed, the raison d'être of shift-share analysis has been to explain regional growth rates on the basis of the distinct sectoral composition of regional economies, any other divergence in a region's growth rate being ascribed to differences in competitiveness. And, as students of the method have pointed out, the more highly disaggregated the data upon which the technique is employed, the more sectoral differences come to account for the entire difference.[10]

A recent effort by Miernyk (1980) to measure the regional concentration of sectors using employment location quotients for 1940 and 1975 in the United States indicates that even at the one-digit scale, industries like agriculture, mining, and manufacturing are still highly unevenly distributed nationwide.[11] While the cross-regional differences in manufacturing employment lessened somewhat during the era, those for mining, and for agriculture in the case of the West North Central region, increased. Miernyk's two-digit sectoral breakdowns by source of personal income also confirm continued high rates of regional specialization, with no systematic tendency for sectors as a group either to increase or decrease their concentration (Miernyk 1980, 107–11).[12] Because these figures still cover a highly aggregated set of sectors, it is impossible to use them to detect systematic concentration or dispersion by profit cycle stage. Case studies of individual sectors do confirm the tendency to disperse, as I have shown at length in a companion volume. A similar argument regarding the skewed spatial concentration of old and new sectors is made by Rostow (1977), who casts his analysis in terms of Kondratieff long-wave cycles.

It is important to note, however, that it is not simply industrial mix that conditions a region's fortunes, but the degree of competitiveness of regions in the sectors which dominate its economic base. The effect of the new international division of labor, with its integration of production across widely disparate labor markets and its acceleration of capital movement in search of more profitable production sites, has been to hasten the redistribution of jobs within sectors across regions. A recent study of regional diversity in the United States found that the regions' job growth depended "far less on industry mix than it did on intra-industry differences between regions" (Jackson et al. 1981, 124–25).

In other words, in the most recent period, the old manufacturing regions have been declining much faster than their industry mix would predict, because they are also losing out in the competition to keep jobs in those sectors. The state of New York suffered competitive job losses (that is, the difference between actual jobs and those that would have existed if the state had grown at the national rate) of some 633,000 between 1958 and 1972, in selected major manufacturing industries. Losses in excess of 10,000 occurred in twelve three-digit manufacturing sectors, including men's and women's apparel, textiles, furniture, paper products, commercial printing, drugs, plastics, office machines, communications equipment, and recreational equipment (Chinitz 1978, 52–53).[13]

In sum, then, the empirical work available to us suggests that sectoral differences are a profound discriminator among regions of the United States. Not only do they differ in product type, but they are developmentally at different stages, with some associated interregional shifting as well as quite skewed patterns of superprofit sectoral growth. The impact of international integration and the military boom seem to be accelerating the displacement and adjustment process. In the interim, at least, regions are becoming more highly differentiated, except insofar as dispersion of profit-squeezed sectors brings the underdeveloped South closer in structure to the North.

Jobs, Joblessness, Migration, and Income

The joint results of the structural changes in the international, sectoral, and military-civilian spheres can be inferred from macroeconomic data on regional change.[14] To begin with, the employment growth experience of regions has clearly been significantly disparate in the postwar period. As table 6.1 indicates, the regions composing the manufacturing belt (New England, Middle Atlantic, and Great Lakes) all grew at rates significantly below the U.S. average throughout the period, while the regions generally considered to constitute elements of the Sunbelt grew at dramatically higher rates throughout. The divergence in job growth rates among regions lessened during the 1960s and increased again in the 1970s, when it exceeded the differential of the 1950s. This pattern suggests that the boom of the 1960s associated with the Great Society social welfare and Viet Nam war stimuli of the federal government had an ameliorating effect on the private sector proclivity for greater rates of accumulation based on Sunbelt employment expansion.[15]

Internal regional homogeneity of job growth experience is evident from the figures for each region. Only five of the twenty-eight states below an arc from Virginia through Alaska failed to host job growth in excess of the national average from 1960 to 1970; and from 1970 to 1975, the single exception to better-than-average growth was West Virginia. In New England from 1950 to 1975, no state grew consistently above the national norm; only brief growth spurts—Vermont and Maine in the 1960s and New Hampshire in the early 1970s—counteracted this common laggardness. All Middle Atlantic states trailed the national growth rate in every decade by more than 40 percent, except New Jersey in the 1950s. Similarly, the Great Lakes states had an almost universally below-par experience through the mid-1970s. Only the Plains states showed no consistency in job growth rates and little internal homogeneity.

The regional experience with unemployment rates presents a somewhat different picture (see table 6.2). The clearest cases of sustained low unemployment rates were in the plains states and in the Southwest. Up through the early 1970s, the picture is otherwise mixed, with some Rocky Mountain states showing high unemployment rates and the Middle Atlantic states showing uniformly lower rates in 1970. By the mid 1970s, however, high unemployment rates (and persistent movements toward them) were systematically showing up in all the manufac-

Table 6.1 Nonagricultural Employment Growth Rates by Region and State, 1950–1982

Region	Percent change 1950–60	Percent change 1960–70	Percent change 1970–80	Percent change 1980–82
New England	10.6	23.0	18.9	1.1
Maine	9.3	19.7	22.1	-1.5
New Hampshire	19.3	29.5	44.7	2.8
Vermont	11.4	37.1	33.1	1.8
Massachusetts	8.2	19.1	15.0	2.8
Rhode Island	-2.3	17.7	14.2	-1.2
Connecticut	19.5	30.8	19.2	-1.3
Middle Atlantic	9.5	18.4	5.4	-0.4
New York	10.9	15.7	-1.0	1.6
New Jersey	21.7	29.3	15.1	0.9
Pennsylvania	1.9	17.1	9.9	-4.3
East North Central	12.3	25.3	15.4	5.8
Ohio	14.0	23.3	13.3	-5.0
Indiana	12.5	29.2	16.3	-5.9
Illinois	11.4	22.9	12.4	-5.4
Michigan	9.1	27.8	16.7	-8.2
Wisconsin	16.6	28.4	25.8	-3.7
West North Central	16.2	27.9	27.9	-2.3
Minnesota	19.5	37.2	32.4	-2.0
Iowa	11.7	29.0	25.8	-5.5
Missouri	13.5	23.6	17.7	-1.9
North Dakota	16.2	29.2	45.8	3.2
South Dakota	1.4	25.2	32.2	-2.3
Nebraska	19.4	26.5	29.3	-2.2
Kansas	20.5	21.1	40.1	-1.6
South Atlantic	29.6	46.5	36.8	2.0
Delaware	27.7	38.5	17.4	-0.9
Marland	25.2	45.1	28.1	-0.7
Virginia	26.4	49.3	38.0	2.1
West Virginia	-12.3	12.3	25.1	-5.8
North Carolina	28.9	49.1	33.1	-1.2
South Carolina	26.2	44.5	39.8	-0.1
Georgia	30.3	48.2	36.6	1.6
Florida	87.5	63.0	63.4	8.4
District of Columbia	7.8	27.7	11.7	-0.6
East South Central	22.8	38.6	34.5	-2.6
Kentucky	17.4	39.2	32.4	-3.4
Tennessee	21.9	43.5	32.0	-3.0
Alabama	25.3	30.1	34.3	-1.4
Mississippi	29.6	42.9	43.9	-2.6
West South Central	28.1	40.1	54.3	6.5
Arkansas	23.3	45.5	39.9	-4.0
Louisiana	24.1	31.9	49.2	4.8
Oklahoma	22.0	32.3	47.0	6.3
Texas	31.8	43.6	59.4	8.4
Mountain	46.7	42.2	66.6	3.3
Montana	11.9	20.7	36.0	6.0
Idaho	17.9	33.9	57.8	-4.1
Wyoming	20.9	12.1	82.4	4.7
Colorado	43.9	44.1	65.0	4.2
New Mexico	55.9	23.9	58.1	1.9
Arizona	106.6	64.0	85.8	3.2
Utah	39.2	35.5	51.3	2.6
Nevada	92.2	96.3	90.3	6.8
Pacific	49.2	41.2	41.8	1.2
Washington	18.9	32.9	46.7	3.0
Oregon	16.4	39.3	47.4	-7.0
California	52.6	41.9	40.1	2.8
Alaska[a]	—	64.5	78.9	4.1
Hawaii[a]	—	55.6	37.4	-0.3
Total United States	20.2	31.0	27.4	-0.1

[a]Not states in 1950.

Source: U.S. Department of Labor, Bureau of Labor Statistics, Employment and Earnings, States and Areas, 1939-1974; and Employment and Earnings, 29, No. 4. (April 1982): 94–104.

Table 6.2   Unemployment Rate, by Region and State, 1950–1984

Region	Unemployment rates relative to U.S. Average					
	1950	1960	1970	1975	1080	1984
New England						
Maine	183	134	116	119	108	81
New Hampshire	137	74	67	81	66	57
Vermont	114	98	100	117	90	69
Massachusetts	120	92	93	147	79	64
Rhode Island	149	121	106	171	101	71
Connecticut	112	101	114	118	83	61
Middle Atlantic						
New York	124	101	91	118	106	96
New Jersey	106	121	93	119	101	83
Pennsylvania	112	145	91	104	111	121
East North Central						
Ohio	91	96	110	100	118	125
Indiana	64	94	102	103	135	115
Illinois	83	76	83	97	117	121
Michigan	112	121	136	162	177	149
Wisconsin	60	70	79	82	99	97
West North Central						
Minnesota	72	83	85	69	80	84
Iowa	37	54	75	67	80	93
Missouri	68	83	67	85	99	96
North Dakota	79	90	93	61	69	68
South Dakota	58	52	67	57	66	57
Nebraska	45	49	63	64	56	59
Kansas	52	74	97	57	62	69
South Atlantic						
Delaware	64	76	97	109	108	83
Marland	81	47	63	95	90	125
Virginia	81	76	69	81	72	67
West Virginia	100	216	124	96	132	200
North Carolina	68	100	87	107	92	89
South Carolina	70	103	102	130	97	95
Georgia	70	105	83	112	90	80
Florida	93	94	89	134	85	84
District of Columbia	81	47	63	95	101	120
East South Central						
Kentucky	75	129	102	90	114	124
Tennessee	81	76	69	81	101	115
Alabama	87	114	95	104	124	148
Mississippi	—	—	98	—	106	144
West South Central						
Arkansas	97	110	102	104	107	119
Louisiana	95	118	134	97	94	133
Oklahoma	79	89	89	72	68	93
Texas	81	96	89	71	73	79
Mountain						
Montana	106	121	112	94	85	99
Idaho	114	98	118	87	98	96
Wyoming	89	79	81	54	55	84
Colorado	87	67	89	64	79	75
New Mexico	112	98	120	91	104	100
Arizona	158	85	89	118	93	67
Utah	108	83	124	88	87	87
Nevada	139	105	120	114	87	104
Pacific						
Washington	139	116	185	109	106	127
Oregon	135	89	91	104	115	125
California	164	105	146	105	96	104
Alaska	204	145	177	101	134	133
Hawaii	197	56	95	87	70	75

Source: Advisory Commission on Intergovernmental Relations, *Regional Growth, Historic Perspective*, June 1980; U.S. Bureau of Labor Statistics, *Labor Force, Employment and Earnings*. 1981, 1984.

turing belt regions, while Rocky Mountain states joined the other Sunbelt regions with across-the-board low rates.

Each macro region harbored internal disparities. The Sunbelt exception was the Far West, which showed higher than average unemployment rates during most of the postwar period, and the South Atlantic region, where five out of eight states posted high rates in the mid-1970s. And in the Northeast, the New England states, New York, and New Jersey had by 1984 dramatically lowered their rates, in contrast to their midwestern counterparts. This wide range of subregional unemployment is indirect evidence that the type of employment decline and growth occurring in each is starkly different and may contribute changing political affinities over the decades.

As low rates of job growth and high unemployment increasingly came to characterize the manufacturing belt, the postwar rate of migration from areas of low opportunity to faster-growing regions quickened. Table 6.3 shows the net rates of migration for regions from 1950 through 1980. As the postwar period progressed, former regions of outmigration such as the east and west south central areas reversed their population outflows, while the northeastern and north central regions became net losers. Both the South Atlantic and the mountain regions substantially increased their net inmigration rates in the 1970s, while the Pacific region's rate fell.

Of course, migration is not only a result of job possibilities—some of it is explained by retirees moving to warmer climes, by households in search of both jobs and lower costs of living, and by stepped up international migration largely across southern borders (into Florida and the Southwest in particular). But it is difficult to argue that jobs are following people rather than vice versa when unemployment rates are highest in the regions of outmigration.[16] Note, for instance, that as unemployment rates rose in the industrial heartland, these states' rate of outmigration overtook that of the Middle Atlantic states, whose losses dropped precipitously in the early 1980s.

All of these disparities are perhaps best registered in the remarkable divergence in population growth rates experienced across regions. Table 6.4 shows the relative growth rates for each region from 1950 through 1984. It indicates a growing divergence in regional growth rates across the postwar period. New England's population growth rate fell from about 70 percent of the national average in the 1950s to about one-third of that rate by the late 1970s. The Middle Atlantic states fell from a growth pace only 20 percent below the national average to a *negative* rate by the late 1970s, a historical first. This was led by a 3.7 percent decline in the population of New York. The east and west north central areas similarly lagged far behind the national growth rate by the 1970s. For the rest of the country, regional population expansion rates were uniformly higher than the national average.

Both the intensity of differences and the common plight within

Table 6.3 Components of Rate of Growth by Regions, 1950–1980 (percent)

Region	1950–1960		1960–1970		1970–1980		1980–1984	
	Total growth	Net migration	Total growth	Net migration	Total growth	Net migration	Total growth	Net migration
New England	12.8	0.2	12.7	3.0	4.2	0.2	1.8	0.0
East North Central	19.2	2.3	11.1	-0.4	3.5	-3.2	-0.2	-3.0
West North Central	9.5	-5.8	6.0	-3.9	5.3	-.7	1.9	-1.1
Mid-Atlantic	13.2	1.0	8.9	0.2	-1.1	-4.9	1.0	-0.7
South Atlantic	22.6	3.1	18.1	5.1	20.4	13.7	6.7	4.2
East South Central	4.9	-12.6	6.3	-5.8	14.5	6.5	2.5	-0.3
West South central	16.2	-4.3	14.0	-0.2	22.9	12.8	9.9	5.2
Mountain	35.0	10.9	20.9	4.5	37.2	25.1	10.4	4.8
Pacific	40.2	21.8	25.3	12.1	19.7	11.9	7.5	3.3

Source: Gregory Jackson, George Masnick, Roger Bolton, Susan Bartlett, and John Pitkin, *Regional Diversity: Growth in the United States, 1960–1990* (Boston, Mass.: Auburn House, 1981); and *Current Population Reports*, Series P-25, no. 970, 1985.

Table 6.4 Population Growth Rates, Relative to U.S. Average, 1950–1984

Region	1950-60	1960-70	1970-80	1980-84
Northeast	71	73	1	28
New England	69	95	36	42
Maine	35	18	120	66
New Hampshire	79	166	223	145
Vermont	15	114	135	85
Massachusetts	56	84	0	26
Rhode Island	49	89	-2	38
Connecticut	137	150	23	35
Middle Atlantic	72	67	-9	8
New York	73	68	-33	23
New Jersey	133	138	24	47
Pennsylvania	44	34	5	7
North Central	87	72	35	9
East North Central	103	83	30	-4
Ohio	117	76	12	-9
Indiana	96	89	52	2
Illinois	84	82	25	16
Michigan	118	106	38	-47
Wisconsin	83	93	58	31
West North Central	51	45	45	45
Minnesota	78	90	63	50
Iowa	28	22	28	-2
Missouri	51	67	46	45
North Dakota	14	-17	51	123
South Dakota	24	-16	33	52
Nebraska	38	40	52	54
Kansas	76	24	46	73
South	89	106	175	164
South Atlantic	122	136	179	159
Delaware	77	78	77	73
Marland	165	198	67	73
Virginia	108	131	134	128
West Virginia	-39	-46	106	2
North Carolina	68	91	140	114
South Carolina	72	68	183	135
Georgia	79	127	172	161
Florida	347	265	390	300
East South Central	27	47	127	59
Kentucky	20	50	123	13
Tennessee	44	80	152	16
Alabama	40	43	116	12
Mississippi	1	14	123	13
West South Central	89	105	201	235
Arkansas	-35	64	169	64
Louisiana	111	95	138	145
Oklahoma	27	78	163	214
Texas	126	130	244	295
West	210	181	209	197
Mountain	189	156	326	247
Montana	79	23	120	111
Idaho	75	56	287	142
Wyoming	77	7	374	211
Colorado	171	192	250	238
New Mexico	193	58	250	221
Arizona	335	258	478	292
Utah	152	142	342	309
Nevada	352	451	571	328
Pacific	217	188	173	178
Washington	105	150	189	123
Oregon	85	143	233	38
California	236	195	166	197
Alaska	317	239	291	581
Hawaii	132	168	228	183

Source: Advisory Commission on Intergovernmental Relations, 1980, table 9; 1980 census of Population and Housing; *Current Population Reports*, series P-25, no. 970, Advance Reports, U.S. Summary

regions seems to have accelerated in the 1970s. While in the 1950s and 1960s, substantial heterogeneity of growth experience was to be found within the southern and mountain states, by the 1970s all were growing more rapidly than the national norm, if Maryland, Delaware, and District of Columbia are excluded. The other exceptions were the three northernmost states in New England—Maine, New Hampshire, and Vermont, all of which increased their populations substantially in the 1970s. In fact on a state-by-state basis, two clean lines could be drawn through the nation's map dividing those regions with greater than average national population growth in the 1970s from those with less (see figure 6.2).

Not only had growth rate differentials worsened by the early 1970s, which clearly gave impetus to regional organizing efforts, but the gap appears to be quite durable. Rates of growth between the Northeast and the Sunbelt diverged even further in the second half of the 1970s. In the early 1980s, the Pacific and west south central regions increased their lead over the national average, while the north central and east south central regions slipped even farther behind.

A SUMMARY AND REFLECTION

The evidence presented in the previous section suggests an interpretation of regional growth differentials in the 1970s as follows. Northeast-

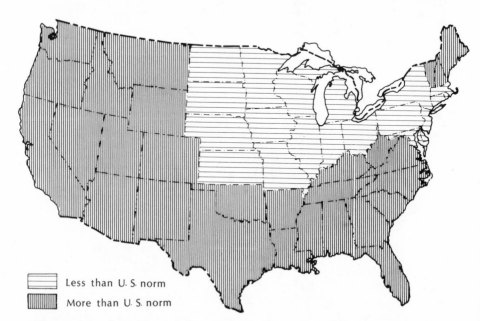

Less than U. S. norm
More than U. S. norm

Figure 6.2 Population Growth Above and Below the U.S. Norm, 1970–1980.

ern decline was associated with an overconcentration of profit-squeezed sectors, and southern and western development with the overlap of three tendencies: (1) the emergence of new centers of superprofit industries, both natural resource and nonresource based; (2) the attraction of profit-squeezed sectors to lower cost areas; and (3) the centrifugal distribution of military expenditures. By the 1980s, New England and the greater New York region had revived, albeit at less than average growth rates and without recouping the losses of the 1970s, on the basis of military-linked expansion and internationally linked business services respectively.

As I have shown in the historical chapters above, regional economic temperaments are a function not only of industrial mix, but also of sectoral dynamics. Of course, these dynamics are preconditioned by unique inherited socioeconomic structures formed in earlier eras. The historical discussion of the North versus the South in chapter 4 shows how distinctive modes of production endowed each region with characteristics that become formative in later stages of economic development. A prime example is the retarding influence that slavery had on southern capitalist development and the subsequent fetter which racism proved to be in the evolution of unionism and a social wage. Indeed, the dispersion hypothesis in the profit cycle argument is predicated upon the existence of lower cost regions to which cost-sensitive sectors in later stages could remove.

A rich and controversial literature debates the role of such "features of regions" in explaining recent capitalist development patterns.[17] The sectoral approach stressed here is designed not to supplant, but rather to complement an approach which first inquires into the characteristics of a place. In the late 1970s and early 1980s, a long overdue literature emerged which argued that regions' fortunes must be studied by looking beyond their boundaries at larger international and industrial forces, as this and the preceding chapter have done. However, the evolved cultures and political structures with which regions meet these larger forces play a considerable role in filtering and modifying their course. Regionalist politics is, of course, one of these.

What normative conclusions can be drawn from this chapter? The data clearly document divergent regional economic growth rates, but do not necessarily prove divergent well-being. The regions whose growth rates have languished in recent years are also those regions whose wealth and income levels have been consistently higher than the national average. Per capita income levels, in fact, have converged dramatically over the course of this century, as figure 6.3 indicates. While significant differentials still characterize class (and ethnic, race, and gender) composition and well-being within regions, this trend is nonetheless striking. For one thing, it shows that great inequalities among regions existed in the past, too, although they were more apt to be registered in disparate standards of living rather than rates of growth. Furthermore, the

Percentage of U. S. Average

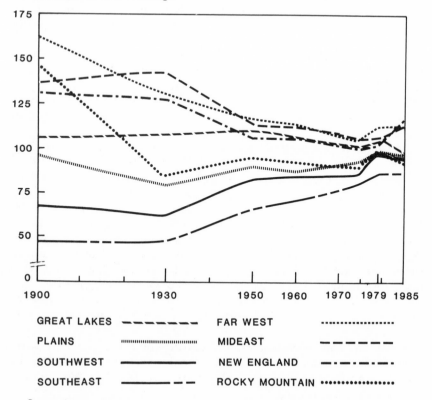

GREAT LAKES ——————   FAR WEST ··················

PLAINS ⅲⅲⅲⅲⅲⅲⅲⅲⅲⅲ   MIDEAST —————

SOUTHWEST ————————   NEW ENGLAND —·—·—·—·

SOUTHEAST ————— — —   ROCKY MOUNTAIN ··················

Source: Advisory Commission on Intergovernmental Relations, Significant Features of Fiscal Federalism, 1987, 1980.

Figure 6.3   Regional Per Capita Income as a Percent of U.S. Average, Selected Years (ACIR).

greatest narrowing of this differential occurred in the period from 1930 to 1950—that is, during the period of substantial federal government guidance of the national economy through the depression and war. In the postwar period, differentials have continued to narrow, but the pace has slackened.

The phenomenon of interregional per capita income convergence has been the subject of hotly debated interpretations. On the one hand, some take it to mean that capitalism does indeed operate in the direction of spatial equilibrium and that normatively, recent growth rates must be judged positive because they achieve this gain in equity.[18] Others argue that per capita income is not a good measure of well-being, since it ignores costs of living differentials which are significantly higher in northern regions.[19] Still others deny any equilibrating impulse in capitalist growth and argue instead that the present convergence is merely the illusion of two trains headed toward each other on adjacent tracks.[20] In my view, the evidence demonstrates simply that capitalist development may indeed produce spatial convergence in developmental outcomes, a tendency entirely consistent with both Marxist and neoclassical contentions that capitalists will endeavor to pay as low a wage (and rent and interest) as possible (Markusen 1977). Such convergence is also compatible with increasing heterogeneity in sectoral composition.

In short, there is no contradiction between a relative convergence in income and an intensification of regional politics. Equalization may occur through processes which require dramatic changes which are politically salient for all the regions involved. Large numbers of local private businesses depend upon capitalist growth for their profitability—especially construction, real estate, utilities (at least under planning practices to date), communications, and transportation. Other depend upon maintenance of employment in other sectors to provide orders from business or consumer clients, as in the case of residential sectors, retail and wholesaling, and services. These sectors provide a ready-made lobby for growth and are presumably quick to join displaced workers and even the indigenous owners of dispersing or abandoning sectors in a regional political effort at rejuvenation. And on the growth side, too rapid rates of development provoke other kinds of conflict which may surface at the regional level. These political manifestations are the topic of the next chapter. Certainly, the regional coalitions examined in the final part of this book are a product, more than of any other cause, of widely disparate growth experience in the postwar U.S. economy.

Notes

1. See Allaman and Birch (1975), Garnick in Chinitz (1978, 151), and Harrison (1982, 36–37).
2. Examples of published volumes concerned with the New England economy in these two periods are Council of Economic Advisors (1951), Miernyk (1954), Estall (1966), Eisenmengar (1967), and Kinnard (1968).
3. See Vernon (1960) for a summary of the New York study.
4. For an excellent review of the New England case, see Harrison (1981).
5. See Liner and Lynch (1977) for evidence on these trends, especially the article by Miernyk.
6. For a detailed account of this subregion and its economic structure, see Markusen (1978). Sale (1975) identifies the six pillars of the Southern Rim economy as agribusiness, defense, electronics, oil, real estate and leisure. Markusen and Schoenberger (1982) survey the history of agriculture and mining and present a framework for sectoral analysis.
7. Tyner and Wallace (1978) offer a full-length case study on western coal. See Kroll (1981) for a bibliography of boomtown effects as well as an empirical

account of the distribution of boomtown costs and benefits across disparate population groups.

8. See Gottlieb and Wiley (1982), Peirce (1972), and Pratt and Ward (1978) for additional power structure characterizations of western states.

9. See Markusen (1978) for an extended analysis of rent in western energy regions.

10. See Stillwell (1969). The reader should keep in mind that this latter point reveals clearly how the shift share technique is not really an explanatory model but a method for decomposing regional growth experience into its constituent elements. For the most recent reviews of the technique, see Stevens and Moore (1980), and Dawson (1981).

11. A location quotient expresses the degree to which employment (or value-added or income) in a region is under- or overrepresented compared to the national norm. A quotient of 1.00 means that the share of that region's total employment accounted for by a sector matches the national rate. A greater rate shows disproportionate concentration of a sector in that region.

12. See similar conclusions for more highly aggregated data in Clark (1980, 111–25). While Miernyk used his quotients for a different purpose, the calculations which he has made are useful for viewing sectoral specialization. Among the more interesting of his figures is that fact that services are more concentrated in the New England and Middle Atlantic regions than in other regions and that this specialization increased from 1969 to 1975, raising questions about the presumed service-led dynamism of the Sunbelt.

13. Norton and Rees (1979) show that some of the shifting is occurring in newer, innovative sectors, perhaps linked to defense expenditures. See also Bergman and Goldstein's (1983) results for metropolitan economies.

14. Other factors such as high energy prices and personal locational preferences also affect these indicators; the profit cycle model is not designed to explain *all* interregional variation.

15. Glickman's (1977) simulations support this argument for the Philadelphia region.

16. For evidence on recent migration trends see Morrison (1980). The conceptual problems are nicely covered in both Muth (1971) and Morrison.

17. Recent contributions, which survey the controversy as well, include Jusenius and Ledebur (1976), Bluestone and Harrison (1980), Weinstein and Firestine (1978), Sternlieb and Hughes (1976, 1978), Birch (1980), Storper (1982), Perry and Watkins (1980), Clark (1978), Mollenkopf (1981), and Watkins and Perry (1977). See Massey (1984) for forceful statement that both sectors and places must constitute primary objects of study for a fully satisfactory regional analysis.

18. See for instance Williamson (1980) and Weinstein and Firestine (1978).

19. See the Northeast-Midwest Institute (1978). A longer run historical discussion of this question can be found in Williamson (1980, 47–53).

20. This colorful analogy is offered by Perry and Watkins (1980, 117). The critique of convergence theory is discussed in chapter 2 above.

7

Economic Impulses to Regional Politics

The economic differentiation of regional space is capable of prompting regionally based politics. In this chapter I explore the translation of postwar economic events into emergent spatial conflicts, particularly those that have taken an explicitly regional form. This chapter presents a framework which uses features of regional economies, as outlined in chapters 5 and 6, to identify the probable members (and opponents) of a regional coalition or conflict and the specific planning and policy issues addressed. The framework also delineates the nature of the political claims put forward and the level of the state to which they are carried. It also permits an assessment of the probable strength of coalition membership, its degree of militance, its goals, and strategy.

In the chapters that follow, this analysis of regional politics is applied to several postwar U.S. cases. Chapters 8 and 9 analyze three suprastate regional organizations that emerged in the 1970s—the Western Governors' Policy Office, Northeast-Midwest Institute, and the Southern Growth Policies Board. Each is shown to be a product of distinct economic stresses upon which each region's unique cultural and political features have been brought to bear. In the final chapter, the emerging geopolitics of defense-based differentiation are sketched out.

The relationships between economic structure and regional politics hypothesized here are not meant to assert that the former is the sole, nor even the primary, determinant of regional politics. As chapter 3 has made clear, traditions that for want of a better term we have called "cultural" are quite significant ingredients in regional struggles. The presence or absence of a unifying culture, a tradition of militance, or a prevailing ideology for or against private enterprise can be the determining factor in the generation or outcome of a particular conflict.[1] Furthermore, not all cases of economic stress will provoke regional conflict. Some conflicts will be fought out solely within sectors, between labor and capital, or among fractions of both, and some will never produce any form of conflict at all.

I do argue that economic differentiation and change are important, often dominant, elements in most regional struggles and that they

139

produce generalizable tendencies toward specific forms of regional politics. Even where the central demands of a region are "noneconomic" in nature (examples are the Catalonian demand for the adoption of Catalan in schools, and the Welsh and Irish desire to reinstitute ancient Gaelic tongues), the basis for the conflict and its emergence at a particular juncture can generally be shown to be highly shaped by underlying economic forces.[2] The framework presented here is designed primarily to trace the specifically economic impulses to regionalism.

Second, this analysis of regionalism is specifically tailored to the contemporary United States. Modern American political structure is a particularly important contextual factor. Since regionalism consists of a set of territorial claims levied on the State, its possible forms and content depend upon the structure of that State and what kinds of territorial politics it currently permits. In the United States, the three-tiered nature of the State, with its federal, state, and local levels, is a primary element assumed in the treatment. Crucial aspects for postwar regional politics include the following: intergovernmental boundaries; intergovernmental allocation of responsibilities and resources; functional rules such as representative democracy; the division of powers among the executive, legislature, and courts; the dual commitment to private property rights and civil liberties; and the two-party system. In the case studies, these various elements will be scrutinized when they are central to the interpretation.[3]

SECTORAL STIMULANTS TO REGIONALISM

In the first place, regional political issues often emerge from the dynamics and nature of individual economic sectors set within the larger events of the international economy. Sectors in specific stages of the profit cycle outlined above manifest a tendency toward certain forms of regional politics. These vary by the nature of the issues raised, the protagonist members of a coalition, and the level of the state to which the demands are addressed. Furthermore, each type of sector—resource, producer, and consumer-oriented—tends to draw together a unique set of combatants, who in turn shape the course of regional politics.

In particular, sectors in two distinct phases of the profit cycle may fuel a major regional conflict. The two correspond to the rapid growth and rapid decline stages of an industry's evolution. At either of these points in time, extraordinary changes in employment (up or down), heavy demands upon resources, and severe multiplier effects on local businesses and residents may culminate in a new form of regional politics, either internally or supraregionally. The major elements of this model of regional politics are tabulated in table 7.1. Throughout the following discussion, examples from recent U.S. history will be drawn upon to illustrate the argument.

Table 7.1 Coalition Membership, Issues and Unity Associated with Profit Cycle Stages

Stages	Coalition Members and opponents	Major issues	Level of government most to least involved	Degree of internal unity within region
II	Incoming corporations, Progrowth coalition vs. residentialists and Traditional Sectors business interests linked to traditional sectors	Land use Infrastructure Environment Housing	1—Local 2—State 3—National	Low
IV/V Region of exit	Workers and local business vs. transregional corporations and other regions	Reinvestment Capital controls Compensation Adjustment aid	1—National 2—State 3—Local	High
III/IV Region of entry	Regional business	Maintenance of low wages and taxes Growth management Unionization	1—State 2—Local 3—National	High

Rapidly Expanding Sectors

Sectors in initial—that is, innovative and growth—stages will tend to produce predeominantly intraregional and local planning conflicts. The primary struggles will surround the transfer and use of local resources. First of all, corporations in the new sectors are apt to bid up the prices for land, labor, and water as they put pressure on an existing stock of these resources. Second, a derived pressure on local resources will operate through the expanded work force, if inmigration accompanies the new sectors' growth, exacerbating the direct growth effects of the sector itself. The housing stock may become inadequate and therefore prohibitively expensive. The transportation system may become overloaded, causing significant delays, wasting communting time, and increasing air pollution. Under these conditions, in an unrestricted capitalist system, the pricing mechanism will tend to shift resources from prior users to new sectors. Those who own the resourcs may be expected to favor the entry of the new sectors, since this development may enhance their wealth. For those sectors and subsistence users whose viability required access to these resources at their previously lower price, and for those who worked in such sectors, the growth or entry of new sectors may be viewed with hostility.

The state becomes the forum for confrontation and arbitration of these issues for two reasons. First of all, it makes decisions regarding the use of land, through regulation of property transfers, permission to change land uses, and permission to build. Second, it makes decisions regarding the public investment that is required for an expanding sector to be viable.[4] Expansion generally requires significant new investment in roads, water, and sewerage, expanded protection services, and new commercial and residential infrastructure. Since both these functions are local responsibilities in the United States, struggle around the transfer and use of resources tends to organize itself around the local level. Thus in initial profit cycle stages, regional politics tends to be intraregional, focused on land use and public investment issues, and composed of pro-growth and slow- or antigrowth coalitions with a distinct sectoral character.

Two exceptions to this pattern may be mentioned at the outset. First, to the extent that the incoming sector is so large that its impact over-reaches local jurisdictional boundaries, it will tend to push the conflict up to the next highest level, in this case the state. If the supralocal impact is differentiated across units, then conflict between the local governments involved may emerge as well, since each may have different dominant coalitions. An example is the energy boomtown phenomenon in which one town hosts the tax-base-enhancing plant or mine while another is burdened with the housing, school, and public-service demands of a growing population of the plant's workers. In cases where jurisdictions suffer the same impact, they may join together in a statewide coalition, or they may still differ about the course of action, depending upon the importance of the particular sector within the region or on the class composition of the community, discussed below.

The second exception is the case in which the federal government owns a significant share of the land whose future is being debated. This is a critical factor in conflict over western U.S. energy development. Since the federal government is a major, sometimes the sole, landowner, it governs the land use issue—who gets it, the terms of using the land (lease stipulations), the price of that use (royalties and rent), and the share that the local jurisdiction will recoup. When federal land is involved, regional conflict around changes in the agricultural, energy, and tourism sectors necessarily involves conflict at the federal, state, and local levels.

Three quite disparate examples of this type of sectorally based re-gional politics can be offered. First, the combination of fast-growing aerospace, electronics, computer, and software sectors in Santa Clara Valley south of San Francisco has set off a process of dramatic competi-tion for land and human resources. The price of land has been bid up so high that firms are increasing workspace densities by building upward and putting two workers in a space previously occupied by one. The lure of the area's concentration of professional-technical jobs has drawn many well-educated inmigrants who have bid up the price of housing, causing particularly severe problems for lower income groups. The area's transportation system has become clogged as workers take on longer and longer commutes. The quality of the air suffers as a consequence. The net result has been a strong residentialist movement to limit the addition of new industrial space—the first example of industrial growth controls in the country. It has also spawned a countermovement by real estate and industrial interests to eliminate environmental and community controls that hamper the construction of new housing.[5]

A second example is the western energy boomtown case, perhaps best exemplified by the remarkable events in southeastern Montana coal fields in the mid-1970s. Here, extensive strip mining and accompanying coal-fired electricity plants raised significant opposition from ranchers, Native Americans, and oldtime members of the community. Issues included land use (especially federal leasing provisions), air quality (a landmark court case stopped construction on two major power plant units), financing of local infrastructure (solved with a 30 percent severance tax on coal mined), and control of development (met with statewide siting legislation). Both interjurisdiction disputes and federal land ownership helped carry the issues from the local level to the state and federal levels.[6]

A third set of examples, less well documented but clearly emerging, are the conflicts in areas where military-related production brings a boom to local economies. One of the factors underlying the City of Santa Monica's strong rent control movement is the upward pressure on housing prices in west Los Angeles Basin communities caused by the burgeoning defense and space-related complexes in El Segundo and other nearby communities. Similarly, opposition to developers' carte blanche is growing in cities like Colorado Springs, as a similar boom propels the rapid conversion of the high plains into sprawling bedroom communities for defense and space-related branch plants.

Sectors in Decline

Sectors in mature and declining stages are apt to produce both intraregional unity and interregional conflict in the region of origin. The tendency toward internal unity arises from the damaging effect that one or more sectors' decline has on an entire local or regional economy, through the depressing effect of its payroll withdrawal on other regional businesses and on the budgets of local and state governments. In this case, it is possible to win the adherence of local businesses, especially those whose assets and markets are unalterably fixed locally. Churches, local banks with lots of mortgage money tied up in local residential and commercial real estate, real estate firms, local insurance salesmen, newspapers whose circulation is purely local—all those institutions that I have identified as the potential territorial lobby above—have an incentive to join ranks with workers displaced from that sector, as well as other local suppliers who sold only to the shutdown sector, such as janitorial services, parts makers, guard services, accountants, and lawyers. Local unity is further abetted by the fact that the immediately offending party is often an outside corporation or conglomerate. This fact tends to generate a form of nativism where the corporation, rather than the capitalist development process, becomes the villain.[7]

If sectoral decline or sectorally related issues are so severe that the entire economic base of a region is threatened, a cross-ethnic working-class coalition may gain control of a government previously in the hands of the region's dominant but exiting or absent capitalists. Examples are successful political challenges at the regional level by iron ore miners on the Mesabi Range in the early twentieth century, by gold miners in the Cripple Creek district of Colorado in the same era, and at the state level by copper workers and farmers in Montana in the 1970s. Generally, however, pure cases of working-class control are infrequent, because some ensemble of business interests almost always complicates regional politics.

Sectors in profit-squeezed stages generate problems for their home regions that readily prompt demands for a policy or planning response at the national level. In contrast, newer, superprofit sectors create pressures that are more often fought out within the region. There are several reasons for this. In the case of outmigration of capital, or sudden plant closings, money capital is not operating within the region, but outside of it. Thus the only resort for a region with a coalition wishing to oppose the outmigration of a sector is to raise the issue in the state forum that governs the larger territory across which sectoral change is occurring.[8]

In the case of newer sectors, the money capital bidding for resources is entering, rather than leaving the region. Thus the terms of its entry are more apt to be written within the region. If an oppositional group succeeds in deploying some mechanism of the local state, such as zoning, to slow its entry or expansion, the growing sector is more apt to possess the resources and motivation to compromise, compensate, buy off, and restructure its plans. In chapter 10, we shall see how this is particularly true of the energy-rich western regions.

Second, the conventional mechanisms for intervening in or softening the pace and intensity of capital migration are mostly not tools of local government. Local tax concessions have been employed to try to convince corporations not to move or to rebuild locally, as in the recent case of GM and Detroit. But most routes require powers and resources not available to the local government. Most cost-reducing measures, for instance, such as better transportation infrastructure or a better trained labor force, are the domain of the bureaucracy of state governments. Measures aimed at stimulating demand, such as import protection, are the province of the national government. Even the power to regulate bargaining between labor and management, another route to dealing with decline, resides at the federal level. Thus the traditional division of powers renders state mechanisms for response to the case of decline more inaccessible than in the growth case.

Third, the complexion of local politics differs sharply in the two cases. In the case off a newly emergent sector, we can expect that those with a base in the older sectors may have a strong hold on the machinery of local government, so that their chances of successful protection of their interests are better. Ranchers in western boomtowns are a good example. In the case of an outmigrating sector, the local government is more likely to have been a collaborator with that sector, through campaign financing, local business ties, and old family connections; thus a prior, it is more difficult for a coalition of the displaced to win a vigorous partisanship from local politicians and their bureaucracies. Unless an unusual turnover has liberalized the prevailing administration and changed the course of its politics (which was true at the state level in Montana), a coalition around plant closings may seek to pursue its cause at higher levels of government. Its success, of course, depends on its antagonists' power at that level as well.

Finally, more radical responses to sectoral decline, such as plant takeovers or economic revitalization, require massive amounts of capital, not only to purchase initially the physical plant vacated by the outgoing sectors but also to refurbish or modernize it. Such funds are not generally available at the local level, particularly when the region is suffering the rounds of economic base shrinkage that follow a sector's wane. In Detroit, an early 1980s proposal to reshape the area's economy on new metal-bending sectors with greater expansionary promise would have committed a large chunk of federal resources to the transition.[9]

The Youngstown case in the late 1970s is an outstanding illustration. When two major steel companies announced the shutdown of multiple facilities within the short span of two years, a broad-based worker-religious-small business coalition was formed. Its object was to reopen the mills, if possible. It forged substantial internal unity, in large part by critiquing the behavior of outside corporations. The coalition correctly understood that to achieve the levels of reinvestment required, they would have to carry their case to the federal government. In the end, the effort failed, both because the steel industry had close ties to the Carter administration and because federal grants to alternative economic development enterprises undercut the business communities' support for the coalition. However, a more sophisticated effort has emerged in Pittsburgh's Steel Valley Authority initiative.[10]

Once escalated to the national level, the politics of regionalism around declining sectors tends to generate two kinds of conflict over the use of the national government to bolster up that region's economy. First of all, the sector whose exit is being protested will generally argue its case through existing bureaucratic and political links. Thus a conflict between workers and the community on the one hand, and the corporations within that sector on the other, emerges at the national level within forums of the state. The balance of this struggle depends upon the support that each contestant gets from other groups in the society. While other corporations will generally support the right of corporations in any particular sector to move, occasional cases may emerge where other sectors support the challenge because of potential adverse effects for them as suppliers or customers. Regional railroads, for instance, may favor the retention of steelmaking capacity or textile firms in the Northeast; northeastern regional utilities are desperate for coal mining to continue in Appalachia versus the West. A well-developed interregional intersectoral coalition around plant closings has not yet developed, but might in the future, a subject we return to in chapter 8.

Regions into which mature sectors are relocating will tend to display a hybrid politics which incorporates elements of each of the two major types just presented. As growth areas, problems of land and resource use will tend to preoccupy them internally. When growth management issues spill over local or state boundaries, they will create pressure for regionwide responses. On these questions, internal regional unity will be strong, led by the indigenous business community. On the other hand, growth management generates significant public sector expenditure demands and erodes the low tax rate which drew relocating firms in the first place. Internal conflict will be greatest around economic features that make the region attractive to profit-squeezed sectors—the low cost of labor (and the absence of unionization), the low cost of land, and the low level of public sector liability. A business-dominated coalition can be expected to place maintenance of its good "business climate" as a central regional planning goal.

Conflict between two regions who are competing over the same mature sectors—one as original host and the other as recent host—will emerge over questions of interregional compensation and aid. Opposition by the latter to national petitions by the former for reinvestment funds, indemnities, controls on capital movement, and amplified aid, may be joined by regions enjoying expansion in innovative sectors. Both types of growth regions will be unsympathetic to demands for channeling public resources to declining regions, on the grounds that the same national resources could better be used to treat their growth problems. This interregional conflict will be exacerbated if the newer, expanding regions are generally relatively underdeveloped—that is, if they have lower standards of living, less developed public sectors, and a higher incidence of poverty. We shall see in chapter 8 that this was the case in the United States in the 1970s.

In the face of this second form of interregional conflict, the internal politics of the regions of origin may change again. If convinced that the battle is over either (1) national policies to bolster the industry (through extended tax breaks or import protection) or (2) the distribution of federal aid among regions, then displaced regional groups, especially workers, may be convinced to join their corporate employers in lobbying for such protection, in the first case, or their regional politicians in arguing for a bigger share of the federal pie in the second case. In the case studies that follow, the tendency toward these different configurations are explored.

Differences by Sectoral Type

In addition to the importance of the stage of maturity of a sector in its profit cycle, the orientation of a sector also influences regional politics. Two distinctions useful for this purpose are natural resource- versus nonresource-dependent sectors, and producer versus consumer goods sectors. The regional issues and their protagonists can be more closely specified by disaggregating sectors in this manner.

Growing or incoming natural resource-based sectors will tend to place competition for such resources at the heart of regional conflict. That is, parties to the conflict will be struggling over the *direct* rather than *indirect* effects of the expanding sector on local natural resources. Furthermore, the most important supply factor at issue will be these resources, particularly land but also water and air quality, rather than labor. Opponents of the incoming sector's aims will be the previous users of these same resources. In the case of intermountain energy development, for instance, the opposition to oil shale, coal stripping, and coal-fired power generation has come from agriculturalists who compete for the same land and water, and the tourist industries and nature lovers who compete for the same environment.

Second, the new sector's demands on the local public sector will be more sharply etched at the local leve, and will focus on production-serving infrastructure. Second round, or indirect, impacts will be important as well, but will tend to take a secondary place behind these immediate conflicts. To the extent that they do become important, they can usually be identified as associated with the growth sector, and may thus become candidates for bargaining with the sector.

Two differences between nonrenewable and renewable resource sectors stand out. First, many sectoral changes in renewable resources do not require a change of ownership or personnel—the obvious case is changes in crop patterns in agriculture. This would diminish regional conflict. Second, the disruption sure to come with exhaustion is not at issue.

The local politics of sectoral confrontation in the natural resource case is complicated if a previously residing group has an ownership claim to the resource while at the same time depending for income upon competing economic uses of the land. Land ownership offers the oldtimer group an opportunity to cash in on the new resource-based activity by extracting some of the superprofits through land rents or sale price.[11]

Several groups come to mind. In the western energy development case, both ranchers and Native American tribes frequently find themselves in this contradictory position. Since sale or lease of land by some members of each group may diminish the income-earning, environmental, or communitarian possibilities for other members, internal strife within these groups may occur. Alternatively, the leverage a group possesses by its ownership of land may enable it to bargain for better jobs in the new land use, such as Native American requirements for quota-hiring reservation members.

In the case of fast-growing, nonresource-dependent sectors, regional conflicts may more often be associated with *indirect* impacts, cycled through the local economy in the form of increased demands on the local housing stock, services for residents, and the commuter-based transportation network. These "urban" impacts are less unambiguously harmful to any particular workplace group; rather than competing with another sector, they tend to produce conflicts between the workers as residents of the region, whose quality of life is deteriorating, and the management of the sector. This conflict may be expressed as environmentalist or no-growth movements.

On the other hand, it is also possible for these aggregate consequences of rapid sectoral growth to become problematic to the sector itself, especially if the deterioration in quality of life is responded to by workers in the form of higher wage demands on the region's employers. In Santa Clara Valley, where extraordinary housing costs, the difficulties of commuting, and the deteriorating quality of urban life have raised the cost of labor to electronics firms, the employers have organized into the Santa Clara County Manufacturers Group, which lobbies for more housing and competes to mold the industrial land-use issues toward its ends (Saxenian 1980). Even in this case, however, the regional politics of the sector itself will most likely diverge from that of its worker-residents, who will levy much different demands on the local government's planning and budgeting process.

In the nonresource-dependent growth sectors, there may be cleavages within the sectors' workforce as well. Different groups of workers may have differential ties to the community and differing abilities to organize their political claims. In sectors with a bifurcated labor force, between substantial groups of professional-technical labor and blue-collar skilled or semiskilled, for instance, or between skilled and unskilled workers (exacerbated by racism), the former groups may be better able to afford the better housing, including locations closer to work (in terms of travel time), to demand salaries or wages to cover escalating housing costs, and to finance local government campaigns. If white-collar, this group may be more apt to consist of people without long-term community goals or commitment, with career goals interregional in nature, and more concerned with property values than with the maintenance of community. The longer the history of the blue-collar workforce in the area, the larger its presence in the sector, and the better organized it is, the more apt it is to have a significant hand in local government land-use and expenditure decisions.[12]

Among declining natural resource-dependent sectors, significant differences in regional politics by sector type can also be hypothesized. The protagonists in each case are apt to be similar—the constituency organizing around a plant closing or sectoral withdrawal will consist of workers in those sectors, members of middle management whose jobs are also at stake, small businessmen in or directly related to the sectors involved, and those classes whose incomes and wealth are derived from direct provision of commodities to the declining sectors and their workforce. In natural resource-based industries, however, there may be a larger constituency of small producers (such as farmers, fishermen, and small lumbering operations) engaged in regional politics than would be the case in most nonresource-dependent industries[13]—the historical product of frontier settlement policies in the nineteenth century.

The substantive issues of regional politics may be significantly different as well. Nonrenewable resource–based sectors have little or no chance to raise the issue of plant reopening or economic revitalization, since the resource will have been economically depleted. This is particularly true when the communities, as in a mining region, are remote from major centers and where a labor pool has been creeated just to extract that resource. In cases where a substantial fixed plant exists (farms, for instance), a regional coalition may have as its goal a set of policies or actions that will permit the start-up of the sector once again, or the use of that productive facility in the cultivation or manufacture of another commodity. The political issues that emerge in each case will be different in kind.

In the nonrenewable resource case, demands will be restricted to requests for the State to intervene in the market for the resulting commodity (through price supports, import controls, government purchase, or land banking) or to act directly to reduce one or more costs of production (tax breaks, government research, cheaper public land rents, more liberal land-use rules, or improved transportation). Recent pressure by the large Pacific Northwest lumber corporations (and sawyer unions) on the National Forest Service to abandon its sustained yield policy, which has increasingly squeezed the profitability of area lumbering, is an example.

While demands for subsidizing a traditional sector may also arise from regions with other types of industries, communities with nonrenewable and one-sector economic bases will have fewer choices. In regions with other alternatives, efforts to attract new sectors may overshadow last-ditch efforts to salvage a declining sector. Cotton fields can be converted to other crops, as in the case of soybeans above, or peanuts in an earlier era. Industrial plants have been converted from one use to another. Another important distinction may hold between the producer and consumer goods industries on the decline end of the profit cycle. In the case of consumer products, it is sometimes possible for a regional coalition of both capital and labor to mount a successful regional or national campaign on the part of consumers to favor the products of an industry simply because it will help save jobs in particular communities. An example of this is the effort by small regional breweries to develop regional pride in their local beer (Iron City, in Pittsburgh, for instance). Another is the effort by the auto manufacturers and unions around the country to convince consumers to "buy American" and save Detroit. Alternatively, if a plant threatens to close or has already closed, a consumer boycott may also be threatened and pursued by labor and community groups. This was broadly discussed in Berkeley as a response to the Colgate plant shutdown in 1980–1981. Similar appeals are usually less successful in a producer good industry, where corporate customers are apt to favor the best product at the lowest price regardless of regional consequences or national origin.

The Pace, Spread, and Coincidence of Economic Change

In addition to sector composition and maturity, there are other aspects of economic change which are systematically related to regional politics. First among these is the pace of change experienced at any particular moment. If a region's economic growth or decline is stretched out over a long period of time and is relatively modest in its impacts, the provocation of regional politics is much less likely. It is where the rate of employment change is most sudden and intense that regional politics is most likely to erupt, as in the Youngstown case cited above. The geographical spread of change is also important in determining the intensity and scale of regional response. If employment growth or cutbacks are highly localized, regional politics will tend to operate on a local level. If employment cutbacks are widely spread, even if differentially, the pressure for a response at any one location will be less, but the possibilities for a broader regional or interregional coalition are greater.

Finally, regional organizing around unique economic dilemmas may be transformed into interregional struggle if decline in one region occurs in tandem with growth in another. If the disparate growth paths are the product of a set of mature sectors moving from one to the other, it may become particularly acute. This, we shall see, is the crux of the postwar North-South antagonism. If the neighbor's growth takes place in complementary sectors, the conflict may also be heated, especially if those sectors sell price-escalating inputs to a hard-pressed set of home industries. This is the crux of postwar East-West conflict.

Ownership and Size Dimensions

The size of plants in a local or regional economy is an important ingredient in regional response. Those sectors with particularly large operations, in either the growth or the decline stage, are more apt to provoke place-based politics around entry or exit. An exodus of many small firms, such as the shoe industry from New England, is more difficult to respond to than the exit of one large corporation that closes out or carries with it many jobs. This is partly because of visibility, but also because of the unity of the workforce that derives from having a common employer. Similarly, small coal mines in Appalachia, even if their environmental and resource-competing consequences are similar to those of large mines in the West, are less apt to fuel a regionwide movement. Small firms, even if entering or leaving a region in tandem, tend to call forth fragmented local responses by workers or community groups, rather than regionwide response.

The geographical locations of ownership of dominant sectors are also contributors to the shape of regional conflict. Economies with a high incidence of local ownership will produce more complicated local responses than sectors with absentee ownership. In the former case, local management and owners can be expected immediately to defend plant closings or new activities and to be powerful in local and regional political forums. They may, on the other hand, favor control of overly rapid development or maintenance of existing operations when an absentee ownership might not. Bluestone and Harrison's finding that cases of corporate ownership showed lower rates of net job destruction than small businesses or conglomerates, seems to suggest this (Bluestone and Harrison 1980).[14]

COMMUNITY RECEPTIVITY

The above discussion offers several hypotheses about protagonist factions, planning issues, and political targets of regional struggles associated with distinct economic structure. These operate at a level of generality that permits an elementary understanding of specific instances of regionalism. In reality, each historical case of regionalism possesses a high degree of specificity; in fact, each is unique. Some instances of regionalism may arise primarily from cultural or political impulses, as shown in chapter 2 above.[15] It is not the aim of this section of the book to explain all cases of contemporary regionalism. The aim is rather to explore the economic roots of regional politics in the postwar United States. In keeping with the commitment to regional complexity, the next two chapters analyze how regional economic differences combine with social and political structures to heighten or dampen regionalist activities.

This synthesis is crucial, because similar economic events may evoke a wide range of responses across regions, from silence to full-scale regional war, depending upon the era, the region's history, its culture, and the political possibilities. In this section I review a set of social, political and cultural features of regions that interact with economic events to shape regional strife. The purpose is to show how these features form a filter between economic change and regional politics. In a similar manner, although not explored here, economic structure may act as a catalyst or a retardant to culturally or politically motivated cases of regionalism. The framework presented here is employed in the case studies which follow.

Class Structure

Perhaps the most important key to the response of a community to a dominant change in its economy is its class structure.[16] At its simplest, this means the division of the population among capitalist, small business (including farmers), and working classes. Each class has a direct material interest in community change; class fractions may furthermore be separable along sectoral lines. Second, the question of class homogeneity is important. Business classes can be divided over issues other than those attached to a particular sector; if so, these cleavages may play an important role. A working class can be divided occupationally, by gender, by race, and by ethnicity. The greater these differences, the less likely that unity around a common regional position will occur. Instead, the negotiation of conflict will tend to take place within the region or within the sector with significant intraclass antagonism. Cases where plant closing struggles devolve into fights among union members about the distribution of the severance package are examples. Any study of sectorally based regional politics must include an investigation of class structure.

Class structure also has a dynamic to it. As sectoral composition of an economy changes, so does the proportional representation of groups within it. Long-term stable class structures are more apt to evoke a protest from abrupt economic change, whereas regions that have already been destabilized through massive in- or outmigration will be less apt to engender a self-conscious regional politics. Thus the framework for study includes an overview of changes in class structure over the last few decades and the importance of the sector in question to that change.

The identification of class composition does not necessarily predict political response. In chapter 3, the distinction between class location and consciousness was made. Often, ethnicity, religion, culture, experience, or sexism intervene to temper or override the class interests that a simple model might predict. Again, the proof of the class concept lies in the case-by-case study of regional politics.[17]

Sectoral Specialization

In addition to its class composition, the degree of specialization in a community or region's industrial structure is a principal determinant of its susceptibility to regional politics. Simply put, the hypothesis here is that the more internally homogeneous the community's industrial structure, the more distinct it is from that of other regions, and the larger the share of the region's jobs which fall into such sectors, the greater the tendency toward a sectorally based regional politics.[18] Clearly, a steel plant closing in a small city will have a more disruptive effect than one in a large city. And two cities of equal size will experience a plant's closing differently depending upon the degree of diversification in the economy. Steel closings in Youngstown, Pittsburgh, and Chicago are examples. Youngstown is the smallest of the three, and the most highly dependent on steel. Pittsburgh is much larger, though its dependence on steel is quite great. The Chicago area is a large steel producer, but its economy is much more diversified than those of the other two. Steel plant closings have provoked greater concern and more identifiable movements in Youngstown than in Pittsburgh, and in Pittsburgh than in Chicago.

The significance of local industrial structure is not merely a function of employment in those sectors whose dynamics are unsettling. It is also a function of the degree of linkages between those sectors and others in the economic base. Sectors that sell to and buy directly from the sector in question may be so tightly tied that their economic fortunes move in the same direction. Thus the total ensemble of industries tied together becomes the focus of an investigation of industrial structure. Regions may vary substantially in the degree of such intersectoral linkages, even around a particular industry. Some auto assembly plants are located near parts producers; others are not. Some steel mills are located near fabricators; others are not.[19] Some coal mines spawn coal-fired electricity plants; others do not. The more spatially concentrated such interindustry links are, the more apt is spatial conflict to emerge over sectoral dynamics. Conversely, while growth or deterioration in one sector will affect the fortunes of a supplier or customer elsewhere, agitation around this linkage will not be registered in a territorial form.

Existing Political and Cultural Infrastructure

In addition to these strictly economic features of a region, institutional and organizational characteristics become important shapers of regional politics. These can be grouped roughly into four types: economic institutions (labor unions, business organizations, and agricultural societies); political institutions (local and regional governments and political parties); cultural institutions (churches and community groups); and informational-ideological institutions (the press and universities). Members of these organizations inevitably become involved in regional politics. Even if new organizations spring up, their membership tends to consist of building blocks of preexisting organizations. Understanding the nature, ideology, relative strength, and leadership potential of each of these is central to understanding the outcome of a specific regional struggle.

A brief catalog of these groups, with emphasis on their importance in different circumstances, is in order. Economic groups are clearly of paramount importance. It is these groups that mold internal class unity or dissension on strategy. They are also the basis of representation on many types of economic development bodies that may play a central role in the unfolding of regional politics. Chief among them are labor unions. In addition to the relative strength of unions among the working-class population in an area, the degree of unity and organization across the region's different unions is an important factor (for example, the presence of a strong state or regional federation), together with the degree of unity or dissension between union locals and their internationals. Business groups are also pivotal institutions.[20] Chief among these is the traditional chamber of commerce, which tends to represent the commercial-financial-real estate classes. In cases of rapid regional change, other business groups may present a significant challenge to the former group; farmers' or ranchers' organizations in energy regions and manufacturers' organizations are examples.

Political institutions of paramount importance are the jurisdictional units that govern the area. If a disrupted region is coterminant with one or more local governments, then its chances of pursuing a solution to regional conflict at that level, or at least gaining the support of local government, are enhanced. The powers of that wing of the state government are relevant as well—what powers to tax, spend, adjudicate, and regulate land use does it have? The extent of local bureaucracy, its structure, and the quality of personnel, including locally elected officials, also shape regional politics. Frequently the pressure to create new regional governments or special services districts, or to create state or federal agencies with powers to intervene in land-use and infrastructure decisions, comes from the lack of congruency between existing political structure and the nature of the sectorally induced problem.

Political parties at the local and regional levels also form a critical element in regional sensitivity. In some regions, one party may long have dominated politics; in this case its refusal to espouse a regional issue will be very difficult to counter. But if it does take up the regional banner, it provides a preexisting structure for political cohesion. In other regions, strong and competitive partisan politics may polarize attempts to achieve internal regional unity. On the other hand, a regionwide minority would have a much better chance of receiving political support for its cause, perhaps winning its claims, under such a system. In yet other regions, party structure may be competitive yet weak, creating many openings for new regional coalitions.

Cultural organizations, for want of a better umbrella designation, include community groups of diverse types, environmental groups, and religious organizations. In many cases of regional politics, such groups have been important foci of organizing efforts. Cultural organizations such as churches and community groups can be vehicles for cross-class coalitions that are difficult to engineer via purely economic interests and linkages. Cultural contributions or constraints on the formation of regional politics operate through more informal channels as well—

folklore, belief systems, attitudes toward authority, dialects or language differences, and so on.

Finally, the role of those insitutions whose product is knowledge, information, and/or ideology in a regional political coalition may be extensive. Newspapers, which are private enterprises with both a pro-business and a pro-local ideology, are generally the major opinion creators in the region as a whole. Their commitment to cover and their editorial position on attempts at regional organizing can have a large impact. Universities and other nonprofit research institutions may lend expertise to one or another regional group in their effort to muster support and documentation for their position.

THE CASE STUDIES OF REGIONAL POLITICS

The importance of economic structure and dynamics in prompting regionally based politics, and the roles of cultural and political structure in filtering it, can be demonstrated by looking at specific cases. While the cases that follow are neither broad nor numerous enough to constitute a full-blown test of the framework presented above, they are written to highlight conformance or nonconformance to the individual propositions. The cases chosen are among the most prominent examples of regional movements in the postwar United States. Each constitutes an outstanding example of the emergence of a vigorous regional coalition or conflict around a set of issues emanating from economic change dominated by one or several distinct sectors.

The cases consist of the emergence of three multi-state regional organizations in the 1970s. They include instances of regionalism originating from a them/us interregional challenge as well as those arising from an indigenous challenge. The development of a northeastern regional caucus arose from a round of sudden adversities in several major sectors. Because these were mature sectors, regional leadership centered its partisan efforts on the federal government's resources, provoking in return an adversary relationship with other regions. In the case of the South and the West, nascent regional organizations which had formed to handle regionally specific internal problems reoriented themselves to answer the northeastern initiative. In these latter cases, then, regionalism was rekindled by the emergence of interregional antagonism as much as by internal regional economic dilemmas.

In each of the cases, I begin by presenting the sectoral structure of the region and the contemporary dynamics which have placed that structure under stress. In addition, the class, ethnic, political, and cultural structure is outlined, to set the stage for assessing the transformation of sectoral impulses into regional politics. The three instances of contemporary regional conflict are organized into two chapters, one on the north-south conflict, and one on the east-west antagonism.

Chapters 8 and 9, then, investigate the heightened regionalism and interregional conflict of the 1970s. In addition to examining the economic impulses to regional politics, these chapters address the ways in which regional self-image and cultural cohesion enter into the process of contemporary regional formation. I have been able to detect how the concerns of each region have changed with interregional antagonism and with the fortunes of their respective economies. The planning issues which dominate each generally confirm the hypotheses offered in this chapter, as do the political forums to which the region has addressed its claims. The analysis reveals some striking differences in the ways contemporary regions build their coalitions and their ideologies, differences which express traditions like states' rights and political affinities as well as the current nature of regional problems.

Notes

1. Lynd (1982) emphasizes the importance of a tradition of rank-and-file dissidence as a factor in rustbelt organizing. Metzgar (1980) stresses the same factor in explaining the difference between the community response to the Youngstown and the Johnstown steel closings in the 1970s. Simon (1980) emphasizes ideology as a factor in the failure of a worker-community-ownership strategy to win adherents in Appalachia.
2. Masterful works combining the cultural with the economic have been produced by those working on Wales (Cooke 1981), Appalachia (Whisnant 1979); Clavel 1982), and Catalonia (Vilar 1978).
3. This means that the model may require respecification in the future as the structure of the state changes. It also limits the applicability of the model to other countries, particularly those without a well-developed territorial decentralization of the state apparatus. As I have argued above, this may be the reason for the divergence between Dulong and myself on the possibilities for a progressive regionalism.
4. These two powers of the state are universal across the United States; in addition, the state may become involved in other ways, such as through economic development programs with special subsidies, through urban renewal–type programs, or through labor training.
5. See Saxenian (1980). Greenberg (1986) offers an in-depth analysis of similar growth politics in nearby Livermore, California.
6. See extended discussion of boomtown cases below in chapter 9.
7. The Kelly and Shutes (1977) analysis of Lyke's role in Youngstown, for instance, while accurate, led to an overly anticorporatist interpretation, as if another, nonconglomerate owner would have acted differently. The subsequent closings of U.S. Steel in the same community demonstrate the limits of blaming conglomeration, and shows that the problem may be endemic to steel under its capitalist form of organization.
8. For a provocative view of how product cycle maturation has produced political pressures at a national scale, see Kurth (1979). Since the appropriate territorial scale is increasingly worldwide, there is some question as to the effectiveness of even national planning in a world capitalist system. Harvey (1982, ch. 13) argues that the system as a whole is headed for global crisis and increasing geopolitical instability.

9. See Luria and Russell (1981).
10. See Lynd (1982); Tri-State Conference on Steel (1984).
11. See Markusen (1978) for a full-length treatment of the question of rent in boomtown energy communities.
12. No a priori distinctions between producer and consumer good sectors are hypothesized here.
13. Some nonrenewable resource-based industries are highly monopolized—copper, for instance, or western coal.
14. One can argue, on the other hand, that conglomerates consistently buy up the already mature plant with the express purpose of extracting liquid capital by running it into the ground. If this is the case, then the problem is not just the conglomerate form, but the underlying dynamics of that sector in that location, as I have argued above.
15. There are specifically political dynamics that yield certain kinds of impulses toward regional political formation. I have argued this point of view previously (1979). A further example is the "winner take all" electoral system, which encourages parties to build strong regional bases. For example, the Republican party may have an incentive to use polarizing regional issues to win over marginal states, even by exacerbating antagonisms with New York, because it makes no difference if it loses the latter state by 49 percent or 32 percent of the vote. I am indebted to David Plotke for this latter example.
16. See also the discussion in chapter 2 on class.
17. See Plotke (1980) for an extended discussion of this point, applied to the United States case.
18. A corollary to this point is that community decisionmaking is more pluralistic when its economy is more diversified, an argument made by Prethus (1964) and Clark (1974). Young and Newton (1980) illustrate the nondiversified case with five single-industry case studies.
19. See the assumption by Isard and Kuenne (1952) that metal fabricating firms would cluster around a new steel complex in the Philadelphia area. In fact, the Fairless works, built in the early 1950s, did not succeed in generating major job growth in metal-using industries.
20. See Arsen (1981) for an overview of the literature on business behavior in local government politics.

8

Postwar Regional Cleavage: The North-South Axis

In previous chapters, I have argued that divergence in regional economic fortunes tends to produce interregional antagonism. Furthermore, the intensity of such conflict will be associated with the degree of trauma experienced by one or more of the diverging economies, whether it be explosive growth or painful shrinkage. In this and the following chapter, the two most prominent instances of postwar regionalism are probed to confirm the extent to which the hypotheses outlined above hold.

To recapitulate, briefly, our model of interregional strife predicts that a region falling behind national growth performance, particularly when outmigration of firms and plants is a major cause, will mount a major appeal to federal government for redress. In contrast, a region enjoying a boom, whether due to inmigration of capital or favorable market conditions for the product of capital or its dominant industries, will become preoccupied with internal conflicts generated by pressures on resources.

We have also anticipated that an aggressive regionalism on the part of the former type of region may call forth a responsive, defensive regionalism on the part of the other, however reluctant. This mutuality will be more robust if there exists a previous history of regional hostility. In both types of region, multiplier effects will broaden the base for the region's organizations effort, although the ambiguity in goals introduced by this expansion will tend to produce alternative leadership vying for control and direction of the regional coalition.

Above, I suggest that the vigor of any region's organizing effort will be enhanced by the presence of a strong one-party system and cultural homogeneity. Alternatively, it will be retarded by internal cultural diversity and conflict, or by the presence of a hotly contested two-party system. The more truly federal the political structure within which these regions operate, and the more fairly represented each is in national power, the more apt regionalism is to levy a set of redistributive claims on the central government, for resources and/or power, rather than engendering separatism.

In the postwar period in the United States, regional growth rates began to diverge dramatically, as shown in chapters 5 and 6. The Northeast became a region of exit and decline, while the South and West grew at rates well above the national norm. This era offers us an opportunity to try out our theories about regionalism. Did growing economic divergence lead to renewed regionalism? Have the booming regions been more self-preoccupied while the slow growth regions have been more aggressive nationally? Have old regional antagonisms played a role in this revival? Have the most heavily affected regional elites succeeded in building regionwide support for their programs? Have alternative groupings emerged to contest regional leadership? Have political parties, cultures, business cycles, and federal structures played the role ascribed to them?

As regional experience diverged in the 1970s, three new and highly publicized regional organizations were formed to address the common interests of their constituents and to marshall energies behind a common platform: The Northeast-Midwest Congressional Coalition (NMCC), the Southern Growth Policies Board (SGPB), and the Western Governor's Policy Office (WGPO). Their official jurisdictions consisted of the states outlined in figure 6.1 above.[1] These three organizations became the chief mouthpieces for articulating the unique needs of each region. Procedurally, I chose to research the context, the issues, the organizational effort, the achievements of, and the challenges to each of these.

Two major areas of interregional antagonism emerged in this period. The first was a struggle over the disposition of federal aid and spending on a geographical basis, a predominantly north-south battle which is the subject of this present chapter. The second was a struggle over the terms on which western energy will be developed, as western regional interests tried to wrangle themselves a better deal from their federal government landlord and from the energy companies exploiting the region's resource base. This was predominantly an east-west issue and is the subject of chapter 9.

These two chapters explore the context, issues, organizational structure, and degree of internal unity or dissension within these organizational representatives of the reemerging regional trichotomy.[2] The studies are organized to illuminate a number of analytical issues from preceding chapters. First, do political claims on a territorially constituted state form an important vehicle for regional identity and expression? Second, how do political and cultural traditions foment or impair regional cohesiveness and organizing? Third, are the regional organizations representative of cross-class interests or are they dominated by one or more segments? Fourth, do rapidly growing regions tend to develop a politics around internal conflicts while stagnating, troubled regions develop an externally oriented politics antagonistic to other regions? At the end of each chapter, I review the substantive validity of the debate and draw some conclusions about regionalism from the evidence presented.

THE NORTHEAST-MIDWEST COALITION

The Context: Industrial Decline in a Rich Region

The northeastern quadrant of the United States is known in common parlance as the manufacturing belt, the frostbelt, and more traditionally, as simply "the East." As we have seen in chapter 6, it has a preponderance of older industrial sectors, many of which have stagnated or diminished in size in the postwar period. Producer goods sectors—chemicals, steel, and machinery or all types—are particularly important in this region. Relative to other regions, it lacks (or has exhausted) a sizable natural resource base, except for agriculture. Its economy is relatively diversified at the regional level, but is much less so at the subregional and local level. Although manufacturing activity has waned in this region, the corporations that participate in these sectors still reside here, maintaining headquarters in the larger metropolitan areas of New York, Philadelphia, Boston, Pittsburgh, Chicago, and Detroit.

The class structure of this region has long been dominated by fully developed capitalist and working classes, with supporting casts of small businesspeople and professional-technical workers. The larger cities host a relatively permanent underclass of largely minority people, often immigrants or rural-to-urban migrants, who serve as a secondary labor force and are often left in poverty. In the countryside, a traditional though declining agricultural population complicates the otherwise quite conflictual capital-labor axis of the region's politics.

Because the region continues to host the major centers of U.S.-based multinational capital, an indigenous capitalist class is very active in its politics. On the one hand, financial and industrial interests have a tremendous stake in the fixed capital assets of the region, particularly those which constitute the urban environment. On the other hand, they are simultaneously making decisions to invest money and physical capital outside the region and nation, contributing to the region's fiscal problems and structural decline. As we shall see below, their leadership in regional politics makes it almost impossible to raise the issue of controlling capital outflow as an effective tool for regional regeneration.

People in the northeastern portion of the country have long demonstrated a strong sense of regional distinctiveness, marked by a pride in their colonial and revolutionary traditions, their success in defending the Union in the Civil War, and their cultural sophistication. Strongly moralistic yet liberal politics, the heritage of New England Protestantism, tend to dominate. Yankee culture is profoundly anti-southern in its moral and political outlook, a legacy of the Civil War conflict which was rekindled during the Civil Rights era. Other unifying features include the region's cold and humid weather, a scarcity of southern whites and blacks, and a history of Yankee-Catholic antagonism (Gastil 1975, 137–74; Garreau 1981, 14–97; Schneider 1981, 211–12). Rather than identify with the larger region, however, residents more often characterize themselves as Bostonians or New Yorkers, engaging in intraregional rivalries in sports, politics, and culture.

In the postwar era, partisan politics have been fierce in this region. Both the Democratic and Republican parties have been broad-based, vigorously competitive, and frequent contributors to national leadership, each producing a postwar president—Kennedy (Democrat from Massachusetts) and Ford (Republican from Michigan). Races for senator, governor, and legislature seats are often hotly contested. Up until the New Deal, "Eastern Establishment" Republicans dominated not only the region's politics, but also the nation's. The New Deal enhanced the already developing urban base of the Democrats by giving the heavily Catholic urban and industrial areas of the Northeast a partnership in national politics with the rural, depressed Deep South and the old progressive states of the upper Midwest. Northern white Protestants began to shift toward the Democratic party in the early sixties, once Kennedy's presidency dislodged religion as a divisive regional issue and Goldwater displaced the Eastern Establishment Republicans in the leadership of the Republican Party (Wattenberg and Miller 1981, 359; Schneider 1981, 203). As a result, the region as a whole has become more Democratic in the past two decades.

This, then, was the context when the quickening of world economic integration, the energy crisis, and an emerging recession of major proportions plunged the region into rapidly worsening economic and fiscal straits. As we have been in chapter 6, this region experienced very low employment growth in the 1970s. Some of its major metropolitan areas suffered absolute population declines, due almost entirely to net outmigration. This traumatic decade prompted a previously optimistic, outward-looking region to reexamine its own internal strengths and weaknesses.

The Issues: How to Reverse Regional Losses

The region's attention was first riveted around the plight of certain northeastern cities, whose population losses, deteriorating employment base, and burgeoning welfare caseload strained the fiscal capacity of their local governments. Detroit's fiscal crisis in the early 1970s was followed by that of New York a couple of years later.[3] The intractability of municipal fiscal crises led inexorably to an analysis of the larger geographical scale in which these problems were embedded, since it became clearer as time went by that the cities' ills could not be coped with internally.[4] A national urban coalition, largely based in the Democratic party, succeeded in crafting federal programs such as countercyclical revenue-sharing, Community Development Block Grants and Urban Development Action Grants.

However, these initiatives began to lose steam by the mid-seventies because not all U.S. cities, particularly those in the South and West, found themselves in the same predicament. Moreover, conditions in many northeastern small towns and even some suburbs began to mirror the problems of the central cities in their regions. The urban coalition reached its peak strength in 1978 and had already begun to give way to the regional realignment by the middle of the decade.[5] Nevertheless, the new regional coalition inherited some of the outlook and favored programs of the urban coalition.

The growing consciousness of a common northeastern cause, distinct from that of other regions, can be detected from mid-decade headlines in the regional press. In early 1976, the New York Times, largest daily circulation paper in the Northeast, published a seven-article series on the "Sunbelt." In May of that year, *Business Week*, another New York City based–publication, published a lengthy article entitled "The Second War Between the States." In June, the *National Journal*, a Washington-based weekly on national politics, published a study under the heading "Federal Spending: The North's Loss Is the Sunbelt's Gain" (*New York Times* 1976; *Business Week* 1976; Havemann et al. 1976).

These articles stressed three themes. One, they expressed alarm that the Sunbelt was growing much faster than the Northeast and documented the magnitude of the differential with impressive statistics. Second, they attributed the differential, accurately, to both population outmigration and higher levels of capital investment in other regions of the country. These outflows, they hypothesized, were prompted by the lower costs of doing business and living in the Sunbelt. Third, they argued that the federal government was in large part responsible for the uneven regional rates of growth because its tax and spending patterns had favored the outlying, faster growing areas.

At the outset, several remedies were offered in these same columns. Under the subheading "A Policy for Domestic Detente," the *Business Week* article outlined a program for regional rejuvenation. It included proposals to redirect federal aid toward slower growth areas and a plea for federal standardization of the social wage. It also stressed internal remedies such as cutbacks of social services, slimming of fiscal profiles, and selective easing of environmental constraints.[6]

In short order, the third theme began to dominate the discussion. A number of research studies attempted to calibrate the magnitude of the federal spending gap.[7] Popular and academic studies alike critiqued the federal government's budgetary and nonbudgetary "favoritism" toward the Sunbelt. Changes that would redirect federal spending back to the Northeast were recommended in the slew of formulas used to allocate grants-in-aid from federal to state and local governments. For example, it was argued that a cost-of-living index should be used to modify a per capita income indicator, since higher northeastern incomes really were necessary to cover the region's higher living costs. Second, tax effort instead of fiscal capacity should be used to distribute revenue sharing funds since northeastern jurisdictions showed a willingness to tax themselves at heavy rates despite their wealthier tax base. A major issue was the disparity between regional levels of welfare funding, a northeastern handicap which should be removed by federal funding of welfare for all states at the higher prevailing levels (Peirce 1976, 1700–1703).[8]

The critique of federal government regional bias also targeted the substance of many federal programs. For instance, arguing that northeastern taxpayers had subsidized cheap sunbelt transportation through the public construction and maintenance of inland waterways, the region's advocates recommended the institution of federal fees for navigational users. Arguing that regulation of natural gas pricing had encouraged industrial users to migrate to the sunbelt states, they proposed to hasten deregulation.

In some cases, the mission of the agency was not challenged but its concentration of resources elsewhere was. They favored rechanneling of Corps of Engineer river and port dredging activities toward the Northeast. They lobbied for repairing old mass transit facilities rather than funding new systems, the latter largely in the Sunbelt. They counseled energy conservation and development of Appalachian coal rather than western coal exploitation. In short, the federal government's role in promoting or retarding the development of the several regions came under intense scrutiny, led by northeastern academics, politicians, organizations, and journalists.

The selection of issues upon which to focus regional energies became the province of the organizations which emerged as the self-appointed voices of the region. There were three sets of issues, with three potential policy targets. First, there were the activities of the private decision makers responsible for the underlying state of the region's economy. Second, there were the region's assets and liabilities as a production environment—its labor force, land, tax rates, cities, and infrastructure— which made up the business climate. Third there was the specter of federal government unfairness. In short order, the agenda that the dominant regional coalition adopted was to stress the importance of this federal role to the exclusion of the other two.

Organizational Form: A Washington-Oriented Coalition

Two groupings emerged in the mid-1970s to address the region's common problems. The initiative in putting together a regional coalition came from those politicians whose jurisdictions were in deepest trouble. The first—the Coalition of Northeastern Governors (CONEG)—was engineered by Governor Carey of New York, whose state lost 239,000 jobs from 1972 through 1975, or 3.4 percent of its total. A congressional counterpart—the Northeast-Midwest Economic Advancement Coalition (NMEAC, later the Northeast-Midwest Congressional Caucus)—was organized by Congressman Michael Harrington of Boston, the most troubled of the larger central cities in the New England region.[9] The success of the latter configuration compared to the former is a function of both the regional political-cultural constraints and the inherent tendencies in the region's economy.

The Northeastern Governors' Coalition

The formation of CONEG (1976) was facilitated by the fact that almost all of the northeastern governors at the time were Democrats. Indeed, those who initially joined all belonged to the Democratic Party—the governors of New York, Connecticut, Massachusetts, Rhode Island, Vermont, New Jersey, and Pennsylvania.[10] The governors' coalition also anticipated that the Democrats might gain the presidency later that year, in addition to maintaining control of Congress. If so, Washington might be adding a receptive ear for the region's interests, especially if the region could help propel the Democrats into power. The prospect of a New Englander—Tip O'Neill—heading the House of Representatives encouraged this national orientation at the time.

Raising the specter of the "cancer of depressed Appalachia" spreading from Maine to Minnesota, the coalition was from the outset aggressive in its designs for regional recovery, emphasizing substantial public investment in the region as a stimulant. It demanded massive infusions of public works funds as well as extension of countercyclical aid. Combining New Deal type ideology with new labels, as in a proposed Regional Energy and Development Corporation, the coalition sought to raise, principally from the federal government, the massive infusions of capital needed to renovate both private and public sectors.

The issue of federal bias quickly escalated to a central position in CONEG's program. It aimed to seek "a united front in Congress and before the national administration on specific economic issues." It convened a major conference on the region's problems in late 1976, which was attended by the seven governors plus more than a hundred businesspeople (especially from banking, insurance, and other regionally tied sectors), academics, economists, and labor and political leaders. It designated "misguided federal policy" as the chief culprit in creating the region's problems (Peirce 1976, 1695, 1699).

Despite its formal aims to represent all of the people of the region, CONEG remained a predominantly business-oriented entity. Its advisory board consisted of one public sector and one private sector representative appointed by each governor. The roster in 1977 showed that without exception, the latter came from the business community, predominantly heads of investment annd commercial banks, utilities, plus one industrial corporate executive (Textron, Inc.) In addition, CONEG was closely identified with business leaders like Felix Rohatyn, who was New York's private sector delegate to the board and an outspoken advocate of antilabor measures and social cost-cutting (Rafuse 1977, 22).[11]

The eclipse of CONEG by its nascent Washington counterpart was chiefly a result of the latter's greater proximity to and power within the federal centers of decision making toward which regional policy demands were tilted. But two other political aspects curtailed its effectiveness as well. First, the Democrats lost two key Middle Atlantic statehouses in the latter 1970s: Pennsylvania and New Jersey. Furthermore, all of the midwestern states had Republican governors by 1980. Partisan politics prevented a joining of these new governors with CONEG. Furthermore, a Republican-sponsored regional body—the Council for Northeast Economic Action—had been organized and funded in 1976 by the Ford administration through EDA, largely as a result of prodding by concerned Republican politicians of the region who feared that the Democrats would ride the regional decline issue into the presidency (Peirce 1976, 1702). The council was headed by the former senior vice-president of First National Bank of Boston and was unabashedly pro-business. Even though its activities remained modest and were oriented toward promoting business issues within the region, the council challenged CONEG's legitimacy as the sole representative of regional economic interests.

The Northeast-Midwest Congressional Coalition

The Northeast-Midwest Economic Advancement Coalition, which shortly after its formation changed its name to the Northeast-Midwest Congressional Coalition (NMCC), was the brainchild of Congressman Harrington. Harrington had requested a study from the Legislative Reference Service of the Library of Congress on the interregional impacts of federal spending. Harrington's vision of a broad, bipartisan regional coalition (Harrington 1976; Harrington and Horton 1977) was designed to overcome the partisanship problem of CONEG and the parochialism of the New England Congressional Caucus. The latter, the first permanently staffed regional caucus in Congress, had been formed in 1972 around issues of the smaller New England region but had difficulties getting its program through the Congress in which its members formed only a small minority.

Harrington convened the new coalition in September of 1976 as a bipartisan body representing all House members from a wide swath of states from Iowa through Pennsylvania to Maine. In subsequent years, the coalition expanded its coverage to eighteen states, including Maryland and Delaware. While a few Republicans declined to join and Democrats were overrepresented among the more active members, the coalition enjoyed wide bipartisan support.[12] It engendered a sister coalition in the Senate (1978) and spawned a nonprofit research wing called the Northeast-Midwest Institute (NEMWI).

The Northeast-Midwest Congressional Coalition became the major publicist for the problems and proposals of the Northeast. It attracted a tremendous amount of press coverage, both within the region and in Washington, on its issues. Its research arm, the institute, was housed at no charge in the House Annex and was funded about equally by individual state contributions (from legislatures or discretionary funds of governors), private foundations such as Rockefeller Brothers and Robert Sterling Clark, and federal agencies such as EDA.[13] The institute researched the region's problems, sometimes contracting out to academic or private groups. The coalition and institute began to publish an annual *State of the Region* (since 1980), a *Regional Data Quarterly,* and an annual regional analysis of the President's budget.

By its own account, the coalition was initially successful on the Hill in several important battles. It pushed through Congress several formula changes that would redirect more federal funds toward the Northeast. The most controversial of these victories was its insertion of the "age of housing" variable into the Community Development Block Grant formula. Since the Northeast, being the oldest region in the country, has more pre-1939 housing stock than any other region, this change clearly redistributed funds toward its constituents. Similar changes were won in new legislation covering food stamps and education.[14] Of the seven major victories the coalition listed on an early 1980s public relations flyer, three concerned formula changes, three defense spending patterns, and one the extension of the investment tax credit (ITC) to rehabilitation of older commercial buildings.

The election of Ronald Reagan forced the coalition into a more defensive position. Implicitly a sunbelt candidate, Reagan won in the Northeast because of widespread disgust with Carter's failure to deliver on his economic promises. Upon assuming office, Reagan proposed budget cuts that heavily penalized older manufacturing regions and their more needy and working-class constituents. In response, the caucus abandoned its aggressive formula-restructuring effort and dug in to protect the last of the Great Society programs.

Defense remained the only program where the coalition actively struggled over distribution, perhaps because it was the only category of expenditure to grow substantially in the 1980s. Its victories on this score included the reversal of decisions to close defense facilities in five states, the reversal of a decision against overhauling four aircraft carriers at the naval shipyard in Philadelphia, and a change in defense contracting to target higher areas of unemployment. Subsequent research by the institute argued that the Pentagon should site more military bases in the Northeast on the grounds that northern climates produce soldiers better equipped to fight in northern European arenas (such as Poland and the USSR) and that missiles launched across the North Pole have a several hundred mile edge if launched from the northern rather than the southern region (CONEG 1977; Mazza and Wilkinson 1980; Merkowitz interview).

Washington waned in significance for the Northeast-Midwest group for several reasons. First, the Senate went to the Republicans in 1980 for the first time in decades. Second, reapportionment will produce a clear shift of congressional votes toward the Sunbelt. As a result, the coalition has considered dropping its regional title and regrouping as a "distressed centers coalition." Increasingly, to win political battles, the coalition has had to recruit support from legislators from other regions—Californians from lumber, auto, steel, and cannery-troubled districts, Alabamians from the steel-depressed Birmingham area, rural areas across the nation with high levels of poverty and poor housing, and suburbs concerned with preserving agricultural lands. Depending upon the issue, the Northeast-Midwest Congressional Coalition expands and shifts its umbrella, in the classic pork-barrelling manner.

With the decline in Washington's ability to solve their problems, the coalition has had to turn elsewhere. Western energy states have become a convenient substitute external scapegoat. The coalition began to study and critique the energy development and taxation programs of these states. The coalition protests that resource levies such as severance taxes on natural gas, oil, and coal are impoverishing northeasterners for the enrichment of western coffers (Northeast-Midwest Institute 1980). We shall return to this issue in the next chapter.

At the same time, the interregional stalemate and the drying up of congressional resources has forced the coalition to search for remedies for economic decline within the region itself. Increasingly, these take the form of traditional business stimuli to "transform initial signs of business-government cooperation into regional competitive strength." The institute issued a joint publication with the formerly competitive and more explicitly business-oriented Council for Northeast Economic Action, entitled "A Northeast Business Agenda for the 1980s." The Agenda embraces five key policy issues: to encourage private investment in older cities, mobilize capital for small business growth, structure public labor training programs to meet business needs, achieve balanced surface transportation in the Northeast, and develop meaningful strategies to cope with foreign competition (NEMWI 1981; NEMWI 1982).

Class Interests and Alternative Approaches

The coalition just described occupied the center of the political stage for the northeastern region in the latter 1970s. It was proud of the fact that it worked with both business and labor, with the Republican (and business-dominated) Council for Northeast Economic Action and with the New Left's National Center for Economic Alternatives. An indication of its success in controlling the regional issue was the failure of any sustained left or working-class-based alternative to develop at the regionwide level. Left groups, in fact, tended to maintain a friendly attitude toward the coalition though they did not count on its support for tactics that challenged basic business practice and control.

The leadership in designing and promoting regional consciousness emanated from within the organizations and media arms of regionally based capital. Indeed, the newspapers and magazines that made so much of the new regional war were themselves important private actors in the regional economy, with a tremendous stake in the preservation of their advertisers and readership. Academics were much slower to jump on the bandwagon, but some did wax enthusiastic about an emerging regional consensus.[15]

The leadership for the actual effort at coalition building arose from within the existing political apparatus of the region. Because these politicians, especially those in the Democratic party, owed their success to a delicately engineered base that included both business and working-class constituents, they had to avoid the two issues which were most closely involved in the well-developed class conflicts of the region. On the one hand, they could not offend their business patrons by talking about effective controls on the movement of capital or novel forms of public investment. On the other hand, they could not alienate their working-class base by espousing an erosion of the social wage and workers' rights in order to improve the region's business climate. The coalition thus focused energies away from the internally conflictual issues of business cost and social control of investment toward the common demand for larger transfers, fairer treatment, and additional social capital from the federal level. Accompanying this strategy, it stressed the abused position of the region within the nation rather than addressing the opposing interests of capital and labor at home.

In the last analysis, however, the coalition's strategy must be seen as more pro-capital than pro-labor. The coalition was not committed during this period to serious research on or support for innovative approaches to a declining capitalist region. For instance, despite the institute's study supporting federal procurement commitments for the proposed Youngstown project, the coalition made no organized effort to help that community-worker buyout attempt. Of dozens of reports undertaken by the institute through 1979, only two tackled clearly labor-oriented issues—one supporting the bailout of Chrysler (which was of course pro-capital as well) and one on the federal role in worker ownership (Zabar and Sullivan 1978; Northeast-Midwest Institute 1979a and 1979b).

Despite the acquiescence of organized labor and left-liberal groups in the coalition's work, progressive alternatives to the coalition's approach did develop within the region. These constitute examples of opposi-tional planning as defined by Clavel (1980). As early as April of 1976, 250 labor leaders met in Trenton, New Jersey to organize a coalition to "provide government and industrial development in our region." Their concerns were immediately job-related. They agreed to lobby to stop the flow of federal contracts to the South and West and to plug tax loopholes that encourage multinationals to redeploy capital outside the United States (Peirce 1976, 1699). While no militant action nor alternatives to capitalist control of production were espoused by this conference, a concern with plant closings, which was to later blossom into movement proportions, was already evident.

Subsequently, the Progressive Alliance was formed at the initiative of the United Auto Workers to address working-class economic issues. Although they aspired to be national in scope, their constituents and issues were largely confined to the Northeast and Midwest. The alliance published the Bluestone and Harrison volume on *Capital and Communities* (1980), which examined in depth the role of private capital in the region's economic ills.[16]

The New Left also attempted to organize on a regional level early in this era. In December of 1976, the Conference on Alternative State and Local Public Policies, a New Left organization based in Washington, sponsored a Northeast Cities Conference. While buying into the federal unfairness argument, the 450 attendees approved a lengthy resolution which called for an end to predatory competition among regions in the form of tax incentives and subsidies, an increase in the level and decentralization of citizen control, an emphasis on new policy instruments that would exert some control over financial and industrial capital, and a commitment to ending economic racism and sexism.[17] However, ongoing organization other than the conference itself, which acts as a national clearinghouse, emerged from this event.

The most successful instances of oppositional organizing have taken place at the state and local levels. A prototype was the Ohio Public Interest Campaign, an umbrella organization of labor, taxpayer, community, environmental, and energy-oriented groups united around the problems of sectoral decline, especially in steel, rubber, and autos. OPIC's agenda included progressive changes in the tax structure, opposition to extended business tax breaks, and efforts to stop plant closings. The Massachusetts Coalition to Save Jobs combined labor with nonworkplace issues such as utility rates, taxes, and housing. These coalitions have pioneered innovative financial and organizational approaches to economic development.[18]

Among workers, these groups more often won support from union locals, district, and state labor organizations, rather than the national and international unions. The leadership of the latter generally repudiated the activist approach of the coalitions, which sometimes include demonstrations around plant closings. The national labor unions' response to the regional crisis, which decimated their ranks, was to step up their organizing effort in the Sunbelt and to push for labor law reform.

On environmental issues, these coalitions attempted to overcome the cleavage between labor and environmental activists. They urged environmentalists and antinuclear movements to address issues of worker displacement. They encouraged the construction trades to stop automatically supporting new projects, such as nuclear power plants, albeit without great success. The reconciliation between labor and New Left groups was aided by the relatively progressive leadership of some unions such as the United Auto Workers, the Oil, Chemical and Atomic Workers, and the white collar and service workers' unions.

With few exceptions, these new coalitions found it easier to organize around state and substate issues. But they also formed a loose alternative network. Best captured in Rifkin and Barber's somewhat chauvinistic title, *The North Will Rise Again,* their vision is one of a restructured, industrial Northeast whose revitalization is built upon innovative approaches to the economy. They explored the use of pension funds to assert worker control over investment priorities, the creation of new public capital institutions, and the pursuit of explicit industrial policies tailored to the special needs in individual sectors and communities. The Youngstown case mentioned above, and Luria and Russell's Detroit plan for new metal-bending industries, constituted community-preserving strategies for particular subregions. Subsequently, both Pittsburgh and Chicago have mounted impressive programs for steel. If economic hardship intensifies, pressures will build for workers and communities, including members of the professional and small business classes, to unify around similar efforts.

Such a coalition might be able to respond to regional ills without resortinng to the regional parochialism which hampered the NMCC and its institute's efforts.[19] The plant closings network, based on union locals and regional offices, religious groups, academics, and public interest groups, links California with the northeastern states.[20] Worker health and safety issues link the Frostbelt and Sunbelt. Environmental issues reach from Woody Guthrie's Redwood forests to the Gulf Stream waters. A movement for economic change, like Youngstown's, can be profoundly committed to preservation of community and region without necessarily blaming other regions for its problems. A successful progressive alternative would have to mount an interregional campaign, but one sensitive to the problems of particular places, with the fundamental reorganization of the economy as its goal.

The Northeast-Midwest Coalition: A Summary

The Northeast-Midwest Congressional Coalition, which emerged as that region's leading organization in the 1970s, was thoroughly state-structured in its composition and intent. The progressive shift of power and visibility from the earlier Coalition of Northeastern Governors to NMCC was a function both of the significance of the national government to the region's strategy and the constraints placed on any organization composed of governors by the region's intense partisan politics. The fact that the coalition operated out of Washington, D.C., its preoccupation with the regional bias in federal spending, and its complaints about the activities of other regions underscore the degree to which this troubled region concentrated on extraregional solutions to its poorly performing economy. The lack of any sustained challenge at the regional level from either the Right or the Left suggests that the coalition succeeded in creating a cross-class program for the region. These findings support the argument of chapter 7—that an economically troubled region will tend to evolve an intraregional cross-class coalition which pursues its claims at higher levels of the State and initiates interregional bickering.

THE SOUTHERN GROWTH POLICIES BOARD

The Context: Rapid Growth in an Underdeveloped Region

The southern region, as we saw in chapter 6, enjoyed a sustained postwar boom which diversified and modernized its economy. The industrialization of the South brought with it many of the problems which had already been experienced by the Northeast and Midwest. But it was also growth of a peculiar sort. The sectors that were moving southward tended to be those in mature stages of their profit cycle, drawn by the lower costs of doing business and the good "business climate." If the southern states were to begin adopting environmental regulations and tax rates similar to the North and were to host unionization on a large scale, they would be less attractive to these relatively profit-squeezed sectors, which might migrate to overshore sites instead. Indeed, by 1974 the growth surge had peaked for every state but Florida. This vulnerability has created unique problems for southern economic development.

Southern class structure has evolved with the region's economy. The new postwar industrial plants have generally been erected by corporations based outside the region. This has meant that the size of the indigenous industrialist class is still relatively small. Home-based regional capital is concentrated in the secondary and supporting sectors such as transportation, utilities, finance, construction, and real estate, and in traditional industries like tobacco, textiles, and timber. Industrialization has contributed to building a wage-earning working class from a largely rural subsistence and sharecropping population of poor whites and blacks. However, the degree of unionization and class consciousness is low, primarily because of the persistence of racism. Racial differences constitute the dominant social cleavage in the South, subordinating class differences.

Unlike the newly emergent regional consciousness in the Northeast, southern regional consciousness has never receded from the area's politics. Slavery, the Civil War, and its aftermath form the single most significant set of events shaping this consciousness, and the inroads of twentieth-century capitalist development do not seem to have eliminated it. In the 1970s, authors writing on the South could still contend that "no region in the country has produced so many people interested in it as a region" and that "the South has seemed to live inside its people like an

instinct" (Gastil 1975, 186; Naylor and Clotfelter 1975, 3).[21] This southern consciousness, at least among whites, has been argued by Reed
(1972) to constitute a solidarity greater than ethnic group bonds, even in
the contemporary period.

This cultural identification has been fostered by the fact that the vast
majority of southerners, both black and white, can trace their roots in
the region back to 1850 and before. Retirees from the North and
immigrants from other nations have settled on the fringes of the South,
rather than in its heartland (Gastil 1975, 174). Among the features of
this culture are "a strong work ethic, an easy-going way of life, manners,
love of place, closeness to nature, sense of God, sense of history, humor
and unpretentiousness" (Southern Growth Policies Board 1981, 11). A
distinctive southern form of Protestantism, conservative and fundamentalist in tenor, has heightened the sense of cultural difference, especially
as against the Northeast.

Interpreters of the South's development problems have viewed this
distinctive culture as both a heritage to be preserved and a handicap.
Since World War II, many interdisciplinary conferences and volumes on
southern development prospects have probed the South's distinctive
resources, underdevelopment, highly developed cultural self-consciousness, and remarkable political structure.[22]

But regional identity is not a timeless, unchanging sentiment. In the
1950s and 1960s, southerners of both races were thrust into the civil
rights movement, an indigenous struggle to restore to black southerners
their political (and social and educational) rights. Indeed, from the
1930s on, fundamental changes took place, captured in the phrase "the
New South." The adjective "New" alluded to two features. One was the
deepening integration of the South into the industrial economy of the
nation. The other was the successful assault on the worst forms of caste
embodied in racially segregated arrangements in politics and public life.

The dramatic upheavals of the New South can best be charted by
looking at changes in the region's politics. A one-party region since the
Civil War, the traditional hegemony of the Democrats began to erode in
the postwar period. From 1900 to 1944, every Democratic presidential
candidate received at least two-thirds of the southern vote. During the
New Deal, southerners gave the Democrats higher margins than did
voters in any other region.

Race was the issue that destroyed the effective north-south coalition of
the New Deal Democrats. The defections began in 1948, when the
national party's battles over civil rights drove some southern Democrats
to oppose Truman and nominate Strom Thurmond on a states' rights
and white supremacy platform. Wallace's American Independent party,
which did so well in 1968, was an inheritor of this disaffection with the
national democrats. Whereas during the New Deal no region rivaled the
South in its support of Democratic presidential nominees, by 1970 no
region was so unsupportive (Ladd and Hadley 1978, 129–34). This

occurred despite the fact that millions of black voters with very strong Democratic affinities were able to exercise their votes for the first time.

While race has been a leading cause of southern political change, it is not the only one. The industrialization of the South has created a new professional and managerial stratum which votes heavily Republican and conservative (ibid., 159). Furthermore, migration has been highly selective in the postwar period, with disproportionate numbers of Republicans moving south. Their voting preferences appear to be closely correlated with class status. Among white migrants, only one quarter of those moving north-to-south were blue-collar workers compared to two-thirds of those moving south-to-north (Converse 1963, 210). These economic changes have produced "the replacement of old agrarian radicalism with new industrial conservatism" (Ladd and Hadley 1978, 139).

The southern shift away from the Democrats also reflects the changing nature of that party nationally. Up through the time of the New Deal, the Democrats had been the party antagonistic to the business nationalism of the Republicans, inherited from the Whigs and the Federalists. Since most of the Eastern Establishment adhered to the Republican party, southerners' support of the Democrats combined an antipathy toward the North with distrust of nationally dominant capitalist interests. But subsequently, many northeastern business elites found they could live with the "new industrial state" and came to tolerate and then support the liberal urban Democratic regimes of the region. As the Northeast increasingly became the most Democratic region, southern objections to the "postindustrial, centralized, welfare-oriented, intellectualist, bureaucratically organized political culture of the Northeast" multiplied (Havard 1972, 714). Despite these changes at the national level, Democratic party dominance at the state and local levels remains strong, particularly in the Deep South.

Organizational Form: A Coalition to Resolve Internal Problems

The Southern Growth Policies Board became a major collective voice for the New South in the 1970s. The SGPB was the brainchild of Governor Terry Sanford of North Carolina, who in 1971 began speaking publicly on the emerging planning needs of the New South. Convening a meeting of southern governors, he emphasized the need to "avoid Northern mistakes in a Southern setting" and urged his colleagues to join together in a new regionwide organization. They complied enthusiastically. In December 1971, nine southern governors signed executive orders creating the board, displaying "the clear feeling that the South was facing a decade of growing pains that would require cooperative study and action (SGPB 1978).[23]

From the outset, this cooperation had a dual thrust. On the one hand, it aimed at solving an unprecedented number of modern growth management problems. On the other, it aspired to supplant intraregional

competition with collaboration in traditional state economic development promotional activities.

The board cast its eligible membership net as widely as possible,
encompassing sixteen states and two territories (Puerto Rico and the
Virgin Islands) as eligible for membership.[24] A marked effort was made
to avoid resemblance to the Old Confederacy, by inviting Oklahoma,
West Virginia, Kentucky, Maryland, Delaware, Puerto Rico, and the
Virgin Islands to join. Yet, those electing to join were more or less the
same states as those with a high incidence of nineteenth-century plantation slavery (see chapter 4). The geographical expanse of SGPB was
almost identical to that of the Confederacy. Thus, despite a desire to
break out of an old regional bind, the SGPB leadership found itself
shunned by peripheral states, reticent to throw their lot in with their
neighbors.

Among those states choosing not to exercise their southern citizenship
were the three who sided squarely with the North (West Virginia,
Maryland, and Delaware) in the Civil War. Texas also demured to join,
largely because its ample finances permitted it to run its own lobbying
operations and because its dominant historical motif is celebrating the
Texas Republic, rather than the Old South.[25] Missouri declined as well.

The extraordinary prevalence of the Democratic party in governor-
ships and legislatures in the South facilitated the rapid formation of the
board, in contrast to the partisanship which hampered CONEG's efforts
in the North. Republican governors did join and remain on the board—
indeed the first chair was Republican Governor Holton from Virginia—
although their participation level in recent years has been assessed as
below average by staff members.

Far more than either of the other two regional organizations studied
here, the Southern Growth Policies Board acknowledged its region's
unique commonality. The opening line of its founding agreement reads:
"The party states find that the South has a sense of community based on
common social, cultural and economic needs and fostered by a regional
tradition" (*Southern Growth Policies Agreement,* Revised and Approved
November 30, 1978, mimeo.). In public presentations, its leadership has
at times unself-consciously alluded to this heritage with phrases such as
"the Southern States of America."

The Board's creators aimed at aggressively speeding the region's
economic integration into the national economy. Yet the political structure of the board reflects a century-old southern commitment to the
federalized state. Its founding document, *The Southern Growth Policies
Agreement,* affirms states' rights: "The independence of each state and
the special needs of subregions are recognized and are to be safe-
guarded."

Reliant on the will and finances of state legislatures, the board has
developed a decentralized representational structure and rotates the
leadership role annually. Originally composed of each governor plus his

or her private appointee, it was expanded to include a legislator from each house of the state legislatures plus an additional governor's appointee, yielding a large board with five representatives from each state. It has also created a separate Legislative Advisory Council of legislators and a cooperative arrangement with the state Municipal Leagues. The result is a somewhat unwieldy board but a strong network of communication between state, local, and regional operations that facilitates internal planning. Swings in sentiment and policy direction at the top are exacerbated by the strong leadership exerted by individual governor chairs, who change each year and sometimes chart dramatically different courses from their predecessors. This turnover has been moderated, however, by relative continuity in staffing, especially in the executive director's position.

At the outset, funding for the board came almost entirely from nonpublic sources. The Ford Foundation provided an initial $225,000 challenge grant. Regional sources such as the Mary Reynolds Babcock Foundation of Winston-Salem provided matching funds. In 1973, southern state legislatures voted to pay dues, which subsequently provided about 50 percent of the board's funding. The rest, particularly during the Washington-oriented years of the late 1970s, came largely from federal agencies such as EDA, HUD, National Science Foundation and national private foundations like the Rockefeller—the same institutions which funded the northeastern effort.

The board assigned itself the task of planning the New South's future. In its initial agreement, the board committed itself to the production of a "Statement of Regional Objectives," which would be updated every six years as conditions changed. The updating has taken place in the form of two Commissions on the Future of the South, one in 1974 and one in 1980. The board was charged with the responsibility for recommending planning and programming initiatives of interstate and regional significance, planning for orderly growth and prosperity of the region, and designing measures for influencing population distribution, land use, development of new communities, and redevelopment of existing ones. Included in its mission was the creation of comprehensive land-use plans for cross-state regions.

The Issues: From Environmentalism to Washington to Boosterism

The issues which preoccupied the New South in the 1970s fall into three distinct groups sequentially. When the board was founded, the leadership adopted the problems of growth management as its centerpiece. By the mid-1970s, largely in response to the initiatives of the Northeast-Midwest region, the board moved half its operations to Washington from Research Triangle Park in North Carolina. In tandem, it shifted its focus to federal monitoring and analysis of federal budget issues. Yet a third period, following Reagan's election, found the board closing its Washington office and once again focusing inward on issues of economic development. The economic and political background to each of these changes is worth discussing in turn.

By the early 1970s, the "New South" began to connote a consciousness of the phenomenal postwar southern growth experience and the new problems it had introduced (see chapter 6). "The New Rich South: Frontier for Growth" was *Business Week*'s title for its 1972 feature on the South. The novel and fragile responsibilities of prosperity confronted the region's planners and politicians. Shifting focus from under-industrialization and rural poverty, the century-long themes of southern economists and regional planners, southern political leadership began to talk about urban crisis, environmental deterioration, capital-labor confrontation, and economic competition among the southern states as the problems of the decade.[26]

The evidence was compelling. States like Florida were running out of water. Coastal states were beginning to worry about despoilation of their natural beauty. Mountain areas were suffering environmental degradation, displacement, and flooding as a result of strip mining. Cities were growing rapidly, exhibiting the urban sprawl of their northern siblings.

In the early 1970s, then, flushed by the sustained boom occurring in the South, the new board asked whether this growth might be better managed. Although the conflict between economic development and environmental needs lurked under the surface, the board aggressively stated that

> Almost every new development, whether it be factory or forestry project, strip mine or stream diversion, imposes some external costs. In most instances, the economic and social benefits outweigh these costs. When they don't, the South must stand ready to reject development which has costs, in terms of human and natural resources, that cannot be justified. [SGPB 1981, 10]

Thus the growth management concern, encompassing issues like coastal protection, environmental preservation, and water supply, flourished in the early years. The report of the first Commission on the Future of the South, in 1974, was preoccupied with land-use and growth control questions:

> We have choices. We can manage growth and attempt to direct it to the benefit of all Southerners while protecting vital resources, or we can stand aside and let come what may, responding with tardy and inadequate reactions. Certainly there are some places better than others for refineries, factories, power plants. Certainly there are places too precious, environmentally or historically, to be ruined by intensive development. Why not identify those places and use each properly? [Commission on the Future of the South 1974, 7][27]

These concerns were reflected in staffing choices. The first NSF-sponsored scholar-in-residence was David Godschalk, a University of North

Carolina planner whose expertise lay in growth management issues. He compiled a directory of growth policy research capabilities, developed a local growth management guidebook, and directed several studies on southern growth policy options during his tenure (Godschalk, Knopf, and Weissman 1978). While some question how seriously the board was committed to growth management all along, and others point out that the growth control constituency within the South was never strong,[28] this effort did parallel the first southern Coastal Area Management Acts and helped to popularize concepts like "carrying capacity," which became a public byword in development-centered debates.

As leadership rotated and the battle calls to federal arms erupted, the board's focus began to shift toward Washington-based issues. The title of a 1976 conference in Florida, "The Sunbelt and Its Critics," nicely captures the board's emerging preoccupation with interregional equity (Rafuse 1977, 4). Shortly thereafter, the board opened up a Washington office, which consumed most of its additional funding and staffing over the next four years. The central thrust of this Washington presence was the defense of existing budgetary formulas and opposition to new ones which would redistribute funds spatially toward the Northeast.

In this era, the board engaged in intensive research on the federal bias issue. The board's scholar-in-residence during these years was Bernard Weinstein, whose expertise lay in the analysis of regional shifts and social indicators. He took on the task of responding to the northeastern challenge on formula issues. Unlike Godschalk, who worked out of Research Triangle, Weinstein was located in the Washington office. Altogether the board published nine reports over a period of four years on federal policy changes and their impacts on the South. Striving to head off more "losses" like the infamous age-of-housing formula change, the board fought for the retention of indicators like poverty and per capita income, indicators on which the South consistently appeared more needy than northeastern states. They prevented "cost-of-living" weights from favoring the northeast, and they won a formula fight on the hefty educational aid issue (SGPB 1978).

But the Washington period found the board reaching beyond simple monitoring of federal activities. It began to apply for federal research and education grants to fund projects like its business seminars on national urban policy and its computer-based *Southern Index*—a data base for improved evaluation of federal programs' impact on the South. It began to develop its own southern initiatives on federal issues like housing, cities, and tax policy. Even more significant, it began to build a critique of the northeastern political economy. In a paper on "The Snowbelt and the Seven Myths," the board's director Blaine Liner rebutted northeastern claims that the South was richer, less poverty stricken, less distressed, and more favored by the federal budget than the North. In an analysis of the cost-of-living issue, a board publication suggested that "many northern states and localities now suffer from an *overdeveloped* public sector" (emphasis added)—a formulation which not so subtly disparaged the social wage in northern regions (Weinstein 1979a).

Yet by 1980, the federal arena lost favor with the SGPB leadership. The demise of the federal focus of the board was the product both of internal pressures and external political events. Internally, the board was increasingly criticized by its membership for its emphasis on the interregional war. Its staff had been caught up in a never-ending quest for more federal grants, plentiful during the Carter years, and with the demanding deadlines for research products that were imposed by the grants. Members felt that the southern economy was being neglected, especially as recession set in. With Reagan's whittling down of EDA, HUD, and other agencies that had participated in the sunbelt-frostbelt controversy, the board's funding for its Washington operations dried up. In addition, the new austerity budget, with its lack of sympathy for northeast problems of industrial decline and its redistribution toward defense spending, removed many of the pie sections over which the regional organizations had been scrapping. The board relinquished its federal monitoring activities to the newly formed Congressional Sunbelt Council (as of January 1981), except for one representative in the Southern Government Association, and closed its Washington office (Congressional Sunbelt Council 1981).[29]

A third "economic development" phase of the board's activities began in 1980 with the second Commission on the Future of the South. This shift reflected the worsening economic condition of the South. The region's postwar gains in per capita income that had been diminishing the gap between the South and the rest of the United States ended in the mid-1970s, leaving the South at only 86 percent of the national average. Branch plant closings, particularly in textiles and shoes, had become more numerous; textile job losses were estimated at 50,000. Especially hard-hit were the Old South states of Kentucky, Tennessee, Arkansas, Georgia, and North and South Carolina—those without the energy endowments of Louisiana, Texas, and Oklahoma, or the retirement, military spending, and immigration induced-growth of Florida. Even Texas' fortunes looked cloudy—industrial production in that state had grown only 0.9 percent in 1979 (compared to a U.S. average of 4.5 percent) and construction activity had fallen.[30] Southern gains on the economies of other regions had halted.

Southern economies not only registered slower growth rates, but their public sectors were beginning to feel the incompatible pressures of overburdened public infrastructure and taxpayer revolt. An added problem loomed in renewed unionization efforts in textiles and other manufacturing industries. In an economy largely dependent on sectors which had been propelled from other regions by profit-squeeze impera- tives for cost cutting, this region's public-private establishment demonstrated predictable concern with preserving the very characteristics which had induced growth in an earlier period.

A shift in southern concern toward promoting domestic economic development was apparent in the work of the 1980 Commission on the Future of the South. Its final report lamented that "the South is inevitably losing some of the advantages it has over other parts of the country in attracting population, business and industry." These advantages were the South's lower wage rates, cheap and abundant energy resources, and lower taxes. Southern planning efforts should respond to "a drive to solve problems at home" and an "impulse for self-sufficiency"; the "time seems to have come for consolidation of growth and for looking inward." Prominent among the commission's goals were methods for encouraging an inflow of capital to support growth (including foreign investment), cutting the fat out of business and political performance, and curtailing unnecessary growth of government (SGPB 1981, 10–12).[31] The new executive director, Jesse White, orated bluntly, "I, therefore, see the Southern Growth Policies Board as being in the business of *economic development* [his emphasis] which lies at the heart of the broader development process" (undated speech, 1982, "The Future Mission and Work of S.G.P.B.").

Class Interests and Regional Alternatives

The swings in issue orientation just documented are understandable in the light of the economic events of the decade and the composition of the board. The governors' private appointees have almost always come from the business community, academic institutions, or the media—reminiscent of the composition of the nineteenth-century commercial conventions and symbolic of the commitment to private-public cooperation. The modal appointee in the period studied was a banker, although utilities, transportation (by, for example, an executive of a major Alabama trucking firm), and industrial corporations (especially lumber, oil, and gas) were also represented. No large corporation with headquarters outside the region was represented. Nor was any labor union, even on the enlarged Commissions on the Future of the South established periodically. The board's composition manifested a strong presence of regionally tied corporate interests. The absence of union members was explained by a staff member interviewed as the product of a desire to keep southern business free from labor problems, the low regard with which southern labor leaders are held, and the unpopularity of unions with southern workers.[32]

The prominence of regional capital's requirements is clearest in the reports of the 1980 Commission on the Future of the South. Its Task Force on the Economy adopted the premise that continued economic growth was the best hope for achieving social equity goals in the southern region. Its formula for action was to "beckon to industry."

Composed of financiers, industrial executives, and economic development directors from member states, the task force recommended an aggressive set of rollbacks on the costs of doing business in the South. Included were elimination of interest ceilings and prohibitions on interstate banking, lighter environmental regulations, decontrol of all energy prices and "amendment" of minimum wages. Most importantly, the task force unanimously recommended a challenge to any and all proposals to "restrict the ability of industry to relocate, to impose restraints on the exercise of workers' rights, and to impose restrictive energy and environmental policies on underdeveloped areas (SGPB 1981, 32–33).[33] In other words, the major issues of workers and environmentalists were solidly opposed by the commission.

Nor were issues of racism and the extraordinary concentration of poverty and unemployment among blacks and women tackled. While the commission had several black members, the only and oblique mention of race relations was the terse statement that "race relations in the South have improved immeasurably in the past 20 years. But no Southerners, white or black, believe they have reached a state of perfection (ibid., 12–13).[34] Equal economic opportunites for blacks and women are conspicuously absent in the commission's vision of the future.

On the whole, the Task Force on the Economy repudiated public sector intervention. However, it was not averse to public aid that might lower the cost of doing business. In addition to coming out in favor of the nuclear breeder reactor and federal export promotion programs, the Commission lauded EDA, the Farmer's Home Administration programs, the Tennessee Valley Authority, and the Appalachian Regional Commission. It supported water resource development programs, tax breaks to strengthen the family farm and encourage long-term investment in private woodland development, the use of public facilities location to create high-wage jobs, activities which promote industrial innovation, and the construction of southern coal slurry pipelines.[35]

Even more purely promotional, the Energy Task Force, composed and staffed almost entirely by the energy industry, embraced almost every pro-energy development planning tenet possible. Included were incentives to encourage domestic oil and coal production, modification of the windfall profits tax, an end to any price regulation, dilution of coal stripping and air quality standards, policies that promote coal exports and pipeline construction, and expansion of nuclear power. Only one person who could be said to represent environmental interests sat on the board—a delegate from the Georgia Conservancy. He felt compelled to dissent from several of the more controversial issues, such as the breeder reactor endorsement. Environmental recommendations were ambiguous—one example reads, "environmental protection efforts should be continued at their present pace, but industry should be given the maximum degree of flexibility in meeting established standards" (Weinstein 1981).

Liberals and growth management advocates on the 1980 commission seem to have been crowded onto two task forces—one on southern children, the other on southern cities. But even here, the recommendations for land-use regulations, especially those forthcoming from the cities group, were watered down in response to organized opposition, led by the chairman of the Economy Task Force, an Atlanta banker and director of Georgia-Pacific lumber company.[36]

Overall, the commission's report was overwhelmingly a statement for a business-oriented economic development strategy, with planning limited to engendering business growth through infrastruture deployment, investment policies, and technological subsidies. My research on the board's record shows that it has solidly opposed unions, has increasingly backed off from serious consideration of environmental problems, and maintains very close and amicable ties with the finance-utility-construction-business complex within its borders.

As in the Northeast, a potential alternative to the board's brand of regionalism is embodied in several coalition groups clustered around decentralized locations. Southerners for Economic Justice, operating out of Durham, North Carolina, organizes around worker issues in the "Central South"—Tennessee, Kentucky, and North and South Carolina. The Southern Poverty Law Center in Montgomery, Alabama promotes efforts at ending racism. For example, it has recently mounted a "Klanwatch" program to monitor explicitly racist organizations and activities. Black activists work in a range of organizations, some national in scope but stronger in the South, from the more established and church-based Southern Christian Leadership Conference and NAACP, to the Southern Organizing Committee, a more radical group. West Virginia, Kentucky, and Tennessee have spawned progressive taxpayer revolts aimed at undertaxation of coal and timber companies.

Many efforts are local rather than regional and are tied to unique problems. Appalachian groups working on workers' rights and environmental issues such as black lung and strip mining are currently coalescing in the Appalachian Alliance.[37] In and around the Tennessee Valley, opposition to the TVA's energy promotion and strip mining policies is growing via the Tennessee Valley Energy Coalition, which argues for citizen control of TVA and reconsideration of TVA's priorities. The most coherent, though often apolitical alternatives, to the board's development vision have been proposed and carried out by a variety of small community development corporations, coops, and worker-owned enterprises in the region.

These community-based and working-class efforts are magnificently chronicled in *Southern Exposure,* a journal dedicated to both cultural coverage and development issues in every corner of the southern realm. While no direct challenge to the Southern Growth Policies Board as the South's regional representative emanates from these groups, their goals clearly contradict the board's vision, emphasizing as they do the rights of

workers to organize, the commitment to multiracial equality while preserving cultural autonomy, the eradication of environmental degradation and worker health hazards, and women's rights.

Yet it remains true that these alternative groups are neither very
strong nor fully regional in their outlook. They have much farther to go
than do their northern counterparts. This difference is underscored by
the fact that the Northeast-Midwest coalition embraces workers' rights to
organize unions and to a modest social wage, while the SGPB explicitly
opposes unions. Whereas plant closings are the major issue for northern
workers, the right to organize is the major one for their southern
counterparts.

In fact, southern worker, race, and community-based groups may find
more in common with counterparts in other regions of the country than
with other southern interest groups, a prospect we will consider in
chapter 10. Union dues from northern workers have helped southern
workers to organize on a plant-by-plant basis. Environmental groups
from the western mountains and the northern forests have contributed
to efforts to save southern coastlines and Appalachian landscapes.
Midwestern farmers sent grain and hay to Southern drought-stricken
farmers. On the other hand, deep-seated provincial prejudices often
hamper cross-regional unity, viz. northern stereotypes of southerners as
rednecks, racists, and right-to-workers. Currently, these southern movements find their common cultural heritage a starting point for organization. Their array, spanning different subregions of and issues in the
South, demonstrates the vitality of place-based politics, frequently arising from specific economic sectors such as coal (Appalachia) or mature
manufacturing sectors like textiles (the Piedmont).

The Southern Growth Policies Board: A Summary

Regional consciousness in the South in the 1970s was restructured
around a new set of problems. Rapid industrialization in the postwar
period had begun to produce environmental deterioration, urban
sprawl, and pressures on local fiscal capacity. The emergent organization which dominated region-level activities, the Southern Growth Policies Board, reflected in ideology and structure many features of distinctive southern political culture which date back to the nineteenth century.
In particular, the hegemony of the Democratic party in state and local
politics and a commitment to states' rights combined to produce a strong
governors' coalition with a weak institutional existence. Unlike the
northern coalition, this one was not cross-class, but carried forward the
goals and sentiments of the regional business elite. The absence of an
active working-class participation—white or black—was a product of
racism's long-term role in retarding unionization. The southern case
offers strong support for the hypothesis that regions in which mature
sectors are growing rapidly, due to interregional shifting, will produce

an internally preoccupied politics aimed at grappling with growth management issues without disrupting the business climate.

THE NORTH VERSUS THE SOUTH REVISITED: AN EVALUATION

The previous sections have documented the formation and evolution of two regional organizations in the 1970s, one encompassing the northeastern and midwestern states from Minnesota to Maine and Maryland, the other spanning the southern states from Louisiana through Kentucky, Florida, and Virginia. The former was nationally oriented, or outward looking, from its inception, while the latter began as a growth management coalition preoccupied with the shape of internal development. To the extent that the two came to face each other as the most visible combatants in a much touted "Second War Between the States," their antagonisms can be traced to both historical clashes and contemporary economic experience. This mutually reinforcing interregional conflict—its evolution and substance—is the subject of this final section. Here, I evaluate the substance of the formal debate.

The economic confrontation between the two rose from an odd sort of sectoral differentiation. The industries which had plumped up the southern economy in the postwar period were precisely those which were depressed, aging, and shrinking as a part of the employment base in the North. The textile and shoe industries had begun to migrate interregionally early in the century. By the 1970s, the South was losing jobs in these sectors as well, though the extent of its losses was nowhere near the North's. Sectors that had thrived in the North as late as the 1950s (metals, autos, machinery, apparel, and brewing) but had since seen substantial layoffs were decentralizing toward southern locations fast enough to provide respectable jobs gains. Thus the South was actually becoming *more* similar to the North in industrial mix.[38]

Yet the South's attractiveness for these mature sectors in the postwar period derived from its exceptional "business climate" resulting low wages, absence of unions, subsidies from local and state governments, and tax concessions. Only by preserving these features would prosperity built on such sectors be maintained.[39] Although the North explicitly identified the electronics, military, and energy sectors as contributors to its adversary's growth, the more narrowly self-defined South that responded to the North's challenge was largely lacking any substantial growth in these sectors and was composed instead of the states of the previously underdeveloped, and once slavery-dominated, Old South economy. Much of the Northeast-Midwest Institute's sunbelt rhetoric was actually directed toward phenomena which better characterized the Southwest, which was not represented in the Southern Growth Policies Board.

The animosities of the 1970s between the North and South were in part a legacy of the Civil War and the antecedent competition between two modes of production. The South's appeal for profit-squeezed northern sectors consisted precisely in the underdevelopment of both its labor force and its local state, traceable in turn to slavery and the subsequent agricultural reconstruction compromise documented in chapter 4. In addition, the distinctive southern regional character and culture which was bred by this historical conflagration proved to be a tenacious source of regional identity and an ongoing context within which new regional antagonisms could flare up.

The proximate cause of postwar antagonism between these two regions was the competition over the locational distribution of the *same* sectors, or put another way, over the social conditions of production. In the North, organized labor and the state-local public sectors constituted highly developed and powerful fetters on a strategy of meeting the South's competitive advantages, although this route was proposed, especially during the New York City crisis and in the American version of enterprise zones, which would forgive some taxes and lift some labor protections in targetted, distressed locations. Some portions of the labor movement saw clearly that the alternative to this prospect was the organization of workers in the South, to eliminate the lower wage, nonunion incentives to migrating capital. But the northeastern coalition was too closely tied to major corporations and their adversarial viewpoint to adopt such a strategy as its explicit program.

It was not surprising, then, that the northern coalition should hit upon the flow of funds issue as a centerpiece to their regional organizing strategy. It was an alternative to changing the underlying economic structure. It seemed an easy way to try to combat state and local budget deficits of crisis proportions. It served as a convenient diverter of attention from corporate culpability. If the cause of northeastern problems could be said to be the southern states stealing "our" jobs, or worse, the federal government robbing northeastern coffers to enrich southern ones, then the heat would be taken off of the indigenous private sector that was most directly responsible for closing plants and financing new jobs elsewhere. This initially worked, although in the longer run, its superficiality became increasingly apparent to progressive groups within the region.

The hue and cry about federal unfairness, then, must be interpreted as an aggressive act by the northeastern coalition against some vaguely designated region called the Sunbelt. The Sunbelt's response was articulated chiefly by the SGPB; western politicans generally concurred in the SGPB's critique but did not spend resources on the controversy.[40] It is worth citing a few journalistic treatments and politicians' statements for the flavor and breadth of the northern attack. *Business Week* (1976) announced "The Second War Between the States." *The Washington Post* (August 9, 1976) chronicled "A New Federal Favoritism for the Sunbelt States." *The Village Voice* (October 11, 1976) headlined "Regional Robbery: How Washington Saps the Northeast." Senator Moynihan in the *New York Times* (August 4, 1977) contended "The crucial point is that . . . the redistributional mode of government, with its bias against New York, is now firmly established in Washington. It is sustained by the rewards it provides to others." Neil Peirce, *National Journal* staffer, warned in the *New York Times* (February 8, 1976), "There's going to be a terrific political issue when the Northeast wakes up to the fact that it's being milked to death for tax money going outside the region." These charges follow a dramatic 1976 *National Journal* article (June 25) which purported to document "Where the Funds Flow: A National Journal Survey Shows that There Is a Massive Flow of Wealth from the Northeast and Midwest to the Faster-Growing West and South" (Havemann, Stanfield, and Peirce 1976). Even union publications picked up the theme; the *Public Employee Press* of March 12, 1976, ran an article by Seymour Melman headlined "The Federal Rip-off of New York's Money," citing a Dreyfus Corporation study as evidence (Melman 1977).

Ironically, this specific form of regional combat also had its precedent in the Civil War epoch, though plaintiff and defendant were reversed. Prior to the Civil War, southern journalists had complained of northern imperialism. The Montgomery, Alabama, *Advertiser* in 1860 calculated the annual cost of southern economic dependence in "Unnecessary Tolls and Tribute the Southern States Pay to the North" (table 8.1). The *Advertiser* concluded, "The establishment of a new Government might cost something, but nothing in comparison to the stream of wealth that would flow to the commercial, manufacturing and mechanical interests, by withholding this annual tribute and working ourselves."

More soberly, *The Richmond Enquirer* of October 7, 1856, urged its readers to vote Democratic in the upcoming presidential election. A Republican accession might rechannel profitable federal contracts for such things as mail carrying and naval supplies to northern businesses.

Table 8.1 Southern "Tolls and Tribute" to the North, 1860

Customs dispersed in the North	$40,000,000
Profit from manufacture of southern raw materials	30,000,000
Profit from imports destined for southern markets	17,000,000
Profit from export of southern goods	40,000,000
Profit from southern travelers	60,000,000
Profit of teachers and others in the South sent North	5,000,000
Profit of agents and brokers and commissions	10,000,000
Capital drawn from the South	30,000,000
Grand total	$231,000,000

Source: The Montgomery *Advertiser,* 1860, cited in Goldfield 1977, 89.

And it would undoubtedly secure and speed the construction of a transcontinental loss from the contracts alone at $50 to 60 million a year.[41]

The similarity between the two epochs is superficial and does not warrant the *Business Week* specter of a second Civil War. The first culminated in a genuine Civil War, that regional conflict turned nationalist which was the subject of chapter 4. The current conflict has flared up between two regions that are *more* similar in economic structure than they have ever been historically. Other historical discontinuities weaken the analogy. One is the reversal of regional roles—the North now claims that it is the victim. A second is that the agent of exploitation indicted has shifted from private capital (albeit with a state backup) to the federal government itself. And, of course, the North is the home of the greatest support for the Democratic party, where the South once claimed this honor.

It is worth pursuing briefly the validity of the flow-of-funds arguments.[42] Two questions must be asked. First, is the Northeast in fact a net loser in the federal flow of funds? The answer to this is a cautious no. There are two major problems with the accounting procedure used to purport unfairness. First, the northeastern accounts always emphasize the regional receipts *net* of taxes paid. By many accounts the per capita receipts of northeastern areas are higher than those of other regions. The differential lies in the uneven distribution of tax payments across the country, a skewness in large part a function of corporate profit tax payments. Yet corporate profits by no means derive from the Northeast, just because the corporations reaping the profits are headquartered there. If corporate profits were reallocated to the place of origin (no small empirical project), then the grounds for the claim of regional robbery might disappear.

Second, the accounts chart only the direct spending patterns of the federal government. Military contracts, for instance, are traced only to the primary contractor's location. Even though these may be disproportionately in the Sunbelt, much of this spending recycles through the northeastern economy in purchases of commodities by primary contractors and in subcontracting arrangements. This is not to deny that southern congressional members have not been successful in postwar military pork-barreling.

A separate question is "*Ought* federal spending to be equalized per capita across regions?" Since the goals of many of the programs subsumed in the debate involve targeted aid to schools, persons in poverty, retirees, resource or transportation development programs, and so on, there is no reason to expect such disbursements to be evenly allocated spatially if the target populations or problems are not also evenly distributed. Clearly, more poor people and more retirees ("per capita") live in the Sunbelt, and many federal land management problems are peculiar to the regions in which they arise.

The superficiality of the flow-of-funds argument is most evident in its fate. Although the Northeast won the first skirmishes, by the decade's end the debate had stalemated in Congress. Indeed, by 1978, the Northeast-Midwest Congressional Coalition, the Coalition of Northeastern Governors, and the Southern Growth Policies Board were holding a series of north-south summits. The "agencies" as they referred to themselves, agreed to work together on the cost-of-living controversy, to cooperate on export development programs, and to pursue federal dollars for maintenance of aging social infrastructure. They also agreed on the "usefulness of regionalism itself as an innovative method to address citizens at the state and local level, the President and the Congress on economic development issues."[43]

To some extent, the regional robbery hoopla may have been chiefly ideologically motivated. Blaming an external force for ills at home has often served as a successful means of muting demands for domestic change. In national forums, politicians from both regions often gave powerful speeches about the ingratitude or aggression of the other. Senator Moynihan from New York suggested that the Northeast had generously financed both westward expansion and the New Deal's southern programs, but that the South was not a thankful stepchild:

> I ask what will become of this tradition of national liberalism if the region from which it emerged should look up two generations later, and find that while other regions were willing enough to accept a transfer of resources when they were the beneficiaries in need, no such reciprocal impulses will appear when the northeast was in need? What if it turns out that the New Deal was a one way street? [Senator Daniel Moynihan, White House Conference on Balanced Growth, 1978]

The South's representative, Governor Busbee of Georgia, retorted, "This is not a divorce proceeding. You can't expect enough alimony to sustain the manner of life you've been accustomed to" (White House Conference on Balanced Growth 1978; Sutton 1978, 37). These statements seem aimed at the press and constituents back home as much as at the other region.

Political changes in Congress and the presidency have weakened the weapons of those battling over federal coffers. The formula fights ended in a standoff. The accession of Reagan, with his lack of an explicit spatial focus and his drive to dismantle the Economic Development Administration and federal aid programs alike, diminished the pie over which to fight. The new federalism which Reagan proposed was, if anything, a movement away from the equalizing of regional social costs envisioned by the Northeast, since Reagan would bestow yet greater responsibility on individual states for determining welfare benefits and eligibility. The only incremental portion of the federal budget available to fight over is the military budget. But defense dollars are largely allocated through the bidding procedures of the Pentagon and through military base location decisions, rather than by formula fashioning in Congress. The competition for military spending thus ends up looking strikingly like the type of competition for private business already well entrenched in states' economic development programs.

So in the end, the real (as opposed to the ideological) thrust of the 1970s north-south regionalism boiled down to a new twist on the old theme of competition over industrial incentives. Both lobbies turned their eyes inward after 1980 to ponder the economic development mechanisms of their member states. There was little to suggest that these might be any different from those that had previously been developed to chip away at corporate costs and woo jobs by bolstering private sector profitability. Indeed, as regional strategies turned homeward in the 1980s, the hostilities between the regions faded once again, and they could be observed pursuing strikingly similar paths.

POSTWAR NORTH-SOUTH REGIONALISM: A SUMMARY

In the postwar period, the industrial mix of the South became more like that of the North, as manufacturers moved south toward the better business climate. Yet, the two regional economies diverged dramatically in the pace of development (chapter 6). The growing disparity in growth rates was exacerbated by the post-Vietnam slowdown of the economy. In response, the harder-pressed region, the Northeast, initiated an aggressive campaign against the Sunbelt to gain better treatment from the central government.

The outward orientation of the Northeast coalition was prompted by internal difficulties. Short on tax revenues and financial capital, the region found it hard to solve its urban and employment crises. Yet the major cause, outmigration of capital, was too difficult and radical for a business-supported political leadership to confront head-on. The federal system facilitated a channeling of demands toward the central State, especially Congress—a political forum in which this region had been traditionally strong. While the strength of the two-party system and the absence of a strong regional self-consciousness proved to be barriers to organizing, the severity of the crisis drove business and political leaders to surmount them in a Washington-based coalition.

The faster-growing southern region entered the decade of widening regional disparity in growth rates with intensive internal debate about the new problems of development. Its attention was drawn into the interregional arena only in response to attacks by the Northeast. Its ability to mobilize in response was facilitated by its durable one-party political structure, its long history of regional self-consciousness, and its traditional hostility toward Yankee culture and economic domination.

Both regional coalitions managed to mount a fairly unified regional front. In the Northeast, initiating elites received broad public support simply because of the regionwide interdependence of the economy and the multiplier effects of sectoral displacement. In the South, vigorous internal conflicts over disruptive economic growth were for a time overriden by another region's aggression and a long memory of interregional strife.

Yet challenges to the dominant business posture of each region emerged in the form of more radical organization efforts on behalf of unions, community groups, and minorities. In the Northeast plant-closing coalitions attempted to shift the onus onto regional and national owners of capital, while in the South vigorous efforts to organize previously nonunionized industries took issue with the good business climate consensus. While these groups could not win control of regionwide political organs, they could and did benefit from the interest galvanized around the latter and often received a wider hearing for alternative programs.

The role of regional economic disparities, in this case in growth rates, is quite clear in prompting regionalism in this era. Interregional hostilities peaked during the latter half of the decade, when restructuring in the Northeast was accelerating. Once the Northeast slide began to halt, around 1980, the vigor of its Washington efforts began to diminish and its anti-Sunbelt campaign languished. In turn, with a stalemate in the flow-of-funds debate, the southern governors' organization turned back to internal development issues.

At the same time, economic differences would not have been sufficient to create this period of regional political drama. The long-standing cultural antagonism between these two groups of states was a powerful shaper of the 1970s debate, as were the political structures and indigenous parties that facilitated it.

Notes

1. The membership of these organizations has been changing over time, generally in the direction of greater inclusiveness. The map and discussion use the membership of each as of 1980, because my purpose is to emphasize the formation and leadership of regional coalitions, rather than their maturity. More recent dropouts and joiners are noted in the text where appropriate. While the notions of "Sunbelt" and "Frostbelt" are quite lumpy and harbor broad disparities across internal boundaries (see Browning and Gesler 1979, and Mellor 1985), these political groups are organizational testimony to a commonly held view of mutuality.
2. These organizations were not the only actors engaged in interregional politics in the 1970s. They were chosen because they were the most visible and most comprehensive, and were more easily compared than other groups. In each region, the presence or emergence of alternative groups will be reviewed, chiefly as a way of evaluating the tenor of regional politics,

particularly the cross-class, cross-sector and cross-ethnic compositional possibilities.

3. See Tabb (1982) on New York City, Ewen (1978) on Detroit, and the articles in Alcaly and Mermelstein (1977) and Burchell and Listokin (1981).

4. In addition to the literature on interregional shifts cited above, two Northeast-oriented research efforts, both funded by EDA, produced significant analysis of the region: Chinitz (1978) and Harrison (1980) (see also New England Economy Project, summary).

5. For a documentation of the rise and fall of the national urban constituency, as registered in the mobilization for and failure of a national urban policy, see Markusen and Wilmoth (1982).

6. This echoed the basic business program for solving urban fiscal crisis by squeezing the social wage and enhancing the attractiveness of the local business climate by both tax incentives and greater social control, which had its showpiece in the Municipal Assistance Corporation's restructuring of the New York City budget. Business organizations such as the Conference Board had been active for some years formulating these types of solutions to city fiscal crisis.

7. For a review of this research, see Markusen and Fastrup (1978).

8. See also Dilger (1982), for an account of these issues.

9. Both were prefigured by a Conference of Legislative Leaders on the Future of the Northeast, held in Albany, New York in December 1975, funded by grants from the federal Economic Development Administration and Environmental Protection Agency, and organized by a leader of the New York State Senate. See Rafuse (1977, 6) and Peirce (1976, 1699).

10. CONEG was scouted by Carey at the National Governors' Conference in Washington, D.C. in February 1976 and officially formed in June of that year. Maine's independent governor participated as an observer and later joined; New Hampshire's Republican governor never joined.

11. For Rohatyn's regional program, see Rohatyn (1977).

12. Interview with David Merkowitz, Northeast-Midwest Congressional Caucus staffer, February 1982. The coalition claimed credit for spawning the Gypsy Moth caucus of dissident Republicans, who began to buck Reagan's program.

13. Ibid. These financial conditions are in flux. In 1983, Congress evicted the institute (and all other nonprofit special interest groups) from their quarters. Furthermore, since EDA and other executive branch funds have dried up, the institute is increasingly seeking private sector support for its work.

14. For an account at the height of the formula debates, see Ehrenhalt, 1977. A lengthier treatment of formula politics is found in Markusen, Saxenian, and Weiss (1981a).

15. The first welcoming of a regional consciousness which I have found in the academic press is found in Sternlieb and Hughes (1978, 34), where they argue that the task is to build a regional constituency over time, a form of "institutionalized advocacy" which "strives to maintain the gathering momentum." See also Wilbur Thompson's article in the same volume.

16. The Bluestone and Harrison work analyzed the causes of plant closing and presented a new agenda that encompassed plant closing legislation, redevelopment, worker buyouts, and selective nationalization as well as collective bargaining and labor law reform approaches. The Progressive Alliance maintained a Washington presence for about two years.

17. Conference on Alternative State and Local Public Policies (1976); also draft of Conference Resolution, in possession of the author.

18. See, for instance, Rifkin and Barber's (1978) articulate argument for pension power, the Conference on Alternative State and Local Public Policies (1976), and Lanigan (1976).
19. Even leftist regionalists sometime succumb to antagonistic expressions toward other regions. See Weiss (1979) on the Rifkin and Barber volume.
20. For a review and examples of the incidence, regulation, and organizing efforts surrounding plant closings see Harrison and Bluestone (1981).
21. Controversy over the psychological and material roots of this consciousness has persisted over the decades, particularly following the publication of Cash's *The Mind of the South* in 1941.
22. Examples of this literature prior to the 1970s include Nicholls (1960), Leiserson (1964), McKinney and Thompson (1965), and Thompson (1967).
23. Observers of southern politics point out that Sanford's initiative was also tied into his national political aspirations (he had been hailed by the eastern seaboard establishment press as presidential material), his connections with corporate liberal circles nationally and the Kennedy clan in particular, and his networking with the liberally minded business leadership across the South.
24. Internally, unique economic features differentiate the coastal, piedmont, and mountain areas, the oil and gas states of Louisiana and Oklahoma, and the military, trade, and retirement-stimulated boom state of Florida from the rest of the Old South states. In addition, great diversity characterizes subregions, some of which, like the Republican sentiment in the southern Appalachians, date back more than a century. Where important, these differences will be sketched out as problems confronting the board's strategies and composition.
25. In the late 1970s, the Texas state office in Washington had three times as many staff members as the SGPB.
26. For a good survey of twentieth-century economic development issues in the South, see Danhof (1964), as well as the edited volume in which it is found. Both Maddox et al. (1967) and Naylor and Clotfelter (1975) emphasize the historical handicaps of southern development—lack of skilled manpower, insufficient investment in education and technology, inadequate capital and insufficient levels of demand.
27. See also Moss (1975) and Teasley (1974).
28. Godschalk et al. report that the Lincoln Institute of Land Policy funded a conference envisioned to pull together state legislators concerned with growth management, but that the draw was so lean that they had to change the conference's topic to "Tax Reform and Southern Development."
29. The council was set up as a counterweight to the Northeast-Midwest Congressional Caucus under the leadership of Texas Democrat Charles Wilson. It saw itself as the junior partner in a David and Goliath struggle with its antagonist and set up its structure in a parallel fashion, with a nonprofit research arm and free House Annex space. In 1981, its members included all the SGPB states plus Texas, and it hoped to attract as new members Arizona, New Mexico, Colorado, California, and Nevada. In July 1982, the Southern Governors' Association voted to move from Atlanta to Washington and to become the region's lead organization in D.C. (letter from SGPB Executive Director Jesse White, October 1982).
30. Weinstein (1979b, 2–4), conversation with Bud Skinner of SGPB, March 1982.
31. Although now it took center stage, concern with business promotion had played a role in the board's activities from the start. In 1973, it hosted a

Conference on Reverse Investment, dedicated to discussion of strategies for promoting foreign investment in the South (SGPB 1973).

32. One SGPB staff member made much of the fact that the head of the North Carolina labor movement was convicted of misusing CETA funds, a charge which unionists contend was purely harassment and was based on a minor technicality rather than on any misconduct involving diversion of funds to other purposes.

33. This position was also embraced in Liner's 1979 presentation outlining and critiquing proposed legislation to restrict business mobility.

34. For an effort to incorporate an analysis of southern race issues into a growth management perspective, see Grigsby (1982).

35. An example of this type of economic development planning is in North Carolina's government-funded $24 million Micro-electronics Center. Like their financially strapped northern neighbors, southern state economic development departments are aggressively pursuing high-tech, military spending, and government contracts. For instance, North Carolina celebrated Small Business Week in May 1982, with a Government Procurement Conference. A Tennessee state office monitors and publicizes every Pentagon bid.

36. Conversation with Tom Schlesinger of the Highlander Center, March 1982.

37. See Whisnant (1979) and Clavel (1982) or a detailed account of the evolution of Appalachian oppositional organizations.

38. Norton and Rees (1979) demonstrate this convergence over the period 1963 to 1976 with shift-share analysis.

39. See Goodman (1979) for a thorough account of how states compete with each other over these cost items.

40. See the next chapter for a further discussion of the western position.

41. Both accounts cited in Goldfield (1977, 89–90). The newspapers took their figures from the sensationalist book by Thomas Kettell, *Southern Wealth and Northern Profits,* cited in chapter 4.

42. For an extended development of these arguments, see Markusen and Fastrup (1978). For an empirical account of federal flows, calculated several different ways, and a political analysis of the formation of the flows components, see Markusen, Saxenian and Weiss (1981a and 1981b). Bellmon (1978, 9) concludes that federal aid has not been regionally biased; Romans (1965) shows how unevenly wealth, and thus property income, is distributed across U.S. regions.

43. At the 1979 summit, the regions agreed to petition the Treasury against any change in the general revenue-sharing formula (an acknowledgment of the standoff), to pursue a pro-rural development policy at the federal level, to mount a public transportation coalition, to support the continuation of EDA, to cooperate in shaping the new CDBG formula, and to work toward a joint policy on toxic waste issues.

9

The Energy-Rich West Versus the Rest

Postwar politics in the United States demonstrates in yet another instance how interregional antagonisms arise when sectors are highly segregated geographically. In this case, the hostilities ran along an east-west axis. Their economic origins were the dramatically diverging growth rates, in the 1970s, between the northeastern industrial belt and the energy-rich Intermountain West. Again, a priori we might anticipate that this latter region, grappling with pyramiding demands on a single, fragile resource base, would turn its political energies to solving internal contradictions. This would not be a region to initiate an interregional challenge. But in response to a challenge from another region, it might defend its special economic situation. Its success would depend upon its existing political structure and its ability to call upon a shared perception of commonality across wide open ranges and formidable mountain barriers.

Across the east-west frontier, regions have traditionally faced each other under conditions of potentially unequal exchange, reminiscent of the original exchange relationship between interior Native Americans and French and British mercantilists. The high concentration of energy sectors in the Intermountain and High Plains West has placed that region in the position of energy supplier to both Pacific Coast and eastern regions. The profitability of downstream sectors in the latter requires keeping energy prices down. But the longer-term viability of the intermountain economy dictates higher prices for its nonrenewable resources.

Historically, the purchasing regions have had the upper hand in this relationship. Their banks financed raw material exploitation. Their railroads controlled access to markets. Their corporate customers (meat packers, grain dealers, oil and coal-using factories, and metal-makers) were furthermore highly oligopolized, permitting them to exercise substantial market power.

But in the postwar period, energy shortages strengthened the exchange position of the West. At least through the 1970s, western states were able to charge hefty severance taxes on many of their resource-based products. Yet the bulk of the profits from more recent energy development accrued to large corporations and property holders in other regions. In the energy boom decade, antagonisms reminiscent of the populist agitation against "eastern money" again erupted. But this time they were more purely regional, "western," in nature than they had been in the late nineteenth century. Here, the east-west regionalism of the 1970s is analyzed in a manner parallel to that of the preceding chapter.

THE CONTEXT: EXTRACTIVE INDUSTRIES AND A HOME-GROWN CULTURE

The economy of the interior or intermountain western states has traditionally been composed of unique and contentious sectors operating within a highly politicized tableau. Agriculture, mining, and tourism comprise the economic base, as chapter 6 detailed. Historically, among land-based activities, the absence of mutually beneficial interlinkages and the competition over scarce natural resources prompted sometimes riotous forms of intraregional conflict.

In agriculture, for instance, land-use incompatibilities between stock raising and crop farming produced the kind of neighborly conflict memorialized in the hit musical *Oklahoma*'s tongue-in-cheek song, "The Farmer and the Cowboy Should Be Friends." Within the ranching sector, cattlemen fought sheepgrowers in sporadically violent outbursts over use of the open range. Mountain-based hydraulic mining techniques and chemical processing of minerals led to soil erosion, flooding, and stream pollution of major proportions in the valleys below, creating tension between mining and agricultural interests. As cities grew up in this arid region, conflicts between urban and rural interests emerged over the appropriation of water.

Contemporary western economic sectors continue to place distinct and competing demands on the relatively fragile environment. Mining companies must displace earth and consume huge amounts of water to refine ores. Ranchers need a renewable groundwater supply and unfenced ranges. Farmers require water for irrigation and fencing to protect tasty crops from wide-ranging livestock. Recreational entrepreneurs count on a pristine and scenic environment. Urban growth coalitions seek water for city consumption and favor accessible recreation areas for their working populations. Particularly in agriculture, whether timbering, ranching or crop-raising, the "carrying capacity" in this often desert-like zone is frequently overreached. Land and water uses are traditionally bellicose topics in western climes. The only successful economic coalitions have been farmed around support for dam, reservoir, and water projects which promise benefits to diverse sectors.

The region's growth and decline has often been engineered by "outside" interests—corporate financiers, managers, and operators whose base is in other regions. Outside ownership, however, does not preclude substantial boosterism within the region favoring resource exploitation. An in-region pro-growth constituency has been closely allied to the nationally based resource companies. The former encompasses not only the local real estate, banking, and commercial sectors, but extensive regional capital in the form of utilities and railroads. Prominent members of this constituency are the construction corporations like Bechtel and Utah Construction, whose business is erecting huge processing plants, dams, and infrastructure. These "built-environment" corporations got their start with the Colorado River Compact, constructing its many dams and reservoirs. Their continued liquidity depends upon the periodic mounting of new large-scale western projects, whether nuclear or coal-fired power generation, new towns, or experimental synthetic fuels plants (Gottlieb and Wiley 1982).

Probably no region has captured the national imagination more than "the West," beginning with Turner's identification of its importance as a formative feature of American character and politics to a raft of twentieth-cenntury books and periodicals. Defending its unity as a region, the West's historians and publicists have emphasized its mountain and desertlike fragility, its beauty, and the remoteness of its human settlements. Howard's title for his history of Montana (1943) captures the elements: *Montana: High, Wide and Handsome*. Protagonists have celebrated the tenacity of the region's successful ranchers, the fluidity of its communities, and the raucous, risk-taking, male lifestyle popularized in cowboy imagery. The love of the land, the nearly anarchist attitude toward government, and the stubbornness and pugnacity of the West celebrated in its literature all color the political style of western organizing.

In reality, no homogeneous western culture exists. Communities have formed around entirely different material bases, and their social lives reflect the traditions and concerns of those activities. The ethnic groups which compose each community tend also to be differentiated spatially and sectorally. Eastern European miners were imported by Rockefeller to work in the southern Colorado coal mines in the early decades of the century. Anglo-American miners flocked to turn-of-the-century gold, silver, and lead mines in the high Rockies. Chicanos were imported to work the New Mexican copper mines. Scandanavian wheat farmers in northeastern Montana became strong advocates of populism, while southeastern Montana stockgrowers of Texas origin have been staunch Republicans. Dozens of Native American tribes with quite distinct traditions and contemporary economies are scattered on reservations throughout the Rockies. Centered in Utah, the Mormon religion forms the basis for strong, exclusive economic, financial, and social ties crosscutting agriculture, mining, and urban areas (Parrish 1980).

While many of these groups trace their roots back a century or more, the majority of westerners are newcomers. In the late 1970s, more than

50 percent of all residents surveyed in the Four Corners states had come from outside the state, except for Utah (Ingram et al. 1980, 27). Many of the region's politicians are not native-born westerners. Newcomers comprised dissimilar groups—retirees, construction workers migrating with energy-related jobs, tourism-oriented entrepreneurs, energy industry and federal government professionals. Some newcomers became ardent environmentalists; some support further development. In smaller towns, the influx of newcomers introduces severe adjustment problems, including increases in unemployment, destabilization of pre-existing social networks, and intensification of social problems like alcoholism, crime, delinquency, and suicide (Massey 1977; Curry 1982; Moen et al. 1981; Kroll, 1981).

The political cultures of western states are highly complex and individual, because of the heterogeneity and lack of interdependence among sectors, uneven rates of subregional growth and decline over the decades, and ethnic skewness in populations. With the exception of New Mexico, neither the Democratic nor the Republican party has been dominant. Initially Republican, many states developed strong third parties during the Populist free silver era. The Democratic party inherited much of these Populist, agrarian attachments and flourished with the New Deal's infusion of capital spending (which brought, for example, Boulder Dam and the national parks) (Donnelly 1940, 8–9). More recently, Democratic support has eroded, from a presidential vote of 61 percent in 1960 to about 44 percent in 1980, although most of the loss has been to self-described independents.[1]

Western states as a whole display four political features. First, their legislatures have tended to be dominated by resource-exploiting interests, either outright as in the case of Montana, or through coalitions, as in the states of Colorado, Utah, and Wyoming.[2] Second, their congressional delegations and governors tend to be more liberal than their legislatures.[3] Third, to the extent that parties attract class, ethnic, and locational allegiances, the Republicans have drawn regional business interests, Anglo-Saxons, suburban residents, and rural ranchers. Democrats have been the party of organized labor (especially miners, railroad, and construction workers), urban and industrial populations, and minority groups. Finally, a strong urban-rural antagonism has characterized legislatures, often arrayed on an east-west axis. But while rural areas have been traditionally Republican, and urban areas Democratic, this appears to be changing as suburbanites swell the Republican ranks and hard-pressed and energy development-threatened farmers and ranchers switch to the Democrats.[4]

The distinctive sectoral and cultural styles of state-level politics can be illustrated by the states of Montana and Utah. The former remained dominated until the mid-1960s by the Anaconda Copper Company, which not only owned the bulk of the state's rich mineral sector but also was the largest landowner of timber acreage, the number one logger and sawmill operator, the parent of the Montana Power Company, and the owner of seven of the state's eight biggest daily newspapers. Anaconda, plus the stockmen, state business and financial interests, and the oil companies who arrived in the 1950s, dominated the state legislature, while the liberal Democrats, who comprised organized labor and the Farmers' Union (mainly northeast wheat farmers), frequently gained the statehouse and the senatorial delegation. With the post-1960s decline of copper, and the rise of lumber, coal and oil interests, the business lobby has become more pluralistic, and sometimes splits internally over issues like public power (Abbott 1940, 99; Payne 1969; Toole 1976).

In Utah, the Republican party has been dominated by a coalition of railroads, utilities, and mining companies, while the Democrats have represented miners, railroad workers and the newer urban businessmen. Democrats attracted many small businesses with their opposition to private utilities, and many stockmen with the advent of New Deal loans and public sector jobs. Most politicians of either party in this state are Mormon (more than 90 percent of all state legislators, for instance), although the Democrats tend to be the party of non-Mormon interests.[5] Other states exhibit similar idiosyncracies in the sectoral and cultural complexion of politics. Arizona, for instance, was proverbially dominated by the three C's: cotton, cattle, and copper (Ingram et al. 1980, 5).

Because of these state-by-state differences, few attempts at regionwide organizing were successful until the 1970s. Indeed, formal regionwide political caucuses in the postwar period were primarily due to efforts by national political parties to secure the region's congressional and presidential votes.[6] As recently as 1960, a scholar of western politics could imagine only the federal government's invasiveness serving as a fulcrum for regional politics (Anderson 1961, 294–95, 298). This all changed with the 1970s energy boom.

THE ISSUES: THE PACE AND BENEFICIARIES OF DEVELOPMENT

Western regionalism in the 1970s was provoked by the new round of energy development, set off by the OPEC oil price hike and the federal government's militant response in Project Independence. The region's economy boomed (see chapter 6). Several issues were key to the new regional self-consciousness. First, effective organizing began around environmental quality. Environmentalists won two early victories. They stopped the proposed 1976 Winter Olympics in Colorado, which threatened a relatively pristine recreational environment, and the Kaiparowitz power plant, which threatened air quality in southeastern Utah.[7] Second, ranching and farming communities became increasingly mobilized in opposition to the strip mining of coal, mine mouth coal-fired generation plants, and high voltage transmission lines, all of which threatened their land, water supply, air quality, and settled community way of life

(Gold 1974).[8] Third, explosive boomtown growth led some mountain towns to fight associated fiscal pressures, community disruption, and the worsening situation of women and minorities. Fourth, Native Americans, encouraged by the strength of a national civil rights movement, contested the terms of leasing of their energy-rich lands, inadequate royalties, and ineffective employment policies.[9] Finally, plant and mine closings, the legacy of past rounds of dynamics of western development, began to produce opposition similar to that in more industrial regions.[10]

With the distinctive energy-based boom, the notion of this region as a resource colony reemerged.[11] References to the mountain West being a national sacrifice area and an internal colony increasingly appeared in the press. Memories of the exploitation westerners had suffered during the era of discriminatory freight rates (remnants of which exist today) heightened sensitivities to the terms of commodity trade between this region and the rest of the country (Jonas 1969, 3).[12]

Western opponents of rapid energy development did not necessarily see eye to eye nor feel their interests opposed to groups in other regions. They did jointly fear the prospective encroachments of a federal government which threatened, under the guise of Project Independence, to preempt newly won state environmental and agricultural preservation laws. This sentiment is not to be confused with the Sagebrush Rebellion, a much later development (from around 1977 on) which was a specific response to the improved and more environmentally protective range and forest management practices of the national Department of the Interior. The Sagebrush Rebels, far from being environmentalists, were primarily the largest grazing and timber interests in the West, supported by a bevy of land interests. They sought transfer of control over western lands from federal sustained-yield agencies to state legislatures. The latter could then sell them outright to the region's largest landowners and land companies. Smaller farmers and ranchers, environmentalists, and urban newspapers tended to oppose this western assertion of rights over land disposal.[13]

The issues of energy development, particularly land policy, energy policy, and community impacts, became the grist of regional politics from the early 1970s on. These were nationally oriented only insofar as the federal government was a major actor in the energy development process. Regional business groups, energy corporations, environmentalists, ranchers, residents—all entered the regional fray for resources and preferred land uses. This was the context which gave birth to a new regional organizing effort.

A NEW ENVIRONMENTAL REGIONALISM: THE WESTERN GOVERNORS' ENERGY POLICY OFFICE

Out of this controversial environment emerged new style western politicians. In Montana, Thomas Judge rode to the governorship in late 1972 on a wave of political reaction to decades of state domination by

Anaconda Copper. The Montana Democratic party took over the state legislature, backed by a coalition of unionized miners, environmentalists, and ranchers. They wrote a new constitution and adopted a series of strong energy development control mechanisms to protect existing sectors like agriculture and tourism against the "exploit and abandon" methods of corporations like Anaconda, whose legacy was quite visible in high unemployment rates and immense craterlike pitting of the land. Committed to going slow on coal, Judge and his legislative counterparts adopted strong strip mining laws, placed a moratorium on diversion of Yellowstone Basin water to industrial uses, set up an Environmental Quality Council, passed a powerful Major Facility Act, and adopted a development-discouraging and impact-financing severance amounting to 30 percent of the value of coal mined (Toole 1976; Hayes 1980, 66–67, 76).

In Colorado, Democrat Richard Lamm was elected governor in 1974 as a strong environmentalist candidate. In the 1960s, Colorado had been a Republican-dominated, "bring business to Colorado" state. But as the skiing industry, dependent on preservation of mountain beauty, expanded the state's tourism sector and as urban growth on the Front Range intensified recreational and water demands on the Rockies, environmentalism began to blossom, crystalizing in the opposition to the proposed 1976 Winter Olympics high on the Continental Divide west of Denver. The voters defeated the Olympics by referendum in 1972 and subsequently supported Lamm as a growth management advocate who favored conservation over energy development.

In Wyoming, Democrat Ed Herschler was elected in the same era on a platform of slow, carefully controlled growth, terminating more than a decade of Republican control of the statehouse. In place of the former governor's invitations to the coal industry:

> Come look in Wyoming . . . We have a lot of coal out there . . . we'd like to have you . . . And I always tell the people who are not particularly friendly to the mineral industries, if you want them all to leave, you'd better be prepared to dig pretty deeply in your pockets to replace that kind of revenue . . .[14] [Hayes 1980, 65]

Herschler's coalition passed new laws stopping coal slurry pipelines from exporting Wyoming water, adopting statewide zoning and water use laws, setting up a stiff Industrial Siting Act, and providing measures for environmental preservation. In Idaho, Cecil Andrus, another Democrat and committed environmentalist, won the governorship in 1974. Andrus later joined Carter's cabinet where, as Interior Secretary, his strong preservationist attitudes helped provoke the Sagebrush Rebellion. In North Dakota, William Guy successfully ran for governor on a platform which included a moratorium on energy company's water applications and a commitment to the environment over profitmaking (Nelson 1979, 21; Hayes 1980, 80, 105).

Lamm first broached the subject of a regional organizing effort in late

1974 at the national Democratic Governors' Conference. Lamm and Judge were dissatisfied with the fragmentation and preoccupations of existing regional organizations. Two EDA-funded regional commissions—The Old West and the Four Corners—clustered Colorado and Montana indifferent spheres despite common problems. The commissions, which each spent about $4.5 million per year on economic development promotional activities, had furthermore shown little interest in merging environmental with growth concerns. The Old West, for instance, advertised in the business press with full-page ads exhorting "Discover the Energy States of America":

> Because the energy is here, these five states are where the next big business boom has started. American needs this energy. And that means things will be happening here. Firms like yours are needed . . . There's Glad-to-see-you energy from state governments that are eager to help you find sites, arrange financing, even train employees . . . Come profit by it. Come prosper in the Energy States of America. [Old West Regional Commission, in *Mainliner* Magazine, June 1977, 23]

The Federation of Rocky Mountain States, a business-government partnership which cost each state $55,000 per year in dues, promoted resource development issues and had supported the Kaiparowitz power plant (Hayes 1980, 59; Western Governors' Task Force 1976, 15).

Judge and Lamm worked out an organizational strategy operating on two fronts. One was internal to the region, an effort to unify states around a strong growth control stance and strengthen the ability of each to deal with large energy companies. The second was external, the effort to present a united front to the federal government, whose policies determined the mineral leasing practices, grazing permits, water and infrastructure development projects, hazardous waste disposal, pollution control, and environmental regulations. The governors were particularly alarmed by the contemporary financial megalomania for large-scale, high-tech, western-based energy developments commencing with Project Independence. The image of two adversaries—one private, one public—was presented in press statements:

> Decisions should be made by the people of this region, not by the federal government or the energy companies. If we sit passively by, we will be a colony for the rest of the United States . . . We've got to organize or the Eastern banks and corporations, helped by the Ford Administration, will pick us off one by one. [Judge, October 1974]

> We won't become the nation's slag heap. I am convinced my election is due in part to a new assertiveness. There is a whole new breed of people out here. . . . We have seen what's happened to Kentucky and Tennessee and West Virginia and other states that have been the nation's coal bin, and we're not going to let that happen to us. [Lamm, early 1975][15]

Arguing a rhetoric of states' rights, and capitalizing on the fact that all the intermountain and high plains states involved had Democratic governors in the mid-1970s, the core leadership successfully recruited the governors of Utah, Nevada, New Mexico, Arizona, North and South Dakota, and Nebraska, which together with Wyoming, Colorado, and Montana made ten original members of the newly formed (July, 1976) Western Governors' Regional Energy Policy Office (WGREPO).[16] The governors won funding from the existing federal regional commissions, while eschewing managerial participation from them. This financial aid permitted them to exclude FMRS from sponsorship, making them fully independent from the private sector whose activities they aspired to control. Adopting a thoroughly decentralized form of organization, they agreed to keep decision making in their own hands and to provide information principally in the form of press releases that would be delivered exclusively to each governor simultaneously for his (there were no women among them) individual use. The governors denied the chairmanship to both Lamm and Judge, of whom the rest were politically suspicious and jealous. The majority of members evidently favored a more gradual, conciliatory and cooperative approach than either man had espoused (Peirce and Hagstrom 1977, 208–19; Hayes 1980, 79, 96–97, 107).

In its infancy, WGREPO was openly environmentalist and championed the preservation of "the Western way of life." Its first five demands were catalogued in WGREPO's first "Statement of Concern": strong strip mining laws, continuation of coal leasing only after strip mining controls are in place, energy conservation as an alternative to energy development, an end to federal preemption of state controls on development, and impact aid from the federal government to compensate communities for adverse boomtown effects. WGREPO advocated an economy built upon a viable agricultural sector and a healthy and attractive tourism sector, while preserving the character of both existing recreational areas and residential communities. The mission was so clear in these early days of the organization that WGREPO's principal (and enthusiastic) biographer could write, "Unhesitatingly the majority of the states in the WGREPO were openly resisting one of the nation's greatest drives toward industrial development in history (Hayes 1980, 96–98, 108).

FROM CONFRONTATION TO PROMOTION: THE WESTERN GOVERNORS' POLICY OFFICE

From the outset, WGREPO sought ways of casting off from the federal trough and launching a permanent, self-financed organization. They tried to maximize political clout by courting the Pacific Rim states of Hawaii, Alaska, and the Pacific Coast, not least because they were interested in capturing the funding sources of three existing regional agencies: the Western Interstate Nuclear Board ($180,000 dues per year per state), the FMRS, and the Pacific Northwest Regional Commission, another of the EDA agencies. To this end, WGREPO's first big project surveyed all existing multistate organizations and suggested remedies for their unwieldy proliferation and their ineffectual, overlapping functions. In the process of trying to supplant existing organizations and to reconcile the differences in regional vision of the plains versus the Pacific states as potential partners, the organization's environmental stance deteriorated and it slowly transformed itself into a balanced growth advocate.

But more importantly, the energy interests themselves rallied their regional suppliers, clients, and other potential beneficiaries to pressure WGREPO leadership to soften their assertive stance against development. Lamm was a good example. In Colorado, Lamm was repeatedly thwarted by a Republican Senate, which defeated most of his growth management proposals, including a severance tax. Lamm, who had initially promised to "drive a silver spike through the heart" of a proposed Denver-area freeway, faced stiff opposition in his 1978 reelection bid. He redesigned the freeway into a parkway. By late 1975, he had begun self-consciously to move away from a confrontational stance and to preach cooperation and negotiation with both the feds and the energy corporations. He had found, he ruefully told the press, that "the oil can is mightier than the sword" (Farney 1978; Hayes 1980, 115).

The lobbying by the energy companies found fertile ground in those members' states that were largely energy consumers rather than producers. As early as 1975, Arizona objected to WGREPO's call for a moratorium on coal leasing, fearful that her electricity-generating utilities would run out of coal. As a result, and with the support of Utah, Nebraska, and South Dakota, the "strip-mining law first" demand of the governors was watered down to read "federal law should conform with the states. . . ." The political leadership of states like South Dakota, Utah, and Arizona had never considered environmental issues a top priority, and their representatives worked persistently to redirect the office's energies in favor of resource development issues.

Energy development interests worked more directly to insert their needs into the regional limelight by working through the Federation of Rocky Mountain States (FRMS). The latter, although it had been excluded from WGREPO, was still bidding to become a partner in the new permanent organization, which was to be called the Western Governors' Policy Office, or WESTPO, for short. An interim Mountain-Plains Task Force was set up with the governors as members and FRMS as staff. The task force's report predictably argued that the proliferation of multistate organizations was a major impediment to successful western unity and forceful representation in Washington. It proposed that WGREPO, FRMS, and the Western Interstate Nuclear Board merge to form one organization. The new body would replace the more environmentally oriented obejctives of WGREPO with five topical task forces—energy, agriculture, human resources, water, and natural resources (Western Governors' Task Force 1976; Hayes 1980, 130–34).[17]

The most difficult issue facing the new organizations was the question of membership. Unlike the regions in the previous chapter, no clear boundary could be drawn around a uniquely "western" region. States like Nebraska and North and South Dakota had gravitated toward WGREPO because they shared problems in agriculture, water, coal development, and power generation and transmission with the Rocky Mountain states. Theirs was a link of common culture as well as economic condition. They desired to break away from the Midwest Governors' Conference to join their fates with the West. At the same time, they were reluctant to see their vote diluted by addition of the Pacific Rim states.

On the western flank, some of the mountain states were well integrated into the southwestern and Pacific northwestern economies. Much of their produce was processed and consumed or shipped out of ports in these states. West coast banks financed the Mountain West's built environment and marketing activities, and their factories shipped most of the assembled autos, canned food, clothing, gasoline, lumber, steel, and construction materials that mountain states consumed.[18] Theirs was a link of economic symbiosis.

The west coast states, however, were fast-growing, energy-consuming areas, worried about getting fuel, electricity, and water from the Intermountain West, enthusiastic about nuclear power, and opposed to severance taxes and other charges that might raise energy prices. California, Oregon, and Washington, defenders of the established Western Governors' Conference, all shunned the new regional organization after several courting sessions, and while Hawaii joined for a short period, it later withdrew. The Pacific states were adamant about preserving the Western Interstate Nuclear Board from cannibalization by the new organization. Alaska was the only noncontiguous state to join, a state with tremendous energy development issues and the greatest proportion of federally owned land in the nation, and thus more similar to WESTPO members.[19]

Ultimately, the new regional organization was to be a full-fledged business-government partnership. It was officially formed in July 1977, a merger of WGREPO and the old public-private Federation of Rocky Mountain States, which was disbanded. WESTPO encompassed eleven western states, with 44 percent of the nation's land area but only 5.8 percent of its population. The new organization was staffed almost entirely by FRMS personnel, which guaranteed a sympathetic hearing for utility interests and symbolized the end of the adversarial relationship between the governors and the private sector.[20]

From its birth, WESTPO became a self-styled "balanced growth" advocate, as evidenced in its first major report, *Balanced Growth and*

Economic Development: A Western White Paper. Explicit mention of the environment became less and less frequent, and antagonistic characterizations of the private sector disappeared. The locus of "exploitation" became a vaguely defined abstraction of "outside investment and ownership," upon which the region was dependent and against which the region needed to organize. The new WESTPO welcomed energy development as an "opportunity to diversify and revitalize the region's economy" and counselled that "the people of the region recognize that their lifestyles will change as the entire nation changes its energy use patterns (WESTPO 1978, 2, 26).

Anticorporate rhetoric had disappeared from the lexicon. Gone, by 1978, was any advocacy of specific leasing, stripping, or siting mechanisms by the states, replaced in official documents by language espousing the establishment of "cooperative procedures." Discussion of conservation and alternative energy development options shrank to on-farm alcohol fuel production for farmers. Increasingly, the governors as a group abandoned their posture of stewards of western resources and arbitrators of land use and resource conflicts. Instead, they lobbied for piecemeal federal programs favored by special interest groups (such as agricultural subsidies and tax breaks and a ban on uranium imports) and impact aid funds to compensate communities for local government stress introduced by energy development (WESTPO 1978, 27, 39).[21]

Even the federal government began to be cast as a cooperative party, rather than a foe, although charges of federal government arrogance were occasionally mounted by one or another governor. Partly, this relaxed attitude toward Washington could be attributed to the ascendancy of a Democratic governor, Carter, to the presidency, but it was also a function of WESTPO's success in negotiations for federal strip-mining legislation and in convincing Carter to propose a $675 million impact aid fund (*Wall Street Journal* 1978; WRAP-UP Issues; *Oakland Tribune* 1980). The governors successfully defeated Carter's attempt to stop large-scale western water projects. They worried loudly about the planning process surrounding new federal initiatives for a $88 billion synthetic fuels program and a $33 billion MX missile program. Cognizant of federal dollars that these two programs would bring the built environment sectors, WESTPO abandoned outright opposition and lobbied instead for a voice in decisions about placement, pace, and impact aid.

By 1981, WESTPO acted as if environmentalism, not economic development, was a dirty word. While formally pledging itself to a balanced consideration of economic development and the environment, WESTPO increasingly became an economic development agency enthusiastic about energy exploitation. It set up a Western Coal Export Task Force, initiated by the once-cautious Judge of Montana and headed up by the governors of Utah and Wyoming. Financed wholly by private money, the task force included seventy private sector members, including coal-producing corporations, railroads, utilities, and construction interests. It sponsored a high visibility trade mission to Japan, Taiwan, and Korea, where it helped secure long-term coal contracts and trade agreements with Asian utility, cement, steel, and trading companies. The task force committed itself to reducing coal transportation costs, to promoting West Coast port development, and to creating a multistate trading company that would be able to circumvent antitrust laws binding on private combines (Polsky 1979, 56).[22]

Similarly, the attitude toward the federal government had become cooperative on energy projects and belligerent on federal environmental and land-use regulations. To facilitate synthetic fuels development, WESTPO pledged itself in 1980 to work together with the feds to accelerate development, streamline the permitting process, and modify environmental standards. Discussions of the environment leaned toward "flexibility" in air quality regulation, "coordination" of development, and "states' rights" in land use and environmental controls, the latter generally a pro-industry response to the tightened federal land management and environmental quality practices of the latter 1970s. WESTPO argued that the federal Synthetic Fuels Corporation ought to internalize some public sector costs of development and that the severance tax was a legitimate public sector charge, which should be passed on to ultimate consumers (WESTPO 1978, 39). Absent was any suggestion that energy corporations might pay for public sector development costs out of profits. Absent, indeed, were any of the earlier criticisms of the private sector's plans for pursuing energy development.

CLASS INTERESTS AND ORGANIZATIONAL ALTERNATIVES

We saw above how the new western regionalism, as articulated by Lamm and Judge, was at its outset explicitly anticorporate. This was possible both beecause of the broad base of indigenous support for existing land uses, founded upon a populist tradition, and because the major energy corporations were not regionally based. The energy development interests had to find a route into regional politics in order to soften this antagonistic stance. They did so energetically, by working through two organizations which represented different configurations of the region's internal class structure.

First, they sought to build upon the normally boosterist attitudes of the region's "built environment ensemble"—the utilities, communications companies, construction interests, and transportation groups. These, long organized as the Federation of Rocky Mountain States, were able to exert their already substantial influence in state and local politics to the extent that, as we have seen, they became partners in the new WESTPO. Their staff members, long accustomed to representing the boosterist point of view, became the governors' staff.[23]

Second, the pro-development shift of the region's leading politicians was due to the successful organization, in the wake of the Kaiparowitz defeat, of the region's largest corporate interests. In 1977, they joined together as the new Western Regional Council (WRC). Composed of an elite of forty-two chief executive officers of corporations operating in the eight mountain states, WRC was committed to looser air quality enforcement, ample coal leasing, regulatory "variation provisions" for the region, improved highway networks, and opposition to extension of wilderness areas and further restrictions on oil companies' acquisitions. Companies represented include sixteen mining corporations (oil and gas, coal, and hard rock), nine utilities, three large construction-related firms, six banks, two railroads, one trucking company, and five manufacturing firms, most of them energy-related. In 1980, the new chair of WESTPO, Scott Matheson of Utah, described WESTPO's relationship with WRC as a "fast-blooming romance" (Gottlieb and Wiley 1980).

In the early 1970s, the new regional coalition forged by Lamm and Judge had widespread support from the environmental and ranching groups who wished to see controls imposed on energy development.[24] But as WGREPO matured into WESTPO and the private sector development interests rose in stature and influence over what can be loosely termed the "western lifestyle" coalition, those oldtimers and newcomers concerned with preserving existing communities and the renewable economic base (ranching and tourism) became increasingly disillusioned with the governors' organization as the mouthpiece and guardian of western interests. They continued to pursue much more militant stands on development through their own state governments, in cooperation or confrontation with federal land management agencies, and in direct action. As in other regions, these organizations and their activities have been active largely at the local and subregional level, although some intraregional coordination exists.

Several individual cases deserve mention, particularly because western regional struggles take on a highly differentiated character depending on the ethnic group, the economic base, and the political infrastructure in each subregion. Among the most well-known and successful are Montana's Northern Plains Resource Council and its sister organizations in Wyoming and North Dakota. Composed primarily of ranchers and committed in practice to membership participation, the Montana group has organized rural ranching "neighborhoods" since the early 1970s around coal development issues in the southeastern portion of the state.

Formerly Republican-leaning, these ranchers became increasingly opposed to coal mining, coal-fired power plant generation, and transmission lines which fouled their air, introduced health hazards, crimped farming practices, and threatened both the water supply and the small town, stable community life they enjoyed.[25] They provided leadership to the coalition which fashioned the state severance tax and the strong siting legislation at the state level. They vowed to fight to maintain these high standards, which from their point of view were designed to help slow or discourage altogether such development. Some of their members have engaged in minor but effective forms of sabotage and harassment, making it difficult, for instance, for energy companies to cross their lands for surveying purposes. To dramatize their issues, NPRC has engaged in populist-type comedy, such as its $2 per plate Chile Reception for James Watt while he spoke downtown at a $500 per plate Republican fundraiser. However, most of its efforts have been nuts and bolts lobbying, testifying, proposing, and organizing.

NPRC is hardly anticapitalist, since it is composed of private landowners and entrepreneurs, some of whom are quite prosperous. But it is frequently opposed to energy corporations' activities and constitutes a clear case of intersectoral politics combined with a commitment to community. NPRC has dealt internally with the contradictory impulse towards collective struggle for preserving the ranching sector and the individual incentive to sell mineral rights and land to energy corporations. It has formed temporary though uneasy alliances with environmentalists and Native Americans on some, though not all, issues. As of 1981, the NPRC was still growing in numbers and had as its major concerns the attacks on state and federal air standards, the grab for Montana water, the perennial attack on reclamation laws, the conflicts between agriculture and mining (both coal and hard rock), eminent domain, and the Northwest Power bill and its multitude of side effects. The incoming chairman in 1981 (the previous chair*man* had been a woman rancher) promised to maintain the tradition of his predecessors in the effective defense of "Montana and its air, water and lifestyle from those who believe they should have free rein to rape and ruin Montana and receive unlimited federal subsidies as they pursue their objectives."[26]

The Northern Plains type of organization has become the basis of a regionwide alternative to WESTPO. Called WORC—Western Organization of Resource Councils—it is a representative body of four such organizations: Northern Plains, Dakota Resource Council, Powder River Basin Resource Council, and the Western Colorado Congress. They organize and lobby on both regional and national levels on issues such as coal leasing policy, federal air quality legislation, and other land and water issues.

A second genre of subregional fights against energy development includes those communities whose sustenance derives from their attractiveness as recreational or historical tourism meccas. Perhaps the most outstanding example in the latter part of the 1970s was the battle between Amax corporation and the town of Crested Butte, Colorado, over whether or not Amax would develop a billion-dollar molybdenum mine two miles away. Crested Butte, with a population of only 1,200, was once a coal mining town, but since the last mine closed in 1952, it had been first a depressed economy and then a skiing town, aided by the National Forest Service's designation of its land as a winter sports site. Like many other skiing towns in Colorado, it attracted a new, environmentally minded and younger population, who came to be militant opponents to further development, especially mining (Williams 1979; Sibley 1980).[27]

In building its coalition locally, the Crested Butte preservationists encountered newcomer-oldtimer antagonisms and suspicion from the surrounding ranchers. Representatives of the Montana NPRC were invited down to help swing this latter group into the anti-Amax camp. By direct action, well-managed publicity, negotiation with Amax (which included a successful request that Amax supply the town planning department with a computer to model impacts), and innovative planning strategies, the town managed to delay the construction of the mine. A court-contested claim that Crested Butte's planning powers encompass the entire watershed supplying the town's drinking water exemplifies the tactics taken by the preservationist group. Crested Butte's efforts encouraged many other towns to raise questions about the style and pace of energy development near their borders.

A third type of subregional struggle in the West is that of Native American tribes over the conditions under which energy corporations may mine on their reservations. Large blocs of land once considered sterile were "ceded" to Native Americans in the latter half of the nineteenth century in return for their forceable removal from more fertile, agricultural areas of the West. It turned out that much of this reservation land had substantial mineral resources under it. For decades, it was leased by the Bureau of Indian Affairs in Washington to energy corporations at bargain rates with minimal royalties.

In the 1970s, some tribes began to challenge the leasing practices. The Northern Cheyenne, in southeastern Montana, successfully fought in the courts for the renegotiation of their coal leases. In addition, the Northern Cheyenne, like some other tribes, entered the air quality debate on the side of the environmentalists. The Northern Cheyenne filed the suit which delayed construction of Colstrip Units 3 and 4, two additional coal-fired power plants that were opposed by NPRC and environmentalists alike.[28]

The Native American struggles over the conditions under which their land could be leased, mined, and built upon also encompassed labor issues. In Arizona, the Navajos negotiated with Peabody Coal for quotas of Navajo miners to be employed in the mines. While direct tribal exploitation of resources has sometimes been discussed, the lack of technical expertise to engage in what is generally a very large-scale process makes this "nationalization" scheme difficult. In Montana, the Northern Cheyenne tried unsuccessfully to cooperatively mine their own coal for heating purposes on their reservation.[29] Most Native American efforts currently aim at improving the economic rents that tribes receive from the exploitation of their minerals. A new group, the Council for Energy Resource Tribes (CERT), represents 26 tribes from the Intermountain and High Plains West, counseling each on the best strategy. Serious internal splits are apparent among these tribes (and even within them) between traditionalists who are opposed to development and those who favor it outright as the only way to ensure a decent income for their people. CERT, while frequently accused of being too sanguine about development, nevertheless represents a remarkable regionwide unifying organization for its Native American constituents.

A final type of regional organizing occurs when the inevitable exhaustion of nonrenewable resources cause plant or mine closings. The West, while enjoying an aggregate energy-induced boom in the 1970s, was not without its shutdowns in the same period. The West, in fact, is peppered with ghost towns which are the natural legacy of resource exploitation. Both workers and secondary sector business people are left without sources of income and with rapidly devaluing assets (homes and shops) when plant closings occur. But unlike the fatalism with which most towns met mine closing announcements, the possibility of worker ownership, pioneered elsewhere and discussed above, reached the Intermountain West in the 1970s. In 1980–1981, the proposed closing in Silver Valley, Idaho of the Bunker Hill Mine, a subsidiary of the conglomerate Gulf Resources, led to a concerted effort to engineer a worker buyout. The object was to save 2,100 miners' jobs and 2,000 to 3,000 related jobs in the valley. Both the union local and several of the area's businessmen were active in trying to organize the buyout, which ultimately failed (Prendergast 1981). The event, however, was a first for the region and may be a precursor of times to come.

Finally, an example of how several of these sectorally and ethnically based groups can coalesce around a development issue is provided by the dramatic struggle against the MX missile in 1979–1981. Slated to span a wide area in southeastern Nevada and southwestern Utah, the MX missile system would have introduced large numbers of construction workers to a truly desertlike area, drawing heavily on the regions' fragile water supplies, and permanently altering the community structure and the access many people had to large areas. Begun by ranchers and miners in the area, a coalition was built which included active participation by the Duckwater Shoshone tribe, environmentalists, and even the Mormon church. The coalition was supported by environmentalists and arms control advocates nationally. Eventually, the areas' politicians, including the governor of Utah, Scott Matheson, had to come out against the missile-basing system, which the Reagan administration then withdrew from consideration. In the process of this remarkable battle, which included publicity, direct action, heated questioning during the Air Force's hearings, and deft use of environmental impact assessment by the opposition, many residents who began by opposing a monstrosity in "my backyard" came to question new military spending initiatives and the arms race in general. This included the Mormon church. Thus a region which has had by far a disproportionate share of military bases also exhibited a will to reject a highly obnoxious instance, despite the federal dollars and jobs it might bring.[30]

THE EAST-WEST ENERGY-BASED ANTAGONISM

By the late 1970s, the conflict between the West and the Northeast over energy issues began to displace the north-south flow-of-funds debate as the foremost interregional issue (Matthews and Beck 1979; Lundstrom 1975).[31] Partly, the new antagonism reflected the fact that the locus of national political power had clearly shifted toward the West. The West's newfound power derived not only from its population gains, which methodically added new western congresspersons every ten years, but also from its economic vigor, concentrated in the energy-producing sectors of oil, coal, uranium, and synthetic fuels.[32]

From the westerners' point of view, two axes of regional conflict can be distinguished. First, subregional antipathies found western agriculturalists, workers, and communities pitted against eastern absentee landowners and operators (included both the federal government and energy corporations). This regionwide conflict centered on the conditions under which energy would be developed and the manner in which social costs would be compensated. A second antagonism centered on the relationship betwen the West and the East as energy producer and consumer respectively. In this case, the issue was whether the terms of trade between the two regions for the commodities of the former were "fair" or cartelized by the western states through mechanisms like the severance tax.

These two sources of interregional antagonism created the potential for two very different regional coalitions. In fact, the narrative above suggests that the original coalition, built around environmental protection, argiculture, and tourism, was displaced by a subsequent pro-energy development coalition, and that the emergence of the buyer-seller interregional antagonism displaced the rancher/labor-outside owners antagonism. The initial regional organizing impetus was led by a new breed of Democratic state governors pledged to control both the short- and long-run developmental costs to their residents. It was an aggressive attempt to change the long history of mineral company exploitation of resources and ghost town legacies. It was a regional movement aimed by-and-large at energy corporations, not at other regions or their residents. It was also an effort to defend far-reaching state growth controls and environmental legislation against a national Republican administration pushing Project Independence.

The shift from this populist politics to an energy boosterist stance was signalled within the individual states by the political troubles of the more progressive governors, who were forced to compromise with regional business interests in the formation of WESTPO. This internal shift was contemporaneous with the aggressive attack by the Northeast-Midwest Coalition on western states' energy taxes. The eastern initiative permitted western politicans to deflect attention from their own increasingly boosterist policies and enlist regionwide sentiment behind WESTPO in a them-us defense of severance taxes.

Aside from the internal political uses of this east-west antagonism to political leaders in each region, what are the merits of the energy cartel argument? It is difficult to evaluate the justice and import of this east-west debate without a careful accounting of the history of and rationale for the western states' actions. In 1975 the Montana legislature passed a 30 percent severance tax on the value of coal taken from the ground in the state's mines. State severance taxes have been levied since the early twentieth century on resources like oil and iron ore; indeed, some thirty-three states currently employ them, including Minnesota, Michigan, and New Hampshire. But Montana's new coal tax rate was the highest in the nation and its designs for the tax proceeds more ambitious than existing uses of the tax elsewhere.[33]

The reasoning behind the Montana tax was that energy companies should fully compensate communities (though not individuals) for extra costs incurred because of their ingress. Furthermore, nonrenewable energy extraction should be charged a premium to help finance the diversification of the economy so that in the aftermath, a depressed economy (like Anaconda's Butte, or the country's primary coal bin, Appalachia) would not be left for the state to cope with. The proceeds were to be divided as shown in table 9.1.[34]

In essence, Montana was adopting an aggressive posture toward any entering corporate activity that might close its "plants" in as short a period as ten or twenty years. The severance tax provided not only compensation for immediate impacts but also a kind of prepaid fund for dealing with the sector's exit. In the state's view, the levy was justified by the present public sector externalities imposed and by the future adjustment costs of its population.[35] The state argued, as well, that since much

Table 9.1 Allocation of Montana's Coal Severance Tax Receipts, 1978

Percent	Allocation
25	Permanent Trust Fund (income but not principal available to the state legislature)
2	County where mine is located
2.5	Alternative energy research development and demonstration
2.5	Local impact and educational trust account (for grants to local governments)
13	Coal area highway improvement
10	State equalization aid for public schools
1	County land use planning
2.5	Loan program to develop renewable resources as water
2.25	Acquisition and management of parks and cultural and aesthetic projects
15	State general fund

Source: Lopach 1918, 1.

of the mining was to occur on federal land, which was not subject to the property tax, the local public sector had little recourse but to use instruments like the severance tax to pay for community adjustments.

The architects of Montana's tax intended it to predistribute some energy company profits from private to public coffers. They did not anticipate that it would become a major bone of contention between regions. They believed that the tax would be absorbed by stockholders, not consumers. Indeed, the initial court challenge to the tax was mounted by four large coal companies—Decker Coal, Westmoreland Resources, Western Energy, and Peabody Coal. Only later, in the appeal to the Supreme Court, were several out-of-state utilities added to the plaintiffs, principally because the plaintiff's case invoked the interstate commerce clause. In a few cases, where long-term coal contracts permit companies to "pass-through" tax hikes to the purchasing utility, the severance tax may have contributed to higher electricity prices for midwesterners. However, the increase amounts to a very small portion of the energy bill, about $1.50 on an annual bill of $359. Other analysts believe that the bulk of severance taxes do come out of profits and increasingly so each year, as pass-through contracts become fewer or as the price of the contract is depressed in consequence (Lopach 1978, 2; Multistate Tax Commission 1981, 7–8; Weinstein 1981a).[36]

Theoretically the severance tax would diminish the attractiveness of the state levying it in favor of mining in lower tax states. Wyoming, for instance, has a severance tax only about half as large as Montana's, and Utah and Colorado have no coal taxes at all. Montana legislators have been willing to see mining activity deflected from their state, arguing that if the coal companies cannot pay their way, they are unwelcome. Montana also took an aggressive position within WESTPO encouraging other states to follow its lead, so that states would not be played off against each other.

Critics sometimes point out that Montana's deposits are more accessible and closer to coal markets than other states, creating a situation of differential rent, capturable in the stiff severance tax. But the reluctance of other states to follow suit is more a function of their political complexion, including coal company influence, than real fear of loss of mining activity. While Montana has not convinced her neighbors to meet her rates (Alaska and North Dakota *have* raised their rates), it has won a strong commitment on the part of WESTPO to defend the right of individual states to adopt their own taxes without ceilings.[37]

The fashioning of the severance tax into an interregional issue was the work of the Northeast-Midwest Institute. In 1980, they produced a staff study of the severance tax issue. In 1981, they published a document entitled *The United American Emirates*, a not so subtle comparison of the western states and their tax arrangements with the cartel of oil-exporting nations. Twenty-four northeastern congressmen filed amicus briefs in the energy companies' and midwestern utilities' Supreme Court case against Montana's severance tax. In July 1981, the Court declared the tax constitutional, since it was applied indiscriminately to both instate and interstate coal transactions and because sufficient precedent existed in the form of severance taxes nationwide. However, the Court suggested that Congress could adopt ceilings for such state taxes if it felt that they were excessive. As a result, Senator Durenberger of Minnesota (a state which levies severance taxes on iron ore, virtually all of which is exported to steel corporations in steel-producing states) introduced a bill which would limit severance taxes to 12.5 percent.[38]

At the same time, states all over the nation began to investigate ways to raise or adopt new severance taxes on land-based resource exploitation. Iowa's governor threatened to impose a tax on his state's corn and soybean crops, arguing that the soils of midwestern states are just as much a nonrenewable resource as are Wyoming's coal fields (a debatable point). Georgia imposed a severance tax in 1981 on lumber exported from its pine woods. New York and Connecticut tried to levy gasoline excise taxes which could not be passed on to consumers, while New Jersey imposed a special tax on petroleum refiners; all three of these were struck down by the courts. Pennsylvania debated a plan to tax electricity exported to other states from nine "mine mouth" electric plants in Pennsylvania's coal fields. Most of these tax proposals are purely retaliatory in nature though some are understandable efforts by hard-pressed governments to capture some of the surplus from lucrative resource-based sectors. None of them are associated with efforts to compensate for production-related social impacts or strengthen their economic base for the future (Coates 1981; *Business Week* 1981a, 94).

The NEMW Institute and northeastern newspapers agreed that an enormous tranfer of resources was taking place via western energy taxes. They cited unpublished projections by the U.S. Treasury that increased revenues for energy-producing states from oil decontrol would amount to $128 billion over the 1980s. The Midwestern Governors Conference claimed that their thirteen member states would be paying more than $2.5 billion in severance taxes by 1985. Critics pointed out that these projections assumed that the real price of energy would rise ad infinitum and that the demand for energy would similarly rise, neither of which was likely to prevail in light of oil gluts and an emphasis on conservation.[39]

The Northeast-Midwest Institute's indictment of the western severance tax included a charge that the tax would distort locational incentives. They argued that it would result in a lower tax burden for business in those states, hastening the migration of business from the highly tax-burdened East to the lower-tax West. Theoretically, the argument is correct. However, there are several reasons to believe that the responsiveness of businesses to lower taxes in the Intermountain West might be limited.

First, the states in question bear heavy transportation cost disadvantages and are among the least industrialized in the nation. Studies of state and local tax differentials almost universally agree that they form a small portion of businesses' total costs and have been ineffective in influencing industrial location.[40] If manufacturing firms have not found intermountain states attractive locations before, it is very unlikely that they will do so under the minimally lightened state and local tax burdens made possible by the severance tax. Secondly, the sectors in which the Northeast is rapidly losing employment—autos, steel, machining, textiles—while hard-pressed by higher energy prices, are not candidates for western locations because of their distance to markets and/or their unsuitability climatically or resource-wise (scarcity of water is one major disadvantage). Third, the severance tax (despite the implied rhetoric) falls on coal and other energy resources *whether or not* it is consumed within the state. Thus any industries attracted to western locations by lower property or corporate income taxes will have to pay the same higher energy prices that any eastern-based company would, if the tax is indeed passed on.[41]

In the east-west energy battles, the South remained neutral. In part, the Southern Growth Policies Board was avoiding a potentially disruptive internal issue. Southeastern states shared energy price fears with their northeastern neighbors, while SGPB members Louisiana and Oklahoma were reaping oil severance taxes themselves. Areas in Texas complained of the coal tax while basking in the warmth of the oil tax. But the reticence of southern leadership to oppose their western counterparts had an historical element as well. Since the populist era, an anti–Eastern Establishment bias had loosely held the South and West together. Indeed, as recently as 1943 the two regions had attempted a joint action to lower freight rates (Garnsey 1950, 257).[42] The "states' rights" ideology of the severance tax defense evoked historical commonalities between the two regions.

The preoccupation of the Northeast-Midwest Congressional Coalition with the severance tax appears to fit the pattern documented above of a business-oriented lobby seeking to divert attention from the larger issues of corporate responsibility and the justification for superprofits toward the specter of regional robbery—blaming individual or collective members of other regions for the home region's ills. In a national debate, Senator Moynihan of New York dramatically cited a bumper sticker "seen in Texas": "Drive fast and freeze a Yankee." This was the evidence for his contention that regional conflict was on the rise in the United States (White House Conference 1978, 118–52). Press accounts from the nation's top media, almost all based on the East Coast, continually suggested that western states' greed and collusion were a major cause of structural problems in the eastern economy. Thus blame for the hardships of the energy crisis were placed on another region rather than on the energy corporations who were taking advantage of it.

Ironically, the efforts by the northeastern coalition to stop the western states' energy initiatives by appeals to federal courts and the Congress provided the western governors with a new villain as well. Caught between renewable resource owners and the major energy corporations, they could now cast the northeastern states as the aggressors. Other possibilities, such as public ownership, slowing energy development, or requiring the energy corporations to absorb adjustment costs without passing them on to consumers, faded from the agenda as westerners were encouraged to close ranks around the modest goal of protecting the rights of states to tax energy development. Since the northeasterners strove to use the federal government to curb western powers, the western governors could fold the old anti-outsider and anti-federal government sentiments of the region into one defensive attitude. While battles over land use continued to dominate internal regional politics, their significance was overshadowed by a regional rhetoric that resurrected old east-west antagonisms.

> We should not be called the sunbelt, but the *match*belt. We are a matchbelt because, unlike the permanence of the sun, our economies burst momentarily into flame, blaze a while, and then are snuffed out, leaving us not with an enduring and robust community but with the ashes of a snuffed-out economy. . . . We would be myopic and ignoring of the lessons of history if we were to give away our resources again. [Governor Lamm, "Some Reflections on the Balkanization of America," Keynote Address at the Annual Meeting of WESTPO, August 18, 1978]

Subtly, the regional leadership claimed that the resources were "ours," rather than belonging either to the nation as a whole or to large energy corporations.

THE NEW MOUNTAIN WEST: A SUMMARY

By the early 1980s, then, the bold western program for curtailing energy-related exploitation had been eviscerated. Nationally, a stalemate had been reached over the energy tax and related land-use issues. Yet some important restrictions had been placed on the worst practices. Of greater significance, however, its conception of its own stewardship had changed.

The West became, in the 1970s, the region with the greatest stake in conservation, wilderness preservation, and controlled development, whether tourism or energy-related. Its traditional insularity and suspicion of the East and the federal government was if anything heightened. In the conflict bred by the national energy crisis, a new ethos emerged across many parts of the West, subscribed to by unlikely political allies. It consisted of a commitment to the preservation of land uses and sustainability of a way of life, and a search for new forms of economic enterprise that might supplant the resource exploitation mode of the past. At times bordering on the chauvinistic, it saw the region as an underdog in this struggle, pitted against outside interests.

It was perhaps best put by Daniel Kemmis, a judge and former Speaker of the Montana House, who in 1983 gave three seminars under the rubric *Democracy at the Headwaters*. Two of these were entitled "Landbased Values as a Source of Political Effectiveness" and "The Future as if Land and People Mattered."

> I am persuaded that the foundation of all our advantages, and the key to understanding how to enhance them, lies in the relationship of this region's people to their natural surroundings . . . [we stand for] the last of what is best in America. [Kemmis 1983, 7, 19]

At the heart of the matter, Kemmis argued, was the need to protect the sustaining power of the land. This could be achieved by building— alongside the necessary evil of the nonrenewable resource develop- ment—a smaller scale, more diverse, more environmentally and socially benign "sustainable economy," compatible with the land. He argued that the region's mission was to insist upon "a national regime of living within our means, to demand that we use our natural resources with the future in mind, and to take the lead here in developing a model for a sustainable economy."

It was also clear to Montanans, stated Kemmis, that this was a project faced with strong and vigilant opponents.

> What I want to emphasize about these conflicts is their essential David and Goliath nature. The fact seems inescapable that the future most of us would choose for this region is inconceivable without some major confrontations with the forces of wealth and power outweighing anything tangible at our command. Our enemies, in sum, are bigger than we are, and they are likely to remain so. The wealth and power concentration in political, industrial and technological entities can never be matched by those committed to preserving and enhancing a quality, people-and-land centered way of life. Which is not to say that the battle is lost, but that we must wage it in new and partly unfamiliar ways. [Kemmis 1983, 7, 8]

Among the new tactics was the need to overcome mutually suspicious special interests within the region and organize on a coalition basis.

> It seems likely that the work will be more successful in engaging a broad cross-section of people if it is carried on in a context where people are creating and nurturing what they value at the same time that they are learning to talk to one another about what matters to them.

Kemmis was speaking here of the strategy of the recently formed Montanans Allied for Progressive Policies (MAPP). This group, aimed at state level issues, education, and elections, brought together members of women's groups, the agricultural community, organized labor, environmentalists, and educators, with outreach efforts extended to Native Americans and poverty groups. Highly participatory and membership education-oriented, the coalition has proved remarkably strong against vested interests in Montana, pushing hard for fairer taxation and alternative economic development.

Nowhere else in the nation, except perhaps Appalachia, has so much thought and experimentation gone into questioning an identity and mapping out a future for the region.[43] That it has is the legacy of the region's unique sectoral makeup, heavily dependent upon nonrenewable resource exploitation and a culture which has engendered strong ties to the land. Despite hard times, many mountain people show greater reluctance to migrate to the nation's larger cities or the booming Sunbelt, and greater interest in alternatives for their own states. Ironically, then, the least industrialized of regions and the one with greatest mobility in the past has been at the forefront of the community preservation movement in the postwar period. It brings, through its regional politics, this priority to national policy-making chambers.

The emergence of east-west conflict over energy development supports a number of theoretical arguments made in previous chapters. This region, in the height of its 1970s boom, organized across state lines to tackle a common set of internal problems wrought by dramatic incursions of energy corporations. The organizational effort was aided by the absence of a strong two-party system and the individualistic style of political leadership, which enabled governors from the various parties to cooperate. As new pro-energy elites began to dominate the official regional organization, grassroots-based ones challenged the leadership and fought for an alternative program.

The federal government was an actor in this drama, because it was a major landowner. On certain matters, such as the leasing of coal lands, it found itself confronted by the new coalition. But the major issues (local government infrastructure crises and competing land-use claims) and solutions to them (the severance tax and facility-siting laws) were homegrown affairs. This confirms the view that rapidly developing regions will be preoccupied with internal conflict.

The east-west interregional hostilities of this era were precipitated by a surprise attack by the Northeast-Midwest Coalition on the severance tax. While architects of the tax had construed it as a legitimate payment by energy companies and their stockholders for irreversibly drawing down the regions' resources, the coalition interpreted it as an unfair tax on the consumers of energy. In response, as the model suggests, the western region did organize to defend its policies. The governor's effort could rely on popular consciousness of western distinctiveness, including a long-standing antipathy toward the East, from whence financial and political power emanated to the disadvantage of the region's residents.

In sum, then, western regional organizing and the interregional conflict over the terms of energy development confirm that regional

218 ■ REGIONS: ECONOMICS AND POLITICS OF TERRITORY

differentials in growth experience and sectoral configuration can provoke regionalism. As anticipated, the harder-pressed region (the Northeast) was again the initiator of political conflict, and in defending itself
the West developed a sharper sense of its distinctiveness in contrast to
other regions. Federal structure, regional politics, and regional cultures
played a supporting role.

Notes

1. See Pomeroy (1965, 191–214) for a discussion of the Progressive movement
   in the West.
2. Ingram et al. (1980, 36) show that state legislators were consistently less
   sensitive to environmental and unemployment issues than voters and more
   enthusiastic about development issues in the 1970s.
3. This may be a result of two factors. One, laggard reapportionment may
   permit rural interests to dominate legislatures beyond the point when
   statewide votes go to liberals. Second, voters may be more liberal on national
   issues than on regional issues, and development interests may be more
   active in regional elections.
4. Treatments of western politics which document these features include
   Donnelly (1940), Jonas (1969), and Peirce (1972). See Bell (1975) for a brief
   review of the often conflicting empirical studies on western political structures.
5. The population of the state as a whole is 70 percent Mormon. Some analysts
   claim that the Mormon church is not all that powerful in state politics (Jonas
   1940, 1969), while others contend that, through extensive church-owned
   businesses which include insurance firms, radio stations, real estate, hotels,
   schools, and manufacturing and data processing firms, as well as substantial
   stock in utilities, department stores, and corporations like Utah International and Utah-Idaho sugar, its influence is overwhelming (Parrish 1980).
6. Both parties launched regional organizations in the 1950s (the Republican
   Western Conference in 1951 and the Western States Democratic Conference in 1959). The creators of the latter stated, "we are trying to create a
   Western bloc which would first benefit the entire West, and benefit the party
   nationally by electing more Democrats" (Anderson 1961, 291).
7. See Gottlieb and Wiley (1982) on the environmental movement in the West.
8. The first nationally publicized confrontation between energy industries and
   farmers is documented in Casper and Wellstone (1981). Agriculturalists on
   the high plains were responding to analysis by groups like the National
   Academy of Science (1973) and the Northern Great Plains Resource Program (1975) indicating that reclamation of strip mining land was a serious
   problem.
9. See Corrigan (1976), *Colorado Springs Gazette Telegraph* (1976), and Massey
   (1980) as examples of accounts of boomtown impacts from both press and
   academia. Widener (1982) and Moen et al. (1981) show that women suffer
   inordinately, both as wives of itinerant construction workers and as objects
   of sexual advances by heavily male populations whether as high school
   women or prostitutes. Native American development issues are surveyed in
   Jorgenson (1978) and Pratt (1978); case studies of the Northern Cheyenne
   and Crow are found in Toole (1976) and Owens and Peres (1980).

10. A planning analysis of declining regions' adjustment can be found in Rust and Alonso (1975). Rabinowitz (1982) documents the persistent high rates of unemployment in the rural West, even in energy-rich counties. Reid (1977), Prendergast (1981), and Associated Press (1977) document plant closings and communities' responses, including cases of a military base and hard rock mines.

11. See Peirce (1972), Caldwell (1977), and Gaffney (1977) for the internal resource colony analysis. Pratt (1978) reviews the internal colony argument critically.

12. The West had always lobbied for high tariffs on imports of beef, metal, sugar, and wool into the United States—gains which led other regions to suspect the West of acting as a cartel, overcharging eastern consumers for these commodities.

13. For the historical antecedents of the Sagebrush Rebellion, see DeVoto (1948) and Garnsey (1950, 204–17). Interpretations of the contemporary movement can be found in Blakemore and Erickson (1981), Sharpe (1980), and Western Governors' Policy Office (1980). Samples of agricultural and regional press evaluation are Kittredge (1980), *Rocky Mountain Journal* (1981), and Leroy and Eiguren (1980).

14. Hayes' extensive study of WGREPO is the source of much of the detail in this section.

15. Both quotes cited in Hayes (1980, 3). See also Lamm and McCarthy (1982) for a virulent statement opposing outside ownership.

16. Andrus of Idaho withdrew in early 1976 because his state's interests did not encompass "the common denominator of coal, oil or shale deposits that mold the interests of the proposed member states together" and because Idaho's links to the Pacific Northwest proved stronger (Hayes 1980, 93).

17. The task force labeled its report *Regional Policy Management*, intimating that it was government policy that must be managed, rather than growth itself.

18. See Gottlieb and Wiley (1982) for a book-length exposition of this interrelationship.

19. The internal antagonisms that remained, and the halfway open door to states farther west, were both dealt with through an "accordion" approach, where participation by any state in a particular task force was voluntary and representatives from nonmember states could be included if the issues were to prove of common concern. In Hayes (1980, 134–39, 152–54). Nevada did not at first join, but later did, and by 1982, Idaho and Washington had finally accepted new invitations.

20. Funding came partly from state dues, captured from FRMS and the former contributions to the Council of State Governments (which had funded these states' dues to the Western Governors' Conference). While some federal money would still be solicited for special projects, the central task of policy development was to be funded from member contributions, to free it from federal influence. Funds also came from the same foundations which had supported sister regions' efforts—Ford and Rockefeller (Western Governors' Task Force 1976, 28.

21. For a comparison of three approaches to boomtown planning, in which impact aid is characterized as the weakest, see Markusen and Glasmeier, 1980.

22. For Judge's growing ties to the Montana International Trade Commission, a similar export promotion group, see Applegate (1977).

23. See Galvin (1969) for an early history of FRMS. For the federation's views, see their publications (1975a, 1975b). For Exxon's position, as an example of

corporate involvement, see Lindauer (1975). For overviews of planning issues, see Markusen and Glasmeier (1980), Shapira et al. (1982), and Siembeda (1978).

24. For instance, Hayes (1980, 85) shows that the Northern Plains Resource Council, discussed below, welcomed the governors' organization.

25. Toole (1976) provides an account of NPRC activities, and Parfit (1980) an insight into its membership. The economics of the region in which NPRC originated is described in Gold (1974), Sullam et al. (1978), and Kroll (1981). The NPRC's newsletter is called *The Plains Truth;* energy politics statewide in Montana was covered by the *Montana Eagle* (which has since folded), while the *High Country News* (Lander, Wyoming) keeps tabs on regionwide efforts.

26. Statement of Bill Gillin, in Northern Plains Resource Council *The Plains Truth* 10, no. 10: 1, November/December 1981.

27. This discussion also benefited from a presentation by Miles Rademan, present community development specialist and former city planner of Crested Butte, at the Regional Conference on New Perspectives on Planning in the West, Arizona State University, March 26–28.

28. See Toole (1976, 33–68) for a discussion of the Northern Cheyenne leasing challenge. Toole also chronicles the differences in development posture between the Northern Cheyenne and the Crow.

29. See Owens and Peres (1980) on the Cheyenne efforts.

30. This account of the MX missile is based upon the presentation by Amy Glasmeier at the Regional Conference on New Perspectives on Planning in the West, Arizona State University, March 26–28, 1982; Glasmeier (1980); and Glasmeier and Schoenberger (1980).

31. Matthews and Beck (1979), Lundstrom (1975). Articles by Joel Kotkin in the *Washington Post* (1979) reported that the "Old Frontier Sees Bright New Future" and explained "Why Power is Flowing to the West." *Newsweek,* May 5, 1975, headlined "Energy: The War Between the States" and profiled "The Angry West versus the Rest."

32. Both Sale (1975) and Phillips (1978) contended that this shift would change the face of national politics. Phillips argued that the southwestward shift in population and power would bring the Republican party back into power after fifty years of Democratic majorities.

33. Agria (1969) surveys the history of the tax. See Weinstein (1981a) for a catalogue of current state levies. Although its rate is higher, Montana collects less in these taxes than states like Texas, Oklahoma, Louisiana, Minnesota, and ten others whose oil, iron ore, and other "exports" are greater in size.

34. Since 1979, the proportions have changed somewhat. The coal highway allocations have been shifted to impact and alternative energy development categories.

35. Congressional Budget Office (1980) found that some states' severance taxes were too low to compensate for current public sectors costs and some, like Montana's, more than sufficient. Krutilla, Fisher, and Rice (1978) showed that sufficiency of existing tax mechanisms depended upon which jurisdiction—city governments, townships, school districts, or counties—were under consideration.

36. See General Accounting Office (1981) for a study that demonstrates how the base, rates, and timing of state changes in mineral taxes can affect the profitability of mines and value of land.

37. Efforts to pass steeper rates than Montana's were mounted in neighboring states. See Dorgan (1977) for the North Dakota proposal.
38. Northeast-Midwest Institute (1980). Weinstein (1981a, 11–12), and *Business Week* (1981a, 94).
39. *Business Week* (1981a, 1981b), Coates (1981), *New York Times* (1981), Weinstein (1981a, 6–7, 25).
40. See Harrison and Kanter (1976) for a survey of this argument.
41. The energy price rise did tend to redirect industry toward regions where energy was cheaper and/or more available. See Miernyk (1975 and 1976), Miernyk et al. (1978), and Hoch (1980) for efforts to model these impacts.
42. They were sabotaged by a Colorado governor who had been elected with railroad receipts.
43. See Eller (1986) for a discussion of parallel Appalachian efforts.

10

Regionalism:
A Review and Prognosis

Sharp differences in economic structure and experience have been major determinants of U.S. regionalism. The translation of differential economic status into interregional antagonism relies heavily upon existing political machinery and the ability of regional organizers to transcend or use to advantage cross-cutting cultural and class differences. This chapter summarizes the arguments of the book and compares the cases of American regionalism investigated in previous chapters. I conclude by speculating on the future of regionalism in the United States and its potential as a conservative or progressive force for change.

THE ECONOMIC BASES OF REGIONAL DIFFERENTIATION

To recapitulate, the economic forces that differentiate regions from each other operate along three axes: (1) growth dynamics, (2) class and ownership structure, and (3) market power. These are listed, along with the most obvious American historical instances, in table 10.1. Contrasts along any one of these dimensions were found to engender self-consciousness and interregional antagonism in the instances studied. Often, two or more worked in tandem to generate regional resentment, chauvinism, or action. Each combination will tend to produce a distinct form of regional politics.

Growth Dynamics

Regions in a capitalist world tend to grow at different rates. While the entire world economy experiences long waves and shorter-term cyclical crises, individual regions often suffer more volatile and sometimes irreversible boom-bust trajectories. Three types of differential growth can provoke regional antagonisms.

First, regions may be growing differentially because one region lags behind in the assembly of appropriate conditions for production and accumulation, while another moves ahead. The nineteenth-century enmity between the North and the South was a product of this type of differentiation. The South's tenacious commitment to a slave mode of

Table 10.1 Economic Sources of Regional Differentiation in Cases of U.S. Regionalism

Source	Instances and era
Differentials in growth dynamics	
Conditions for accumulation	North-South, mid-19th century
Sectorally based differentials	East-West, late 19th century
Agriculture vs. industry	North-South, mid-19th century
Profit-squeezed vs. superprofit	Southwest-Northeast, 1970s
Geographical relocation	West-East energy sector shifts, 1970s
	Southeast-Northeast, 1970s
Differentials in class and ownership	
Structure	
Regional class segregation	U.S., mid-20th century
Absentee ownership	North-South, mid-19th century
	East-West, late 19th century
	East-West, 1970s
Differentials in market power	
Productive vs. financial and distributive sectors	North-South, mid-19th century
	East-West, late-19th century
Producer vs. producer	U.S., Appalachia, mid-20th-century
	West-East, 1970s

cash crop production prevented it from offering capitalist entrepreneurs the capital, labor, infrastructure, and legal inducement to industralize. Similarly, the incomplete development of free wage labor in the Appalachian coal fields retarded capitalist development in that subregion. In these cases, regional ruling elites and clever politicians were often able to blame the poor performance of their regions on "outsiders" and thus divert attention from internally archaic economic structures.

Second, interregional growth differentiation is sometimes the compound result of sectoral specialization. The precipitous decline of Appalachia in the last forty years bears testimony to the role of sectoral specialization—in that case, coal. And within the world economy of the time, the heavy dependence of southern planters on cotton demand rendered their economy vulnerable and less dynamic than their northern, more diversified neighbors.

The rise of new sectors with different geographical proclivities also contributes to sectorally lodged growth rate disparities. The center of gravity of industrial production may shift, as it has from the Frostbelt to the Sunbelt, because entirely new industries are fostered in a new region. These shifts are often connected with new technologies or forces

Table 10.2 Instances of Economically Induced Regional Politics in the United States

Type	Instances and era
Repudiation of regionalism	
Politically dominant and prosperous regions	Northeast, 19th and early 20th centuries (Ch. 4)
	Sunbelt, late 20th century (Ch. 8)
Regions with broadly similar experiences	U.S., 1930s–1960s (Ch. 4)
Regional separatism	
Booming regions with unique imperatives but ineffective control of central government	South, mid-19th century (Ch. 4)
Claims for regional special treatment	
Regions for adverse economic conditions due to sectoral obsolescence	Appalachia, 1950s–1960s (Ch. 3)
Oligopolized and profit-squeezed sectors, locational shifts	Northeast, 1970s (Ch. 8)
Outside ownership, absence of market power	West-South, late 19th century (Ch. 9)

of production. Examples are plastics displacing steel, high-tech communications revolutionizing business services, and western coal mining techniques supplanting those in Appalachia. Another source of territorially differentiated sectoral growth has been the military orientation of some segments of manufacturing.

Industrial specialties may also have a retarding effect upon growth if market power has accompanied their evolution. Some regions' predicament is made worse by the distorting effect that large oligopolistic sectors have had on subregions (steel in Pittsburgh, and autos in Detroit) by crowding out other entrepreneurs and overconcentrating production.

A third form of interregional growth differential occurs when two or more regions compete over the *same* sectors. In this case, the development of heightened class conflict and working-class organization propels capitalist production, particularly in more mature sectors, from the region of origin to others where the social and political structure is more amenable. This is the type of growth differential which has prompted contemporary antagonism between the North and the South.

Regardless of the particular form of growth differential, the political responses of the respective regions are relatively predictable. Regions with superior growth performance may develop a consciousness about their own uniqueness, but will tend to be preoccupied with internal conflicts over land use and public resources. To the extent they foster a sense of regional identity, distinctiveness, or unity, it will only incidentally be aimed antagonistically outward, at other regions.

Regions with lagging growth records, on the other hand, will exhibit a strong sense of injury, of distinctiveness, and of common cause. They are more apt to be the initiators of interregional conflict, especially when they can rely upon effective political presence at the center.

The protagonists in the Civil War are good examples of this difference. The rapid growth region, the North, was ridden with internal conflicts over land development, factory life, commercial versus industrial priorities, agricultural versus urban interests. Numerous political parties sprang up to carry forward odd configurations of class and cultural interests. Northerners had little sense of themselves as a group. Indeed their Civil War rallying cry "the Union forever" referred to the entire nation, not just the North. White southerners, on the other hand, saw themselves as southerners and their neighbors as Yankees. They developed a strong affinity for the Democratic party and increasingly closed ranks around the defense of their economy and institutions against the Yankee imperialists.

Similarly, the Northeast became the region of laggard economic growth in the postwar period. This condition produced a sense of common plight and a regional esprit which had not existed since the Civil War. Through a remarkable historical reversal, it had become the region claiming injury and precipitating a new round of interregional conflict. In the same era, the South and Intermountain West had begun to experience reinvigorated growth rates after decades of outmigration and decline in many subregions. They became preoccupied with the internal conflicts and new problems of rapid growth. Their participation in the interregional hostilities of the 1970s was largely defensive, parrying the northeastern attack on federal aid flows, energy issues, and military spending differentials.

The point to be made here is that differences in regional growth experience can lead to interregional antagonism, even when the "cause" of the problem is internal (underdeveloped capitalist institutions) or systemwide (a result of capitalist crisis and dynamics). These conflicts can occur even if the economic structures of the regions involved have been growing increasingly similar over time.

Differential Class and Ownership Structures

Divergent growth rates are often contemporaneous with, even linked to, significant differences in regional class and ownership structures. There are two ways in which these enter into and mediate regional politics: internal class homogeneity and external ownership of resources and productive assets.

First, as noted in chapter 2, there are few instances in the United

States where particular classes are heavily regionally concentrated. When a region is predominantly working class, as in mining areas, the possibility for class-based politics to dovetail with regional politics is present. However, regions with heavily working-class populations are notably underrepresented in interregional and national politics, in part because of less well-developed leadership and political capabilities. Furthermore, few regions have purely working-class structures.

An example of class-based regional politics was the populist movement of farmers, both poor and "middle class" in the late nineteenth century. Their success in organizing was fueled by severe economic crisis and vulnerability to monopolistic practices in their markets. Their struggle was not just against merchants, financiers, and railroads, but against what they termed the "Eastern Establishment." Yet in the long run the populist challenge lost its explicitly regional dimension, principally because the western region became increasingly complex in its class structure and because cross-cutting regional hostilities, inherited from the Civil War, bolstered the existing two-party system.

Two more recent instances show the difficulty faced by a predominantly working-class regionalism. The effort in the 1970s to form a worker-community union in Appalachia could not transcend the political complexities posed by small coal owners and operators and a large small business community. The efforts in the Youngstown and Pittsburgh areas to build an alternative to steel shutdowns have faced tough opposition from indigenous capital, regional banks, and small business sectors.

Yet if there was a politics of the organized working class in this era, it was quite regionally based in the quadrant of the Midwest and North Central states. Labor's candidate, Mondale, won the Democratic party primaries almost exclusively in this region, while losing to challenges outside of it.

A second form of class-based interregional animosity arises from ownership and control of regionally based activities by corporations or individuals residing outside the region. Outside ownership is perceived to be disadvantageous to the local economy for several reasons. First, profits from production will flow directly out of the region with no prospect of local reinvestment. Second, absentee owners may not understand the local economy and its culture. They may not care about the particularly disruptive effects of operating in a certain manner (mine disasters and boom-bust ghost towns are the pervasive image). Or, they may simply make stupid mistakes. Evidence from both past and present work, cited in previous chapters, suggests that at least historically, local ownership has resulted in relatively more local reinvestment, more "normal" paths of resource exploitation, and greater entrepreneurial concern with the health of the local economy and its residents.

Several instances of heavily resented absentee ownership have contributed to U.S. regionalism. The antebellum southerners were in part correct when they charged the northeastern commercial establishment with siphoning off a portion of cotton profits, though the major problems of the southern economy were internal. The western Populists castigated eastern owners of banks and railroads. Yet, in both instances, the outside owners' success lay in their market power in the realm of circulation, rather than production, a source of differentiation addressed later in this chapter. These problems would not have evaporated had these institutions been owned within the region. Home-based corporations are not necessarily more virtuous than absentees.

Increasingly, charges of outside ownership and control ring hollow in this age of integrated world capitalism. In the nineteenth century, locally accumulated profits often were reinvested in local enterprises (New Bedford's whaling receipts went into textile mills; Great Lakes timber profits financed Minneapolis grain mills). But with modern capital markets and large conglomerate corporations, profits earned by individuals or plants in any one place have little chance of remaining there. Regional vulnerability to corporate decisions is indeed a problem, but has less and less to do with those corporations being "outsiders," and more to do with the lessening importance of place to capitalist activity across the board. Nevertheless, because of old injuries, prevailing ideology, and contemporary opportunism, political leaders still find it advantageous to villainize "eastern" corporations and "foreign" ownership of agricultural lands.

These forms of class differentiation across space, either directly through geographic concentrations of producing classes or indirectly through absentee ownership, have the potential to generate a regionalism which explicitly addresses issues of exploitation and the social structure of production. Populism, with its demands for public banks, public utilities, and nationalization of the railroads, came closest to mounting a challenge to the ownershp structure of American capitalism. Indeed, producer co-ops created by farmers have proved a durable, if limited, alternative. Yet because the bulk of its adherents were small farmers, sharecroppers, and small businesspeople, populism never evolved an effective critique of wage labor and industrial capitalism.

Regions where absentee ownership is an issue, but largely among entrepreneurs in other sectors, may find innovative routes to ensure that some percentage of profits will stay within the region. The contemporary West has found such an instrument in the severance tax. But some supporters of the tax—ranchers and businesspeople—are not likely to support a demand for socialization of production. By and large, westerners are not calling for public ownership of the large energy corporations, although it has been suggested for utilities. Indeed, they are outspoken in their criticism of the federal government's Synthetic Fuels Corporation. They can be expected to eschew issues of ownership restructuring, just as northern businessmen were loathe to support redistribution of plantation lands to former slaves in the post–Civil War

South. To dispossess one segment of capital of its property easily leads to questions about the rights of others to their holdings.

Spatially Uneven Market Power

A third material basis of regional differentiation is the uneven distribution of market power among regions that maintain exchange relationships with each other. This type of regional irritant presupposes differences in the sectoral composition of trading regions and operates in the realm of circulation rather than production. Within this category, there are two types of market power: (1) the uneven distribution of market power between production versus circulation sectors—generally the domination by commercial, financial, and transportation sectors of agricultural, mining, and manufacturing sectors; and (2) the uneven distribution of market power among productive sectors between commodity suppliers and their business customers, or between producer and consumer goods sectors.

The first form, monopolistic control of finance and commercial capital over productive capital, is the more important for explaining late nineteen-century regional antagonisms. As we recounted in previous chapters, northern mercantilists profitted tremendously from their region's strategic position as trader, banker, and shipper of southern cotton in the Atlantic arena. Similarly, western farmers and southern sharecroppers balked under the yoke of exploitative freight rates, extraordinary interest rates, and vulnerability to price gouging by grain dealers. In both cases, the demand for government (though not necessarily federal) intervention in these market relationships became a powerful mobilizer in the regionalism of each era.

The second form of exploitation is more germane to the twentieth-century experience. Midwestern and western farmers have persistently confronted oligopolies in supply markets (farm machinery, fertilizers, and energy) and in selling markets (meatpackers and food processors). Similarly, small coal operators faced large oligopolistic consumers like the steel corporations, curtailing profitability and contributing to that region's underdevelopment.

Generally, less capital-intensive, more competitive sectors are more apt to be handicapped in interregional trade. Historically, these have been chiefly on the raw materials end of the spectrum, as in agriculture and mining. Thus, resource-rich regions have often been on the exploited end of this exchange relationship. However, the contemporary struggle over energy prices and policy shows that roles may be reversed. In the U.S. case, the energy-rich Intermountain West appears to have the upper hand in this crucial market. It can, for instance, levy relatively hefty severance taxes without fear of substantial loss of market. This reversal is in part a function of the increasing capital intensiveness of modern energy extraction and the emergence, for a decade, of an extraordinary international oligopoly in the energy sector.

Regionally uneven distribution of market power will tend to fuel interregional antagonism if the effects of the resulting unequal exchange are severe enough to threaten the viability of an entire regional economy. This was the case with eastern capitalists' domination of westward agricultural markets in the nineteenth century and with western-operated (though often eastern-owned) energy sectors in the postwar period. It also contributed to southern rebellion in the Civil War era.

This form of interregional antagonism is most purely a struggle among corporate owners and regional business elites in regions relying upon the respective contentious sectors. Working-class residents may be drawn in if the imbalance threatens jobs, but the outcome of a regional conflict over market power will at most be a redistribution of proceeds among sectors rather than a restructuring of underlying economic relationships. In the most successful case, populist agitation by western farmers resulted in dramatic institutional changes, including the regulation of financial and commercial oligopolies and, much later, national intervention into agricultural markets via price supports and stockpiling. Yet even here, while slowing the rate of displacement of family farmers, no real changes in the structure of production ensued.

Combinations and Permutations

A region's economic status can be assessed by looking collectively along these three axes—growth dynamics, class structure, and market power. There do exist pure cases where economic stagnation and decline; high concentrations of working-class people; absentee ownership; and external control over financial, commercial, and industrial markets plague a single regional economy. This was the position of Appalachia from the Great Depression to the late 1960s. Conversely, there have been instances where a single region is favored along all of these lines, as was the North in the mid-nineteenth century. But more often, regional economies will tend to diverge in varying directions along the major axes.

For instance, regions enjoying rapid growth may simultaneously suffer from adverse class and ownership structures and unfavorable positions in interregional markets. The American West was growing explosively, if quite cyclically, during the latter half of the nineteenth century. Yet though crop yields, gross regional income, and similar measures of regional growth climbed rapidly, large numbers of producers suffered the insecurity, poverty, and periodic bankruptcy that resulted from the absentee ownership and market power of corporations in the realm of circulation.

In another example, the Intermountain West has enjoyed extraordinary rates of growth, the highest in the nation, since 1960. In addition, it is relatively well-situated in interregional commodity markets because of the energy crisis and the structure of the energy industry. However, the bulk of the profits generated from its nonrenewable resources flow to corporate coffers outside the region and are destined for rapid deployment in any global location which promises higher profits.

Alternatively, a rapid growth region may have a relatively strong indigenous entrepreneurial class but be hemmed in by fierce competitive conditions in the interregional marketplace. This is best illustrated by the South in the postwar period. While its output expands and its commercial classes thrive, its growth is predicated upon continued maintenance of low-cost conditions of production, namely keeping wages and taxes low and unions out. Growth is thus more tenuous.

Both the previous instances of rapid growth with adverse class and ownership or market structures lead to the phenomenon of poor and worsening internal income distributions within "healthy" expansionary economies. This deterioration contributes to the internal conflicts which tend to preoccupy these types of rapidly growing regions. Those groups suffering adversely from the sectoral displacement or the income distributional consequences of rapid growth form the constituencies for the progressive politics which emerged during the Populist era. Conflict around growing internal disparities are also evident in the postwar West and South, the nation's faster-growing areas.

In yet another permutation, slow growth regions may house relatively strong indigenous capitalist corporations and enjoy a dominant position in at least some segments of interregional trade. The Northeast in the contemporary period is an example. While its indigenous industrial sectors and working class suffer from heightened international competition, its large contingent of corporate headquarters and internationally leading financial institutions continue to prosper from their market power. The complaints of the region's leadership about its troubled economy have been justly viewed with suspicion by workers and entrepreneurs in other regions, who continue to view it as the locus of power over the conditions of and compensation for work across far-flung regions.

ECONOMICALLY INDUCED BRANDS OF REGIONAL POLITICS

Three distinct postures towards regionalism are available to regions. Schematically, these can be catalogued as (1) repudiation of regionalism, (2) regional separatism and (3) claims for regional singularity. Preferences for one over another can be associated with the variants in economic status just reviewed. These are heavily shaped by the existence of the American federal political system with its highly decentralized, formal democratic powers and its interregional two-party politics.

The Repudiation of Regionalism

Regions which have the good fortune to be favored under uneven development will tend to eschew regionalism and embrace nationalism. This is particularly true when they have relatively strong political representation within the State and if their prosperity depends, in part, on a favorable position in interregional trade. The most obvious example is the North during the nineteenth century. In a series of political postures dating back to the national banking schemes of Hamilton and the national program of the Whigs, the dominant mercantilist classes in the Northeast favored national integration, a strong central government, a national currency, and subordination of state interests to the project of building a strong national economy. Regional affinities were viewed as provincial by these advocates of nationalism. Ironically, eastern nationalism has been provincial in its own right, oblivious to the uniqueness of outlying regions and often equating its own regional requirements with national needs.

Nationalism, or more accurately, sentiment for national integration, is not necessarily synonymous with prosperity. If an economic crisis, such as the Great Depression, hits all regions equally hard, it is possible that regional differences will become muted. This happened in the New Deal. The Roosevelt administration was able to build particularistic regional concerns into a national program for economic revitalization: credit for western farmers, TVA for a cotton- and coal-depleted South, and public works for eastern cities. The New Deal consensus was made possible by a depression of such massive proportions that it profoundly affected the growth rates of all regions. This has not been true of most other downturns.

In general, a nationalistic posture is characteristic of those regions that either enjoy a relatively strong position with respect to comparative regional growth rates, class-ownership structure, and power in sector-specific markets, or in those cases where all regions are positively or adversely affected by similar circumstances. In all other cases where an interregional economy is highly differentiated by class-ownershp differences, maldistributed market power, or uneven growth dynamics, hostile interregional politics will emerge, when initiated by a region which claims to be exploited by the existence of interregional differentials and holds other regions accountable.

Regional Separatism

Sentiment for regional separatism will tend to be strongest in regions where the economy is prospering but where basic sectors face adverse market power or operate with substantial outside ownership of crucial sectors and where the region in question does not dominate the national state.[1] The separatist impulse may be of a mild form, aimed at devolution of political power or defending the status quo against greater centralization of state power. Or it may take a more severe form, even evolving into an independence movement. Regions whose populace supports a form of separatism presumably stand a better chance of controlling the conditions of production, prices, and profit flows in their major sectors under a more decentralized political structure.

The most extreme example of a separatist movement in U.S. history was the southern effort to secede from the Union. As we have seen in chapters 3 and 4, the South was enjoying a shortlived boom in cotton markets during the immediate prewar period, giving its planter elite an illusion of economic robustness. Confederate leaders believed that an independent South would be economically viable. In addition, they planned to seize control of their own banking and commerce and to recoup their tax contributions to the national government. For all these reasons, they anticipated that the southern economy would be strengthened by the severance of political partnership with the North. Once autonomous, they could eliminate the manufactured goods which cost them dearly due to their dependence upon imports of machinery, tools, and consumer goods. And they could play off English against Yankee textile buyers in a cotton market which they would dominate.

In the postwar resurgence of regionalism, those regions whose growth rates are comparatively favorable have adopted mildly separatist and states' rights political postures. The contemporary South, whose regional elites operate through the Southern Growth Policies Board, enjoyed stronger growth rates than its northern neighbors, at least in the 1970s. At the same time, it marketed its output in highly competitive markets. It did comparatively well because prices of its standard commodities are lower, in large part due to the good "business climate." Confronted with a Northeast-Midwest coalition which desired to impose uniform labor laws, federal welfare takeovers, and new redistributive formulas for federal spending, southern leadership championed states' rights, federal fiscal conservatism, and lower social spending.

The ensemble of differential economic attributes in the Intermountain West leads to another variant of separatism. Like the postwar South, this region grew rapidly from the late 1960s on, largely due to the energy crisis. But unlike the South, its dynamic sectors were more thoroughly directed by corporate managers lodged outside the region. Unlike the South as well, its lead sectors commanded a relatively dominant position in their interregional and international markets. The West has also been relatively separatist, particularly over issues of land use and energy taxation. The WESTPO coalition frequently resorted to states' rights arguments to legitimate its claims to control its own development.

Claims for Regional Special Treatment

A third type of interregional politics emerges in those regions whose recent growth experience has been poor both absolutely and relatively. Adversity in regional economic growth experience, whether it arises from a concentration of profit-squeezed sectors, the desire of corporations to escape well-developed working-class institutions, the exhaustion of natural resources, profit-draining outside ownership, or some combination of these, will pressure regional leadership to petition the federal government for special treatment. If all regions suffer similar economic ills, then a national program like the New Deal could be engineered. But if the regions in question are atrophying while their counterparts are booming, they will be forced to make their case for special regional consideration.

Examples of this kind of regional claim for special assistance are Appalachia in the 1950s and 1960s postwar period, the Northeast beginning in the late 1960s, and the Midwest beginning the late 1970s. Youngstown, Ohio is a graphic example of a subregion in distress compelled to entreat the federal government directly for specially tailored aid. In the cases of Appalachia and Youngstown, the residents suffered not only the demise of critical sectors (coal and steel) but also wielded little or no control locally over the resources and productive assets involved. This gave their demands a particular urgency and cogency which have been more difficult to achieve in larger, more complex geographical entities such as Detroit, Pittsburgh, or the Northeast as a whole.[2]

The boundaries between these three types of regionalism are not rigid. The first two—repudiation of regionalism and regional separatism—tend to be longer-term postures based on significant differences in mode of production, sectoral structure, market power, or maturation of capital-labor relations. Periods of great regional hostility are often characterized by regions on opposing sides of this boundary, each creating an ideology about its politics ("the Union Forever," "states' rights") that lasts well beyond the period of conflict. Regions with this inherited posture may also, in response to shorter-term displacement or trauma, claim singularity and demand special treatment. Thus the Northeast in the 1970s, long the champion of national integration, found itself lobbying for compensatory aid in the 1970s. In the same decade, the relatively states' rights-ist Intermountain West asked for impact aid to ameliorate the effects of rapid energy development.

THE DETERMINANTS OF SUCCESSFUL REGIONAL ORGANIZING

A central theme of this book is that differential economic experience may be the primary, but not the sole, determinant of regionalism. In some instances where a group has succeeded in creating powerful regional sentiment around economic differences, its goals have been defeated. The South's loss in the Civil War is the best example. In other cases, efforts to revive an older regionalism or create a new one, again around economic issues, have languished. The recent northeastern effort is a good illustration. In this section, we reflect on the evidence from these cases that illuminates the translation of economic hostilities into organized instances of regionalism. The conclusion is that successful regional organizing efforts must be able to rely upon a relatively strong economic base, find a way of building inter- and intraclass unity, bridge internal social and cultural differences, and marshall political powers equal to its aspirations.

Economic Viability and Leadership

A region must have an economic base that is resilient enough to enable prosecution of its regional case. The southern leadership failed to understand the weaknesses in its own economy in the pre–Ciivil War period. Its cash crop economy turned out to be a hopeless provisioner of military supplies, particularly food and clothing for its troops, while the Confederacy's most liquid asset, cotton, was easily blockaded and rendered useless by its opponents. The North, on the other hand, had an economy which was not only sufficient to its goal of preserving the Union, but was stimulated by the war effort. In another instance, the strength of their energy-boosted economy enabled the western governors to defend their environmental and tax instruments and to fend off federal government preemption of state and local jurisdiction over energy development.[3]

In addition to economic strength, regional organizing efforts do better under circumstances where the affected parties have previously exercised a leadership role in economic matters and are politically well-seasoned. In the Intermountain West, for instance, the ranchers and farmers affected by energy development in the 1970s moved more easily into the forefront of the protest movement because they had long histories of participation in cattlemen's associations and the Farmer's Union, fighting for a better deal in prices, transportation, and agricultural policy. Furthermore, the agricultural and ranching communities had existing organizations which they used as springboards to build new ones more appropriate to the issues at hand. Residents of mountain towns were less well equipped to assume leadership, like their Appalachian counterparts in an earlier period. In the Northeast, commercial and industrial interests that had traditionally been active in national business lobbying found it easy to assert leadership in regional advocacy, while newly distressed industrial communities found it more difficult.

Intra- and Interclass Unity

Regional organizing efforts which confront few perceived interclass differences will tend to be more successful than those which are ridden with internal conflict. The extraordinary solidarity among southern elites in the nineteenth-century was a function of the dominance of its landowning class, the weakness of indigenous merchant and commercial classes, and the ability of planters to convince white farmers farming on a small scale of their commonality of interests. Solidarity among business classes in the North in the same era was more difficult to achieve, precisely because the commercial classes often opposed the nascent industrial capitalists and because formidable intraregional differences existed among each faction (for example, the New England textile mills versus the Pennsylvanian ironmakers). Western unity in the contemporary period is harder to achieve than southern unity for similar reasons.

Interclass antagonisms within a region often form a barrier to the successful mobilization of regionalism. In the nineteenth-century South, for example, the planter class had to use coercion to force slaves to fight. Large numbers of poor white, independent farmers deserted. Indeed, the flight of massive numbers of slaves to the Union side was a factor in the war's military outcome. While the Unionists had to put up with draft riots by workingmen and some desertion by farmboys, their losses from internal class dissension were much fewer. Certainly, their draft dodgers and deserters did not race to join the enemy.

In some cases, the amelioration or prevention of interclass discord may itself be the motivation for regional elites and politicans to engage in interregional animosities. Certainly, the call to regional arms had this effect in some cases, regardless of whether or not this was the intent. Southern planters tied poor whites to them by villifying the North. Contemporary northern elites may be diverting working-class attention from the underlying crisis tendencies in capitalist structure by attempting to blame other places for domestic ills. We return to this possibility in the final section of this chapter.

Political and Cultural Media
Economic impulses to regional politics are heavily mediated by existing political and cultural forms. I have elaborated upon these at length in chapters 3 and 7, but it is worth summarizing the variants which have occurred in American instances of regionalism, drawn from the case studies.

The U.S. political system is perhaps the most significant institutional force shaping the course of American regionalism. Yet its role is contradictory. In its structuring of the State, it provides a ready apparatus for distinctly regional politics. National legislative leadership is explicitly territorial in composition. Even the presidential vote is toted up on the basis of geographical units. The evolution of state governments, their constitutional powers, and the parallel growth of strongly state-based political parties further facilitate the formation of regionalist politics. Since power and resources have been heavily concentrated in the central State, this federal system has created a remarkable tension between regionally distinct needs and national consensus. Indeed, a hallmark of the American political system versus its European progenitors is the dominance of place-based over class-based politics. On the other hand, the political party system tries to bridge regional differences. Given an extraordinarily stable two-party system, the mission of a national party is to create cross-regional coalitions which will remain durable and will supply both congressional delegates and electoral votes. When one or both parties are successful in this effort, regionalism as a divisive force is muted. When regional differences are fiercest, the two-party system tends to fall apart and parties become strongly regionally based.

Illustrations of these tendencies abound. In the Civil War era, the

Whigs and Democrats alike sought to coalesce disparate classes and cultures across regions to hold sway nationally. Both failed. While the Whigs gave way to a series of new parties and finally to an exclusively northern republicanism, the Democrats became the party of the South. In the postwar period, the North attempted to rebuild a national coalition by investing southern political power in a new Republican party consisting of blacks and former Whigs.

Political parties also rose and fell with regionalism in the eighty-year stretch between the Civil War and World War II. The emergence of a significant third party challenge in the Populist Progressive era was closely tied to the regional animosity between the West and the East. The submergence of regional conflict in the New Deal was the product of an enormously successful Democratic effort to recruit depression-pressed classes in all regions.

In the most recent postwar period, a relatively balanced rivalry between the two major parties has endured. Each has been relatively well represented in all regions, with the exception of the South. However, in the 1970s, a decade of growing economic divergence and revived regional conflict, the parties began to become relatively more regional in character once again, with striking shifts in geographical base. The Democrats, once strongest in the South, now became increasingly the dominant party of the Northeast for reasons detailed in chapter 8. In response, southerners increasingly voted for Republican presidential candidates even though their indigenous political machines remained largely Democratic. At the same time, the Republicans strengthened their hold on the West. Mirrored best in presidential voting patterns, the Frostbelt has become predominantly Democratic and the Sunbelt predominantly Republican. Regional hostilities seem to have been, in this case, a major catalyst in the reshaping of the geography of political parties, rather than vice versa.

This contemporary jockeying for position demonstrates how powerfully the system works to constrain the prospects for regionalism. Political parties must build multiregional bases to win the presidency or to ensure success in the national Congress. This is less important in political systems where the presidency or parliamentary rule are won by strictly national vote. Within a region, then, a party may chose to emphasize regional priorities and antipathies, but to gain national power it must moderate these views lest it appear to be purely provincial. Ironically, given the predominance of place-based politics in the United States, there are simultaneously fewer instances of true regional separatism than in most other democratic industrialized nations.

A good example of the contradictory role of federalism is the dilemma faced by the Democratic party in the 1980s. Increasingly the party of urban areas and mature industrial states, the Democrats have agonized over the position of issues like import protection, plant closing legislation, industrial policy, urban aid, and labor law reform in their platform.

Too strong an advocacy of these remedies for northeastern decline would offend the Southeast, where a newly built Republican party could cut deeply into the congressional Democratic caucus. Indeed, the relative failure of the Northeast-Midwest coalition to win its major positions in Congress in the early 1980s demonstrates the limits to purely regionally based politics, especially in an era where regionally laggard growth rates are shifting the center of gravity of power toward the newer, Sunbelt regions.

Cultural differences have been a secondary factor in the initiation of regional strife in the U.S., particularly in the twentieth century. Profound differences in outlook did characterize the elites of the two major regions in the pre–Civil War period, in ways that make cultural rancor difficult to separate from economic warfare in retrospect. Yet ethnic and religious differences among elites were not a major shaper of Civil War animosities. Indeed, religious bonds were broken asunder by the war. The Protestant churches fractured along regional lines over the issue of slavery during that period.

Differences in lifestyle and regional self-conception have contributed to regionalist sentiment in the twentieth century, but they cannot be credited with causing renewed regional tensions. Indeed, the homogenization of American culture in the postwar period through national media such as television and movies and via large-scale interregional migration has muted differences in regional cultures. Those cultural distinctions and affinities which continue to operate in the United States are often not regional in nature and may be the basis instead for cross-regional political coalitions (the Moral Majority is an example).

One cultural difference which has played a pivotal role in maintaining regional hostilities is the difference in attitude toward formal race relations between North and South. Franklin Roosevelt held his fragile New Deal together by avoiding a head-on collision on this issue (see chapter 4). And as we saw in chapter 8, the attempt by the northern liberals and President Kennedy in particular to destroy southern institutions of segregation resulted in the loss of southern votes for national Democratic candidates and reignited southern resentment of Yankee arrogance. Southerners argued that northern cities practice an equally effective form of economic and spatial segregation. While racism is a very serious problem in both regions, different views on how to eliminate it continue to divide regional leadership.

Another cultural distinction contributes to Frostbelt-Sunbelt cleavage. The older manufacturing belt has evolved a way of doing business which relies upon adversarial negotiation between capital and labor, heavily ethnic patterning of urban life, and machine politics with its institutionalized graft and patronage systems. In states like California, Colorado, and Florida, politics are more fluid, union-management confrontations less ubiquitous, and ethnic and racial rivalries less embittered.[4] In the boom states, a more recently assembled population tends to be more forward-looking and open-minded, less organized, and less politicized. Politics in Chicago versus San Francisco or Denver amply demonstrate this difference.[5]

Region Building: A Summary

Geographical areas of the earth are uniquely marked by differential endowments in nature. They become regions when societies build distinct economies and political systems within their boundaries. Regions are thus built environments, rather than strictly natural ones, and they change over time in size, shape, and significance. Regionalism is the consciousness of a resident population about its commonalities across a geographical space and in distinction to groups in other regions. This book offers a framework for understanding the origins of regionalism and has held it up to scrutiny by examining the most prominent instances of regionalism in American history.

The cases of regionalism studied generally support the first nine theses laid out in chapter 1. (The final thesis, on the political potential of regionalism, is addressed in the final portion of this chapter.) Disparities in economic structure and growth rates have been the most prominent causes of American interregional antipathies. However, their translation into vigorous interregional conflict has been heavily mediated by the federal structure of government and politics.

Regionalism generally emerges in one region and evokes a defensive response from another. The initiation of interregional conflict is more apt to come from a hard-pressed region than one currently flush with economic success, unless the latter believes that it is discriminated against in the national power structure. Booming regions are more apt to develop an internally oriented regionalism preoccupied with solving new developmental problems.

Efforts to organize a region around its singular economic needs have been more successful in regions with a history of strong cultural affinities, lacking significant cross-cutting class antagonisms, and free of strong interparty rivalries. Furthermore, regionalist demands have tended toward separatism or redistribution of powers if the initiating region believes itself to be economically robust, but toward redistribution of funds and special treatment if it is economically depressed.

The internal complexity of regional economies and social structure guarantees that any regionalist coalition will be relatively variegated in its composition. Even when a minority of residents are directly affected, broad regional support for their economic predicament may emerge due to the multiplier effect. However, class and other social differences may be encompassed within the coalition. Thus, room is provided for contention over the leadership and program of such a coalition.

It is this final observation that makes the question of the political content of regionalism so interesting. As the cases show, some of the most sigsnificant social issues in American history have been fought out along geographical lines (Native American survival, slavery, and the family farm are examples). Political organization along regional lines, and the tension between regional and national priorities, has strengthened and elaborated the federal structure of the state as well as producing some extraordinary innovations in settlement patterns, cultural institutions, and public programs. What is the future of regionalism in the United States?

THE OUTLOOK FOR REGIONALISM

Regionalism has been a durable and complicating factor in American politics. In this assessment of its future, we address two questions: (1) will regionalism continue to be a significant force in American politics? and (2) will the construction of coalitions along regional lines be progressive or reactionary?

The Significance of American Regionalism in the Future

The instances of regionalism studied in this book suggest that regional cleavage is a relatively persistent phenomenon in American politics.[6] However, the demands registered by the regions of unrest seem to be of successively milder substance. It is not likely that a regional conflagration on the scale of the Civil War will be repeated in the United States for the foreseeable future. The north-south conflict of that era was based on two contesting modes of production. Subsequently, all regions of the United States became more similar in their almost universal adoption of free wage labor in a predominantly capitalist economy.

Yet, capitalism has been highly uneven in its degree of development across regions. This unevenness was analyzed by some scholars with a core-periphery model which viewed the process as one in which the wealthier regions or centers of monopoly capital became increasingly richer at the expense of poorer regions. More recently, the extraordinary reversals of previously leading regions such as the northeastern United States (and entire countries such as Britain) suggest an alternative interpretation. The more internally developed and conflictual working-class institutions in these regions have precipitated a dramatic outmigration of capital which "causes" poorer regions to grow relatively faster. While the former may still house the world's leading corporations and enjoy relatively higher per capita incomes, large groups within their borders may suffer long-term displacement.

Indeed, the hypermobility of capital may systematically create the conditions for renewed regionalism and regional conflict. A tension exists between free geographical mobility and organized reproduction processes, which must remain fixed, secure, and largely immobile to be functional.[7] Regionalism is a form of defense, on the part of those with the greatest stake, in this immobile built environment. In periods when capital mobility is accelerating, as it has since the late 1960s, greater displacement and growth disparities among regions will ensue, evoking greater territorially based protest. Similarly, the centralization of policy making in the State, a complement to the growing centralization of capital, may systematically reinforce the significance of territorial representation and conflict.[8]

Thus, the tendency toward regionalism will persist. However, the identity of the regional antagonists may change. Territorial conflicts may not remain regionalized at all, but give way to other geopolitical antagonisms at the national or local level. As an example, the particular regional conflicts that marked the stormy decade of the 1970s are not apt to persist in as virulent a form. Let's look briefly at each in turn.

The east-west conflict was predicated on scarcity of energy, high energy prices, rapid exploitation of energy resources in the West, and efforts by western political leaders to ameliorate the disruptive effects and to internalize at least some of the development costs in the price of extraction. By the mid-1980s, energy prices had again plunged, and many of the projects slated for the West were shelved. Furthermore, because of large-capacity additions, particularly of nuclear power plants, and the decline in industrial demand due to plant closings and increasing dependence upon imported products, an energy surplus began to appear across large portions of the manufacturing belt. While the fundamental and potentially adversarial relationship between these regions remained—the one the supplier, the other the buyer—the immediacy of the conflict had waned.

The north-south antagonism may prove more durable. It is a prototype of a much larger international struggle over the conditions of further development of the capitalist economic order. The struggle pits those who would preserve the gains of organized labor and the welfare state in the more industrially advanced regions, against the flight of capital toward the poorer, less internally conflictual regions of the world where precapitalist forms of production have until recently retarded capitalist development. The issue is whether capital must recognize the rights of workers and pay wages prevailing in advanced capitalist countries, or whether the lack of working-class institutions such as labor unions will be allowed to lure capital toward higher profits. The North and South will probably become more similar in both sectoral composition and growth rates. However, whether northern institutions like labor unions and the welfare state are dismantled or preserved will depend much upon the outcome of these regions' struggle over the machinery of the federal government and its deployment in support of or restraint of capital flight, including internationally.

However, new sources of territorial differentiation threaten to dislodge these conflicts from the center of the stage and raise others, more complex, in their stead. The most powerful of these is the militarization of the American economy, which has been a major factor in skewing high-tech and capital goods production to the defense perimeter (chapter 5), drawing a remarkable number of interregional migrants along with it, many of them from the more educated classes. At the same time, the vitality of this government-dependent segment of manufacturing has obscured the deterioration in the basic nonmilitary capital goods sectors, which have experienced disastrous losses in both international and domestic markets through the mid 1980s.[9] The industries most adversely affected are heavily concentrated in the Midwest. As a result, growth rate differentials have widened during the 1980s, although not along simple Frostbelt-Sunbelt lines. The major difference fell along coastal-heartland lines, as income growth in the former outstripped that in the latter by 4 percent to 1.4 percent, creating a gap of 10 percent by 1984 (*Chicago Tribune* 1986).

The military build-up and accompanying deterioration in the rest of the manufacturing base occurs unevenly within regions and metropolitan areas as well. Pockets of boom accompany military expenditure in states like Florida, Texas, Alabama, Colorado, and parts of New England, while other communities in the same states suffer decline and outmigration. California, which is the single largest recipient of military-related funds, has been one of the states worst hit by deindustrialization in the 1980s, with disproportionate numbers of plants closing in the timber, auto, rubber, steel, and related industries.[10] Around metropolitan areas, some suburban jurisdictions are growing rapidly from military-induced activity, while inner cities and other suburbs languish with plant closings. Texas shares this same unevenness as the oil slump has plunged much of its economy into recession (Weinstein 1983, 66–72).

It is difficult to see how this extraordinary military repatterning of manufacturing space might elicit a territorially based response. Possibly, critique of the economic consequences of military spending might emerge from the Midwest or, alternatively, among networks of inner-city-based organizing efforts.

Another emerging form of spatial differentiation is the product of a second specialty of the United States in international trade—the management and control of capital mobility. "World cities" like New York, Los Angeles, and Miami have hosted tremendous office-based booms associated with the proliferation of business services needed to finance, market, transport, communicate, and account for the growing share of product traded internationally. Other manufacturing-era cities are eclipsed, and inner-city problems are etched yet more sharply in contrast to the affluence of these business quarters and their denizens. These differences cut across regional boundaries and create commonalities among internationally oriented regions that may diffuse traditional regionalist sentiment. One manifestation of this trend was the unprecedented 1986 meeting of legislators from "the mega-states" of California, Texas, and Florida, which accounted for over half of the nation's total population growth in the first half of the 1980s.

Great institutional inertia in the American political system augers well for the maintenance of regionalism in the United States. So does the tenacity of regional caricatures. Both the heavily territorialized federal apparatus of government and cultural antipathies nurtured over time lend themselves to renewed regionalist sentiment and actioin. However, we have also argued that the root causes in all prominent instances of U.S. regional conflict have been economic in character. The persistence of more than residual regionalism, therefore, depends upon the continued unevenness of capitalist development, in any of the several forms distinguished above. In the postwar period, it has been sectoral differences and growth rate differentials which have provided the impetus. In fact, the resurgence of regionalism in the 1970s is directly attributable to accelerated rates of restructuring at a time when respective regions were distinctly differentiated by industries in the most volatile portions of their profit cycles. The power of regionalism in the future depends upon the extent to which this type of uneven development continues, and whether the major manifestations will be regional, rather than urban-rural or coastal-interior.

The Conservative and Progressive Potential of Regionalism

The question of the tenor, or normative qualities, of a particular instance of regionalism has been hotly debated, as we saw in chapter 3. Within the Marxist tradition, the debate has favored the repudiation of regionalism, which has been evaluated by the revolutionary-minded as a deflector from international working-class solidarity. Among the New Left, there has been greater disagreement, the fruit of reevaluation of ideological rigidity in traditional Marxist praxis and of pragmatic responses to immediate situations. Both groups measure the degree of progressiveness of a regional movement by its contribution to the transformation of the capitalist economic order as opposed to reinforcement of its prevailing exploitative and crisis-prone dynamics. Working within the second tradition, I define as progressive those institutional innovations which challenge abuses of capitalism and are democratic in nature. Examples are unions, antitrust legislation, minimum wage laws, social security, cooperatives, and public ownership.

Has American regionalism played a conservative or a progressive role in transforming the capitalist economy? Ammunition can be found in the cases studied here for either position. The negative interpretation would emphasize the fact that leadership in most cases of interregional conflict has devolved upon regional capitalist elites. In the American West of recent years, a ranching and environmentally originated regionalism was taken over by regional elites who have bent anti-eastern and anti-outsider sentiment to their own ends, including quiet agreements in favor of energy exploitation with large outsider corporations. It is not far from the truth to conclude that all instances of successful U.S. regional organizing to date against some outside agent or other region have been led by, or at least ended up being hospitable to, the accumulation needs of a regionally dominant economic elite. A corollary is that no case of American regionalism has been a purely working-class (or slave or tenant farmer) phenomenon.[11]

Critics might go on to argue that regionalism has also consistently deflected the energies of potentially progressive groups toward cross-class coalitions which end up reinforcing the hold of the regional elites and advancing their narrow sectoral or boosterist goals at the expense of more progressive innovations. It is true, as I have documented in various cases, that regional elites will often try to unify all residents of the region around a common program that suits their ends. In some cases, such groups have drawn upon preexisting regional hostilities to deflect incipient challenges from other quarters. Perhaps the best example of this was the way in which western Republican regional elites cast populism as a southern Democratic plot and "waved the bloody shirt" of Civil War affinities to dissuade tenant farmers from voting for a third party, while the ex-planter southern leadership of the Democratic party tried to discredit populism in the South as a Republican (that is, northern) plot (Goodwyn 1978, 18–19).[12]

There are two objections, it seems to me, to this indictment of American regionalism. First, it is not always true that a regional elite is successful in tying exploited classes to its program. Black slaves in the Civil War South are a good example. Indeed, the war between the states provided an extraordinary means of liberation for black slaves which might not have been as sweeping under other circumstances. It permitted them to make their refusal to work a stunning blow to the South while their flight in large numbers to aid the Unionists made the Emancipation Proclamation mandatory. Similarly, workers in the North were not always willing cannon fodder for nascent capitalist Unionist leadership, as the draft riots showed.

Second, the attempt on the part of a regional elite to raise the issue of "them against us" on a regional rather than a class or sectoral basis does not prove that it is effective, even when it is correlated with the failure of organization along other lines. The failure of populism, for instance, to forge an interregional unity against financial and mercantile capital (or as a proxy, a South-West coalition against the Northeast) cannot clearly be laid to the successful waving of the bloody shirt and invocation of the Lost Cause. There are a number of other explanations of this failure, including educational and organizational failures, and underestimation of the political power and mobilization of eastern capital.

But apart from these problems of fact or interpretation, there is one additional weakness in a position that dismisses regionalism a priori as a pathway toward progressive change. This is the failure of a purely class analysis to comprehend the ways in which the fortunes of a regional economy as a whole really do have important interactive effects on the various members of the region. A political position which endorses only cross-regional class unity rejects out of hand the ways in which economic and social life are governed by relationship and qualities which are common to particular places and peoples—features which may be truly territorial in nature. Most obviously, through a whole range of reproductive institutions from the family through the schools and local governments, economic adversities that hurt one set of workers or employers will ricochet through the local economy so that many more people are affected. Thus all residents of a particular region do have a serious stake in, say, the timber or mining industries, or in steel or auto manufacture, that cannot be reduced simply to a critique of capitalism. Under any conceivable socialist scenario, the dilemma of maintenance of their communities, with these existing infrastructure and social networks, would remain.

What makes regionalism such a complex expression is its singular interplay with the contested role of the State. The one institution which plays a persistent central role in the formation of regionalism in the United States is the State. It is precisely its territorial nature, which ambivalently straddles the principles of democracy and the capitalist State, that makes regionalism a possible route toward progressive transformation—though not perhaps the regionalism of full-blown proportions, as in the Civil War or the media-hyped "Second War Between the States" of the 1970s. It is regional organizing efforts as training grounds and routes to political power that are promising in this sense. Let me cite a few examples.

The Civil War provided a budding northern working-class movement an arena in which to formulate its demands and broadcast its predicament. The southern planters actually helped through their critique of "wage slavery," as they termed northern free wage labor. Unions were quick to point out the similarities between slaves and wage workers, underscoring the hypocrisy of northern leadership in condemning the former while engaging in the exploitation of the latter. While the Union cause was an excuse for very repressive measures taken against draft resisters and union efforts to organize plants, the northern critique of exploitation in another region proved very functional in the long run as a means of strengthening labor's claims against capital. In addition, once slavery was eradicated, wage labor could no longer been seen as superior to a worse fate. This is not to argue that the war was on balance a positive milestone in the history of the northern working class, but that its effect on the organizational unity and strength of that class was not unambiguously adverse.

Similarly, western ranchers and environmentalists have not been disarmed by the Western Governor's Policy Office and the pro-development tack it has taken recently. In the earlier days of the recent energy boom, the office offered them a voice and a way to get in touch with other groups. When it began to go soft on energy development, these groups had already built strong intraregional networks which permitted them to pursue their ends through other channels as well as by keeping pressure up on WESTPO. And while they maintain an autonomous stance organizationally, they continue to support regional claims such as defense of the severance tax and state siting control that potentially strengthen their hand.

In other words, participation in a regional cause, in addition to addressing directly the macroeconomic condition of the home economy, may serve as an apprenticeship in regional economics and the exercise of political power. It may be a way in which groups with a stake in the region learn about the mechanics of the regional, national, and international economies in which they are embedded. It may be the only possible stepping stone to a more autonomous, class-conscious organization with a clearer economic agenda. It may be a way of discovering that regional elites cannot be counted on to take effective steps to clean up the mess left in the wake of capital flight or rapacious energy development. New interregional alliances may then be formed, without abandoning the roots of distinctive regional origins.

Yet the case for the progressiveness of regionalism ought not to be made on grounds of apprenticeship alone. In the final analysis, miners, farmers, and autoworkers—even those with well-developed class consciousness—are more apt to consider themselves Kentuckians, Minnesotans, or Detroiters than members of a particular class. The preservation of place, and its relative health, remains a very central issue for most people, even the latest migrants to and from a place. People are proud of where they live and have lived, are concerned that their neighbors fare well, and want their children to have the choice of a future in the place. That emotional bond, wrapped up in the conditions of reproduction and culture of entire groups of people, is not chauvinist in essence, although it can become so at certain historical moments.[13]

The cases studied in this book illustrate that co-optation of regional feeling into narrow support for the interregional demands of a regional elite occurs most often when (1) some previous regional conflict has drawn in the bulk of the population in an active way or (2) nonelite classes are demobilized in the current era. The collaboration of active unions, farmer organizations, and environmentalists in a regional effort less often derails an impulse toward expression of progressive demands and is more a stepping stone to other—often cross-regional—forms of political action.

What may be said, then, is that a progressive regionalism is one which transcends the simple formula of them-us and creates links between progressive interests in distinct regions without destroying the legitimacy of uniquely regional claims. This was an important ingredient in the success of the New Deal. Indeed, a savvy progressive movement in our own times might take advantage of cleavages among regional capitals and fashion a cooperative national program which might encompass the following. Western environmentalists, ranchers, and communities would be assured of orderly, ecologically respectful methods of energy extraction even if it costs energy consumers and users a bit more. Eastern and midwestern unionized workers would be guaranteed an industrial policy which would forcefully stem capital flight and experiment with new forms of worker ownership and control, even if it were to cost western consumers of manufactured products a bit more. Southern workers would be guaranteed the right to organize and to a social wage equivalent to that in more developed regions, even if it cost consumers in other regions a bit more.[14] Such a movement would thus transcend regional lines. Yet it would be strongly indebted to regional consciousness and preexisting regional organizing efforts as instruments in its creation.

A national program could be built around these regionally initiated demands. It would have as its common theme the stability and preservation of community, counterposed against the hypermobility of capital and waste of human and physical resources left in its wake.[15] It would respect and champion the uniqueness and diversity of individual communities and regions.

In the early 1980s, a number of authors have written creatively on the subject of a progressive and democratic economic transformation.[16] A major weakness in most of these proposals is that they ignore or at least sidestep the particularities of regions, ethnicities, and cultures, proposing a common rubric, such as "growth with equity," around which disparate progressive groups might coalesce.[17] Yet these agendas have gone undeservedly unnoticed and have not been integrated into the mainstream of political debate. In the view of this author, one of the chief reasons for this poor response is the failure to acknowledge individual and group priorities in coalition-building and to place them first, rather than last, in the organizing effort.

A notion like "growth with equity" will not propel a ranching organization faced with strip mining into a political coalition. But a commitment to acting on that issue, in combination with a host of other issues, might. This necessarily means compromise among diverse constituents. It also means that a great deal of energy must be spent educating and communicating among potential members. Indeed, a major tactical mistake of left progressive efforts in the United States is the formulation of nationally focussed political agendas, aimed at politicans and the press, in the absence of a grassroots participatory process.

Such grassroots participation can work, even over long distances. As a prototype of a regionally based democratic, grass-roots coalition-building effort, the Montana Alliance for Progressive Policies has taken on the hard work of educating its diverse constituents (women, agriculturalists, organized labor, educators, environmentalists, Native Americans, and the poor) about each other's issues. They bring groups face-to-face, as much as is possible, to experience directly the priorities and problems of their "neighbors," many of whom live hundreds of miles from each other. It is not always possible to get all groups to support every priority of each caucus in the coalition, and the coalition does not force those issues which are too explosive.

The Union victory in the Civil War era and the successful New Deal coalition of the 1930s offer other political lessons. Both took up the causes of disparate groups across the regions and wove them together to create an unbeatable national program. As we saw in the case of the North, this involved an extensive campaign to instruct western farmers about the need for a tariff while convincing easterners to support western physical improvements. In the New Deal, farmers were asked to support workers' rights to organize and unemployment aid, while workers were encouraged to support agricultural relief programs.

In both these historical instances, existing political parties were either replaced by new ones that represented an emergent progressive coalition or dramatically overhauled. And in both cases, dramatic progressive reforms were achieved—the elimination of slavery in the former, the creation of a social welfare society in the latter. In each case, the political program of the new configuration prevailed for nearly half a century, although much of its progressive and activist content eroded overtime.

The creation of a new national coalition with a progressive economic agenda faces great obstacles, as the 1980s popularity of Reaganism with its militaristic, free enterprise, and antigovernment ideology has demonstrated. Like the New Deal and the Republican party in the Civil War crisis, compelling ideas and innovations will undoubtedly come from below, from local and regional experiments which provide successful prototypes, increase comprehension through failure, and educate people in the process. Contemporary examples are the Pittsburgh area's Steel Valley Authority, Montana MAPP's alternative economic agenda, and California's Plant Closing Project. Each was borne out of desperation and acute crisis, and each has become a landmark for groups in other localities and regions.

The most powerful common theme is community preservation. Yet communities differ markedly from each other in origin, historic role, and current predicament. Explicit acknowledgment of regional differences will have to be built into any successful coalition-building effort. Instead of animosity and suspicion, the fruit of past regional antagonisms, a successful coalition will have to sew seeds of understanding, respect and friendship—across races, across cultures, across urban-rural splits, across humid and arid climes; between miners and ranchers, steelworkers and environmentalists, peace advocates and construction workers. Such a joint project might then reap the benefits of regional integrity, economic progress, and world peace. This is the political challenge of regionalism.

Notes

1. Gourevitch, 1977, argues for the European and Canadian cases, that separatism may also occur where a region exercises economic but not political leadership (for example, Catalonia). In the United States, because of the flexibility of the political system, this has not been the case.

2. In these latter cases, the ownership of the resource and shutdown plants *is* indigenous. Arguing that a region whose own economic elites are responsible for its problems might also be asked to solve them, spokespersons for other regions have criticized special aid infusions like the Chrysler bailout loan, a national urban policy that lopsidedly helped northeastern cities, and import protection for industries like steel and autos.
3. Economic vigor automatically pays off in enhanced political power, decade by decade, in the United States. Economic growth multiplies job opportunities and prompts inmigration, which via reapportionment translates into greater congressional clout.
4. California is exceptional for hosting great ethnic differences and a strong union movement and yet continually innovating politically and culturally.
5. Sunbelt cities have enjoyed widening "pro-growth" coalitions for most of the postwar period; in contrast, slower-growing cities have evolved more exclusive coalitions whose job it is to see that their members get contracts, jobs, and neighborhood improvements. See Mollenkopf (1981) and Fainstein and Fainstein (1983).
6. For a similar view, see Phillips (1982, 74–770.
7. This argument has been made by David Harvey (1982, 29–34).
8. For an elaboration of this view, see Tarrow et al. (1978, 1–27).
9. In addition to the evidence in chapter 5 above, see Markusen (1986d) for an elaboration of this argument.
10. See Shapira (1986) for an extensive empirical account of this restructuring in California. See also Teitz (1984).
11. Nor has any other dominant American political movement, for that matter.
12. Goodwyn makes much of the function of north-south sectionalism preventing a rise of west-south unity around populism. He has not, however, satisfactorily analyzed the east versus west–south rivalry, which did facilitiate as well as complicate the movement.
13. The tendency to deprecate political actions that arise from defense of the sphere of reproduction is a serious political mistake, in my view, and stems from the incorrect emphasis given to production over reproduction in Marxist economic theory (see Hartmann and Markusen, 1980). The urban social movements literature has helped to correct this problem, but much of the regional literature continues to repeat the error.
14. Such a program would have to be tied up with international goals of a similar sort—controls on trade, for instance, from plants in countries where workers are highly exploited. Distinctive regional issues may not be the only planks in the platform—justice and opportunities for minorities, women, seniors, and gays; opposition to increased defense spending; an end to nuclear proliferation; a progressive human rights policy around the world; and many others could be included.
15. See Markusen (1977 and 1979a) for the formal economic justification for this strategy, on grounds of efficiency as well as equity.
16. Bowles, Gordon, and Weisskopf (1984), Carnoy and Shearer (1980), Alperovitz and Faux (1984), and Bluestone and Harrison (1982). In Europe, their counterparts have come from among Eurocommunist Socialists, and the left wing of the Labor Party in Britain.
17. Bluestone and Harrison are more sensitive to regional and community issues and deserve credit for helping to start the community versus capital movement in the United States. For an interesting academic counterpart from Poland, see Ciechocinska (1983); she advocates an emphasis on "living conditions" as a normative priority in regional planning in contrast to the technocratic emphasis on growth poles and production complexes.

Appendix:
Alternative Approaches to the Study of Regions and Regionalism

A set of quite disparate approaches have been employed historically by students of regions and regional politics. In this appendix, four major methodological schools are briefly surveyed. In addition to the explicit study of phenomena at the regional level, there are relevant bodies of scholarship aimed at interpreting nationalism and urbanism, each of which is reviewed for its insights and analogies with regionalism.

THE LITERATURE ON REGIONS AND REGIONALISM

A profuse literature acknowledges the prominence of regional differentiation and regionalism in the United States and tries to cope with it theoretically. Four efforts can be distinguished: the history of sectionalism, regional organicism, regional science, and Marxism. Each has attempted to understand regional complexity, albeit with a different object in mind. While each has contributed to the conceptual approach to regions, all suffer from similar shortcomings. First, each tends to pursue abstraction at the cost of explanatory power and justice to the real complexity of regions. The regional organicism of Odum is least offensive on this score. Second, each tends toward a monocausal account of regional form, and in doing so, ignores or discounts the insights of previous paths of scholarship. Marxism and regional organicism are less culpable here than regional science. Third, each group of regional scholars (some regional economists excepted) has tended to treat regional differentiation as a universal and permanent phenomenon. In what follows, I survey these traditions of regional analysis, placing each within its larger theoretical and social context.

The Regional Historians

Regional distinctiveness as a topic of historical study is as old as academic history in the United States. The most famous academician of sectionalism[1] was Frederick Jackson Turner, whose provocative essay, "The Significance of the Frontier in American History," in 1893 launched a generation of scholarship and brought Turner fame. For Turner, regions were created as a function of the moving frontier—that ill-defined westward area where European stock had not yet established their material culture. Turner's essay contained three ideas which attained the status of basic truths for generations. First, he argued that the American regional experience differed from the European because of the availability of cheap, extensive land on the frontier and because of the resistance of Native Americans. These conditions rendered obsolete the heritage of British institutions and prompted the construction of new political and economic forms. Second, Turner suggested that the frontier was an escape valve for urban industrial conflict and thus replaced class consciousness with a regional orientation. Third, Turner asserted that the frontier experience encouraged distinctive cultural values, such as self-reliance, ingenuity, and participatory democracy (Turner 1894; Hofstader 1968).

Since Turner wrote, historiographers have documented the weaknesses of Turner's formulations. While he was justifiably reacting to the history he was taught, which interpreted the American experience as singularly derived from the European, he went overboard in rejecting the latter. He elevated "the frontier" to a timeless abstraction, contrasted with the urban settled areas of the country. He lumped the southern and northern frontier together, writing as if the same white, "independent," farmer aspirants were the major agents of development in each arena. As historians later pointed out, this hardly held in the American Southwest (Louisiana and Texas), where planters owning and managing large numbers of slaves controlled the development process and black labor farmed the land. In his fervor, Turner turned major the axis of U.S. sectional conflict by 90 degrees, dismissing the north-south antipathy and replacing it with an east-west rivalry (Hofstader 1949; Taylor 1971).[2]

Despite Turner's limits, his work offers several insightful approaches to regions. First, his frontier argument implicitly views regions as social constructions, not as physiographic (or homogeneous) entities. Second, his break with the European tradition stresses the necessity for particularity and concreteness in the analysis of regions. While his generalizations on national character were overly simplistic, his insights into aspects of western American culture were perceptive.[3] Third, Turner's interpretation implies that cultures can be reshaped by the peculiarities of regional experience (and vice-versa).[4] Each of these aspects of his work was analytically and empirically sound.

Among historians, Turner's interest in the primacy of American regional issues was carried on by William Hesseltine. Hesseltine was preoccupied with conflicts within regions among classes. He viewed national politics and growth as the product either of a coalition of regional ruling classes (compromising to secure domination within their regions), or less often, of the enmity between regional ruling classes. "The contest between groups for the control of the region has been the moving force of American history," he wrote (1944, 37).[5] Despite the monocausality of his economic elites approach, Hesseltine's work was valuable for its sophisticated understanding of the differential complexities of regions and his refusal to treat regions as internally homogeneous.

Unlike Turner, who was a partisan of the West, Hesseltine deplored sectionalism (which he, like Turner, saw as a permanent phenomenon). Hesseltine even went so far as to suggest that regions might exploit each other. "Sectionalism," he wrote, "is the combination of comparable dominant groups in contiguous regions in order to exploit other regions or the nation as a whole" (1944, 42).[6] He saw sectionalism as competitive rather than cooperative, particularistic rather than national, divisive rather than unifying in its tendencies. Hesseltine's views were formulated in an era of wartime national consensus, and expressed an affinity with the centralism, materialism, and nationalism of depression-era New Deal policies.

The Regional Organicists

Analysts from geography to sociology have envisioned regions as organic units. This view, traceable to the older philosophical traditions of both naturalism and Darwinism, became particularly strong in the United States in the early decades of the twentieth century. Several quotes cited in Odum and Moore (1938, 20) will suffice to illustrate:

> A "region" is the geographer's term for an "environmental type" in which the "geographic elements are combined in certain definite and constant relations." [B. A. Botkin]

> A *region* may be defined as an area where nature acts in roughly uniform manner. [Stuart Chase]

> . . . those areas that show within their boundaries essential uniformity in dominant physical conditions and consequently in dominant life responses. [Mabel C. Stark]

> . . . a complex of land, water, air, plant, animal and man [sic] regarded in their special relationship as together constituting a definite, characteristic portion of the Earth's surface. [A. J. Herbertson]

To this rather "natured" regionalism, others grafted on an appreciation for history and culture, arguing that regions are organic units:

> My conception of a region is one in which vegetation, animal and human life have acquired a character due to a permanent association; to the fact that the struggle for existence had brought about some sort of equilibrium among the competing and co-operating organisms. [Robert E. Park, cited in ibid.]

> An organic region may thus be described as an area whose people are bound together by mutual dependencies arising from common interests. [V. B. Stanbery, cited in ibid.]

> The kernel characteristic of a region is that it is an area within which certain types of socioeconomic adjustments to the [environment] have been made by man so generally as to constitute the real "regionality" of the area, and therefore to provide the reason for separating that area from adjacent areas which are characterized by different types of adjustments to the [environment]. [Renner 1935, 37]

Organic regionalism culminated in the 1930s in the advocacy of individually tailored regional plans based on the assumed dominance of natural factors in differentiating regions, reinforced by evolved cultures. An image of people living together in harmony and autonomy supplanted the incessant regional rivalry stressed by the historians. This approach was politicized by Howard Odum, the southern regionalist, who argued that the South was a unique, organic region whose cultural singularity must be nurtured by policies responsive to the region's history and environment (Odum 1935; Odum and Moore 1938).[7] The southern regionalists' approach was taken up by the National Resources Committee in the 1930s and subsequently fashioned into plans for regional river basins which would engineer comprehensive development by building upon the particular resource base of each region. TVA was the most successful of these plans, although its goals were considerably narrowed in practice.[8]

While the topography and differential resource endowments of regions are certainly forces in shaping regional differences, organicist thinking tended to subordinate other determinants of regional distinctiveness to physical factors.[9] While separate histories mattered, and regions were celebrated for their unique institutions and ways of life, culture was seen as derived from long years of interaction with the region's natural environment. The school offered a highly Darwinian-colored view of cultural evolution and had little to say about the impact of human volition, class structure, and politics on a relatively tractable environment.

The organic school's prominence at this historical juncture had much to do with contemporary economic and political forces. For one thing, the era of inexhaustible frontiers had come to an end. The legacy of prior methods of exploitation—timber ravaging, strip and hydraulic mining, decimation of animal populations, and soil erosion—focused planning and political attention on the increasingly fragile environment.[10] At the same time, resources were still a wellspring of American economic growth, so that the development of untapped natural resources—in the form of water power, navigation, and soil conservation—could and did form a central pillar of economic policy, especially during the Great Depression. Territorial planning, clothed in organicist visions, in practice integrated regions with disparate cultures and resource bases into the larger American industrial economy, eroding cultural distinctiveness in the process.[11] Nevertheless, the organic school did lend to regional analysis an appreciation of the concrete reality and uniqueness of each region. That appreciation was submerged in the subsequent rise of regional science.

Regional Science and Planning

In what has aptly been dubbed the emergence of "Social Physics" (Friedman and Weaver 1979, 175),[12] post—World War II regional science further emptied the concept of region of its social content. Regional science increasingly substituted an abstract notion of space for that of region, devoting its energies to the abstract modelling of spatial form and the advocacy of one or more criteria as the "best" delineators of regions.

While regional science proper did not assume an organizational form until the 1950s,[13] its roots reached back into the late 1930s and early 1940s, when rural agronomists and sociologists first applied statistical techniques to mapping regions (Lively and Almack 1938; Hagood, Danilevsky, and Beum 1941; Mangus 1940). Subsequently, regional scholars from the social sciences and geography enthusiastically searched for empirical regularities, tendencies or "laws" that would remain invariant over a wide spectrum of possible observations. The design of regional definitions and empirical characterizations became an end in itself, marked by an anxiety about rigor and bias:

> It is fortunate that the regionalist has this rigorous technique (principal components analysis) at his command if for no other reason than to demonstrate that regions are not to be determined on the basis of whim and personal predilections. [Vance 1951, 132]

Thus regions became defined, in regional science, as mere spatial units with scale attributes: "spaces which are larger than any single urban area, that is, as supra urban space. At the same time, a region is contained within a nation and is thus a sub-national space" (Alden and Morgan, 1974, 2)[14]

Some regional science analysts turned toward deductive methods to generate theoretical models of regional structure. Teitz, for instance, applied set theory to regions, demonstrating how a number of different types of regions could be handled conceptually (1962).[15] Economists also made contributions to regional science, seeing in the regional realm an opportunity to apply microeconomic models to new material. But to the economists, the project of defining region lost meaning, and "regional" became a mere adjective:

> Regional economics is the study of man's economic behavior in space. [Siebert 1969, 1]

> Regional economics is the study of the neglected spatial order of the economy. It is the study of the geographic allocation of scarce resources.[16] [Nourse 1968, 1]

The regional economists replaced maps of geographic regions with graphs and diagrams in which geometric regularities filled spaces which had no boundaries except where one geometric figure intersected another.[17]

Those analysts who were more empirically minded drew up typologies of regions which, while inspired by the location models, more closely corresponded to popular regional images. Friedmann and Alonso, for instance, classified regions as metropolitan, development axes, frontiers, or depressed areas (1964, 3). Meyer, Richardson, and Boudeville each espoused some variant of three basic regional forms: homogeneous, nodal (or polarized), and programming (or administrative) regions (Meyer 1963, 22; Richardson 1973, 6–8; Boudeville 1966 and 1979, 19). Hoover collapsed the programming reigons into the other two, emphasizing behavioral criteria:

> Basic to the idea of a region is a high degree of correlation of behavior among its various parts. Since this correlation can reflect either of two quite distinct features of internal structure, we distinguish two different types of regions, the homogeneous and the nodal. [Hoover 1971, 122]

The ascendancy of the behavioral approach initiated a relentless search for *the* dominant criterion which could demarcate regions.[18] Examples ranged from indicators such as population density, to economic variables (income) and social characteristics (percent nonwhite). At times this quest amounted to crude empiricist plumbing of the data. The method yielded an incessant shifting among contending qualities, ranking them to choose one or another as the winning contestant. When no one factor emerged, umbrella concepts like agglomeration economies were substituted for aspects of human behavior.[19] Since agglomeration was never adequately defined, regional definition became less precise. Even if boundaries cannot be exactly drawn, wrote Richardosn, they are to be found "in the no man's land at the spatial limits of the geographic spread of agglomerating forces internal to contiguous regions" (1969, 6).[20] The moving force had become macroeconomic and unspecified, while the human presence was explicitly rendered inconsequential.

Those regional scientists who became actively involved in regional planning turned toward more pragmatic definitions of regions.

> I should like to suggest that the most helpful region in many instances is what might be called the *economic development region* . . . [where] . . . the emphasis is on the development of policies, programs and actions to move the region from where it is economically toward predetermined economic objectives. [Fisher 1955, W-6]

In textbook treatments aimed at planners, scholars like Isard (1975, 1–12) and Hoover (1971, 120–26) advocate drawing regional boundaries to correspond with the nature of a problem at hand. For instance, economies in public service provision suggest one type of regional unit, such as the SMSA, while efficiency in water quality protection calls for another, the watershed. But, they continued, planners might discover that they cannot employ such procedures because data bases may be compiled on a nonmatching territorial scale, or political boundaries may traverse an economic region. In such cases, they counseled, planners would want to redesign their regional definitions to use existing information, to fashion workable policy, and to test their theories and the success of their prescriptions. This elasticity of definition, required in practice, nevertheless continued to worry regionalists like Perloff, who feared that the ambiguity of the subject matter had led to popular skepticism regarding the validity of regional planning as a field and practice (1968).[21]

Regional science carried the analysis of regions far afield from an earlier grounding in history, natural factors, and culture. Consider, for instance, Isard's invitation to the historyless region:

> For the moment, assume that the region of study for a particular problem has been prescribed for us, or can be easily determined, or suppose it is delineated because of a deadline that existed as of one minute ago, which forced us to immediately define our regions. [1975, 2]

It shies away from the concrete, embodying few insights from the institutional economists.[22] It is completely silent on the presence of conflict as a source of regional definition or meaning. But neither has it been devoid of accomplishments.

For one, its efforts at precision, while perhaps immodest, serve as a corrective to the sloppy regionalizing of many a journalist and historian. So central a question as "was the South self-sufficient prior to the Civil War?" can be answered in a contradictory manner, depending upon whether the historian includes the states of Texas, Kentucky, and Tennessee in definition of the "South" (Sexton 1975). Second, the introduction of economic models to regional analysis has strengthened the field immensely, even if we choose to stress other features of economic behavior than those settled upon by the neoclassical school.

Third, the attention to spatial structure is clearly regional science's most outstanding contribution. It has developed the insight that the proximity or remoteness of economic agents to each other (be they firms, workers, or consumers—though not, alas, governments) is a central feature of regional life. While we may legitimately question the politics of a "science" which plays with regional structure as if its elements[23] were so many tinker toys (in practice as well as in theory) we must also recognize it as the innovator of the spatial dimension, as a *theoretical* pioneer in regional analysis.

Marxists on Regions

Since this book incorporates a great deal of Marxist analysis throughout, I briefly summarize here the contemporary contributions of Marxists to regional studies. The revival of Marxism in the 1970s, especially among younger scholars who brought to it the experience of the New Left, has produced a serious critique of the reification of both cities and regions under prevailing social science approaches. As a group, the Marxists have argued that regions could not be studied in isolation from their larger national and world settings. Causal forces driving regional development are situated outside the place per se, not embodied in characteristics of regions.[24] In fact, few contemporary Marxists have been concerned with explaining the phenomenon of regions at all. Two themes have dominated the Marxist literature: deriving current regional experience from a larger capitalist dynamic and explaining persistent regional differentiation.

With respect to the first theme, considerable debate exists within Marxism. Many Marxists argue that regional change is derivative of the laws of motion of capitalist development.[25] This school sees regional underdevelopment as just one of several forms of uneven development under capitalism.[26] Its proponents argue that uneven development is a corollary, a constant companion, and even a precondition, to the somewhat undialectically named "logic of accumulation."[27]

> [regional imbalances] have a positive role to play in maintaining the class divisions and the property rights of capitalists, continued capital accumulation and the generation and expropriation of surplus value. [Clark 1980, 226]
> . . . the continued reproduction and indeed worsening of these regional problems is a necessary condition of accelerated accumulation. [Carney 1980, 44]

At the empirical level, this position remains undemonstrated. Since almost any phenomenon can be roped in under the rubric of "uneven development," almost any regional oddity can be identified as a product of the capitalist economy. And, since development is left undefined, the quality of unevenness is highly ambiguous. As a result, historical accounts of regional development often slip into descriptive adventures where capitalist logic is responsible for every turn of events.

Yet another group of Marxists have contested the "laws" approach. More empirically minded, they begin inductively with specific regions and inquire into the set of forces shaping the development of each. This group uses the same methodological categories—mode of production, class, state, and ideology—as the former group, but is more apt to rely on historical and detailed case studies. This tradition really begins with Vilar, whose monumental study of Catalonia (1977) remains the best single example of a European regional study.[28] Vilar's work stresses the necessity to examine regions in their concrete form, as complex social entities whose significance and interrelationships defy generalization. By the early 1980s, some Marxists began to argue this as well, in case studies of particular regions which offered much new analytical insight.[29] Such studies have recently proliferated and have been dubbed variously "locality studies" and "the new regional geography."

But perhaps the stronger suit of Marxism is its insights into the coexistence of regions at different stages of development. Here, Marxists have recently gone beyond the model of accumulation to seek causes of regional differentiation. Several of these forays have generated vigorous internal debates. One group argues that areas of the world with older, slower-developing modes become victims of imperialist exploitation by advanced capitalist countries. Another group stresses the persistence of prior modes of production as barriers to regional development under capitalism.[30] Yet another has focused on unequal exchange of labor power and value embodied in commodities as a barrier to capitalist development (Emmanuel 1972). These models have been designed with developing countries in mind, but some applications to regions within countries like the United States and Britain have been made.[31] Within advanced capitalist countries, Marxists have done pioneering work on industrial differentiation of regions and their divergent experiences over time, on the size of corporations, and on the division of labor within the corporation and its concomitant use of regional space.[32]

With few exceptions, however, the focus remains on what happens to regions, not on what they are. Marxists, at least in the United States, have done little work on the theoretical status of regions or on regional politics.[33] For the most part, Marxists are uneasy about regional politics. They tend to view regional movements, at least in advanced capitalist countries, as secondary to class politics at best and confounding of progressive change at worst. This tendency arises, I believe, from the traditional hierarchy of theoretical, and therefore, political, priorities in Marxism (not unlike the impulse toward monocausality discussed above), which places economism first, followed by the political and only then the cultural. Only recently, as I have recounted in chapter 3, have a significant number of Marxist scholars challenged this economism.[34]

In summarizing this relatively new and rich literature, two problems stand out. First, Marxists in different countries stress different determinants of regionalism, and express opposing views on its desirability. Second, scholars working in the Marxist tradition have come to entirely contradictory positions on as fundamental an issue as whether regions are converging in advanced capitalist countries.[35] The dilemma presented by these problems—whether or not generalizations can be made regarding regions—is reminiscent of an older Marxist debate on the concept of nation. It is worth asking what analytical light might be cast on the problems of regions by the extensive work on nationalism.

THE NATIONAL QUESTION

Unlike the bulk of regional work, the conceptual work on nations and nationalism has tended toward the normative rather than the definitive.[36] It has been preoccupied with evaluating nationalism rather than with determining what a nation is.[37] But several themes running through the Marxist literature on nations provide insights into regional questions raised above.

To begin with, the concept of nation is not a central feature of the basic Marxist model of society. Yet Marxists, being committed to political activism, have continually had to confront nationalism as a reality. As Vilar ruefully observes, despite his belief in class encounters as the most progressive form of struggle, all major conflicts in his lifetime have been among nations rather than antagonistic classes. The same has been true in the main since Marx's time, even though Marx and almost all of his successors continually and optimistically predicted the demise of national separateness and antagonism. Citizenry in a nation-state has become the primary identifying mark of most peoples of the world. Socialists, as well as other "-ists," have had to accept and use the national settings in which they have found themselves.[38]

But Marxists are quite clear that they have not developed an adequate theory of nations or nationalism.[39] Part of the problem lies in the inability to encompass culture, economy, and state in a unified notion. Although Marx himself often interchanged the words "country," "nation, people," and "society," his adherents in the Second International debated the proper definition of nation vigorously. Three quotes will illustrate:[40]

> The nation is defined as the totality of people who are united by a common fate so that they possess a common [national] character; the common fate means primarily a common history and a common national character, i.e., at least a uniformity of language; common territory is not a part of the definition. Socialism must embrace self-determination. [Otto Bauer 1907]

> Language is the primary basis for a nation, not national character. Many social organizations are communities of fate and have a common culture and character, but these will tend to disappear with the growth of nation-states and the growing importance of class struggle. Proletarian internationalism is the socialist route. [Karl Kautsky 1887–1907, 159]

> A nation is an historically evolved, stable community of language, territory, economic life, and psychological make-up manifested in a community of culture. [Joseph Stalin 1913, 163]

Note that language is cited by all three, but they do not agree on territory, on the comprehensiveness or importance of elements, nor on the correct posture of socialists toward nations. Marx, however, specifically excluded the linguistic requirement, as would most contemporary Marxists, although from Canada to India language differences underlie strong movements toward regional autonomy (Davis 1967, 150, 159, 163). If anything, definitions offered by Marxists have become vaguer with time, as in the nation as "an individual society which functions with a considerable degree of autonomy, integration and self-consciousness" (Bloom 1941, 19),[41] or as

> those persons who compose a political community or other ethnic aggregation of individuals having particular characteristics. . . . It is not only the bearer of culture, but it is a unifying influence around which men's [sic] efforts may suitably crystallize for the benefit of man's [sic] individual collective development. [ibid., 17]

Remarkably prominent in all these definitions, however, is the cultural category. In most of the literature, Marxist and non-Marxist alike, an adamant distinction is made between the *nation* and the *State* (Davis 1955, x, 15). "Nation" connotes aspects of a human community apart from the political institution of the State, even though the elements of that community remain analytically elusive. However, more recently, the cultural connotation of "nation" in the literature has dwindled in stature and the distinction between "nation" and "State" has nearly vanished. Both Nairn and Hobsbawm, in their debate, equate the nation with the nation-state, and speak of nationalism as the equivalent of self-determination and as in essence a claim to separate nation-state status.[42] Nearly absent in the definitional debate is any economic category (Nairn 1977; Hobsbawm 1977),[43] even though today we might intermingle the term "economy" with Marx's synonyms listed above.

But if Marxists have not included economic characteristics in their definition of nation, they have offered us at least two theories about the way in which economic forces have historically created (and threaten to destroy) nations. Both theories are strongly normative in nature, rather than purely descriptive. Both also demonstrate the Marxist commitment to historical vision and a dynamic comprehension of human institutions. Perhaps in this same history lies the key to the relative decline of the cultural connotation, and rise of the political, in the term "nation."

The first begins with Marx and has most recently been expanded by Hobsbawm. Marx's contribution verged on the purely normative. According to Hobsbawn, Marx evidently believed that there was some historically specific optimal size to a capitalist "economy." The right to separate statehood was possessed only by those nations of his time which were in a position to develop modern economies. The geographic limits of a nation should be drawn to meet the needs of operating an advanced economy, not by historical, traditional or legal factors, military defense requirements, fear of aggression or conquest.[44] Hobsbawm argues that the optimality impulse led to a form of bourgeois nationalism which forged *unification* in the nineteenth century (for example, of Germany and Italy). That form of nationalism, and its causes and merit, he distinguishes from contemporary nationalism, which is largely *separatist* in nature. The latter, he argues, is made possible by the disintegration of the national economy as a building block of world capitalism, creating a situation in which peoples may actually be more manipulable by multinational corporations and world powers as separate, small, sovereign, but economically dependent states (Bloom 1941, 20, 35). Note that this argument constitutes a functionalist hypothesis about the outcome of separatist movements today, but does not explain why they arise. Not surprisingly, Hobsbawm is quite negative toward contemporary nationalism and separatism.

The second economic theory, and one which Hobsbawm sharply disputes, is Nairn's similarly historical distinction between nineteenth-century nationalism and what he calls "neonationalism." Nationalism was the counterpart to an expanding capitalism, while neonationalism is a response to its extraordinarily uneven development in the current era. As peoples respond to their own particular grievances, rooted in this uneven development, they set into motion a process of sociopolitical fragmentation, which is the inevitable setting within which socialists must act. In his home country, this is leading to the break-up of Britain (via the imminent secession of Scotland and Wales), a prospect which Nairn views as positive as well as inevitable (Hobsbawm 1977, 5–6).

Yet while Marxists have pioneered economic theories of national formation, many have been insistent that there remains a profound cultural aspect to nationalism which cannot be interpreted on purely economic grounds. They argue that nationalism is not just a dependent variable, but plays a semi-autonomous role in history. Non-Marxists tend to treat nationalism as a psychological phenomenon—an emotion, an attachment, a state of mind, a cohesiveness—which can be objectively analyzed in an empiricist fashion but which must be distinguished from the institutional form which it takes (Nairn 1975a, 1975b, 1977).[45] Marxists have struggled to find some material explanation for it, with limited success. The community has always been a part of the Marxist vision; Marx's Gemeinschaft, the classless human society, originally connoted a small-scale, face-to-face association whose members knew each other personally in all respects (Potter 1968, 36, 40–41). And despite the change in human scale that capitalism has wrought, many Marxists cannot suppress the kind of language in their work that affirms the sacredness of community, the validity of a people's tradition, and the drive toward survival (Davis 1967, 203). The contemporary moral values of democracy, civil rights, anti-authoritarianism, fear of centralized power, and habitability keep cropping up in Marxist work as precepts not necessarily secondary to economic liberation. Nairn, for instance, embraces "the real values of smaller, more recognizable communities."[46]

At the same time, Marxists exhibit a number of justifiable misgivings about nationalist sentiment. For one, they tend to find it reprehensible in its competitive, smug, superior forms, where nationalism becomes an invidious comparison with other groups and can be mobilized against them. In addition, they note and fear its plasticity, which can be demonstrated in numerous historical cases. Marx himself claimed that one could easily change one's nationality and that at times there were good grounds for doing so (Nairn, 1977, 253). The content of nationalism can be changed, too, and can span disparate ends. Early twentieth-century Czech nationalism, for instance, encompassed economic protection for an emerging capitalist sector, political rights and the franchise for Slav nationalities, national education, and use of the vernacular as the official language (Bloom 1941, 22, 75). A third suspicion is that contemporary nationalist sentiment is fundamentally conservative, since it represents the resistance of older, even archaic, classes to the onward (and presumably upward) progression of human society. For these reasons, Marxists have found it generally impossible to support the unqualified right of self-determination.

But an even deeper reason, and insight, lies beneath that refusal. And that is the observation that any nationalism encompasses a group of people who are necessarily divided in other ways. The internal heterogeneity of any nation means that by definition no unity of condition or purpose binds it together. The question of who comprises the nation and who claims to speak for it is foremost in Marxist analysis. This is a far more profound principle than the assertion that economic oppression is primary. It contends that two forms of oppression may lurk under the nationalism banner: the oppression of the minority within the nation, and the oppression of one nation by another. Thus any particular incidence of nationalism must be judged by its content and its protagonists, and in the case of international confrontations, by identification of the aggressor(s). The fear of nationalism is thus rooted in this potential for nationalist collectivity to obscure and even create other forms of inhumanity.

The nationalism debate leaves us with an illustrative method for interpreting territorial movements. It has much to offer a student of regions. Its participants have insisted on historical specificity and have tried to comprehend all the complex determinants of national form and activism. They reject an economistic determinism, while showing at the same time how a theory of the economy can inform a theory of nationalism. They remain ambiguous about the degree of independence of nationalism as an historical force. But an inkling persists that there exists a realm of human practice not captured by existing economic categories, and yet concretely connected to physical place.

Can regional issues be subsumed within the same debate? I believe, despite the methodological similarities, that the answer is no. Several distinctions can be asserted at the outset. First, the wealth of the national literature compared to the paucity of the regional suggests that the regional question is simply much more modest in scale and historical import. This does not mean it is not worth studying, nor that its historical role is unchanging.

Second, the political content of regionalism is clearly different, in that it bears a quite subordinate position with respect to the nation-state. For the required analytical specificity, students of regions and regionalism must thus work with the internal apparatus of a nation-state—its federal or centralized structure, its form of representation, its political parties, and its degree of territorial policy making and practice—to a much greater extent.

Third, regions are definitely territorial, I would argue, in a way that the perceived notion of nation is not. One's nationality does not generally change if his or her location does, but the one's "regionality" is often less durable and more readily discarded. Fourth, the region can rarely be treated as "an economy," as countries increasingly cannot as well, but a region almost always comprises a distinct subset of economic activities which thus form the heart of the economic component of study.

Fifth, the environmental and cultural content of regionalism, while it may shade into or more rarely transform itself into nationalism, is apt to be different in kind from nationalism. Natural features of the landscape, for instance, are more likely to have a causal and effective role than in modern nationalism, as are traditions grown up around productive roles like agriculture, mining, or auto-making. Finally, the internal anatomy of regional politics is apt to be much more visible, and the power of patriotism much diminished, for regions. Multiple claims to regional leadership may emerge, and regionalism may thus prove even more malleable than nationalism. These are the distinctions to which the method and results of this book are addressed.

THE URBAN LITERATURE

Urban political economists, socialists, geographers, planners, and historians have greatly enriched our understanding of cities and metropolitan areas in recent years. But for a number of reasons, the intersections with the regional literature are few. While I have drawn upon work from this field in the course of the book, it is worth briefly outlining the different and complementary orientations of the two fields here. First of all, most of urban literature addresses urban structure (Davis 1967, 145). The resulting body of work is quite rigorous and rich empirically, with its own demanding debates.[47] But it also restricts itself to urban phenomena—the integration of economic activities within one labor market, the segregation of productive from reproductive space, the class differentiation of neighborhoods, and the dynamic of capital accumulation through the continual destruction and reconstruction of the built environment. Accompanying work on urban politics deals with the struggles around these structures—that is, it concerns social movements of people *in* cities, but not *about* cities.

Regional analysis must tackle quite a different animal. Regions have a very different structure than urban areas, one which centers on the nature of its unique productive apparatus much more closely. Yet regions may not possess a unified labor market. Regional struggles may occur over some of the same issues battled in cities, but their political form is generally distinct. Moreover, the phenomenon of regionalism has no counterpart in urbanism, a word which bears no connotation of a territorial group asserting some form of territorial identity and rights. Unlike cities, regions are more apt to have strong antagonisms to or at least self-conscious differences wtih other regions. Thus there is a relational realm *among* regions that must be investigated, a major object of the book.

Notes

1. While the historians and early regionalists differentiated sectionalism from regionalism, largely in normative terms, I use them synonymously in this appendix. See Odum and Moore (1938, 34–51) and Elazar (1966, 142–50) for efforts to distinguish between regionalism and sectionalism.
2. Turner's passionate academic advocacy of the frontiersman, and by association, of the western region, can be traced to his partisanship with the populist movements of his time and his membership in the progressive school of historians. His original insight can be laid to his Wisconsin background, and his consequent antipathy to the European school during his graduate studies at Harvard. See Hofstadter (1968).
3. See Elkins and McKitrick (1954) for an interesting defense of Turner's insights into the shaping of frontier democracy. While they overstate the homogeneity of frontier communities, their empirical studies of several frontier regions support the idea that rapid settlement forced broader political participation than would have occurred otherwise.
4. In later life, in times when Presidents Harding and Wilson both pronounced the end of sectionalism as a national force, Turner was still convinced that his beloved sections would prove a permanent feature of American life (Turner 1932). By this time, he had adopted a richer view of the determinants of regional formation, including both political and cultural factors, although his work was still merely suggestive.
5. Hesseltine waffles between seeing regions as divisive forces in national unity and as complementary elements composing national cohesiveness. Of course, they can be either, at different historical movements, but Hesseltine seems to have wanted badly to have it one way or the other.
6. Here the formulation suggests that some regions must be among the exploited, rather than exploiters. Yet he ignores this implication in the rest of his analysis.
7. Odum was a sociologist of southern culture and a passionate advocate of southern distinctiveness. Odum and Moore's opening chapter on the "Implications and Meanings of Regionalism" is the best overview written to date. Friedmann and Weaver (1979) offer the best secondary account of this tradition and are the modern protagonists of organicism. See also Weaver's discussion of the utopian and anarchist precursors (1984, ch. 3), and Matthews' review of the sociological contribution (1983, 38–41).
8. United States National Resources Committee (1935). The Tennessee Valley Authority was also a political payoff by Roosevelt for southern support and became, under his appointees, an out-and-out boosterist agency, focusing

on power generation, improvement of navigation, and agricultural aid for the more prosperous area farmers. See Whisnant (1979). Another classic on resource-based regional planning is Hansen and Perloff (1942); Weaver (1984, ch. 4) gives a retrospective account.

9. See the discussion in chapter 3 of Phillips' interpretation of the pre–Civil War South, where he begins "Let us start with the climate . . ." which leads to cotton and thus to slavery and thus to civil war (1936).

10. See Gore (1984, 229–32) for a critique of Friedmann and Weaver's contemporary celebration of organicism.

11. Friedmann and Weaver (1979) argue that regional planning in the 1930s took a partisan "territorial" form which strove to preserve and protect regional cultures in contrast to post–World War II functional planning, which integrated backward regions into the American mainstream at the expense of indigenous cultures. I believe that the earlier "territorial" planning efforts turned out to be profoundly integrating as well. TVA, for example, led the industrialization of its region. Friedmann and Weaver's tendency to romanticize the territorial planning era results from their concentration on the ideology of planners, rather than the political realities of the time, as their object of study.

12. See also Olson (1974) for a critique of positivism in regional science.

13. Regional Science had its roots in the 1940s, in efforts by economists to apply economics to regional problems; the Regional Science Association was formed in 1954 and subsequently became both interdisciplinary and international. See Isard (1975, 6–7, and 1980).

14. See also Richardson (1973, 6). Note that the conception here is residual—that which resides between city and nation.

15. See also Gale and Atkinson (1980) and Fischer (1980).

16. See Dubey (1964) for an elaboration of this interpretation. Isard, 1980, documents the leadership of economists in establishing regional science.

17. See, for example, Isard (1956). Friedmann and Weaver (1979, 179) argue that this innovation completely changed the visual images used by planners, who for the first time "could actually 'see' a regional landscape that had 'structure' but no boundaries." The models built upon were actually not new, but had been pioneered in the preceding century and a half by Von Thunen, Weber, and Losch.

18. Meyer (1963) extensively documents this effort.

19. Richardson (1973) is the best full-length treatment of agglomeration in space.

20. See also the work of Soja (1971) and Gale and Atkinson (1980) on "fuzzy spaces."

21. Indeed the multiplicity of offerings on the notion of region had become a standard source of apologetic introductions by regionalists:

> The problem of defining what is meant by the term "region" has absorbed a very great deal of interest and debate, particularly amongst geographers. However, not all of this energy has been fruitful and there is now a remarkable but potentially disconcerting variety of meanings associated with the term. [Alden and Morgan 1974, 2]

> Many hundreds of thousands of words have been written on this topic without coming to a fully satisfactory answer. [Richardson 1973, 6]

> A substantial, possibly redundant, literature has been devoted to this question, and the resulting definitions are legion. [Hoover 1971, 122]

22. An exception is Gale and Atkinson's (1980) attempt to introduce institutional considerations into regional science via set theory.
23. Witness the deployment of highways across the Appalachian landscape in harmony with the growth pole theory and designs of Appalachian Regional Commission planners.
24. For examples, see Massey (1978, 1979), Scott and Roweis (1977), Jones and Stillwell (1980), Gordon (1978), Molotch (1979), Edel (1981), and Castells (1977).
25. Harvey (1982), Dunford, Geddes, and Perrons (1981), Smith (1981), Taylor (1981), Walker (1978), Collective for the Special Regional Issue (1978), Kay (1975).
26. In addition, there has been a long overdue revival of political geography in the 1980s, much of it benefitting from Marxist insights. See in particular, Agnew (1981), Taylor (1982), Taylor and House (1984), and Knight (1982b). Claval (1984) offers an interpretation of the rise and fall of, or "cycles of interest" in political geography.
27. See for example, Walker (1978), Soja (1980), Clark (1980), and Carney (1980). For a more recent debate on this position, see Browett (1984) and Smith (1986). Other Marxist critics of the view that space is a wholly subordinate category include Urry (1981) and Cooke (1983, 161–63).
28. Cardoso and Faletto (1974) offer another example, in this case for Latin America.
29. See, for example, Bagnasco (1981), Simon (1980), Markusen (1978), and Cooke (1981), on Italy, Appalachia, the Intermountain West in the U.S., and Wales respectively, and the collection in Sawers and Tabb (1984). Harvey (1984) makes the case for an historical materialist approach to geography.
30. See for example, Brenner (1977), Wallerstein (1979), Amin (1976).
31. See, for instance Persky (1972) on the U.S. South, and Hechter (1975) on Wales; both use the notion of internal colony.
32. Massey and Meegan (1978) in England, and Bluestone and Harrison (1980) in the United States have pioneered the sectoral work; Hymer (1973) in the United States initiated work on the internal functions of corporations and their spatial needs; Holland (1976) in England introduced the notion of mesoeconomic corporate functions.
33. Two exceptions to the former are Soja (1980) and Markusen (1982), which are dealt with at greater length below. The topic of the politics of regions is taken up in the final section of this chapter.
34. Sociologists have led the counterattack against this version of Marxism. See the dialogue in Gregory and Urry (1985) between sociologists and geographers on the relationship of space to society. Equally challenging are the strength of "noneconomic" yet progressive groups on the political side of the equation.
35. For example, much more than any other group, scholars in the French regionalist tradition emphasize the state, particularly its national form (Lebas 1977; Dulong 1978).
36. Dulong (1978) analyzing France, Chorney (1977) on Canada, and Markusen (1979b) on the United States all argue that regions seem to be converging, at least in terms of the penetration of capitalist relationships and the resulting homogenization of society, while others, Holland (1976) for instance, anticipate the opposite.
37. Most, though not all, of what follows draws on the seminal Marxist works in

this field. While Marxist work, such as Nairn, reviews and draws upon the non-Marxist work, the reverse is not generally true. I include Potter's essay both because it builds on non-Marxist interpretations and also because I find its ability to deal with both normative and substantive issues remarkable and clear, which cannot be said of most of the nationalism literature.

38. This tendency can be traced back to Marx. See Bloom (1941, 11), and Davis (1967, 76).
39. Vilar (1979), Potter (1968, 35), Davis (13–15, 20), Bloom (1941, 27).
40. See, for instance, Hobsbawm (1977, 21) and the editorial introduction to his article in the same *New Left Review*.
41. I am indebted to John Friedmann for the latter insight.
42. See especially Vilar (1979) on this point.
43. Some still hold the former notion; Catalonians consider themselves a nation but one fighting for devolution not secession.
44. Except, of course, the ruling class, which Marx frequently equated polemically with the nation from the first (Bloom 1941, 65). Such political dismissal of the nation assumes its identity with the State, and stands in stark contrast to the definitions just reviewed.
45. Nairn (1975a, 1975b, 1977). I have not room here to probe this fascinating clash, which is embedded in the protagonists' respective positions in the Old and New Left. At the root of the difference is the latter's profound pessimism about the progressiveness of capitalist evolution compared to the optimism of the former, and the latter's recognition of forms of oppression such as sexism, racism, environmental degradation, and so on as generators of progressive struggles on their own, even preoccupying, grounds. See Anderson (1976) for a compelling description of this split. In the case at hand, Hobsbawm is issuing warnings that undoubtedly arise from the experience of seeing European socialist and communist movements quashed twice during and after nationalist world wars.
46. See in particular Debray's (1977) impassioned plea.
47. Brownell and Goldfield (1977, 19) for example, conclude that "the extent and type of communications, the degree of functional segregation, the presence of an organized commercial-civil elite, the existence of an urban consciousness, and the extent of urbanity (that is, service and marketing establishments) have signified "city" to various writers.
48. See in particular the essays and studies in Clavel, Goldsmith, and Forester (1980), Cox (1978), Dear and Scott (1981), Harvey (1975, 1973), Harloe (1977), Pickvance (1976), Tabb and Sawyers (1978).

Bibliography

Abbott, Newton Carl. 1940. "Montana: Political Enigma of the Northern Rockies." In *Rocky Mountain Politics,* edited by Thomas Donnelly, 189–217. Albuquerque: University of New Mexico Press.

Abernathy, William J. 1978. *The Productivity Dilemma: Roadblock to Innovation in the Automobile Industry.* Baltimore: Johns Hopkins University Press.

Adams, Gordon. 1981. *The Iron Triangle: The Politics of Defense Contracting.* New York: Council on Economic Priorities.

Advisory Commission on Intergovernmental Relations. 1980. *Regional Growth: Historic Perspective.* Washington, D.C.: ACIR.

Agnew, J. A. 1981. "Structural and Dialectical Theories of Political Regionalism." In *Political Studies from Spatial Perspectives,* edited by Alan D. Burnett and Peter J. Taylor, 201–36. New York and Chichester, U.K.: Wiley.

Agria, Susan R. 1969. "Special Tax Treatment of Mineral Industries." In *The Taxation of Income from Capital,* edited by Arnold Harberger and Martin Bailey, 77–122. Washington, D.C.: Brookings Institution.

Alavi, Hamza. 1975. "India and the Colonial Mode of Production." In *Socialist Register,* edited by Ralph Miliband and John Savelle, 160–197. London: Merlin Press.

Alcaly, Roger, and David Mermelstein. 1977. *The Fiscal Crisis of American Cities: Essays on the Political Economy of Urban America with Special Reference to New York.* New York: Random House.

Alden, Jeremy, and Robert Morgan. 1974. *Regional Planning: A Comprehensive View.* New York: John Wiley.

Allaman, P. M., and David Birch. 1975. *Components of Employment Change for States by Industry Group, 1970–72.* MIT and Harvard University Joint Center for Urban Studies, Working Paper no. 5. Cambridge.

Allswang, John. 1978. *The New Deal and American Politics.* New York: John Wiley.

Alperovitz, Gar, and Jeff Faux. 1984. *Rebuilding America: A Blueprint for the Future.* New York: Pantheon Books.

Amin, Samir. 1976. *Unequal Development: An Essay on the Social Formations of Peripheral Capitalism.* New York: Monthly Review Press.

Anderson, James. 1983. *Bankrupting American Cities: The Tax Burden and Expenditures of the Pentagon by Metropolitan Area.* Lansing, Mich.: Employment Research Associates.

Anderson, Perry. 1976. *Considerations on Western Marxism.* London: New Left Books.

Anderson, Totten J. 1961. "The Political West in 1960." *Western Political Quarterly* 14, no. 1: 287–99.

Applegate, Rick. 1977. *Information Alert X: The Montana International Trade Commission.* Bozeman, Mont.: Center for Public Interest.

Arnold, Vic, ed. 1980. *Alternatives to Confrontation: A National Policy Toward Regional Planning.* Lexington, Mass.: Lexington Books.

Arsen, David. 1981. *Public Choice and Business: The Impact of Firms on Municipal Budgets.* Ph.D. diss., University of California, Berkeley.

Associated Press. 1977. "Mine Closing Hits Town Hard at Christmastime." *Denver Post,* December 27.

Bagnasco, A. 1981. "Labour Market, Class Structure and Regional Formation in Italy." *International Journal of Urban and Regional Research* 5, no. 1: 40–44.

Baldwin, Malcolm. 1973. *The Southwest Energy Complex: A Policy Evaluation.* Washington, D.C.: Conservation Foundation.

Balibar, Etienne. 1971. "From Periodization to Modes of Production." In *Reading Capital,* edited by Louis Althusser and Etienne Balibar, 209–24. New York: Pantheon Books.

Banaji, Jairus. 1972. "For a Theory of Colonial Modes of Production." *Economic and Political Weekly* (Bombay) no. 52: 2498–502.

Barney, William. 1972. *The Road to Secession: A New Perspective on the Old South.* New York: Praeger.

Bateman, Fred; James Foust, and Thomas Weiss. 1974. "The Participation of Planters in Manufacturing in the Antebellum South." *Agricultural History* 48, no. 2: 277–97.

Beale, Calvin. 1975. *The Revival of Population Growth in Nonmetropolitan America.* Economic Research Service, U.S. Department of Agriculture, ERS-605, Washington, D.C.

Bean, Walton. 1973. *California: An Interpretative History,* 2d ed. New York: McGraw-Hill.

Beard, Charles. 1913. *An Economic Interpretation of the Constitution of the United States.* New York: Macmillan.

Beard, Charles, and Mary Beard. 1927. *The Rise of American Civilization,* vol. 1. New York: Macmillan.

Beer, Samuel. 1973. "The Modernization of American Federalism." *Publius* 3, no. 2: 49–95.

Bell, Charles. 1975. "Politics in the West." *Western Political Quarterly* 28, no. 2: 237–39.

Bellmon, Henry. 1978. *Patterns of Regional Change: Interpretations and Highlights.* Report prepared by the Library of Congress for the Senate Committee on Appropriations, Ninety-fifth Congress, September. Washington: Government Printing Office.

Benson, Lee. 1972. "Explanations of American Civil War Causation: A Critical Assessment and a Modest Proposal to Reorient and Reorganize the Social Sciences." In *Toward the Scientific Study of History: Selected Essays of Lee Benson,* 225–333. Philadelphia: Lippincott.

Bergman, Edward, and Harvey Goldstein. 1983. "Dynamics and Structural Change in Metropolitan Economies." *American Planning Association Journal* (Summer) 263–79.

Bernstein, Barton J. 1966. "Southern Politics and Attempts to Reopen the African Slave Trade." *Journal of Negro History* 51 (January): 16–35.

Berwanger, Leon. 1967. *The Frontier Against Slavery.* Urbana, Ill.: University of Illinois Press.

Bezdek, Roger. 1975. "The 1980 Impact—Regional and Occupational—of Compensated Shifts in Defense Spending." *Journal of Regional Science* 15, no. 2: 183–198.

Billings, Dwight, and Kathleen Blee. 1986. "Bringing History Back In: The Historicity of Social Relations." *Current Perspectives in Social Theory* 7: 51–68.

Birch, David. 1980. "Regional Differences in Factor Costs: Labor Land, Capital and Transportation." In *Alternatives to Confrontation: A National Policy Toward Regional Change.* edited by Victor Arnold. Lexington, Mass.: Lexington Books.

Blakemore, Richard, and Robert Erickson. 1981. "The Sagebrush Rebellion: A Response to Federal Land Policy in the West." *Journal of Soil and Water Conservation* (May-June): 146–48.

Block, Fred. 1984. "The Myth of Reindustrialization." *Socialist Review* 14, no. 1: 59–76.

Bloom, Solomon F. 1941. *The World of Nations: A Study of the National Implications in the World of Karl Marx.* New York: Columbia University Press.

Bluestone, Barry, and Bennett Harrison. 1980. *Capital and Communities: The Causes and Consequences of Private Disinvestment.* Washington, D.C.: Progressive Alliance.

———. 1982. *The Deindustrialization of America.* New York: Basic Books.

Bokemann, D. 1974. "A Framework for the Technological Theory of Regional Development." *Papers, Regional Science Association* 33: 33–58.

Boudeville, J. R. 1966. *Problems of Regional Economic Planning.* Edinburgh: Edinburgh University Press.

Bowles, Samuel, David Gordon, and Thomas Weisskopf. 1984. *Beyond the Waste Land.* Garden City, N.Y.: Anchor Press.

Bradby, Barbara. 1975. "The Destruction of Natural Economy." *Economy and Society* 4, no. 2: 127–61.

Brenner, Robert. 1977. "The Origin of Capitalist Development: A Critique of Neo-Smithian Marxism." *New Left Review* 104 (July-August): 25–92.

Brock, William R. 1975. "Reconstruction and the American Party System." In *A Nation Divided: Problems and Issues of the Civil War and Reconstruction,* edited by George M. Frederickson. 81–112. Minneapolis: Burgess Publishing.

Browett, John. 1984. "On the Necessity and Inevitability of Uneven Spatial Development Under Capitalism." *International Journal of Urban and Regional Research.* 8, no. 2: 155–76.

Brown, Dee. 1971. *Bury My Heart at Wounded Knee: An Indian History of the American West.* New York: Holt, Rinehart & Winston.
Brown, Richard. 1966. "The Missouri Crisis, Slavery and the Politics of Jacksonianism." *South Atlantic Quarterly* 65 (Winter): 55–72.
Brown, Roy. 1940. "Colorful Colorado: State of Varied Industries." In *Rocky Mountain Politics*, edited by Thomas Donnelly, 51–87. Albuquerque, N.M.: University of New Mexico Press.
Browne, Lynn. 1980. "Regional Investment Patterns." *New England Economic Review*, July/August: 5–23.
Browning, Clyde, and Wil Gesler. 1979. "The Sun Belt-Snow Belt: A Case of Sloppy Regionalizing." *Professional Geographer* 31, no. 1: 66–74.
Bruchey, Stuart. 1965. *The Roots of American Economic Growth, 1607–1861: An Essay in Social Causation.* London: Hutchinson University Library.
Buck, Trevor W. 1979. "Regional Class Differences: An International Study of Capitalism." *International Journal of Urban and Regional Research* 3, no. 4: 516–26.
Buell, Barbara. 1980. "Sunnyvale Rebuffs Industry." *Peninsula Times Tribune*, January 9.
Burchell, Robert, and David Listokin. 1981. *Cities Under Stress: The Fiscal Crises of Urban America.* Rutgers, N.J.: The Center for Urban Policy Research.
Burns, Arthur F. 1934. *Production Trends in the United States.* New York: Bureau of Economic Research.
Caldwell, Lynton. 1977. "Freedom, Justice and Self-Determination: Reflections on Domestic 'Colonialism.' " *Western Wildlands* 3, no. 3: 30–36.
Cannon, Lou, and Joel Kotkin. 1979a. "Old Frontier Sees Bright New Future." *Washington Post*, June 17.
———. 1979b. "Why Power is Flowing to the West." *San Francisco Chronicle*, July 4, F1.
Cardoso, Fernando, and Enzo Faletto. 1979. *Dependency and Development in Latin America.* Translated by Marjory Mattingly Urquidi. Berkeley: University of California Press.
Carney, John. 1980. "Regions in Crisis: Accumulation, Regional Problems and Crisis Formation." In *Regions in Crisis: New Perspectives in European Regional Theory*, edited by Carney, Ray Hudson and Jim Lewis, 28–59. London: Croom Helm.
Carnoy, Martin, and Derek Shearer. 1980. *Economic Democracy: The Challenge for the 1980s.* White Plains, N.Y.: M. E. Sharpe.
Cash, J. 1941. *The Mind of the South.* New York: Alfred A. Knopf.
Casper, Barry, and Paul David Wellstone. 1981. *Powerline: The First Battle of America's Energy War.* Amherst: University of Massachusetts Press.
Castells, Manuel. 1977. *The Urban Question: A Marxist Approach*, translated by Alan Sheridan. Cambridge, Mass.: M.I.T. Press.
———. 1980. *Multinational Capital, National States, and Local Communities.* University of California, Institute of Urban and Regional Development, Working Paper no. 334. Berkeley.
Caughey, John Walton. 1969. *The American West: Frontier and Region.* Los Angeles: Ward Ritchie Press.
Chinitz, Benjamin. 1960. "Contrasts in Agglomeration: New York and Pittsburgh." *American Economic Association, Papers and Proceedings*, 50: 279–89.
———. ed. 1978. *The Declining Northeast: Demographic and Economic Analyses.* New York: Praeger Publishers.
Chorney, Harold. 1977. "Regional Underdevelopment and Cultural Decay." In *Imperialism, Nationalism, and Canada*, edited by C. Heron, 108–141. Kitchener, Toronto: New Hogstown Press/Between the Lines.
Christiansen, Bill, and Theodore Clack, Jr. 1976. "A Western Perspective on Energy: A Plea for Rational Energy Planning." *Science* 194 (November 5): 578–84.
Ciechocinska, Maria. 1983. "The Living Conditions Approach to Regional Sociology." In *Dilemmas in Regional Policy*, edited by A. Kuklinski and Y. G. Lambody, 115–39. Berlin, New York, Amsterdam: Moudan.
Clammer, John, ed. 1978. *The New Economic Anthropology.* London: Macmillan.
Clark, Gordon. 1980a. "Capitalism and Regional Disparities." *Annals of the American Association of Geographers* 70, no. 2: 521–32.
———. 1980b. "Capitalism and Regional Inequality." *Annals of the Association of American Geographers* 70, no. 2: 226–37.
———. 1984. "The Changing Composition of Regional Employment." *Economic Geography* 60, no. 2: 175–93.

Clark, Terry. 1974. "Can You Cut a Budget Pie?" *Policy and Politics* 3, no. 2: 3–32.

Clark, Thomas. 1978. "Regional Development: Strategy from Theory." In *Revitalizing the Northeast,* edited by George Sternlieb and James Hughes, 405–43. New Brunswick, N.J.: Center for Urban Policy Research, Rutgers University.

———. 1981. "Regional and Structural Shifts in The American Economy Since 1960." In *The American Metropolitan System,* edited by Stanley O. Brunn and James O. Wheeler, 111–26. New York: John Wiley.

Claval, Paul. 1984. "The Coherence of Political Geography: Perspectives on its Past Evolution and its Future Relevance." In *Political Geography: Recent Advances and Future Directions,* edited by Peter Taylor and John House, 8–24. London: Croom Helm.

Clavel, Pierre. 1980. "Opposition Planning." In *Urban and Regional Planning in an Age of Austerity,* edited by Pierre Clavel, John Forester and William Goldsmith, 206–18. New York: Pergamon Press.

———. 1982. *Opposition Planning in Appalachia and Wales.* Philadelphia: Temple University Press.

Clavel, Pierre, William Goldsmith, and John Forester, eds. 1980. *Urban and Regional Planning in an Age of Austerity.* New York: Pergamon Press.

Clelland, Donald, and William Farm. 1964. "Economic Determinants and Community Power: A Comparative Analysis." *American Journal of Sociology* 69, no. 5: 511–21.

Coalition of Northeastern Governors Policy Research Center and the Northeast-Midwest Research Institute. 1977. *A Case of Inequality: Regional Patterns in Defense Expenditures, 1950–1977.* Washington, D.C.: Mimeo, House Annex.

Coates, James. 1981. "A New Civil War Looms Over State Taxes on Natural Resources." *Washington Post,* August 19, A7.

Coben, Stanley. 1959. "Northeastern Businessmen and Radical Reconstruction." *Mississippi Valley Historical Review.* Reprinted in *The Economic Impact of the Civil War,* edited by Ralph Andreano, 125–33. Cambridge, Mass.: Schenkman Publishing.

Cochran, Thomas. 1962. "Did the Civil War Retard Industrialism?" In *The Economic Impact of the American Civil War,* edited by Ralph Andreano, 148–60. Cambridge, Mass.: Schenkman Publishing.

Cohen, Robert. 1977. "Multinational Corporations, International Finance, and the Sunbelt." In *The Rise of the Sunbelt Cities,* edited by David Perry and Alfred Watkins, 211–26. Beverly Hills: Sage Publications.

Cohen, Stephen. 1970. "From Causation to Decision: Planning as Politics." *American Economic Review* 60, no. 2: 180–94.

Cole, Arthur Charles. 1934. *The Irrepressible Conflict: 1850–65.* New York: Macmillan.

Collective for the Special Regional Issue. 1978. "Uneven Regional Development—An Introduction." *Review of Radical Political Economics* 10, no. 3: 1–12.

Collins, Linda. 1978. *Okies in Socio-Historical Perspective.* University of California, Department of Sociology Working Paper. Berkeley.

Commission on the Future of the South. 1974. *The Future of the South.* Chapel Hill, N.C.: Southern Growth Policies Board.

Conference on Alternative State and Local Public Policies. 1976. *Northeast Cities Conference: A Reader.* Washington, D.C.: CASLPP.

Congressional Budget Office. 1980. *Energy Development, Local Growth and the Federal Role.* Staff Working Paper. Washington, D.C.: Congressional Budget Office, June.

Congressional Sunbelt Council. 1981. *History, Goals and Membership.* Mimeo. U.S. House of Representatives, House Annex, Washington, D.C.

Conkin, Paul. 1959. *Tomorrow a New World: The New Deal Community Program.* Ithaca, N.Y.: Cornell University Press.

Conrad, Alfred H., and John R. Meyer. 1958. "The Economics of Slavery in the Antebellum South." *Journal of Political Economy* 66, no. 2 (April): 95–130.

Converse, Philip E. 1963. "A Major Political Realignment in the South?" In *Change in the Contemporary South,* edited by Allan P. Sindler, 195–222. Durham, N.C.: Duke University Press.

Cook, S. F. 1971. "Conflict Between the California Indian and White Civilization." In *The California Indians,* edited by R. F. Heizer and M. A. Whipple. Berkeley: University of California Press.

Cooke, Philip. 1981. *Class Relations and Uneven Development in Wales.* University of Wales Institute of Science and Technology, Department of Town Planning, Working Paper. Cardiff, UK.

———. 1983. *Theories of Planning and Spatial Development.* London: Hutchinson.

———. 1985. "Class Practices as Regional Markers: A Contribution to Labour Geography." In *Social Relations and Spatial Structures,* edited by Derek Gregory and John Urry, 213–341. New York: St. Martin's Press.

Corrigan, R. 1976. "Western Boom Towns—'Going Crazy, Going It Alone.' " *National Journal* October, 1150–52.

Coulter, E. Merton. 1947. *The South During Reconstruction.* New Orleans: Louisiana State University Press.

Council of Economic Advisors. 1951. *The New England Economy: A Report to the President.* July. Washington, D.C.: Government Printing Office.

The Council for Northeast Economic Action and the Northeast-Midwest Institute. 1981. *A Northeast Business Agenda for the 1980's.* Washington, D.C.: NEMWI.

Cox, Kevin. 1977. "Location and State in Market Societies." Ohio State University, Department of Geography Discussion Paper no. 61.

———. ed. 1978. *Urbanization and Conflict in Market Societies.* Chicago: Maaroufa Press.

Cuneo, C. J. 1978. "A Class Perspective on Regionalism." In *Modernization and the Canadian State,* edited by Glenday, H. Guindon, and A. Turoweitz, 132–56. Toronto: Macmillian.

Curry, Bill. 1982. " 'Voting With Their Feet' Leaves Migrants Unshod." *Los Angeles Times,* January 16, 1–8.

Czamanski, Daniel Z., and Stan Czamanski, 1977. "Industrial Complexes: Their Typology, Structure and Relation to Economic Development." *Papers of the Regional Science Association* 38: 93–111.

Danhof, Clarence. 1964. "Four Decades of Thought on the South's Economic Problems." In *Essays in Southern Economic Development,* edited by Melvin Greenhut and W. Tate Whitman, 7–68. Chapel Hill, N.C.: University of North Carolina Press.

Danhof, Clarence. 1969. *Change in Agriculture: The Northern United States 1820–1870.* Cambridge: Harvard University Press.

The Data Center. 1981. *Understanding and Combating Plant Closures.* Oakland, Cal.: Investigative Resource Center.

Davey, Brian. 1975. "Modes of Production and Socio-Economic Formations." *South Asia Marxist Review* 1, no. 2: 23–39.

David, Paul, Herbert Gutman, Richard Sutch, Peter Temin, and Gavin Wright. 1976. *Reckoning with Slavery: A Critical Study in the Quantitative History of American Negro Slavery.* New York and London: Oxford University Press.

Davis, David Brian. 1969. "The Comparative Approach to American History: Slavery." In *Slavery in the New World,* edited by Laura Foner and Eugene Genovese, 61–68. Englewood Cliffs, N.J.: Prentice-Hall.

———. 1975. *The Problem of Slavery in the Age of Revolution, 1770–1823.* Ithaca, N.Y.: Cornell University Press.

Davis, Horace. 1967. *Nationalism and Socialism.* New York: Monthly Review Press.

Dawson, John. 1981. *Shift-Share Analysis: A Bibliographic Review of the Technique and Applications.* Monticello, Ill.: Vance Bibliographies. April.

Debo, Angie. 1970. *A History of the Indians of the United States.* Norman: University of Oklahoma Press.

Dear, Michael, and Gordon Clark, 1980. *Dimensions of Local State Autonomy.* John F. Kennedy School of Government, Working Paper. Cambridge, Mass.

Dear, Michael, and Allan Scott, eds. 1981. *Urbanization and Urban Planning in Capitalist Society.* Chicago: Maaroufa Press.

Debray, Regis. 1977. "Marxism and the National Question." *New Left Review* no. 105 (September-October): 25–41.

Decker, Leslie. 1969. "The Great Speculation: An Interpretation of Mid-Continent Pioneering." In *The Frontier in American Development,* edited by David Ellis, 357–80. Ithaca, N.Y.: Cornell University Press.

Degler, Carl. 1974. *The Other South: Southern Dissenters in the Nineteenth Century.* New York: Harper & Row.

DeVoto, Bernard. 1948. "Sacred Cows and Public Lands." *Harper's Magazine,* July, 44–55.

Dilger, Robert. 1982. *The Sunbelt/Snowbelt Controversy: The War Over Federal Funds.* New York: New York University Press.

Dillon, Merton, 1969. "The Abolitionists: A Decade of Historiography, 1959–69." *Journal of Southern History* 35 (November): 500–22.

Donnelly, Thomas, ed. 1940. *Rocky Mountain Politics.* Albuquerque, N.M.: University of New Mexico Press.

Dorgan, Byron. 1977. *A Program for a 33 1/2% Coal Severance Tax in North Dakota: Planning for North Dakota's Future*. Bismarck, N.D.: State Tax Commission.

Dorsett, Lyle. 1977. *Franklin D. Roosevelt and the City Bosses*. Port Washington, N.Y.: Kennikat Press.

Dowd, Douglas. 1974. *The Twisted Dream: Capitalist Development in the United States since 1776*. Cambridge: Winthrop.

Driver, Harold E. 1969. *Indians of North America*. 2d ed., rev. Chicago: University of Chicago Press.

DuBois, W. E. B. 1935. *Black Reconstruction in America*. New York: Russell and Russell.

———. 1970. *The Suppression of the African Slave-Trade to the United States of America, 1638–1870*. (Originally published 1896.) New York: Dover.

Duberman, Martin, ed. 1965. *The Anti Slavery Vanguard*. Princeton: Princeton University Press.

Dubey, Vinod. 1964. "The Definition of Regional Economics." *Journal of Regional Science* 5, no. 2: 25–30.

Duchacek, Ivo D. 1970. *Comparative Federalism: The Territorial Dimension of Politics*. New York: Holt, Rinehart & Winston.

Dulong, R. 1978. *Les Régions, l'état et la société locale*. Paris: Presses Universitaires de France.

Dunford, Michael, Mike Geddes, and Diane Perrons. 1981. "Regional Policy and the Crisis in the UK: A Long-Run Perspective." *International Journal of Urban and Regional Research* 5, no. 3: 377–410.

Earle, Carville, and Ronald Hoffman. 1977. "The Urban South: The First Two Centuries." In *The City in Southern History*, edited by Blaine Brownell and David Goldfield, 23–51. Port Washington, N.Y.: Kennikat Press.

Easterlin, Richard. 1960. *Trends in the American Economy in the Nineteenth Century*. Princeton, N.J.: National Bureau of Economic Research.

———. 1961. "Regional Income Trends, 1840–1950." In *American Economic History*, edited by Seymour Harris. New York: McGraw-Hill.

Edel, Matthew. 1981. "Accumulation and the Explanation of Urban Phenomena." In *Urbanization and Urban Planning in Capitalist Societies*, edited by Michael Dear and Allan Scott, 19–44. Chicago: Maaroufa.

Ehrenhalt, Alan. 1977. "Regionalism in Congress: Formulas Debated." *Congressional Quarterly*, August 20.

Eisenmengar, Robert. 1967. *The Dynamics of Growth in New England's Economy: 1870–1964*. Middletown, Conn.: Wesleyan University Press.

Elazar, Daniel. 1966. *American Federalism: A View from the States*. New York: Thomas Crowell.

Elkins, Stanley, and Eric McKitrick. 1954. "A Meaning for Turner's Frontier." *Political Science Quarterly* no. 69 (September-December): 321–53.

Eller, Ronald D. 1986. "The Search for Community in Appalachia." Chairman's Keynote Address, Ninth Annual Appalachian Studies Conference, Appalachian State University, Boone, North Carolina, March 21. Mimeo.

Emmanuel, Arghiri. 1972. *Unequal Exchange*. London: New Left Books.

Engerman, Stanley. 1967. "Effects of Slavery Upon the Southern Economy: A Review of the Recent Debate." *Explorations in Entrepreneurial History* 4, no. 2 (Winter): 71–97.

———. 1971. "The Economic Impact of the Civil War." In *The Reinterpretation of American Economic History*, edited by Robert W. Fogel and Stanley Engerman. New York: Harper & Row.

Enmale, Richard, ed. 1961. *The Civil War in the United States by Karl Marx and Frederick Engels*. 3d ed. New York: International Publishers.

Erickson, Rodney. 1980. "Corporate Organization and Manufacturing Branch Plant Closures in Non-Metropolitan Areas." *Regional Studies* 14, no. 6: 491–501.

Erickson, Rodney, and Thomas Leinbach. 1979. "Characteristics of Branch Plants Attracted to Nonmetropolitan Areas." In *Nonmetropolitan Industrialization*, edited by Richard Lonsdale and H. L. Seyler, 57–78. New York: Halsted Press.

Estall, R. C. 1966. *New England: A Study in Industrial Adjustment*. London: G. Bell.

Ewers, H. J., and R. W. Wettmann. 1980. "Innovation-Oriented Regional Policy." *Regional Studies* 14, no. 3: 161–179.

Fainstein, Norman, and Susan Fainstein. 1983. *Restructuring the City: The Political Economy of Urban Redevelopment*. New York. Longman.

Fainstein, Norman, and Susan Fainstein. 1985. "Is State Planning Necessary for Capital? The U.S. Case." *International Journal of Urban and Regional Research*. 9, no. 4: 485–507.

Farney, Dennis. 1978. "Whether Coloradans Hate Pollution or Red Tape More Vehemently May Decide Governorship Race." *Wall Street Journal,* October 31, 40.
Federation of Rocky Mountain States, Inc. 1975a. *Energy Development in the Rocky Mountain Region: Goals and Concerns.* Denver, Col.: Federation of Rocky Mountain States.
———. 1975b. *Regionalism and the Nation: Our Rights and Responsibilities.* A Summary Report of the 11th Annual Meeting, October 15–16. Denver: Federation of Rocky Mountain States.
Feller, Irwin. 1974. "The Diffusion and Location of Technological Change in the American Cotton-Textile Industry, 1890–1970." *Technology and Culture* 15, no. 4: 569–93.
Fischer, Manfred. 1980. "Regional Taxonomy: A Comparison of Some Hierarchic and Non-Hierarchic Strategies." *Regional Science and Urban Economics* 10: 503–37.
Fisher, Joseph. 1955. "Concepts in Regional Economic Development Programs." *Papers and Proceedings of the Regional Science Association* 1: W1–W20.
Fishlow, Albert. 1965. *American Railroads and the Transformation of the Ante-bellum Economy.* Cambridge: Harvard University Press.
Fogel, Robert W. 1964. *Railroads and American Economic Growth: Essays in Econometric History.* Baltimore, Md.: Johns Hopkins University Press.
Fogel, Robert W. and Stanley Engerman. 1971. "The Relative Efficiency of Slavery: A Comparison of Northern and Southern Agriculture in 1860." *Explorations in Economic History* 8: 353–67.
———. 1974. *Time on the Cross.* 2 vol. Boston: Little-Brown.
Foner, Eric. 1970a. *Free Soil, Free Labor, Free Men.* London: Oxford University Press.
———. 1970b. "The Causes of the Civil War: Recent Interpretations and New Directions." *Civil War History* 20 (September): 197–215.
Forbes, Jack D. 1970. *Native Americans of California and Nevada.* Healdsburg, Cal.: Naturegraph Publishers.
Foster-Carter, Aidan. 1978. "The Modes of Production Controversy." *New Left Review* 107 (January–February): 47–77.
Franklin, John Hope. 1967. *From Slavery to Freedom.* 3d ed. New York: Alfred A. Knopf.
Frederickson, George. 1975. "Blue Over Gray: Sources of Success and Failure in the Civil War." In *A Nation Divided: Problems and Issues of the Civil War and Reconstruction,* edited by George Frederickson, 57–80. Minneapolis: Burgess Publishing.
Freehling, William W. 1972. "The Founding Fathers and Slavery." *American Historical Review* 77 (February): 81–93.
Freeman, Christopher, John Clark, and Luc Soete. 1982. *Unemployment and Technical Innovation.* London: Frances Pinter.
Freidel, Frank. 1965. *F.D.R. and the South.* Baton Rouge: Louisiana University Press.
Friedmann, John. 1973. *Urbanization, Planning and National Development.* Beverly Hills: Sage.
———. 1980. *Urban Communes, Self-Management, and the Reconstruciton of the Total State.* University of California, School of Architecture and Urban Planning, Working Paper. Los Angeles.
———. 1981. *Life Space and Economic Space: Contradictions in Regional Development.* University of California, School of Architecture and Urban Planning, Working Paper. Los Angeles.
———. 1986. "The World City Hypothesis." *Development and Change.* 17, no. 1: 69–84.
Friedmann, John, and William Alonso. 1964. *Regional Development and Planning: A Reader.* Cambridge, Mass.: MIT Press.
Friedmann, John, and Clyde Weaver. 1979. *Territory and Function: The Evolution of Regional Planning Doctrine.* London: Edward Arnold.
Friedmann, John and Goetz Wolfe. 1982. "World City Formation: An Agenda for Research and Action." *International Journal of Urban and Regional Research.* 6, no. 3: 309–44.
Frobel, Folker, Jurgen Heinrichs, and Otto Kreye. 1979. *The New International Division of Labor.* Translated by Pete Burgess. Cambridge: Cambridge University Press.
Gaffney, Mason. 1977. "Counter-Colonial Land Policy for Montana." *Western Wildlands* 3, no. 3: 16–25.
Gale, Stephen, and Michael Atkinson. 1980. "Toward an Institutionalist Perspective on Regional Science: An Approach Via the Regionalization Question." *Papers of the Regional Science Association* 43: 59–81.
Gale, Stephen. 1976. "A Resolution of the Regionalization Problem and its Implications for Social Justice and Political Geography." *Geografiska Annaler,* Series B, 5B: 1–16.

Galvin, Donald L. 1969. "The Federation of Rocky Mountain States: A Test of Regionalism." Ph.D. diss., University of Colorado.

Garnsey, Morris. 1950. *America's New Frontier: The Mountain West.* New York: Alfred A. Knopf.

Garreau, Joel. 1981. *The Nine Nations of North America.* Boston: Houghton-Mifflin.

Gastil, Raymond. 1975. *Cultural Regions of the United States.* Seattle: University of Washington Press.

Gates, Paul Wallace. 1942. "The Role of the Land Speculation in Western Development." *The Pennsylvania Magazine of History and Biography* 66: 314–33.

———. 1965. *Agriculture and the Civil War.* New York: Alfred A. Knopf.

———. 1979. "Indian Allotments Preceding the Dawes Act." In *The Rape of Indian Lands,* edited by Paul Gates. New York: Arno Press.

Gaventa, John. 1980. *Power and Powerlessness: Quiescence and Rebellion in an Appalachian Valley.* Oxford: Clarendon Press.

General Accounting Office. 1981. *Assessing the Impact of Federal and State Taxes on the Domestic Minerals Industry.* Washington, D.C.: Office of the Comptroller General.

Genovese, Eugene D. 1967. *The Political Economy of Slavery.* New York: Random House.

———. 1968. *In Red and Black: Marxian Explorations in Southern and Afro-American History.* New York: Vintage Books.

———. 1971. *The World the Slaveholders Made.* New York: Vintage Books.

———. 1974. *Roll, Jordon, Roll: The World the Slaves Made.* New York: Pantheon Books.

Gilman, Rhoda R. 1970. "Last Days of the Upper Mississippi." *Minnesota History* 42, no. 4.

Ginsburgh, Patty. 1980. "Industry Group a Major Force in Santa Clara County Politics." *The Peninsula Times Tribune,* February 15.

Glasmeier, Amy. 1980. *A Socio-Economic Impact Study of the Proposed MX Missile Project.* University of California, Department of City and Regional Planning, Unpublished Professional Report.

Glasmeier, Amy. 1986. *The Structure, Location and Role of High Technology Industries in United States Regional Development.* Ph.D. dissertation, University of California, Berkeley.

Glasmeier, Amy, and Erica Schoenberger. 1980. "Selling the MX: The Air Force Asks Nevada to Move Over." *The Progressive* (Madison, Wisc.), April.

Glenn, N. D., and J. L. Simmons. 1967. "Are Regional Differences Diminishing?" *Public Opinion Quarterly* 31: 176–93.

Glickman, Norman. 1977. *Econometric Analysis of Regional Systems.* New York: Academic Press.

Godschalk, David, Bruce Knopf, and Seth Weissman. 1978. *Guiding Growth in the South.* Research Triangle Park, N.C.: Southern Growth Policies Board.

Gold, R. 1974. *A Comparative Study of the Impact of Coal Development on the Way of Life of People in the Coal Areas of Eastern Montana and Northeastern Wyoming.* Missoula, Mont.: Institute for Social Science Research.

Goldfield, David R. 1977. "Pursuing the American Urban Dream: Cities in the Old South." In *The City in Southern History,* edited by Blaine Brownell and David Goldfield, 52–91. Port Washington, N.Y.: Kennikat Press.

Goldin, Claudia Dale. 1975. "Urbanization and Slavery: The Issue of Compatibility." In *The New Urban History: Quantitative Exploration by American Historians,* edited by Leo Schnore, 231–46, Princeton, N.J.: Princeton University Press.

Goldin, Claudia, and F. Lewis. 1975. "The Economic Cost of the American Civil War: Estimates and Implications." *Journal of Economic History* 35 (June): 299–326.

Gomez, Rudolf. 1969. "Utah: The Different State." In *Politics in the American West,* edited by Frank Jonas, 327–79. Salt Lake City: University of Utah Press.

Goodman, Robert. 1979. *The Last Entrepreneurs: America's Regional Wars for Jobs and Dollars.* New York: Simon & Schuster.

Goodwyn, Lawrence. 1978. *The Populist Moment: A Short History of the Agrarian Revolt in America.* New York & London: Oxford University Press.

Gordon, David. 1978. "Capitalist Development and the History of American Cities." In *Marxism and the Metropolis,* edited by William K. Tabb and Larry Sawers, 25–63. New York: Oxford University Press.

Gore, Charles. 1984. *Regions in Question: Space, Development Theory and Regional Policy.* London & New York: Methuen.

Gottlieb, Robert, and Peter Wiley. 1980. "The New Power Brokers Who Are Carving Up the West." *Straight Creek Journal* 9, no. 12 (March 2): 1–3.

———. 1982. *Empires in the Sun: The Rise of the New American West.* New York: Putnam.

Gourevitch, Peter. 1977. *Politics, Economics, and the Reemergence of Peripheral Nationalisms: Some Comparative Speculations.* McGill University, Department of Political Science Working Paper, September. Mimeo, Montreal.

———. 1979. "The Re-emergence of Peripheral Nationalism: Some Comparative Speculations on the Spatial Distribution of Political Leadership and Economic Growth." *Comparative Studies in Sociology and History* 21: 303–22.

Gray, Lewis. 1933. *History of Agriculture in the Southern United States to 1860.* Vols 1 and 2. Washington, D.C.: Carnegie Institution.

Green, Fletcher. 1965. "Introduction." Thomas P. Kettell, *Southern Wealth and Northern Profits.* University, Ala.: University of Alabama Press: IX–XXV.

Green, James. 1972. "Behavioralism and Class Analysis: A Review Essay on Methodology and Ideology." *Labor History* 13 (Winter): 89–106.

Greenberg, Douglas. 1986. "Growth and Conflict at the Suburban Fringe: The Livermore-Amador Valley." Ph.D. dissertation, University of California, Berkeley.

Greene, Jack. 1973. "The Social Origins of the American Revolution: An Evaluation and an Interpretation." *Political Science Quarterly* 88 (March): 1–22.

Greene, Lorenzo. 1942. *The Negro in Colonial New England.* New York: Columbia University Press.

Greenwood, Michael, and Gary Hunt. 1984. "Migration and Interregional Employment Redistribution in the United States." *American Economic Review* 74, no. 4 (December): 957–69.

Gregory, Derek, and John Urry. 1985. *Social Relations and Spatial Structures.* New York: St. Martin's Press.

Grigsby, J. Eugene. 1982. *Planning and Managing Growth in the Sunbelt.* University of California, School of Urban Planning and Architecture, Working Paper. Los Angeles.

Gutman, Herbert G. 1975. "The World Two Cliometricians Made: A Review Essay of F + E + T/C." *Journal of Negro History* 60 (January): 53–227.

Hacker, Louis. 1935. "The First American Revolution," part 1. *Columbia University Quarterly* 27 no. 3: 259–95.

———. 1940. *The Triumph of American Capitalism.* New York: Simon & Schuster.

Hackney, Sheldon. 1969. *Populism to Progressivism in Alabama.* Princeton, N.J.: Princeton University Press.

Hagood, Margaret J., Nadia Danilevsky, and Corlin Beum. 1941. "An Examination of the Use of Factor Analysis in the Problem of Subregional Delineation." *Rural Sociology* 6 (September): 216–33.

Hall, Peter. 1982. "Innovation: Key to Regional Growth." *Transaction/Society* 19, no. 5 (July/August).

Hall, Peter, and Ann Markusen, eds. 1985. *Silicon Landscapes.* London: Allen & Unwin.

Hall, Stuart. 1981. "The Great Moving Right Show." *Socialist Review* 11, no. 1: 113–37.

Handlin, Oscar, and Mary Handlin. 1950. "Origins of the Southern Labor System." *William and Mary Quarterly* (3rd series) 7: 199–222.

Hansen, Alvin H., and Harvey Perloff. 1942. *Regional Resource Development.* Washington, D.C.: National Planning Association.

Hansen, Niles. 1973. *The Future of Non-Metropolitan America: Studies in the Reversal of Rural and Small Town Population Decline.* Lexington, Mass.: D.C. Heath.

———. 1978. "Economic Aspects of Regional Separatism." *The Regional Science Association, Papers and Proceedings* 41: 143–52.

———. 1979. "The New International Division of Labor and Manufacturing Decentralization in the United States." *Review of Regional Studies* 9, no. 1: 1–11.

———. 1980. "Dualism, Capital-Labor Ratios and the Regions of the U.S.: A Comment." *Journal of Regional Science* 20, no. 3: 401–3.

Harloe, Michael, ed. 1977. *Captive Cities: Studies in the Political Economy of Cities and Regions.* London and New York: John Wiley.

Harper, Lawrence. 1942. "Mercantilism and the American Revolution." *Canadian Historical Review* 23, no. 1: 1–15.

Harrington, Michael J. 1976. "Regional Economic Trends: A Profile of Problems." Paper presented at the Conference on Alternative State and Local Public Policies, Washington, D.C., October, 1976.

Harrington, Michael, and Frank Horton. 1977. "Rescuing the Region." *New York Times,* July 1.

Harris, Seymour. 1952. *The Economics of New England.* Cambridge, Mass.: Harvard University Press.

Harrison, Bennett. 1980. *The Changing Structure of the New England Economy Since World War II: A Review and Analysis of Some Numerical Indicators.* Cambridge, Mass.: Joint Center for Urban Studies of MIT and Harvard University Working Paper. Cambridge, Mass.
———. 1981. *Rationalization, Restructuring and Industrial Reorganization in Older Regions: The Transformation of the New England Economy Since World War II.* Cambridge, Mass.: Joint Center for Urban Studies of MIT and Harvard University.
———. 1984. "Regional Restructuring and 'Good Business Climate': The Economic Transformation of New England Since World War II." In *Sunbelt/Snowbelt: Urban Development and Regional Restructuring,* edited by Larry Sawers and William K. Tabb. New York: Oxford University Press.
Harrison, Bennett, and Barry Bluestone. 1981. *The Incidence and Regulation of Plant Shutdowns.* Joint Center for Urban Studies of MIT and Harvard University Working Paper. Cambridge, Mass.
Harrison, Bennett, and Sandra Kanter. 1976. "The Great State Robbery." *Working Papers for a New Society* 4, no. 1 (Spring).
———. 1978. "The Political Economy of States' Job-Creation Business Incentives." *Journal of the American Institute of Planners* 44, no. 4: 424–55.
Hartmann, Heidi, and Ann Markusen. 1980. "Contemporary Marxist Theory and Practice: A Feminist Critique." *Review of Radical Political Economics* 12, no. 2, (Summer): 87–94.
Hartz, Louis. 1955. *The Liberal Tradition in America.* New York: Harcourt, Brace & World.
Harvey, David. 1973. *Social Justice and the City.* Baltimore: Johns Hopkins University Press.
———. 1975. "The Geography of Accumulation." *Antipode* 7, no. 2, (September): 9–21.
———. 1982. *The Limits to Capital.* Oxford: Basil Blackwell.
———. 1984. "On the History and Present Condition of Geography: An Historical Materialist Manifesto." *The Professional Geographer* 36, no. 1: 1–11.
———. 1985. "The Geopolitics of Capitalism." In *Social Relations and Spatial Structures,* edited by D. Gregory and J. Urry, 128–63. New York: St. Martin's Press.
Havard, William C., Jr. 1972. "From Past to Future: An Overview of Southern Politics." In *The Changing Politics of The South,* edited by W. C. Havard. Baton Rouge: Louisiana State University Press.
Havemann, Joel, Rochelle Stanfield, and Neil Peirce. 1976. "Federal Spending: The North's Loss is the Sunbelt's Gain." *National Journal,* June 26, 878–91.
Hayes, Lynton. 1980. *Energy, Economic Growth and Regionalism in the West.* Albuquerque: University of New Mexico Press.
Hechter, M. 1975. *Internal Colonialism: The Celtic Fringe in British National Development, 1536–1966.* London: Routledge & Kegan Paul.
Heizer, Robert, and Alan Almquist. 1971. *The Other Californians: Prejudice and Discrimination under Spain, Mexico and the United States to 1920.* Berkeley: University of California Press.
Henry, David. 1983. "Defense Spending: A Growth Market for Industry." *U.S. Industrial Outlook 1983,* xxxix–xlvii.
Herndon, G. Melvin. 1967. "Indian Agriculture in the Southern Colonies." *North Carolina Historical Review* 44.
Hesseltine, William. 1944. "Regions, Classes and Sections in American History." *Journal of Land and Public Utility Economics* 20 (February): 35–44.
Hesseltine, William B., and David L. Smiley. 1960. *The South in American History.* 2d ed. Englewood Cliffs, N.J.: Prentice-Hall.
Hicks, John D. 1931. *The Populist Revolt: A History of the Farmer's Alliance and the People's Party.* Minneapolis: University of Minnesota Press.
Hindess, Barry, and Paul Hirst. 1975. *Pre-Capitalist Modes of Production.* Boston: Routledge & Kegan Paul.
Hirsch, Seev. 1967. *Location of Industry and International Competitiveness.* London: Oxford University Press.
Hirst, Paul. 1979. *On Law and Ideology.* Atlantic Highlands, N.J.: Humanities Press.
Hobsbawm, Eric. 1964. "Introduction." Karl Marx, *Precapitalist Economic Formations,* translated by Jack Cohen. London: Lawrence & Wishart.
———. 1972. "Some Reflections on Nationalism." In *Imagination and Precision in Social Sciences: Essays in Memory of Peter Nettles.* 385–406. London: Faber & Faber.
———. 1975. *The Age of Capital: 1848–1875.* London: Weidenfeld & Nicolson.
———. 1977. "Some Reflections on 'The Breakup of Britain.'" *New Left Review* no. 105 (September-October): 3–23.

Hoch, Irving. 1980. "Role of Energy in the Regional Distribution of Economic Activity." In *Alternatives to Confrontation: A National Policy Toward Regional Change,* edited by Victor Arnold. Lexington, Mass.: Lexington Books.

Hofstadter, Richard. 1938. "The Tariff Issue on the Eve of the Civil War." *The American Historical Review* 44: 50–55.

———. 1949. "Turner and the Frontier Myth." *The American Scholar* 18 (October): 433–43.

———. 1968. *The Progressive Historians.* New York: Alfred A. Knopf.

Holland, Stuart. 1976. *Capital Versus the Regions.* London: Macmillan.

Holt, Michael. 1973. "The Politics of Impatience: The Origins of Know-Nothingism." *Journal of American History* 40 (September): 329–31.

Hoover, Edgar. 1948. *The Location of Economic Activity.* New York: McGraw-Hill.

———. 1971. *An Introduction to Regional Economics.* New York: Alfred A. Knopf.

Horowitz, David. 1978. *The First Frontier: The Indian Wars and America's Origins: 1607–1776.* New York: Simon & Schuster.

Horsman, Reginald. 1967. *Expansion and American Indian Policy, 1783–1811.* East Lansing: Michigan State University Press.

Hotelling, Harold. 1929. "Stability in Competition." *Economic Journal* 39, no. 1: 41–57.

House, John, ed. 1983. *United States Public Policy: A Geographical View.* Oxford: Clarendon Press.

Howard, Joseph. 1943. *Montana: High, Wide and Handsome.* New Haven: Yale University Press.

Howard, Robert. 1979. "Going Bust in Youngstown." *Commonweal,* May 25, 301–5.

Howes, Candace. 1979. *Notes on Classical and Neo-Marxist Theory on Ideology and Struggle.* University of California, Department of Economics, Berkeley, Mimeo.

Hymer, Stephen H. 1973. "The Multinational Corporation and the Law of Uneven Development." In *Economic and World Order,* edited by J. W. Bhagwati, 113–40. New York: Macmillan.

Ingram, Helen, Nancy Laney, and John McCain. 1980. *A Policy Approach to Political Representation: Lessons from the Four Corners States.* Baltimore: The Johns Hopkins University Press, for Resources for the Future.

Innes, Harold. 1970. *The Fur Trade in Canada: An Introduction to Canadian Economic History.* Rev. ed. Toronto: University of Toronto Press.

Isard, Walter. 1956. *Location and Space-Economy.* New York: John Wiley and Sons.

———. 1960. *Methods of Regional Analysis.* Cambridge, Mass.: MIT Press.

———. 1975. *Introduction to Regional Science.* Englewood Cliffs, N.J.: Prentice-Hall.

———. 1980. "Notes on the Origins, Development, and Future of Regional Science." *Papers of the Regional Science Association* 43: 59–81.

Isard, Walter and Robert Kuenne. 1953. "The Impact of Steel Upon the Greater New York-Philadelphia Region: A Study in Agglomeration Projection." *Review of Economics and Statistics.* 35, no. 4: 289–301.

Jackson, Gregory, George Masnick, Roger Bolton, Susan Bartlett, and John Pitkin. 1981. *Regional Diversity: Growth in the United States, 1960–1990.* Boston, Mass.: Auburn House.

Jensen, Merrill, ed. 1951. *Regionalism in America.* Madison: University of Wisconsin Press.

Joint Economic Committee. 1982. *Location of High Technology Firms and Regional Economic Development.* Washington, D.C.: Government Printing Office.

Johnson, Michael P. 1977. *Toward a Patriarchal Republic: The Secession of Georgia.* Baton Rouge: Louisiana State University Press.

Johnson, P. S., and D. G. Cathcart. 1979. "New Manufacturing Firms and Regional Development: Some Evidence from the Northern Region." *Regional Studies* 13: 269–80.

Jonas, Frank. 1940. "Utah: Sagebrush Democracy." In *Rocky Mountain Politics,* edited by Thomas Donnelly. Albuquerque: University of New Mexico Press.

———. 1969. *Politics in the American West.* Salt Lake City: University of Utah Press.

Jones, Evan, and Frank Stillwell. 1980. *When is an Urban Problem not an Urban Problem? Some General Propositions and Australian Illustrations.* University of Sydney, Department of Economics, Working Paper. Sydney, Australia.

Jones, S. J. 1971. "Some Regional Aspects of Native California." In *The Calfornia Indians,* edited by R. F. Heizer and M. A. Whipple. Berkeley: University of California Press.

Jorgensen, Joseph. 1978. "A Century of Political Economic Effects of American Indian Society: 1880–1980." *Journal of Ethnic Studies* 6 (Fall).

Jorgenson, Joseph, Richard Clemmer, Ronald Little, Nancy Owens, and Lynn Robbins.

1978. *Native Americans and Energy Development.* Cambridge, Mass.: Anthropology Resource Center.

Jusenius, C. L., and L. C. Ledebur. 1976. *A Myth in the Making: The Southern Economic Challenge and Northern Economic Decline.* Washington, D.C.: Economic Development Administration.

Kanter, Sandra. 1978. "A History of State Business Subsidies." *National Tax Association/Tax Institute of America Papers and Proceedings.* Columbus, Ohio.

Karaska, Gerald. 1967. "The Spatial Impacts of Defense-Space Procurement: An Analysis of Subcontracting Patterns in the United States." *Peace Research Society, Papers,* 8: 108–22.

Kay, Geoffrey. 1975. *Development and Underdevelopment.* London: Macmillan.

Kelley, Edward, and Mark Shutes. 1977. "Lykes' Responsibility for Closing the Youngstown Campbell Works." Cleveland: Ohio Public Interest Campaign. November.

Kemmis, Dennis. 1983. *Democracy at the Headwaters.* Series of papers presented at Northern Lights Institute, Montana, July, August, and September. Mimeo.

Kesselman, Mark. 1981. "Regionalism and Monopoly Capitalism: A New Approach to the Study of Local Power." *International Journal of Urban and Regional Research* 5, no. 1, March: 107–16.

Kettell, Thomas. 1965. *Southern Wealth and Northern Profits.* "Southern Historical Series." Vol. 5. University, Ala.: University of Alabama Press.

Kinnard, William, Jr. 1968. *The New England Region: Problems of a Mature Economy.* Storrs: University of Connecticut Center for Real Estate and Urban Economic Studies.

Kittredge, William. 1980. "The Family Ranch and Other Serious Matters: An Editorial." *Rocky Mountain Magazine,* January–February, 66–67.

Knight, David. 1982a. "Canada in Crisis: The Power of Regionalisms." In *Tension Areas of the World,* edited by D. G. Bennett, 254–79. Champaign, Ill.: Park Press.

———. 1982b. "Identity and Territory: Geographical Perspectives on Nationalism and Regionalism." *Annals, Association of American Geographers* 72: 514–31.

Kousser, J. Morgan. 1974. *The Shaping of Southern Politics: Suffrage Restriction and the Establishment of the One-Party South, 1880–1910.* New Haven: Yale University Press.

Kraenzel, Carl F. 1955. *The Great Plains in Transition.* Norman: University of Oklahoma Press.

Kroeber, A. L. 1963. *Cultural and Natural Areas of North America.* Berkeley: University of California Press.

———. 1971. "The History of Native Culture in California." In *The California Indians,* edited by R. F. Heizer and M. A. Whipple, Berkeley: University of California Press.

Kroll, Cynthia. 1981. "The Local Distributional Effects of Energy Development: Coal Boom Towns in the Northern Great Plains." Ph.D. diss., University of California, Berkeley.

Kurth, J. 1979. "The Political Consequences of the Product Cycle." *International Organization* 33, no. 1 (Winter): 1–34.

Krutilla, John, Anthony Fisher, and Richard Rice. 1978. *Economic and Fiscal Impacts of Coal Development: Northern Great Plains.* Baltimore: Johns Hopkins Press, for Resources for the Future.

Kuznets, Simon. 1930. *Secular Movements in Production and Prices.* Boston: Houghton-Mifflin.

Laclau, Ernesto. 1979. "Democracy and Socialist Struggle in Latin America." *Latin American Research Unit Studies.* January–April.

Ladd, Everett Carl. 1981. "The Shifting Party Coalitions—from the 1930s to the 1970s." In *Party Coalitions in the 1980s,* edited by Seymour Martin Lipset, 127–49. San Francisco: Institute for Contemporary Studies.

Ladd, Everett Carl, Jr., with Charles Hadley. 1978. *Transformations of the American Party System: Political Coalitions from the New Deal to the 1970s.* 2d ed. New York: W. W. Norton.

Laird, Melvin, moderator. 1976. *Energy Policy: A New War Between the States?* Washingotn, D.C.: American Enterprise Institute.

Lamm, Richard D., and Michael McCarthy. 1982. *The Angry West: A Vulnerable Land and Its Future.* Boston: Houghton Mifflin.

Land, Aubrey. 1970. "Economic Base and Social Structure: The Northern Chesapeake in the Eighteenth Century." In *Class and Society in Early America,* edited by Gary Nash, 126–30. Englewood Cliffs, N.J.: Prentice-Hall.

Lanigan, Christine. 1976. "Connecticut's Push for New Products." *The New Englander,* February, 31–32.

Lebas, Elizabeth. 1977. "Regional Policy Research: Some Theoretical and Methodological Problems." In *Captive Cities,* edited by Michael Harloe, 79–88. New York and London: John Wiley.

Leiserson, Avery, ed. 1964. *The American South in the 1960s.* New York: Praeger Publishers.

Leontieff, Wassily, Alison Morgan, Karen Polenske, David Simpson, and Edward Tower. 1965. "The Economic Impact—Industrial and Regional—of an Arms Cut." *Review of Economics and Statistics* 47, no. 3: 217–41.

Leroy, David, and Roy Eiguren. 1980. "State Takeover of Federal Lands—The Sagebrush Rebellion." *Rangelands* 2, no. 6 (December): 229–31.

Leuchtenburg, William. 1963. *Franklin D. Roosevelt and the New Deal, 1932–1940.* New York: Harper & Row.

Lever, W. F. 1975. " 'Mobile Industry' and Levels of Integration in Subregional Economic Structures." *Regional Studies* 9: 265–78.

Lindauer, R. L. 1975. *Solutions to Economic Impacts on Boomtowns Caused by Large Energy Development.* Denver: Exxon Company, U.S.A.

Liner, E. Blaine. 1979. *Overview of Legislation to Restrict Business Mobility and Defense Issues of Concern to the South.* Research Triangle Park, N.C.: Southern Growth Policies Board. Mimeo, November.

———. 1976. *The Snowbelt and the Seven Myths.* Research Triangle, North Carolina: Southern Growth Policies Board. Mimeo.

Liner, E. Blaine, and Lawrence Lynch. 1977. *The Economics of Southern Growth.* Research Triangle Park, N.C.: Southern Growth Policies Board.

Litwack, Leon. 1961. *North of Slavery.* Chicago: University of Chicago Press.

Lively, C. E., and R. B. Almack. 1938. *A Method of Determining Rural Social Subareas with Application to Ohio.* Ohio Agricultural Extension Station. Bulletin no. 106. Columbus.

Lockridge, Kenneth. 1973. "Social Change and the Meaning of the American Revolution." *Journal of Social History* 6: 403–39.

Lopach, James. 1978. *The Coal Tax Challenge.* University of Montana, Department of Political Science, Montana Public Affairs Report, no. 24, June. Missoula.

Lovering, John. 1978. "The Theory of the 'Internal Colony' and the Political Economy of Wales." *Review of Radical Political Economics* 10, no. 3: 55–67.

Luger, Michael. 1981. *Regional Employment Effects of Federal Business Tax Incentives.* Ph.D. diss., University of California, Berkeley.

Lundstrom, Meg. 1975. "Energy and States' Rights." *The Nation,* September 11, 208–10.

Luria, Dan, and Jack Russell. 1981. *Rational Reindustrialization.* Detroit: Widgetripper Press.

Lynd, Staughton. 1967. *Class Conflict, Slavery, and the United States Constitution.*

———. 1979. "Investment for Whom? Steelworkers Fight to Save 'Our Steel Mill.' " *In These Times,* March 21–27.

———. 1982. *The Fight Against Shutdowns: Youngstown's Steel Mill Closings.* San Pedro, Cal.: Singlejack Books.

Maddox, James, E. E. Liebhafsky, Vivian Henderson, and H. M. Hamlin. 1967. *The Advancing South: Manpower Prospects and Problems.* New York: Twentieth Century Fund.

Main, Jackson Turner. 1961. *The Antifederalists: Critics of the Constitution, 1781–88.* Chapel Hill. University of North Carolina Press.

———. 1970. "The Economic Class Structure of the North." In *Class and Society in Early America,* edited by Gary Nash, 100–17. Englewood Cliffs, N.J.: Prentice-Hall.

Malecki, Edward. 1984. "Military Spending and the U.S. Defense Industry: Regional Patterns of Military Contracts and Subcontracts." *Environment and Planning C: Government and Policy,* 2: 31–44.

Malone, Michael. 1980. "Electronics Executives, Officials Clash over Jobs-Housing Issues." *San Jose Mercury,* April 23, 13D.

Mandel, Ernest. 1963. "The Dialectic of Class and Region in Belgium." *New Left Review* 20: 5–31.

———. 1975. *Late Capitalism.* (Originally published in French, 1972.) London: New Left Books.

Mandle, Jay R. 1978. *The Roots of Black Poverty: The Southern Plantation Economy After the Civil War.* Durham, N.C.: Duke University Press.

Mangus, Arthur. 1940. *Rural Regions of the United States.* Washington, D.C.: Government Printing Office.

Markusen, Ann. 1977. "Federal Budget Simplification: Preventive Programs vs. Palliatives for Local Governments with Booming, Stable and Declining Economies." *National Tax Journal* 30, no. 3 (September).

———. 1978. "Class, Rent and the State: Uneven Development in Western U.S. Boomtowns." *Review of Radical Political Economics* 10, no. 3: 117–29.

———. 1979a. "Regional Economic Contraction and Intergovernmental Finance: A Theoretical Perspective." *National Tax Association/Tax Institute of America, Papers and Proceedings,* Columbus, Ohio: 87–94.

———. 1979b. "Regionalism and the Capitalist State: The Case of the United States." *Kapitalistate* 7 (Winter): 39–62.

———. 1980. "Regionalism and the Capitalist State: The Case of the United States." In *Urban and Regional Planning in an Age of Austerity,* edited by Pierre Clavel, William Goldsmith, and John Forester. New York: Pergamon Press.

———. 1983. "Regions and Regionalism: A Marxist View." In *Regional Analysis and the New International Division of Labor,* edited by Frank Moulaert and Patricia Wilson Salinas, 33–55. eds. Boston: Kluwer-Nijhoff.

———. 1985a. "Defense Spending: A Successful Industrial Policy?" In *The Politics of Industrial Policy,* edited by Sharon Zukin. New York: Praeger Publishers.

———. 1985b. "Military Spending and Urban Development in California." *The Berkeley Planning Journal.* 3, no. 1.

———. 1985c. *Profit Cycles, Oligopoly and Regional Development.* Cambridge, Mass.: MIT Press.

———. 1985d. *Steel and Southeast Chicago: Reasons and Remedies for Industrial Renewal.* Northwestern University, Center for Urban Affairs and Policy Research. Report to the Mayor's Task Force on Steel and Southeast Chicago. Evanston, Ill.

———. 1986a. "Defense Spending and the Geography of High Tech Industries." In *Technology Regions and Policy,* edited by John Rees, 94–119. New York: Praeger Publishers.

———. 1986b. "Empirical Research in the Marxist and Schumpeterian Traditions: Reflections on Explaining Spatial Change." In *Marx, Schumpeter, Keynes: A Centennary Celebration of Dissent,* edited by Susan Helburn and David Bramhall. New York: M. E. Sharpe.

———. 1986c. "The Military Remapping of the United States." *The Built Environment.* 11, no. 3: 171–80.

———. 1986d. "Military Spending and the U.S. Economy." *World Policy Journal.* 3, no. 3: 495–516.

———. 1986e. "Neither Ore, Nor Coal, Nor Markets: A Policy-Oriented Analysis of Steel Siting in the U.S." *Regional Studies.* 20, no. 5: 449–62.

Markusen, Ann, and Jerry Fastrup. 1978. "The Regional War for Federal Aid." *The Public Interest* 53 (Fall): 87–99.

Markusen, Ann, and Amy Glasmeier. 1980. *The Case Against Boomtown Impact Aid.* University of California Institute of Urban and Regional Development, Working Paper no. 296, February. Berkeley.

Markusen, Ann, Peter Hall, and Amy Glasmeier. 1986. *High Tech America: The What, How, Where and Why of the Sunrise Industries.* London: Allen & Unwin.

Markusen, Ann, Annalee Saxenian, and Marc Weiss. 1981a. "Who Benefits from Intergovernmental Transfers?" In *Cities Under Stress: The Fiscal Crises of Urban America,* edited by Robert Burchell and David Listoken. New Brunswick, N.J.: Rutgers University Center for Urban Policy Research.

———. 1981b. "Who Benefits from Intergovernmental Transfers?" *Publius,* 2, no. 1 (Winter): 5–3.

Markusen, Ann, and Erica Schoenberger. 1982. "The Political Economy of Regional Development in the Western United States." In *An Inquiry Into Critical Perspectives in Planning,* edited by Joochul Kim. Tempe: Arizona State University.

Markusen, Ann, and David Wilmoth. 1982. "The Political Economy of National Urban Policy in the USA: 1976–81." *Canadian Journal of Regional Science* 5, no. 1: 145–63.

Marris, Peter. 1976. "The Ideology of Human Settlements." Seminar on Social Work, Education and Human Settlements, University of British Columbia. *People and Places: Social Work Education and Human Settlements.* International Association of Schools of Social Work.

Martin, Calvin. 1974. "European Impact on the Culture of a Northeast Algonquin Tribe: An Ecological Interpretation." *William and Mary Quarterly* (3rd series) 31, no. 1.

Massey, Doreen. 1978. "Regionalism: Some Current Issues." *Capital and Class.* no. 6: 106–25.

————. 1979. "In What Sense a Regional Problem?" *Regional Studies* 13: 233–43.

————. 1984. *Spatial Divisions of Labor: Social Production and the Georgrpahy of Production.* New York: Methuen.

Massey, Doreen, and John Allen, eds. 1984. *Geography Matters: A Reader.* Cambridge: Cambridge University Press.

Massey, Doreen, and Richard Meegan. 1978. "Industrial Restructuring Versus the Cities." *Urban Studies,* 15, no. 3: 273–88.

————. 1982. *The Anatomy of Job Loss.* London: Methuen.

Massey, Garth. 1977. *Newcomers to an Impacted Community in Wyoming.* Laramie: University of Wyoming, Center for Urban and Regional Anaylsis.

————. 1980. "Critical Dimensions in Urban Life: Energy Extraction and Community Collapse in Wyoming." *Urban Life* 9, no. 2: 1878–99.

Matthews, Ralph. 1983. *The Creation of Regional Dependency,* Toronto: University of Toronto Press.

Matthews, Tom, and Melinda Beck. 1979. "The Angry West vs. the Rest." *Newsweek,* September 17, 31–40.

Mayer, Margit, and Margaret Fey. 1977. "The Formation of the American Nation-State." *Kapitalistate* no. 6 (Fall): 39–90.

Mazza, Jacqueline, and Dale Wilkinson. 1980. *The Unprotected Flank: Regional and Strategic Imbalances in Defense Spending Patterns.* Washington, D.C.: Northeast-Midwest Institute.

McBreen, Maureen. 1977. "Regional Trends in Federal Defense Expenditures: 1950–1976." Report to the U.S. Senate Committee on Appropriations Ninety-fifth Congress, In *Selected Essays on Patterns of Regional Change,* October: 511–41, Washington, D.C.: Government Printing Office.

McCormick, Richard. 1975. "Political Development and the Second Party; System." In *The American Party Systems: Stages of Political Development,* 2d ed., edited by William Chambers and Walter Burnham. New York: Oxford University Press.

McDonell, Terry. 1979. "The Noise Under the Brown Cloud." *Rocky Mountain Magazine,* October, 5.

McEachern, Doug. 1976. "The Mode of Production in India." *Journal of Contemporary Asia* 6, no. 4: 444–57.

McKinney, John, and Edgar Thompson, eds. 1965. *The South in Continuity and Change.* Durham, N.C.: Duke University Press.

McManus, Edgar J. 1973. *Black Bondage in the North.* Syracuse, N.Y.: Syracuse University Press.

McNeill, William. 1976. *Plagues and Peoples.* Garden City, N.Y.: Anchor Press/Doubleday.

McNickle, D'Arcy. 1962. *The Indian Tribes of the Untied States: Ethnic and Cultural Survival.* New York and London: Oxford University Press.

————. 1971. "Americans Called Indians." In *North American Indians in Historical Perspective,* edited by Eleanor Leacock and Nancy Lurie. New York: Random House.

————. 1979. "Indian and European: Indian-White Relations from Discovery to 1887." In *the Rape of Indian Lands,* edited by Paul Wallace Gates. New York: Arno Press.

Meier, August, and Elliott Rudwick. 1966. *From Plantation to Ghetto: An Interpretative History of American Negroes.* New York: Hill & Wang.

Mellors, Graham. 1985. "Sunbelt/Snowbelt: Occupational Aspects of a Current Controversy." Paper presented at the Annual Meetings of the Association of American Geographers, April 20–24. Detroit.

Menard, Russel. 1973. "From Servant to Freeholder: Status Mobility and Property Accumulation in 17th Century Virginia." *William and Mary Quarterly* 30, no. 1: 37–64.

Mensch, Gerhard. 1979. *Stalemate in Technology.* Cambridge, Mass.: Ballinger Publishing.

Merriner, Jim. 1977a. "Second Civil War: The Issue is Money." *Altanta Constitution,* October 15.

————. 1977b. "Sunbelt Lobbying Mapped." *Atlanta Constitution,* October 16.

Metzgar, Jack. 1980. "Plant Shutdowns and Worker Response: The Case of Johnstown, Pennsylvania." *Socialist Review* no. 53: 9–49.

Meyer, John R. 1963. "Regional Economics: A Survey." *American Economic Review* 50, no. 1: 19–54.

282 ■ Bibliography

Miernyk, William. 1954. *The People of New England and Their Employment.* Boston: The New England Council.

———. 1975. "Regional Employment Impacts of Rising Energy Prices." *Labor Law Journal* 26, no. 8: 518–23.

———. 1977. "The Changing Structure of the Southern Economy." In *The Economics of Southern Growth,* edited by E. Blaine Liner and Lawrence Lynch. Research Triangle Park, N.C.: Southern Growth Policies Board.

———. 1976. "Regional Economic Consequences of High Energy Prices in the United States." *Journal of Energy and Development* 1, no. 2: 213–39.

———. 1980. "Regional Shifts in Economic Base and Structure in the United States Since 1940." In *Alternatives to Confrontation: A National Policy Toward Regional Change,* edited by Victor Arnold. Lexington, Mass.: Lexington Books.

Miernyk, William, F. Giarratani, and C. F. Socher. 1978. *Regional Impacts of Rising Energy Prices.* Cambridge, Mass. Ballinger Publishing.

Miner, H. Craig, and William Unrau. 1978. *The End of Indian Kansas: A Study of Cultural Revolution 1854–1871.* Lawrence: Regents Press of Kansas.

Mintz, Sidney W. 1969. "Slavery and Emergent Capitalisms." In *Slavery in the New World,* edited by Laura Foner and Eugene Genovese, 28–35. Englewood Cliffs, N.J.: Prentice-Hall.

Mitchell, Braodus. 1968. *Rise of Cotton Mills in the South.* New York: DaCapo Press.

Moen, Elizabeth, et al. 1981. *Women and The Social Costs of Economic Development: Two Colorado Studies.* Boulder, Col.: Westview Press.

Mollenkopf, John. 1981. "Paths Toward the Post-Industrial Service City: The Northeast and the Southwest." In *Cities Under Stress: The Fiscal Crises of Urban America,* edited by Robert Burchell and David Listoken. New Brunswick N.J.: Rutgers University, Center for Urban Policy Research.

Molotch, Harvey. 1979. "Capital and Neighborhood in the United States: Some Conceptual Links." *Urban Affairs Quarterly* 14, no. 3 (March): 289–312.

Montgomery, David. 1967. *Beyond Equality: Labor and the Radical Republicans: 1862–1872.* New York: Alfred A. Knopf.

Moore, J. Barrington. 1966. *Social Origins of Dictatorship and Democracy.* Boston: Beacon Press.

Moore, Wilbert E. 1971. *American Negro Slavery and Abolition: A Sociological Study.* New York: Third Press.

Morrison, Peter. 1977. "The Functions and Dynamics of the Migration Process." In *Internal Migration: A Comparative Perspective,* edited by Alan Brown and Egon Neuberger, 61–72. New York: Academic Press.

———. 1980. "Current Demographic Change in Regions of the United States." In *Alternatives to Confrontation: A National Policy Toward Regional Change,* edited by Victor Arnold. Lexington, Mass.: Lexington Books.

Moss, Alice, 1975. *Growth Mangement in the South.* Research Triangle Park, N.C.: Southern Growth Policies Board.

Multistate Tax Commission. 1981. "Coal Severance Tax Impacts." *Multistate Tax Commission Review* (Boulder, Col.) 1, no. 1: 7–8.

Muth, Richard. 1971. "Migration: Chicken or Egg?" *Southern Economic Journal* 37: 295–306.

Nace, Theodore. 1978. "State Politics and the Northern Plains Coal Boom, 1971–1975: Montana, Wyoming and North Dakota." Berkeley, Cal.: University of California, Department of City and Regional Planning.

Nairn, Tom. 1975a. "Old Nationalism and New Nationalism." In *The Red Paper on Scotland,* edited by Gordon Brown. Edinburgh: EUSPB.

———. 1975b. "The Modern Janus." *New Left Review* no. 94 (November-December): 3–29.

———. 1977. *The Break-up of Britain: Crisis and Neo-Nationalism.* London: New Left Books.

Nash, Gary. 1974. *Red, White and Black: The Peoples of Early America.* Englewood Cliffs, N.J.: Prentice Hall.

———, ed. 1970. *Class and Society in Early America.* Englewood Cliffs, N.J.: Prentice-Hall.

Nash, Henry Smith. 1950. *Virgin Land: The American West as Symbol and Myth.* Cambridge, Mass.: Harvard University Press.

National Academy of Science. 1973. *Rehabilitation Potential of Western Coal Land.* Cambridge, Mass.: Ballinger Publishing.

Naylor, Thomas, and James Clotfelter. 1975. *Strategies for Change in the South.* Chapel Hill. University of North Carolina Press.

Nelson, Bryce. 1979. "Cecil Andrus—The West's Best Friend?" *San Francisco Chronicle,* Monday, October 1, 21.

Nevins, Allan. 1950. *The Emergence of Lincoln.* New York: Scribner.

New England Economy Project. 1981. *Case Study Summaries, Policy Analysis and Research Methodology.* Cambridge, Mass.: Joint Center for Urban Studies of MIT and Harvard University.

Nicholls, William. 1960. *Southern Tradition and Regional Progress.* Chapel Hill: University of North Carolina Press.

Norman, Ellen. 1978. "Industrial Growing Pains Hit Sunnyvale 15 Years Early." *Palo Alto Times,* September 28.

North, Douglas C. 1961. *The Economic Growth of the United States, 1790–1860.* Englewood Cliffs, N.J.: Prentice-Hall.

Northeast-Midwest Institute. 1978a. *Focus on Regional Cooperation: North-South Summit, Boston August 24–25.* Washington, D.C.: NEMWI.

———. 1978b. *Per Capita Income is Not a True Measure of Health.* Washington, D.C.: NEMWI.

———. 1979a. *Employees to the Rescue: The Federal Role in Worker Ownership.* Washington, D.C. NEMWI.

———. 1979b. *The Regional Impact of the Crisis at Chrysler.* Washington, D.C.: NEMWI.

———. 1980. *The Effects of Rising State Severance Tax Revenues: 1980–1990.* Regional Energy Impact Brief no. 10. Washington, D.C.: NEMWI, House Annex.

———. 1981. *The United American Emirates.* Washington, D.C. NEMWI.

———. 1982. *The 1982 User's Guide to Government Resources for Economic Development.* Washington, D.C.: NEMWI.

Northern Great Plains Resources Program. 1975. *Effects of Coal Development in the Northern Great Plains: A Review of Major Issues and Consequences at Different Rates of Development.* April. Denver: Northern Great Plains Resources Program, A Consortium of the Department of Agriculture, Interior and the Environmental Protection Agencies and the states of Nebraska, North Dakota, South Dakota, Montana and Wyoming.

Northern Plains Resource Council. 1977, 1978, 1981. *The Plains Truth* 6, no. 9, (November); 6, no. 11 (January); 10, no. 10 (November/December).

Norton, R. D., and J. Rees. 1979. "The Product Cycle and the Spatial Decentralization of American Manufacturing.' *Regional Studies* 13, no. 2 (141–51).

Nourse, Hugh O. 1968. *Regional Economics.* New York: McGraw-Hill.

Noyelle, Thierry. 1983. "The Implications of Industry Restructuring in the United States." In *Regional Analysis and the New International Division of Labor,* edited by Frank Moulaert and Patricia Wilson Salinas. Boston: Kluwer-Nijhoff.

Noyelle, Thierry, and Thomas Stanback, Jr. 1983. *Economic Transformation of American Cities.* Totowa, N.J.: Rowman & Allanheld.

Nugent, Walter T. K. 1963. *The Tolerant Populists: Kansas Populism and Nativism.* Chicago: University of Chicago Press.

Oakey, R. P., A. T. Thwaites, and P. A. Nash. 1980. "The Regional Distribution of Innovative Manufacturing Establishments in Britain." *Regional Studies* 14: 235–53.

O'Connor, James. 1973. *The Fiscal Crisis of the State.* New York: St. Martin's Press.

———. 1975. "The Twisted Dream." *Monthly Review* 26, no. 1: 41–54.

———. 1976. "A Note on Independent Commodity Production and Petty Capitalism." *Monthly Review* 28, no. 1: 60–63.

———. 1979. "The Democratic Movement in the United States." *Kapitalistate* no. 7: 15–26.

O'Connor, Kevin. 1974. "The Industrial Structure of a Growth Center: An Outline for Research." In *Spatial Aspects of the Development Process,* vol. 2, edited by Frederick Helleiner and Walter Stohr. "Proceedings of the Commission on Regional Aspects of Development of the International Geographers Union." London, Ontario.

Odum, Howard. 1935. *The Regional Approach to National Social Planning.* New York: Foreign Policy Association.

———. 1936. *Southern Regions of the United States.* Chapel Hill: University of North Carolina Press.

Odum, Howard, and Harry Estill Moore. 1938. *American Regionalism: A Cultural History of National Integration.* New York: Henry Holt.

O hUallachain, Breandan. 1986. *Some Regional Implications of Recent Growth in the American Military-Industrial Complex.* Northwestern University, Department of Geogrpahy, Working Paper. Evanston, Ill.

Olson, Gunnar. 1974. "Servitude and Inequality in Spatial Planning: Ideology and Methodology in Conflict." *Antipode* 6, no. 1 (April): 16–21.

Otterbein, Keith F. 1964. "Why the Iroquois Won: An Analysis of Iroquois Military Tactics." *Ethnohistory* 11, no. 1.

Owens, Nancy; and Ken Peres. 1980. *Overcoming Institutional Barriers to Economic Development on the Northern Cheyenne Reservation.* Lame Deer, Mont.: Northern Cheyenne Research Project.

Owsley, Frank L. 1949. *The Plain Folk of the Old South.* Baton Rouge: Louisiana State University Press.

Paddison, Ronan. 1983. *The Fragmented State: The Political Geography of Power.* New York: St. Martin's Press.

Parfit, Michael. 1980. "Last Stand at Rosebud Creek." *Rocky Mountain Magazine,* May/June, 65–70.

Parrish, Michael. 1980. "The Saints Among Us." *Rocky Mountain Magazine,* January/February, 17–32.

Parsons, Stanley. 1973. *The Populist Context: Rural Versus Urban Power on a Great Plains Frontier.* Westport, Conn.: Greenwood Press.

Patterson, S. C. 1966. *The Political Culture of the American States.* Iowa City: University of Iowa Press.

Payne, Thomas. 1969. "Montana: Politics Under the Copper Dome." In *Politics in the American West,* edited by Frank Jonas, 203–30. Salt Lake City: University of Utah Press.

Peirce, Neal. 1972. *The Mountain States of America.* New York: W. W. Norton.

——. 1976. "Northeast Governors Map Battle Plan for Fight over Federal Funds Flow." *National Journal,* November 27, 1695–1703.

Peirce, Neal, and Jerry Hagstrom. 1977. "Western States Join in Forming a United Energy Front." *National Journal,* February 5, 208–10.

Perloff, Harvey. 1968. "Key Features of Regional Planning." *American Institute of Planners Journal* 34, no. 3: 153–59.

Perry, David and Alfred Watkins. 1980. "Contemporary Dimensions of Uneven Urban Development in the U.S.A." In *City, Class and Capital: New Developments in the Political Economy of Cities and Regions,* edited by Michael Harloe and Elizabeth Lebas, 115–42. London: Edward Arnold.

Perry, David, and Alfred Watkins, eds. 1977. *The Rise of the Sunbelt Cities.* Beverly Hills: Sage Publications.

Persky, Joseph. 1972. "Regional Colonialism and the Southern Economy." *Review of Radical Political Economy* 4, no. 1: 70–79.

——. 1978. "Dualism, Capital-Labor Ratios and the Regions of the U.S." *Journal of Regional Science* 18, no. 3: 373–81.

Phillips, Kevin. 1969. *The Emerging Republican Majority.* New Rochelle, N.Y.: Arlington House.

——. 1978. "The Balkanization of America." *Harpers,* May, 37–48.

——. 1982. *Post-Conservative America: People, Politics and Ideology in a Time of Crisis.* New York: Random House.

Phillips, Ulrich Bonnell. 1936. *American Negro Slavery.* New York, London: Appleton and Company.

Pickvance, Christopher S., ed. 1976. *Urban Sociology: Critical Essays.* New York: St. Martin's Press.

Piore, Michael. 1979. *Birds of Passage: Migrant Labor and Industrial Societies.* Cambridge: Cambridge University Press.

Plotke, David. 1980. "The United States in Transition: Toward a New Order." *Socialist Review.* 10, no. 6 (November-December): 71–124.

Plummer, James. 1977. "The Federal Role in Rocky Mountain Energy Development." *Natural Resources Journal* 17 (April): 241–60.

Policy Analysis Staff Group, National Forest Service. 1980. "The Sagebrush Rebellion—Concerns and Approaches." Internal memo, July.

Polsky, Anthony, 1979. "The American West Looks East." *Far Eastern Economic Review,* November 2, 56.

Pomeroy, Earl. 1965. *The Pacific Slope: A History of California, Oregon, Washington, Idaho, Utah and Nevada.* Seattle: University of Washington Press.

Pope, Polly. 1966. "Trade in the Plains: Affluence and Its Effects." *Kroeber Anthropological Society Papers* 34.

Post, Charles. 1982. "The American Road to Capitalism." *New Left Review:* 1, 33: 30–51.

Potter, David. 1968. "The Historian's Use of Nationalism and Vice-Versa." In David Potter, *The South and the Sectional Conflict.* Baton Rouge: Louisiana State University Press.

———. 1976. *The Impending Crisis, 1848–1861.* New York: Harper & Row.

Pratt, Raymond. 1978a. "Developing Nations or Internal Colonies? Tribal Sovereignty and the Problem of Resource Exploitation." Paper presented at Western Political Science Association meetings. Los Angeles, March 16–18.

Pratt, Raymond, and Dwayne Ward. 1978. "Corporations, the State and Energy Development in the Northern Rockies." Paper presented at the American Political Science Association meetings. August 30. New York.

Pred, Allan R. 1976. "The Interurban Transmission of Growth in Advanced Economies: Empirical Findings vs. Regional-Planning Assumptions." *Regional Studies* 10: 151–71.

Pred, Allan R. 1977. *City Systems in Advanced Economies: Past Growth, Present Processes, and Future Development Options.* New York: John Wiley.

Prendergast, Alan. 1981. "Gimme Shelter." *Rocky Mountain Magazine,* December, 30–31.

Prethus, Robert. 1964. *Men at the Top: A Study in Community Power.* New York: Oxford University Press.

Prucha, Francis Paul. 1962. *American Indian Policy in the Formative Years: The Indian Trade and Indian Intercourse Acts, 1790–1834.* Cambridge, Mass.: Harvard University Press.

———. 1976. *American Indian Policy in Crisis: Christian Reformers and the Indian, 1865–1900.*

Rabinowitz, Alan. 1982. "Urban and Rural Unemployment in the Western States." Paper presented at the Regional Conference on New Perspectives on Planning in the West, March 26–28, at Arizona State University, Tempe.

Rabinowitz, Howard. 1977. "Continuity and Change: Southern Urban Development, 1860–1900." In *The City in Southern History,* edited by Blaine Brownell and David Goldfield, 92–122. Port Washington, N.Y.: Kennikat Press.

Rafuse, Robert, Jr. 1977. *The New Regional Debate: A National Overview.* Washington, D.C.: National Governors' Conference.

Ransom, Roger, and Richard Sutch. 1975. "The Impact of the Civil War and Emancipation on Southern Agriculture." *Explorations in Economic History* 12, no. 1: 1–28.

———. 1977. *One Kind of Freedom: The Economic Consequences of Emancipation.* Cambridge: Cambridge University Press.

Reed, John Shelton. 1972. *The Enduring South: Subcultural Persistence in Mass Society.* Lexington, Mass.: D. C. Heath.

Rees, John. 1982. "Defense Spending and Regional Industrial Change." *Texas Business Review.* January-February, 40–44.

Rees, John, and Howard Stafford. 1983. *A Review of Regional Growth and Industrial Location Theory: Toward Understanding the Development of High-Technology Complexes in the United States.* Washington, D.C.: Office of Technology Assessment.

Reid, T. R. 1977. "Trusting Rural Town Survives ABM Boom and Bust." *Washington Post,* Monday, February 28, A1, A14.

Renner, George T. 1935. "The Statistical Approach to Regions." *Annals of the Association of American Geographers* 25, no. 3 (September): 137–52.

Rey, Pierre-Philippe. 1971. *Colonialisme, Neocolonialisms et Transition au Capitalisme.* Paris: F. Maspero.

Richardson, Harry W. 1969. *Regional Economics.* New York: Praeger Publishers.

———. 1973. *Regional Growth Theory.* London: Macmillan.

Richardson, Harry, and Joseph Turek. 1985. *Economic Prospects for the Northeast.* Philadelphia: Temple University Press.

Rifkin, Jeremy, and Randy Barber. 1978. *The North Will Rise Again: Pensions, Politics and Power in the 1980s.* Boston: Beacon Press.

Rohatyn, Felix. 1977. "Reviving the Northeast." *The Washington Post.* April 17: C8.

Romans, J. Thomas. 1965. *Capital Exports and Growth Among U.S. Regions.* Middletown, Conn.: Wesleyan Press.

Rostow, Walt. 1977. "Regional Change in the Fifth Kondratieff Upswing." In *The Rise of the Sunbelt Cities,* edited by David Perry and Alfred Watkins, 83–103. Beverly Hills: Sage Publications.

Rothblatt, Donald. 1971. *Regional Planning: The Appalachian Experience*. Lexington, Mass.: Heath Lexington Books.

Rowthorne, Robert. 1971. "Imperialism in the 1970s: Unity or Rivalry." *New Left Review* no. 69.

Rundquist, Barry. 1983. "Politics' Benefits and Public Policy: Interpretation of Recent U.S. Studies." *Environment and Planning C: Government and Policy* 1: 401–12.

Rust, Edgar, and William Alonso. 1975. *Adaptation or Reversal: Policies for the Quality of Life in the Economically Declining parts of Montana, North Dakota and Wyoming*. Berkeley: Berkeley Planning Associates (February 28).

Sack, Robert. 1974. "The Spatial Separatist Theme in Geography." *Economic Geography* 50: 1–19.

———. 1980. *Conceptions of Space in Social Thought: A Geographical Perspective*. Minneapolis: University of Minnesota Press.

———. 1981. "Territorial Bases of Power." In *Political Studies from Spatial Perspectives*, edited by Allen Burnett and Peter H. Taylor, 53–72. Chichester and New York: John Wiley.

Sale, Kirkpatrick. 1975. *Power Shift: The Rise of the Southern Rim and its Challenge to the Eastern Establishment*. New York: Random House.

Salpukas, Agis. 1977a. "U.S. Funds Available to Reopen Plants, Steel Group is Told." *New York Times*, November 26.

Santa Clara County Manufacturing Group. 1979. "Views on Land Use and Transportation Recommendations." February 21, Mimeo.

Sassen-Koob, Saskia. 1982. "Recomposition and Peripheralization at the Core." *Contemporary Marxism* no. 5 (Summer): 88–100.

Saunders, Peter. 1979. *Urban Politics: A Sociological Interpretation*. London: Hutchinson.

Sawers, Larry, and William K. Tabb. 1984. *Sunbelt/Snowbelt: Urban Development and Regional Restructuring*. New York and Oxford: Oxford University Press.

Savage, Robert. 1973. "Patterns of Multilinear Evolution in the American States." *Publius*. 3, no. 1: 75–108.

Saxenian, Annalee. 1980. *Silicon Chips and Spatial Structure: The Semiconductor Industry and Urbanization in Santa Clara County, California*. Master's thesis, Department of City and Regional Planning, University of California at Berkeley.

Sayer, Andrew. 1985. "The Difference that Space Makes." In *Social Relations and Spatial Structures*, edited by Derek Gregory and John Urry, 49–65. New York: St. Martin's Press.

Schneider, William. 1981. "Democrats and Republicans, Liberals and Conservatives." In *Party Coalitions in the 1980s*, edited by Seymour Martin Lipset, 179–231. San Francisco: Institute for Contemporary Studies.

Schultze, Robert. 1958. "The Role of Economic Dominants in Community Power Structure." *American Sociological Review* 23, no. 1: 3–9.

Schwartz, Mildred A. 1974. *Politics and Territory: The Sociology of Regional Persistence in Canada*. Montreal: McGill-Queens University Press.

Scott, Allan, and Shoukry Roweis. 1977. "Urban Planning in Theory and Practice: A Reappraisal." *Environment and Planning* 9: 1097–119.

Sellers, James. 1962. "The Economic Incidence of the Civil War in the South" (originally published 1927). In *The Economic Impact of the Civil War*, edited by Ralph Andreano, 79–89. Cambridge, Mass.: Schenkman Publishing.

Sexton, Robert. 1975. "Regional Definitional Problems in the Antebellum South." University of Colorado, Department of Economics, Working Paper. Boulder.

Shapira, Philip, Nancey Leigh-Preston, Edward Blakely, and Ted Bradshaw. 1982. "Western Urban and Rural Development: Emerging Conflicts and Planning Issues." Paper presented at the Regional Conference on New Perspectives on Planning in the West. March 26–28, at Arizona State University, Tempe.

Shapira, Philip. 1979. "The Uneven Economy and the State in Massachusetts." Master's thesis, Department of Urban Studies and Planning, Massachusetts Institute of Technology.

Shapira, Philip. 1986. *Industry and Jobs in Transition: A Study of Industrial Restructuring and Worker Displacement in California*. Doctoral dissertation, Department of City and Regional Planning, University of California, Berkeley.

Sharkansky, Ira. 1970. *Regionalism in American Politics*. Indianapolis: Bobbs-Merrill.

Sharkey, Robert. 1959. *Money, Class and Power: An Economic Study of Civil War and Reconstruction*. "Studies in Historical and Political Science" Series 77, no. 2. Baltimore, Md.: Johns Hopkins University.

Sharpe, Maitland. 1980. "The Sagebrush Rebellion: A Conservationist's Perspective." *Rangelands* 2, no. 6 (December): 232–34.

Sherry, Robert. 1976. "Comments on O'Connor's Review of *The Twisted Dream:* Independent Commodity Production Versus Petty-Bourgeois Production." *Monthly Review* 28, no. 1: 52–60.

Shortreed, Margaret. 1959. "The Anti-Slavery Radicals: From Crusade to Revolution, 1840–1868." *Past and Present* no. 16 (November): 65–87.

Sibley, George. 1980. "Crested Butte, Amax and the Bird is Dead Bar & Grill." *Rocky Mountain Magazine,* April 19–30.

Siebert, Horst. 1969. *Regional Economic Growth: Theory and Policy.* Scranton, Pa.: International Textbook.

Siembeda, William, ed. 1978. *A Changing Enchantment: Public Policy Issues in the Southwest.* Albuquerque: University of New Mexico, School of Architecture and Planning.

Simon, Rick. 1979. "The Development Faith and Economic Development in West Virginia: Lessons from the Coal Miner's Strike of 1977–78." West Virginia Department of Environmental and Urban Systems Working Paper. Blacksburg.

———. 1980. "The Labor Process and Uneven Development: The Appalachian Coalfields." *International Journal of Urban and Regional Research.* 4, no. 1 (March): 46–71.

Smaby, Beverly P. 1975. "The Mormons and the Indians: Conflicting Ecological Systems in the Great Basin." *American Studies* 16, no. 1: 35–48.

Smith, Neil. 1981. "Degeneracy of Theory and Practice: Spatial Interactionism and Radical Eclecticism." *Progress in Human Geography* 5, no. 1: 111–18.

———. 1986. "On the Necessity of Uneven Development." *International Journal of Urban and Regional Research* 10, no. 1: 87–104.

Smith, T. Lynn. 1954. "The Emergence of Cities." In *The Urban South,* edited by Rupert Vance and Nicholas Demerath, 24–37. Chapel Hill: University of North Carolina Press.

Soja. Ed. 1971. *The Political Organization of Space.* Association of American Geography, Commission on College Geography Resource Paper no. 8. Washington, D.C.

———. 1980. "The Socio-spatial Dialectic." *Annals of the Association of American Geographers* 70, no. 2: 207–25.

———. 1981. *A Materialist Interpretation of Spatiality.* University of California, School of Architecture and Urban Planning Working Paper. Los Angeles.

Southern Growth Policies Board. 1973. *Reverse Investment in the South: Proceedings of a Southern Growth Policies Board Workshop.* June 19–20, Columbia, S.C. Mimeo.

———. 1978. *Annual Report.* Chapel Hill, N.C.: SGPB.

———. 1979. *Report from the North/South Summit.* September 13, 14, Asheville, N.C. Research Triangle Park, N.C. SGPB.

———. 1981. *Report of the 1980 Commission on the Future of the South.* Chapel Hill, N.C.: SGPB.

Spicer, E. H. 1969. *A Short History of the Indians of the United States.* New York: Van Nostrand.

Stampp, Kenneth M. 1956. *The Peculiar Institution: Slavery in the Ante-Bellum South.* New York: Vintage Books.

———. 1980. *The Imperiled Union: Essays on the Background of the Civil War.* New York: Oxford University Press.

———. ed. 1974. *The Causes of the Civil War.* Rev. ed. Englewood Cliffs, N.J.: Prentice-Hall.

Starobin, Robert S. 1969. *Industrial Slavery in the Old South.* New York: Oxford University Press.

Stein, Jay. 1985. *U.S. Defense Spending: Implications for Economic Development Planning.* Georgia Institute of Technology, City Planning Program Working Paper. Atlanta.

Stephenson, George M. 1967. *The Political History of the Public Lands from 1840 to 1862: From Pre-emption to Homestead* (originally published 1917). New York: Russell & Russell.

Sternlieb, George, and James Hughes. 1976. *Post-Industrial America: Metropolitan Decline & Interregional Job Shifts.* 75–127. New Brunswick, N.J.: Rutgers University, Center for Urban Policy Research.

———. 1978. *Revitalizing the Northeast: Prelude to an Agenda.* New Brunswick, N.J.: Rutgers University, Center for Urban Policy Research.

Stevens, Benjamin, and Craig Moore. 1980. "A Critical Review of the Literature on Shift-Share as a Forecasting Technique." *Journal of Regional Science* 20, no. 4: 419–37.

Stevenson, Garth. 1979. *Unfulfilled Union: Canadian Federalism and National Unity.* Toronto: Gage Publishing.

Stillwell, Frank. 1969. "Regional Growth and Structural Adaptation." *Urban Studies* 15, no. 3: 162–78.

———. 1979. "Australian Urban and Regional Development in the Late 1970's: An Overview." *International Journal of Urban and Regional Research* 3, no. 44: 527–40.

Stocking, George. 1954. *Basing-Point Pricing and Regional Development*. Chapel Hill: University of North Carolina Press.

Storper, Michael. 1982. *The Spatial Division of Labor*. Ph.D diss., University of California, Berkeley.

Sullam, Carolla, Michael Storper, Donna Pittman, and Ann Markusen. 1978. *Montana: A Territorial Planning Strategy*. University of California, Institute of Urban and Regional Development, Working Paper no. 294. Berkeley.

Sutch, Richard. 1975. "The Breeding of Slaves for Sale and the Westward Expansion of Slavery, 1850–1860." In *Race and Slavery in the Western Hemisphere*, edited by Stanley Engerman and Eugene Genovese, 173–210. Princeton, N.J.: Princeton University Press.

Sutherland, Stella. 1936. *Population Distribution in Colonial America*. New York: Columbia University Press.

Sutton, Horace. 1978. "Sunbelt vs. Frostbelt: A Second Civil War?" *Saturday Review*, April 15, 28–37.

Swanton, John Reed. 1952. *The Indian Tribes of North America*. Washington, D.C.: Government Printing Office.

Sweirenga, Robert. 1968. *Pioneers and Profits: Land Speculation on the Iowa Frontier*. Ames: Iowa University Press.

Sydnor, Charles S. 1948. *The Develoment of Southern Sectionalism, 1819–1848*. Baton Rouge: Louisiana State University Press.

Tabb, William K. 1982. *The Long Default: New York City and the Urban Fiscal Crisis*. New York: Monthly Review Press.

Tabb, William, and Larry Sawers, eds. 1978. *Marxism and the Metropolis*. New York: Oxford University Press.

Takaki, Ronald. 1971. *A Pro-Slavery Crusade*. New York: Free Press.

Tarrow, Sidney, P. Katzenstein, and L. Grazionom, eds. 1978. *Territorial Politics in Industrial Nations*. New York and London: Praeger Publishers.

Taylor, George, ed. 1971. *The Turner Thesis*. No. 2, "The Amherst Problems in American Civilization." Lexington, Mass.: D.C. Heath.

Taylor, M. J. 1975. "Organizational Growth, Spatial Interaction and Locational Decision-Making." *Regional Studies* 9: 313–23.

Taylor, Peter. 1981. "A Materialist Framework for Political Geography." *Transactions of the Institute of British Geographers*. 7, no. 1: 15–34.

Taylor, Peter, and John House. 1984. *Political Geography: Recent Advances and Future Directions*. London: Croom Helm.

Teasley, Colleen. 1974. "Onward! Commission's Aim is South's Gain." *Atlanta Constitution*, May 6, 7-D.

Teitz, Michael. 1962. "Regional Theory and Regional Models." *Papers and Proceedings of the Regional Science Association*. 9: 35–50.

———. 1984. "The California Economy: Changing Structure and Policy Responses." In *California Policy Choices, 1984*, edited by John Kirlin and Donald Winkler. Sacramento: Sacramento Public Affairs Center.

Temin, Peter. 1976. "The Post-Bellum Recovery of the South and the Cost of the Civil War." *Journal of Economic History* 36 (December): 898–907.

Thomas, G. E. 1975. "Puritans, Indians and the Concept of Race." *New England Quarterly* 47, no. 1.

Thomas, Peter. 1976. "Contrastive Subsistence Strategies and Land Use as Factors for Understanding Indian-White Relations in New England." *Ethnohistory* 23, no. 1.

Thompson, Edgar, ed. 1967. *Perspectives on the South: Agenda for Research*. Durham, N.C.: Duke University Press.

Thompson, Wilbur. 1965. *A Preface to Urban Economics*. Baltimore: Johns Hopkins University Press.

———. 1969. "The Economic Base of Urban Problems." In *Contemporary Economic Issues*, edited by Neil Chamberlain, 1–47. Homewood, Ill.: Richard Irwin.

Thwaites, A. T. 1978. "Technological Change, Mobile Plants and Regional Development." *Regional Studies* 12: 445–61.

Tiebout, Charles. 1966. "The Regional Impact of Defense Expenditures: Its Measurement and Problems of Adjustment." In *Defense and Disarmament,* edited by Roger Bolton, Englewood Cliffs, N.J.: Prentice-Hall.

Toole, K. Ross. 1976. *The Rape of the Great Plains.* Boston: Little, Brown.

Trigger, Bruce. 1969. *The Huron: Farmers of the North.* New York: Holt, Rinehart & Winston.

Tri-State Conference on Steel. 1984. *A Community Plan to Save Pittsburgh's Steel Industry.* Homestead, Pa.: The Tri-State Conference.

Trounstine, Philip. 1979. "A Task Force Proposal to Centralize Land Use Planning is Branded Politically Impossible." *San Jose Mercury News,* October 21.

Turner, Frederick Jackson. 1894. "The Significance of the Frontier in American History." In American Historical Association, *Annual Report for 1893,* 199–277. Washington, D.C.

———. 1932. *The Significance of Sections in American History.* New York: Henry Holt.

———. 1961. *Frontier and Section: Selected Essays of Frederick Jackson Turner* (originally published 1894). Englewood Cliffs, N.J.: Prentice-Hall.

Tyner, Wallace E., and Robert J. Kalter. 1978. *Western Coal: Promise or Problem?* Lexington, Mass.: Lexington Books/D. C. Heath.

United States Commission on Civil Rights. 1978. *Energy Resource Development: Implications for Women and Minorities in the Intermountain West.* Denver, Col.: Government Printing Office.

United States National Resources Committee. 1935. *The Regional Factors in National Planning.* Washington, D.C.: Government Printing Office.

Urry, John. 1981. "Localities, Regions and Social Class." *International Journal of Urban and Regional Research* 5, no. 4: 455–74.

———. 1985. "Social Relations, Space and Time." In *Social Relations and Spatial Structures,* edited by Derek Gregory and John Urry, 20–48. New York: St. Martin's Press.

Van Duesen, Glyndon. 1965. "Why the Republican Party Came to Power." In *The Crisis of the Union,* edited by George Harmon Knoles, 3–20. Baton Rouge: Louisiana State University Press.

Van Every, Dale. 1966. *Disinherited: The Lost Birthright of the American Indian.* New York: William Morrow.

Vance, Rupert B. 1951. "The Regional Concept as a Tool for Social Research." In *Regionalism in America,* edited by Merrill Jensen. Madison: University of Wisconsin Press.

Vernon, Raymond. 1960. *Metropolis 1985: An Interpretation of the Findings of the New York Metropolitan Region Study.* Cambridge: Harvard University Press.

———. 1966. "International Investment and International Trade in the Product Cycle." *Quarterly Journal of Economics,* 80, no. 2: 190–207.

———. 1971. *Sovereignty at Bay: The Multinational Spread of United States Enterprises.* New York: Basic Books.

Vilar, Pierre. 1978. *Cataluna en la Espana moderna.* Barcelona: Editorial Critica.

———. 1979. "On Nations and Nationalism." Translated from the French by Elizabeth Fox Genovese. *Marxist Perspectives* 2, no. 1 (Spring): 8–29.

Vining, D. R., and A. Strauss. 1977. "A Demonstration that the Current Deconcentration of Population in the United States is a Clear Break with the Past." *Environment and Planning A,* 9: 751–58.

Voakes, Paul. 1978. "Housing-Job Imbalance Poses Problem." *Palo Alto Times,* November 8, 31.

Wade, Richard C. 1964. *Slavery in the Cities: The South, 1800–1860.* New York: Oxford University Press.

Walker, David, ed. 1980. *Planning Industrial Development.* New York: John Wiley.

Walker, Richard. 1978. "Two Sources of Uneven Development under Advanced Capitalism: Spatial Differentiaiton and Capital Mobility." *Review of Radical Political Economics* 10, no. 3: 28–37.

———. 1985. "Class, Division of Labour and Employment in Space." In *Social Relations and Spatial Structures,* edited by Derek Gregory and John Urry, 164–89. New York: St. Martin's Press.

Wallerstein, Immanuel. 1976. "American Slavery and the Capitalist World Economy." *American Journal of Sociology* 81, (March): 1199–213.

———. 1979. *The Capitalist World Economy.* Cambridge: Cambridge University Press.

Watkins, Alfred, and David Perry. 1977. "Regional Change and the Impact of Uneven Development." In *The Rise of the Sunbelt Cities*, edited by David Perry and Alfred Watkins, 19–54. Beverly Hills: Sage Publications.

Wattenberg, Martin, and Arthur Miller. 1981. "Decay in Regional Party Coalitions: 1952–1980." In *Party Coalitions in the 1980s*, edited by Seymour Martin Lipset, 341–67. San Francisco: Institute for Contemporary Studies.

Weaver, Clyde. 1981. "The Limits of Economism: Toward a Political Approach to Regional Develoment and Planning." In *London Papers in Regional Science*, vol. 2, edited by R. Hudson and J. Lewis. London: Pion.

Weaver, Clyde. 1984. *Regional Development and the Local Community*. New York: Wiley.

Webb, Walter Prescott. 1931. *The Great Plains*. Waltham, Mass.: Blaisdell Publishing.

Webber, Melvin, 1963. "Order and Diversity: Community Without Propinquity." In *Cities and Space: The Future Use of Urban Land*, edited by Lowdon Wingo. Baltimore: Johns Hopkins Press.

Webber, M. J. 1972. *Impact of Uncertainty on Location*. Cambridge, Mass.: MIT Press.

Weinstein, Bernard. 1979a. *Cost-of-Living Adjustments for Federal Grants-in-Aid: A Negative View*. February. Chapel Hill, N.C.: Southern Growth Policies Board.

———. 1979b. "The Current Recession and Its Impact on the South." Testimony before the Subcommittee on Fiscal and Intergovernmental Policy of the Joint Economic Committee, Ninety-Seventh Congress, First Session. October 16. Mimeo.

———. 1981a. *Conflicts of U.S. Energy-Producing and Consuming Regions: A Search for Resolution*. University of Texas, Department of Economics, Dallas. Mimeo.

———. 1981b. *Report of the Task Force on the Southern Economy*. Research Triangle Park, N.C.: Southern Growth Policies Board.

———. 1983. "The Eyes of Texas are Bloodshot." *Texas Business*. April: 66–72.

Weinstein, Bernard, and Robert Firestine. 1978. *Regional Growth and Decline in the United States: The Rise of the Sunbelt and the Decline of the Northeast*. New York: Praeger Publishers.

Weiss, Marc. 1979. "Review of 'The North Will Rise Again: Pensions and Power in the 1980s' " *In These Times*, 4, no. 8, January 10–16.

Weltfish, Gene. 1971. "The Plains Indian: Their Continuity in History and Their Indian Identity." In *North American Indians in Historical Perspectives*, edited by Eleanor Leacock and Nancy Lurie. New York: Random House.

Western Governor's Policy Office. 1978. *Balanced Growth and Economic Develoment: A Western White Paper*, vol. 1. Denver: WESTPO.

———. 1980. *WRAP-UP* (Newsletter of WESTPO). Denver: WESTPO.

Western Governors' Task Force on Regional Policy Management. 1976. *Regional Policy Management: The Task Ahead*. Executive Summary, vol. 2, December 10.

Whisnant, David. 1979. *Modernizing the Mountaineer: People, Power and Planning in Appalachia*. New York: B. Franklin.

The White House Conference on Balanced Growth and Economic Development. 1978. "Beyond Sunbelt-Frostbelt: Regional Policy for a Changing Economy." *Final Report*, vol. 1. app. 118–66. Washington, D.C.: Government Printing Office.

Widener, Sandra. 1982. "Boom Town Women." *This World*, February 21, 18–26.

Wiener, Jonathan M. 1978. *Social Origins of the New South: Alabama, 1860–1885*. Baton Rouge: Louisiana State University Press.

Williams, Eric. 1961. *Capitalism and Slavery*. New York: Russell & Russell.

Williams, Raymond. 1973. "Base and Superstructure in Marxist Cultural Theory." *New Left Review* 82, (November-December): 80–86.

Williams, Roger Neville. 1979. "A Tiny Town Battles a Mining Giant." *New York Times Magazine*, March 4, 17–40.

Williams, William Appleman. 1981. "Radicals and Regionalism." *Democracy* 1, no. 4 (October): 87–98.

Williamson, Jeffrey. 1980. "Unbalanced Growth, Inequality and Regional Development: Some Lessons from U.S. History." In *Alternatives to Confrontation: A National Policy Toward Regional Change*, edited by Victor Arnold. Northeast-Midwest Institute, April 3, Washington, D.C. Lexington, Mass.: Lexington Books.

Wolfe, Alan. 1977. *The Limits of Legitimacy: Political Contradictions of Contemporary Capitalism*. New York: Free Press.

Woodward, C. Vann. 1938. *Tom Watson: Agrarian Rebel*. New York: Macmillan.

———. 1951. *Origins of the New South 1877–1913*. Baton Rouge: Louisiana State University Press.

Wright, Gavin. 1978. *Political Economy of the Cotton South: Households, Markets and Wealth in the 19th Century.* New York: W. W. Norton.

Yoachjim, Susan. 1980. "Sunnyvale Cuts Job Growth with Industry Limits." *San Jose Mercury,* March 27.

Young, John, and Jan Newton. 1980. *Capitalism and Human Obsolescence.* Montclair, N.J.: Universe Books/Allanheld, Osmun.

Zabar, Laurence, and Michael Sullivan. 1978. *The Use of Federal Procurements in Revitalizing the Economy of Youngstown, Ohio.* Washington, D.C.: Northeast-Midwest Institute. Mimeo.

Zilversmit, Arthur. 1967. *The First Emancipation.* Chicago: University of Chicago Press.

Business Week. 1972. "The New Rich South: Frontier for Growth." September 2, 30–37.

———. 1976. "A Second War Between the States." May 17, 92–113.

———. 1981a. "Disparity Marks 1980 Growth." April 13, 146.

———. 1981b. "A Drive to Cap Severance Taxes." July 27, 94.

———. 1981c. "Now Energy is What Counts in the War Between States." October 26, 166–70.

Chicago Tribune. 1986. "Study Finds Growth Primarily on Coasts." July 11, B1.

Colorado Springs Gazette Telegraph. 1976. "Grants Bursting with Boom." November 14, 1-d.

High Country News. 1968. Lander, Wyo. Selected issues.

Montana Eagle. 1981. Helena, Mont. Selected issues.

New York Times. 1976. "Jobs and Revenues Shifting Toward Sunbelt." April 7.

New York Times. 1981. "Taxes by Energy States Causing East-West Split." October 15.

Newsweek. 1975. "Energy: War Between the States." May 5.

Oakland Tribune. 1980. "Western Governors Open Policy Meeting." September 5, A-9.

Rocky Mountain Journal. 1981. "No Sagebrush Sympathy." Editorial from January, reprinted in *Congressional Record,* January 22, 1981, E 117.

Shale Country. October 1975; February 1978. Denver: Mountain Empire Publishing Company.

Wall Street Journal. 1978. "Carter Proposes $675 Million Plan to Aid Energy-Rich Areas' Rapid Development." May 5.

Washington Post. 1979. "Old Frontier Sees Bright New Future" and "Why Power is Flowing to the West." June 17, 18.

Western Wildlands. 1977. Vol. 3, no. 3 (Winter). Missoula, Mont.: University of Montana, Forest and Conservaiton Experiment Station.

Author Index

Subject Index